Queering Reproduction

Queering Reproduction

Achieving Pregnancy
in the Age of Technoscience

Laura Mamo

DUKE UNIVERSITY PRESS   *Durham & London 2007*

© 2007 Duke University Press
All rights reserved
Printed in the United States of America
on acid-free paper ∞

Designed by Jennifer Hill
Typeset in Carter and Cone Galliard by
Keystone Typesetting, Inc.

Library of Congress Cataloging-in-
Publication Data appear on the last
printed page of this book.

In memory and honor of
Dr. Adria E. Schwartz (1946–2002)
For teaching me intellectual curiosity and . . .

And to
Helen Fitzsimmons
For providing laughter, love, and family

Contents

Acknowledgments

THIS PROJECT HAS BENEFITED FROM the assistance and support of many people. Most important has been my partner, Helen Fitzsimmons. I am deeply grateful for her willingness to move with me from our "promised land" of San Francisco to the District of Columbia: both places have come to represent for us the extent of queering and the oppressive force of conformity and false tolerance of difference. It has been quite a ride.

I was drawn to the topic of queer reproductive practices as a second-year doctoral student in the department of sociology at the University of California, San Francisco (UCSF). I worked at the time as a research assistant in the Center for Reproductive Health, where heterosexual assumptions were built into almost every research project. Therefore, as part of my qualitative-methods training, I decided to conduct an exploratory qualitative study on queer reproductive practices. Although I knew of many studies of lesbian mothers, I was not aware of any studies along the lines I proposed. The project eventually became my doctoral dissertation. I was fortunate to have had an outstanding committee: Adele Clarke, Virginia Olesen, Gay Becker, and Val Hartouni. I thank each of them for their unique contributions.

Since that time, I have benefited from the support of numerous individuals and organizations. Most recently, the department of sociology at the University of Maryland, where I am currently an assistant professor, generously provided time, resources, and assistance. In 2002 I received funding from the University of Maryland Graduate Research Board. The department of sociology granted me two additional summers of support and a third-year, semester-long teaching release to write this book. The research assistance of Vrushali Patil, Michelle Corbin, Leigh Bryant, and Amber Nelson was invaluable. I thank Bill Falk, George Ritzer, and the late Richard Harvey Brown for reading earlier drafts of this book. Several other faculty members at the University of Maryland became my local, intellectual community: Elizabeth Marshall, Katie King, Bonnie Dill, Meredith Honig, Melissa Milkie, Meyer Kestnbaum, Marilee Lindemann, and William Cohen.

I received generous funding through UCSF, including a Regents Fellowship, a Health Sciences Fellowship, a Graduate Student Research Award, and the Diane Forsyth Memorial Dissertation Award. I could not have accomplished my analysis without the transcription support of and comments from Joyce Umamoto and Barbara Tashima and the editorial assistance of Juliane Baron. I especially thank Rima Shore for seeing me through the eleventh hour when I needed help the most. I literally could not have done it without her.

I owe gratitude to members of the qualitative methods and writing groups I have participated in over the years: Janet Shim, Jennifer Fosket, Paula Lum, Leslie Martin, Melanie Egorin, Teresa Scherzer, Jennifer Fishman, and Kristen Karlberg. Several others provided important conversations about my research: Shelly Adler, Amy Agigian, C. L. Cole, Ronnie Eversley, Anne Figert, Lisa Handwerker, Ellen Lewin, Lisa Jeane Moore, Cloe Ohme, Maureen Sullivan, and Carolyn Weiner. I thank Mary Rose Mueller for treating me as her equal and giving me a job when I needed one.

Special acknowledgments go to my friends, colleagues, and intellectual soul mates at UCSF, Jennifer Fosket and Janet Shim, who read and commented on every word included in and cut from this project. My piano teacher, Margaret Fabrizio, taught me that sometimes the only, and most difficult, way to get a work of art to the next level is to "white out" those parts that feel the most creative and clear. Starting fresh is a constant challenge when rewriting a manuscript.

I would like to thank my East Coast colleagues and friends: Kelly Joyce, Jackie Orr, Celine Marie Pascale, Elizabeth Marshall, Juliane Baron, Meredith Honig, and Morva McDonald. The feedback on early drafts by Kelly, Celine, Beth, and Juliane helped me realize their full potential. Kelly read every word of the final manuscript and clarified sentences I could no longer see. Kelly, you're the best.

I also wish to thank the editors, staff, and reviewers from Duke University Press. I am most grateful to the acquisitions editor Raphael Allen for his belief in this project. I thank Ken Wissoker for his willingness to take it on and the anonymous reviewers for their very thorough and encouraging review of early versions of this manuscript.

Beyond the academic walls have been the support, conversation, and life force provided by many friends and family members. I would like to thank in particular my three lesbian mothers: my mother, Ann D'Ercole; my not-mother, Adria E. Schwartz; and my stepmother, Linda Brady. Although Adria died before I finished this book, her voice, encouragement, and intellectual curiosity remained ever present. Together and in various ways my mothers have exemplified how lesbian families can blur and morph, at times mirroring the idealized family and at times steadfastly resisting it. I also thank my grandmother Rose D'Ercole for her reminder that love conquers all. I miss her every day. Finally, I thank my chosen family—Mary Cain and Chris Bettinger, Don Lusty, Janet Smith, Eleanor Palacios, Elizabeth Marshall and Michael Maneer, Kelly Joyce, Rima Shore, Alex Schwartz, and especially Jennifer Fosket—for providing vacations, books, music, discussion, laughter, and all those things that go into a well-lived life.

Finally, I would like to recognize the many women who volunteered their time to tell me their stories, for without them this book would not have been possible. More women volunteered than I was able to interview, and I thank all of them for doing so. Not all of the women I interviewed were able to become "lesbian mothers," but each had the courage to contemplate the complex meanings of motherhood and queer identity. In addition to the individuals who shared their stories, several organizational directors and staff also met with me to explain the histories and missions of their services, as well as their individual thoughts on queer reproduction. I owe particular thanks to Sherron Mills and staff members at Pacific Reproductive Services, Maura Riordan and staff members at the Sperm Bank of California, Leland Traiman of Rainbow Flag Health Services, 1996 members of the Prospective Queer Parents organization, Kim Toeves and Stephanie Brill of Maia Midwifery, and the staff of the Alternative Family Project.

Earlier versions of parts of chapters 2 and 7 appeared as "The Lesbian 'Great American Sperm Hunt': A Sociological Analysis of Selecting Donors and Constructing Relatedness," in *Uncoupling Convention: Psychoanalytic Approaches to Same-Sex Couples and Families*, edited by Ann D'Ercole and Jack Drescher (Hillsdale, N.J: Analytic Press, 2004). An earlier version of chapter 7 appeared as "Biomedicalizing Kinship: Sperm Banks and the Creation of Affinity-ties," in *Science as Culture*, 14, no. 3 (2005): 237–64. Parts of earlier versions of chapters 5 and 6 appeared as "Negotiating Conception: Lesbians' Hybrid-Technological Practices" in *Science, Technology and Human Values* 32, no. 3 (2007): 369–93.

Introduction

THE QUESTIONNAIRE SEEMED TO GO ON FOREVER. Renee looked around at the other patients who had come to San Mateo Fertility Associates and wondered who they were. Was she the only lesbian here? Her friends Jan and Marilyn had told her that lots of lesbians used the doctors at this clinic. Renee and her partner had spent the last month going through the donor catalog and had arranged to have three vials of sperm shipped to this office. Renee refocused on the form: she knew the date of her last menstrual cycle, but was it diabetes that had killed her uncle? As she waited, she tried to focus on the baby she was so eager to conceive.

Renee is a lesbian in the Bay Area of San Francisco, California. Hers is the story of a significant cultural group, one with its own fascinating history, assumptions, mores, ethics, practices: she is part of a large population of lesbians who are bearing and/or raising children. Lesbian identifications have to some extent shifted, one is told, from flannel and softball to strollers and day care. In the United States an estimated 1.5 to 5 million lesbian mothers reside with their children (Hequembourg and Farrell 1999).

Despite these numbers, the research literature is relatively silent on how lesbians (or gay men) go about reproducing and forming families. How do lesbian women negotiate their paths to motherhood? How do they conceptualize family? How do they go about conceiving children? What kinds of medical assistance do they seek? What other routes do they take to building a family? As K. R. Allen and D. H. Demo noted, "Where these families have been studied, they have been problematized and their diversity has been overlooked" (1995, 11). While researchers have begun to fill this gap, much more remains to be known, especially in the realm of "chosen families."

Renee's story is about cultural change, about the ways that feminism in general, and lesbian feminism in particular, has influenced the contemporary culture(s) of lesbian lives; once geared to resist dominant culture, lesbian feminism now appears to embrace parenthood and all the tropes of normalcy that accompany it. But Renee's story is also about historic social change: the separation of reproduction from heterosexual intercourse; the medicalization and demedicalization of homosexuality; the emergence of gay and lesbian social identities; and the normalization of fertility services that lend a helping hand to all women seeking pregnancies. Finally, hers is a story about the evolving relationship between Americans and biomedical interventions and technologies. Biomedical sciences and their medical applications no longer focus exclusively on the treatment and cure of pathology in the form of illness, but increasingly on the amelioration of life difficulties through transformations of one's self. While Renee and the other lesbians featured in this book largely accept biomedical assistance on their paths to pregnancy, they are also strategic in how they negotiate the process, at once resisting and accepting medical ideas, techniques, and services. Renee's story—and lesbian insemination in general—is a fascinating lens through which to view the changing relationships between Americans and biomedicine.

After all, Renee does not *need* to be in that waiting room. She is not infertile according to the medical classification. Her problem, if one chooses to call it that, is social. She needs a substance that is by no means scarce. And the procedure of vaginal insemination is uncomplicated, requiring the simplest of technologies, which Renee can learn about from friends, the Internet, and other media resources.

Renee has grown up in America after and with *Our Bodies, Ourselves,* that is, in an era when empowerment in the realm of women's health issues was a core tenet of feminism in general and lesbian feminism in particular. Yet, despite the success of women's health movements, Renee is filling out the new-patient forms at the San Mateo Fertility Associates, a medical group of "fertility specialists" that offers comprehensive diagnosis and treatment of infertility and reproductive endocrinology disorders. In other realms of medicine and healthcare, one might suspect that advertising influenced Renee, but society is not yet at the point where reassuring TV doctors say, "Ask your doctor about lesbian insemination." Perhaps Renee has been influenced by the wave of self-help literatures that are written as personal narratives of empowerment, yet advocate expert services to overcome personal obstacles. Or perhaps she is following the advice of friends or her primary-care physician or gynecologist.

So what has brought Renee to seek specialist services? How do these services interact with her sense of who she is and her goal of pregnancy? And how does she benefit? Citing theory, research, and ethnographic material, *Queering Reproduction* explores these questions in the context of both medical and social trends. It describes the medical therapies and social movements that have led Renee and many others to turn to specialists. It chronicles the changes in medical knowledge, feminism(s) and women's health movements, healthcare services economies, and political ideologies that have influenced the options and actions of women choosing motherhood outside the bounds of heterosexual relationships. In particular, it shows how advances in assisted reproduction have "biomedicalized" a relatively simple process. It shows how, by gaining access to these interventions, lesbians have destabilized the dichotomy between heterosexual and homosexual experience and the institution of the family, the grounds upon which dichotomous gender is reinforced and maintained.

In the process, this book explores many of the cultural forces and patterns that shape and are shaped by Americans' evolving ideas, behaviors, and life journeys. At one time, Renee's story might have seemed unusual, but today her story is becoming routine for many with access to medical services and the capital to negotiate all that these services offer. Furthermore, when one looks deeply at the contours of her actions and the forces that shape them, one finds many of the same immense, interrelated forces that influence so many other aspects of American life.

Renee's Story and American Life in the New Century

Renee's story shares many qualities with those related to me by the other thirty-five lesbians I interviewed for this book. First, her story reflects a heightened concern with security and uses the rhetoric of risk management that has saturated public discourse. There are several kinds of risks managed by the lesbians I interviewed: reducing risk of disease transmission with the promise of technoscientific advances in sperm testing, washing, and storage; reducing risk of reduced social dominance by selecting sperm with the "right" genetic and social characteristics; and reducing risk of unstable parental rights by accessing and creating legal documentation stating intentional parenthood and by following state legislation declaring and defining parental status.

Second, Renee's story echoes current health care discourses which emphasize not only illness, treatment, and cure but also health, enhancement, and personal responsibility and fulfillment.[1] Similarly, the women interviewed were knowledgeable about medical issues and their own bodies; they were enterprising in the ways they gathered resources, initiated health care actions, and responded to new information; they were pragmatic in the ways they engaged their bodies and selves with medical, legal, and cultural worlds; and they were calculating in their attempts to maximize benefits to themselves and their children. These characteristics were clear in the ways women decided to become parents, sought donors, and selected anonymous sperm. As women select sperm donors, for example, they are encouraged to consider enhancing the next generation by reducing both the risk of potential illnesses and that of perceived cultural liabilities such as short stature, acne, academic weakness, lack of athleticism, lack of musical talent, or even being black or Asian.

Third, Renee's story speaks to a consumer society marked by ideals of ownership, presumed individual choice, and consumption as means to fulfill one's desires, identities, and life-goals. Consumption infuses all aspects of our lives, including our reproductive lives. Healthcare has extended in ways that emphasize consumer processes of pleasure and transformation: there is no choice but to exercise choice. Healthcare encompasses any and all issues concerning health and lifestyle with a goal of meeting assumed market demands. The lesbians interviewed describe interactions that are pragmatic negotiations taken as they reach toward an end goal/desire: to become pregnant and attain motherhood. For many lesbians, buying sperm — and all that sperm embodies — becomes a route not only to achieving parenthood, but also to realizing their imagined senses of self and their hope for the future.[2]

Fourth, Renee's story reflects anxieties about social connection and belonging in the age of "bowling alone" — a trend toward less civic engagement and more isolated (often electronic) activity both at home and in the workplace (Putnam 2000) — and in a culture in which healthcare services facilitate lesbians' reproduction while simultaneously legally and politically contesting their right to exist. In this context, women like Renee are seeking to redefine and create family in ways that render them legible as full participants in the United States and in ways that might be used to gain legitimacy in a largely heterosexist culture. In doing so, the boundaries between family and community are blurred as the field of procreators extends beyond traditional mothers and fathers.

Fifth, the story reflects a culture that places immense value on technoscientific progress, measured by the continual introduction and professional

oversight of new technologies that promise to be more advanced, successful, and efficient (and, yes, more expensive!). Yet the implications of adopting such technologies are consequential for older technologies, as many
become obsolete; for medical practices, as newer technologies are built into
standard protocols; and for the cost of delivering and receiving healthcare
services.

Finally, Renee's story illuminates the ways in which people interact with
the world around them and make meaning out of those interactions. It
shows that the everyday behavior of ordinary people is not calibrated either
to follow or to subvert American ideals or the ideals that animate social
movements (e.g., feminism) or organizational discourses (e.g., fertility
medicine). Rather, individuals act in ways that seem likely to achieve their
most deeply held goals and dreams. Their actions, as well as the meanings
that shape them, reflect strategic and intentional navigations of the enabling
and constraining stratifications of society.

While the immediate goals of lesbian reproductive practices are parenthood and the formation of families, they are also part of a politics of seeking
recognition and belonging. I use the term *queering reproduction* to draw
attention to processes by which lesbian reproductive practices simultaneously alter and maintain dominant assumptions and institutions. I argue
that while lesbians and other nonheterosexual actors and groups variously
push and pull their way into normativity, doing so does not solidify the
normal, but instead makes its borders far more porous and opaque, thereby
recasting the meaning of reproduction itself. The stability and assumed
naturalness of reproduction, and by extension the family form, has undergone substantial cultural reworking and is today finally queered. Lesbian
reproductive practices have contributed significantly to this destabilization.

Crafting New Family Forms

Nothing within biology demands the nuclear family. It is a cultural and
social system enforced by regulations and reinforced by legal discourse,
medical practices, and cultural norms. Yet in the United States it is the
nuclear family, bound by blood and legal arrangements of marriage and
adoption, that represents social order, idealized kinship, and legitimate relations. But, as Gayle Rubin (1975) argued, cultural rules are alterable rules.

For more than three decades, new family forms have proliferated in the
United States and many other countries. There are intentional single par-

ents, blended (step-parent) families, interracial families, older-parent families, families headed by grandparents, and other variations. Such variety is not the result of individual choices alone, but is shaped by historical social forces and ideologies, which themselves do not reflect a single historical moment, but represent expanding and contracting changes over time. Nonetheless, these new family forms collectively destabilize the myth of the U.S. (white) nuclear family (Coontz 1992; Stack 1974), show that families comprise both immediate *and* extended kin (Stack 1974), and demonstrate that families take a diversity of forms (Stacey 1990, 1996; Collins 1999).

Like other emergent family arrangements, gay and lesbian families have only recently been the subject of social-science research. Most of the research on lesbian families has emphasized the normalcy of these families, of their relationships, and of their effects on children when they are compared with the "normal" heterosexual nuclear family (see Stacey and Biblarz 2001). Social scientists have focused primarily on the increased visibility of gay, lesbian, and queer communities and their participation in marriages, domestic partnerships, and child-rearing (see for example Lewin 1993, 1998a; Carrington 1999). They have tended toward a general theorization of gay, lesbian, and queer social (and family) life (Stacey and Biblarz 2001; Stacey 2003). In contrast, Maureen Sullivan (2004) has eloquently argued that dual-mother families are agents of social change undoing the gendered social order. Families in which both parents are of the same sex undo gender by refusing the relationality through which dichotomous gender is defined.

I examine lesbian processes of becoming parents and constructing families through the use of assisted-reproduction technologies. My focus lies on the complex ways in which such technologies and the family structures they engender both "trouble the normal" and reinforce the normalization of traditional gender, sexuality, and family constructs. That is, I ask how, and in what ways, do these practices construct new and old ways of knowing about kinship, of becoming related, of being recognized as belonging to social life, and of being and doing gender, sexuality, and family.

Complicating Identity Matters

Within studies of sexualities, assumptions of the unity of gay identities and experiences were displaced in the 1980s and 1990s. Susan Krieger (1983), Jennifer Terry (1991), Kath Weston (1991), Ellen Lewin (1993), and others conducted empirical research that destabilized homogeneous, universal views of lesbians. Other scholars further differentiated lesbian "identity" and revealed how race and class dimensions participate in the multiple bases of lesbian identities (see, for example, Kennedy and Davis 1993; Lewin 1996; Anzaldúa 1987). Judith Butler (1990, 1993) conceptualized the very meaning of gender and sexuality as reiterative performances. As Virginia Olesen (2000) pointed out, this was similar to earlier articulations by the sociologists Erving Goffman (1959) and Candace West and Don Zimmerman (1987). By viewing sexual identities as processes, scholars displaced the dualistic conceptions of gender and sexuality, prioritizing instead a questioning of "the notion that sexual subjects share a sexual core (a preference or orientation), that underneath the skin they have the same kind of self" (Gamson 2000, 352).

The theoretical assumption that one could locate the "truth" of sexuality and thus study it was eroded in favor of distinguishing the social and interactional processes by which bodies and desires are given meaning and transformed into social categories with political significance. This had long been understood by qualitative researchers working in phenomenological, interactionist, and other constructionist or labeling-theory traditions. What these perspectives share is an understanding of sexuality as a powerful system of regulation whose very categories (the dominant being heterosexual and homosexual) function as regulatory ideals that produce, discipline, and mark the bodies they govern and underpin all aspects of contemporary life.

In many ways, U.S. culture continues to assume heterosexuality and to emphasize the channeling of sexual expressions into "legitimate" forms and "proper" settings, that is, within marriage and for the purposes of procreation. Heterosexism, with its assumptions of what constitutes normal and deviant behaviors, desires, and lifestyles, continues to shape social-science literature, social policy, and social ideas. Heteronormativity, the equation of humanity with heterosexuality, operates as a hegemonic or taken-for-granted assumption in U.S. society and is embedded into many of its social institutions, including the family (Warner 1993). Heteronormativity operates as a system of power that variously affects, through privileging and constraining, heterosexuals, gay men, lesbians, bisexuals, transgendered persons, and everyone else.

Queering Reproduction is critical social theory that engages central questions facing groups of people placed in unequal systems of political, social,

institutional, and historical contexts. Lesbians continue to be denied full
citizenship in U.S. society—they are denied the right to marry, to visitation
of their partners, to transfer property and assets on death, to immigrate to
the United States, and so on—and are faced with heterosexist and heteronormative logics of gender and sexuality that constrain their daily lives.

Lesbian identities and lesbian politics form a scope through which this
book looks. Yet the very concepts of "lesbian" and "lesbian process" are
problematic. Lesbians represent a multitude of understandings, practices,
and standpoints. *Lesbian* encompasses an experiential diversity that is extremely complex, that is shifting, situated, and intersectional with other axes
of difference such as race, gender, class, nationality, age, and geographic
place. *Lesbian* itself is a linguistic convenience, a placeholder that might seem
to suggest a fixed set of characteristics and meanings associated (in a world
that tends toward binary categories) with the concepts not male–not heterosexual. The distinction between *lesbian* as a linguistic category productive of
power and as a group-based identity reflects the difference between "post"
projects that emphasize the ways meanings are materially and discursively
produced based on linguistic and embodied repetitions—what Butler
(1990) terms "performativity" (see also West and Fenstermaker 1995; West
and Zimmerman 1987)—and meaning derived from one's standpoint(s) in
social locations.[3]

I use *lesbian* as both identity and linguistic construct. At times, I use the
term as a convenient marker to describe the women and experiences that are
the subject of this study (and the subject of a political group). This takes into
account the complexity of lesbian subjectivities. At other times, I grapple
with *lesbian* as a more dimensional concept that is given meaning through its
linguistic position in relation to heterosexuality, thus examining the ways
that binary categories work to construct and normalize the social order and
how these are "built in" to institutions, discourses, and practices. As a result,
I centralize how the very meaning of human reproduction is brought forward, stabilized, and shaken through its tight coupling with the meanings of
heterosexuality, family, and nature.

While I have no choice but to complicate matters, power relations are
never as transparent and clear as one hopes to make them. At times, they are
invisible and embedded in the categorical names assigned to persons and the
social practices and institutions that those individuals encounter in everyday
life. Subjectivities are sociohistorical constructs, varied and distinctive in

their specificities across time, place, and culture. They are categories of meaning shaped by historical processes and systems of knowledge (see, for example, Omi and Winant 1994 on racial formation). As a result, lesbian subjectivities are ongoing social formations shaped by historical processes and systems of knowledge, including the histories of "infertility" and "homosexuality" as medical classifications, the politicization of lesbian identities, shifting gendered and social norms, and the rise of "Fertility Inc."[4]

Yet at times I force a "unity" of the lesbian subject that does not exist; I do so deliberately and thoughtfully as a project of critical social thought. The term *lesbian* is both experienced materially on the bodies of human actors and (re)produced in social (inter)actions. My goals are to reveal the ways in which such subjectivities negotiate regulatory practices and to uncover the ways in which heterosexuality continues to operate as a system of normalization.

The influence of the French philosopher Michel Foucault is highly significant to my argument. Foucault (1980a) argued that definitions in the realm of sexuality and reproduction are cultural categories as well as systems of regulation that change over time and place. Bodies and their subjectivities and identifications are constituted in and through relations of power-knowledge. The classifications of "infertility" and "homosexuality," for example, do not arise in nature, but are constituted by social and cultural systems of meaning, codified in cultural rules that define what is normal and abnormal. These discourses in turn shape subjects — and their identities — through their labeling practices. Through the lens of Foucault's thought, one sees how declaring same-sex sexuality to be unnatural is a line-drawing mechanism through which heterosexuality is naturalized.

Constituting Subjects, Making Biomedical Belonging

This book traces some of the historical processes and discourses that have shaped and continue to shape lesbian subjectivities and the unfolding of lesbian motherhood as a technological achievement. As part "archaeology of knowledge" (Foucault 1972), this book attends to the ways various knowledges produce new forms of subjects and practices. It emphasizes those discourses in which lesbian reproductive practices have been embedded and shaped over the past century, particularly in the last thirty years. As such, it proceeds from the assumption that lesbian reproductive practices are situated in and shaped by various disciplinary discourses and power relations.

I make use of the work of feminist poststructuralists (see especially Balsamo 1996; Sawicki 1991; Lock and Kaufert 1998) who draw heavily on Foucault's work to argue that subjectivities in general and gendered subjectivities in particular are entangled within power relations. Foucault (1980a, 1980b) argues that modern power is enacted through regulations of the population. *Biopower* is his term for an important shift from control over death to the regulation of life processes such as birth, health, sex, and mortality through methods of administrative calculation that, in effect, arrange life into standards of normalization. Biopower operates inside the minds and bodies of populations, affecting how they think of themselves and their social relations. That is, modern power makes selves, identities, and ways of being.[5] Subjectivities, of course, are intimately connected with the material, lived realities of gender, race, class, and other systems of privilege and inequality. As long as race, class, and gender stratifications are part of social life, individuals are constrained in the ways in which they can shape their bodies and identities.

Discourses of (medical) reproduction and sexuality co-produce lesbian subjectivities and social forms of biomedical belonging. At the same time, the ways women respond to power relations are varied, ranging "from selective resistance to selective compliance," as Margaret Lock and Patricia Kaufert (1998) describe. Yet, while there may be choice and freedom, these are neither universally applied nor meaningful; people's imaginings of their selves, and their abilities to create themselves anew, are limited. I make claims of agency that account for the structural constraints of power relations.[6]

What might appear to be emerging freedoms and choice offered by new technological practices are concurrently forged *within* power relations, not outside them. This idea marks much of feminist technoscience studies approaches: the meeting of bodies with technological and scientific practices are part of culture and power; they do not exist outside of culture and power. Bodies and their subjectivities are conceived, technologized, and debated within politically and socially meaningful contexts by people who face different and multiple situations of power (Grosz 1993; Pitts 2005).

Although I examine lesbian practices of achieving pregnancy as "eyes wide open" and intentional, I nonetheless argue that despite idealist visions, structural constraints continue to be imposed. In an effort not to falsely emphasize agency over structural constraint, I attend to the messy workings of power and culture in shaping these practices. For example, as I underscore in chapters 4 and 5, practices of getting pregnant are "choreographies" of body-subject relations (see Thompson 2005), which include willful agency and external and unconscious forces of power. It is my goal throughout the book to demonstrate that in examinations of lived, material practices, power shapes what can be known and what remains invisible and presumably unknown.

Biomedicalization of Life Processes

A central avenue through which power-knowledge-body relations are addressed is through the medicalization and biomedicalization of reproduction and other life processes. Medicalization refers to the extension of medical knowledges, practices, and techniques into people's daily lives by labeling aspects of social life as "illness" or "disease" and placing them under the jurisdiction of medicine (Law 1987; Conrad and Schneider 1980; Ehrenreich 1978; Zola 1972).

Throughout most of the twentieth century, the complex processes that constituted medicalization shifted certain social issues into the realm of the medical. This transformation in American medicine (following Starr 1982) coalesced into *bio*medicalization (Clarke et al. 2003), which continues to this day. It encompasses the cumulative impact and cultural pervasiveness of technoscience and a commodity culture, as well as a focus on risk and surveillance, an increase in customized and "lifestyle" medicines, and other social processes that take place as medicine travels in new ways and into new places.

Like medicalization, biomedicalization privileges expert knowledge and ensures professional jurisdiction over the labeling, classification, and treatment of bodies and behaviors. As Foucault (1980a) eloquently argues, biopower enacts the regulation of private and public life through the elaboration of expertise in the form of specialized knowledges. These knowledges then create their own "objects" of analysis. That is, medicine and medical experts label bodily states, behaviors, and desires, thereby opening up spaces for the deployment of expert knowledges in the service of "cure." Foucault terms this cure *normalization*. Those who do not fit within normalized categories are ready targets for the intervention of expert knowledge.

However, neither medicalization nor biomedicalization is destiny. People variously possess agency, the ability to exert influence over, if not shape, their own lives (see Foucault 1988a, 1988b). Individuals or patients are able to selectively take on, resist, or negotiate its classifications and interventions. Biomedical knowledges and practices are not neutral social forces; they encompass power relations that define, shape, and control individuals and populations. Moreover, corporate interests act as dominant forces in biomedicalization, as companies encourage consumers to surf the Internet to locate knowledge, find communities, and make their health selections.

It follows that lesbian reproduction is not technologically determined; it is not the next step in medicalizing human reproduction. Rather lesbian reproduction is a social and cultural achievement that has unfolded within and through layers of social processes constituted within, yet also beyond, medicine. This story of lesbian reproduction is situated, partial, and produced through multiple social fields including, but not limited to, biomedicine. As a result, lesbians living child-free and seeking pregnancies are neither bound by the discourses of biomedicalization and its reliance on expert knowledge and consumer practices, nor entirely free of them. Instead, cultural ideals that come into being in the context of biomedicalization shape the way all of us think about, experience, and put into practice our bodies, health, and illness. At the same time, the expert classifiers who emerge in the context of biomedicalization produce new identities and create new languages that the very people they classify can appropriate to live and speak on their own terms.

The power relations between the classifiers and the classified are complex. Negotiation of and resistance to expert knowledges take many forms, and in the process hybrid knowledges and practices are created and deployed. Biomedical processes are not entirely hegemonic and can no longer be conceptualized as a distinct and identifiable social world. Instead, biomedical knowledges, services, and discourses are cultural practices that travel widely. Lesbian reproductive practices, then, do not simply involve the classifiers speaking and the classified responding. The histories of homosexuality and infertility, for example, are produced as much by those who live and feel these "aberrations" as they are by experts who label and define them. Constructions of homosexuality and infertility are collaborative and ongoing social processes that take place outside as well as within the porous boundaries of sciences and biomedicines. Similarly, lesbian reproductive practices are also not entirely bound by discourses of lesbian and gay political movements and theories; they are embedded within them and variously shaped by them. As a subject and social practice, lesbian reproduction is the product of several social forces coalescing in neat *and* messy ways that are profoundly social.

I argue that the biomedicalization of reproduction and sexuality are co-constituted and ongoing cultural practices.[7] Despite different outcomes, the medicalization of infertility and homosexuality are not parallel processes, but overlapping systems of meaning that continue to shape the landscape of family formation. Competing ideologies have resulted. On the one hand, these histories have supported the ideology that all can, and therefore all should, reproduce. On the other hand, they have led to a reliance on Fertility Inc. for the needed technology, thereby sharply limiting access to assisted reproduction. Because assisted reproduction continues to garner legitimacy primarily as a means of allowing heterosexual couples to overcome childlessness, lesbians must navigate a landscape that only implicitly accepts them as users of these technologies. In biomedicalization, economic forces of consumer culture welcome almost anyone in their fee-for-service medical system: the new professional gatekeeping of Fertility Inc. is to provide services to anyone with money and cultural capital.

The Genesis of This Book and My Politics of Engagement

Like many feminist scholars interested in women's health, reproductive rights, and social justice, my politics of engagement are intertwined with my political commitments, personal biography, and the social locations in which I am situated. Searching for justice, particularly in the realm of healthcare, has always been a concern in my work. I have long participated in addressing reproductive and sexual health issues and I have worked in gay and lesbian health organizations. My work has taken me from AIDS services to teen reproductive healthcare to sexual human rights.

Assisted reproduction is an issue of women's health that intersects with reproductive politics more generally. As Monica Casper asserts, reproductive politics include the "multiple ways in which human reproduction, particularly as women experience it, is shaped by power, inequality, and social location" (1998, 10). Assisting reproduction and creating families are embedded in the politics of reproductive and sexual health, where significant race and class disparities exist between those who have access to health information and healthcare and those who do not. It is ironic and unjust that in an age of expensive, high-tech healthcare, many women (mostly poor, immigrant, black, or Latino) cannot and therefore do not receive even basic medical services such as routine check-ups and prenatal care. Reproduction is historically a key site of social control over women and women's agency, as well as a site in which stratifications have been profoundly exercised. In the United States and elsewhere, reproductive processes are contested and stratified at multiple levels of social life: interpersonal, community, biomedical, cultural, economic, social, and global (Ginsburg and Rapp 1995).[8] Reproductive politics take many forms, including battles over abortion, sex education, menopause and the use of hormone-replacement therapies, teenage pregnancy, and so on.

Lesbian reproduction embodies a particular configuration of these reproductive politics. It conjoins a historical proliferation of technologies to assist conception, debates over the proper and legitimate place of human procreation, and ideas regarding "appropriate" family forms. It is also a fee-for-service practice shaped by one's ability to pay. Lesbian reproductive practices are situated in and shaped by women's health issues, technomedical worlds, and the politics of sexual and reproductive rights.

In terms of my own personal biography and social locations, these issues are deeply personal for me, as they in some ways trace my life history. I contend, however, that engaging in a reflexive feminist sociology demands that researchers no longer assume that they can stand apart from the external world and transform it into an object of scientific study. Instead, they must be willing to examine the ways their own life journeys and assumptions shape their interpretations of the social world.

People often ask me why I selected this research project. What is it about my life and life journey? Do I share the experiences of the people whose lives I investigate? My answers are as complicated and partial as the stories of those participants: my story and theirs is not an authentic truth, but a partial story captured at a particular time.

I was born in 1969 into a white, working-class family. My parents met in Catholic school and were married shortly after their high-school graduation. Neither of my parents attended college. My mother was a stay-at-home mom who cared for me and my two older brothers while my father worked as a traveling salesman. By 1974, my parents were separated, and my now single mother began to attend community college in New Jersey, where she found an active women's center—or perhaps they found her. After my parents' divorce, in the context of 1970s "lesbian-feminist" ideals, my mother declared her lesbian identity. Still, we remained a suburban family: my mother, her "friend," my brothers, and me. I was toted around to Holly Near concerts, Adrienne Rich readings, and my brothers and I soon found ourselves to be part of the lesbian world. In the early 1980s my mother's relationship ended, and she fell in love with another woman, who became my "not-mother" and second parent. In the mid-1980s, my not-mother chose to become a lesbian mom herself and adopted her son, Alex. At the time, "turkey-baster babies" had gained momentum, "alternative family" play groups had formed, and lesbian mothers no longer embodied contradictory terms. Alex and his mom were part of a community of alternative families who celebrated gay pride and were out at school, camp, and health appointments.

In 1987 I went away to college and became sexually involved with women. For me and the other young lesbians with whom I created community, this era marked the beginning of boundary crossing and fluid sexual practices. Whether we identified as dykes, lesbians, queer, or bisexual, we shared a common assumption: desiring and loving someone of the same sex was not a fixed identity, nor would it preclude motherhood; these were not irreconcilable possibilities. In fact, by the late 1980s and early 1990s, many of us espoused a new story: of course we would have kids, too! It was our right, after all. We could have them in any number of ways: sleep with a man, adopt, or find a donor (anonymous or known) and use a turkey baster. We could be single parents, co-moms, or co-parents with a gay man (or couple) who also wanted to have children.

Turning attention inward, I began to view this narrative as at once an emergent social force and a peculiarly conventional perspective. As a community, we had expanded the number of options, but in some ways the story we then constructed was utterly traditional. Did this represent a mainstreaming of lesbian lives? No questions, no analysis, just reproduction and motherhood for all! This mainstreaming was in full view in my college town—Madison, Wisconsin—where playgrounds were visited by children with their two moms. These experiences led me to the questions that were the genesis for this book.

First, I wondered in what ways could I understand and give meaning to my own childhood. But other questions drew me, with equal power, into this inquiry. As an observer and participant in "lesbian cultures" throughout the 1970s, 1980s, and 1990s, I often questioned whether having a child was a transgressive act for a lesbian. Or did it represent another variant of the enduring social norms of gender and of dichotomous gender's concomitant social form, heterosexual reproduction? It seemed to me that lesbians having children reaffirmed the sociocultural expectation that women would reproduce, thereby naturalizing women's bodies as reproductive. My own background also confirmed that the idealized nuclear-family kinship structure (with two parents of the opposite sex) was no longer salient in social practices, at least in my own social life. Yet, its dominance remained ideologically hegemonic.[9]

Of course no childhood—including my own—takes place in a vacuum. Experiences happen and meaning evolves in the context of the heterosexual surround. And so, I came to wonder, in what ways were lesbian reproduction and parenting shaped by cultural norms? What were the factors that shaped the decisions of lesbians choosing motherhood? In what ways did lesbian reproductive practices challenge and destabilize the long-standing ideological structure? And in what ways did they participate in its very reinforcement by providing the deviant other on which its meaning was formed?

The methods and engagement of this topic follow feminist in-depth interviewing and multi-sited analysis.[10] As a feminist, qualitative researcher I work against positivistic claims to truth and objectivity by attending to subjectivities and lived experience. Yet, experience is always already interpreted (as Joan Scott 1992 so eloquently argued) and knowledge is always multiple and partial (Haraway 1991). In bringing forward material practices, I do not accept narratives as "truth," but instead analyze the ways practices are embedded in and shaped by cultural forces.

My primary data sources include in-depth interviews with thirty-six women who self-identified as lesbian, gay, bisexual, or queer and who were seeking to achieve pregnancy, as well as in-depth interviews with key local actors providing related services to these respondents. Drawing on the interviews with lesbians seeking pregnancies, I followed the data to three local sperm banks, one biomedical infertility practice, and one pre-conception and midwifery practice. I conducted six formal interviews with providers to determine the state of the practice of assisted reproduction and the construction of "appropriate" users of these services. The interviews included questions about the overall mission, practice, and organization of the services offered as well as the tools and techniques used in assisted reproduction.

I followed the general principles of grounded theory and multisited ethnography. Grounded theory, as developed by Barney Glaser and Anselm Strauss (Glaser and Strauss 1967; Glaser 1978; Strauss 1987; Strauss and Corbin 1990), emerges from the central tenets of symbolic interactionism and is an inductive method of analysis that emphasizes discovery and theory development. Its core components are to simultaneously conduct data collection and analysis and to allow conceptual understandings to emerge from the data. Multisited ethnography is a strategy for capturing complexity and multiplicity while attending to validity (Rapp 1999). In many ways, the use of a single data source can elicit impressions that there is only one "truth" to be told. Multiple sources of data help to shatter this impression and reveal heterogeneous positions. By utilizing multiple data sources and a process of constant comparison within each source, I was able to trust that the conclusions I drew were representative of the multiplicity and variety of experiences included in this specific and localized phenomena. While grounded theory allows for this type of "validity" check in that it requires one to constantly compare codes within each interview itself and with codes assigned to interviews with other respondents, it does not implicitly attend to issues of partial knowledges. While "objectivity" was abandoned in my research process, I replaced it with "adequacy" and "credibility." Thus, by interviewing a diverse range of respondents in terms of personal characteristics such as race or ethnicity, class, and partner status, as well as in terms of differing positions or circumstances along the insemination-pregnancy trajectory, I was able to confidently draw conclusions about their relative accuracy. Yet, at the same time, I understood that these conclusions were my interpretations about shifting and already interpreted experiences. Thus, what I present are partial knowledges: they must be read with the understanding that there can be no complete truth, no unity, and no single objective experience.

Plan of the Book

This book presents situated accounts of "getting to pregnant" as described in thirty-six in-depth interviews. I recruited respondents using a snowball sampling method. I placed flyers in local bookstores and at fertility offices, and I placed an advertisement in two sperm-bank newsletters. In addition, word-of-mouth contacts were generated during the interview process. I received phone calls from many more women than I was able to interview. The thirty-six respondents who appear in this book share a goal of pregnancy for themselves or their partners, yet their lives and perspectives differ in many ways. While many occupy middle-class backgrounds and many identify strongly with lesbian cultures, these are not universal characteristics. (See table 1 for a sketch of their racial, occupational, and relationship status as self-described in interviews; although reductive, these descriptions provide a starting point for their stories that follow.) Collectively, their histories constitute the heart of the story of lesbian reproduction.

My ethnographic analysis centers technoscientific practices to explicate relations among cultural meanings and material actions.[11] I take users of biomedicine seriously in this research, account for and value their perspectives, and make their views, decision making, and actions the "object" of focus.[12] In chapter 1 I place this ethnographic material in historic context. Since the lesbians depicted in this book were by no means the first homosexuals to become the objects of medical attention, nor were they the first prospective parents to turn to medical providers for assistance, I begin at a crossroads — at the unintended meeting of sex without reproduction and reproduction without sex. I examine the sociocultural histories of medical reproductive technologies and the medicalization and demedicalization of (homo)sexualities. I then trace the 1970s emergence of a lesbian alternative-insemination movement, with its espousal of women's empowerment and reproductive rights.[13] The story of lesbian alternative insemination as a lay social movement, exemplified by do-it-yourself turkey-baster babies, is quickly complicated as lesbian lives and identities become ever more culturally accepted, as medical providers become open to providing services to these women, and as assisted-reproduction technologies (including sperm banking) increasingly offer anonymity, efficiency, safety, and other desirable qualities.

In chapter 2 I examine the forces that shape lesbians' thinking and decision making as they pursue parenthood. I consider the ways that lesbians, as individuals and couples, consider the possibility of parenthood, make sense of the information and options available to them, and actively prepare for getting pregnant. Highlighting struggles with identity, as well as generational differences in identity formation, I explore how parenthood as a goal

Table 1 Description of Participants (Self-Report)

NAME	AGE AT TIME OF INTERVIEW	RACE/ ETHNICITY	RELATIONSHIP STATUS	OCCUPATION
Carla	37	White	Single (dating)	Nurse
Chloe	31	White	Partner (Arlene)	Transcriptionist
Arlene	48	White	Partner (Chloe)	Photographer
Dana	38	African American	Single	High School Teacher
Rachel	36	White	Partner	Physician's Assistant
Renee	36	White	Partner	Animal Caregiver
Deborah	34	Jewish	Single	Graduate Student
Marilyn	37	White	Single	Nurse
Heather	34	White	Partner (Judith)	Nurse
Judith	40	White	Partner (Heather)	Nurse
Angela	37	White	Partner (Carmen)	Legal Assistant
Carmen	35	White	Partner (Angela)	Unknown
Marie	31	White	Partner (Roslyn)	Physical Therapist
Roslyn	39	American Indian	Partner (Marie)	High School Teacher
Diane	36	Jewish	Partner	Physician
Ray	37	White	Partner	Activist, Manager
June	40	White	Partner (Raquel)	Business Consultant
Raquel	33	Latina	Partner (June)	Musician, Teacher
Lynda	38	White	Partner	Physician
Paula	29	Jewish	Partner	Public-Relations Consultant
Sara	38	Jewish	Partner (Kim)	Physician
Kim	36	Korean American	Partner (Sara)	Physician
Kaye	33	White	Partner	Management Consultant
Esther	35	Jewish	Single (dating)	Nonprofit Manager
Beatrice	32	Latina	Partner (Megan)	Accountant
Megan	34	White	Partner (Beatrice)	Unknown
Joyce	36	White	Single	Customer Services
Shari	35	White	Partner (Robyn)	Unknown
Robyn	38	Latina	Partner (Shari)	Executive Assistant
Leslie	44	White	Partner	IT Specialist
Janella	32	White	Partner (Michelle)	Architect and Carpenter
Michelle	37	Italian	Partner (Janella)	Public-Health Researcher
Tina	33	White	Partner (Elizabeth)	Investment Banker
Elizabeth	34	White	Partner (Tina)	Investment Banker
Bonnie	38	Jewish	Partner (Audrey)	Grant Writer
Audrey	40	African American	Partner (Bonnie)	Professor

is pursued by individuals and couples, with an emphasis on how couples deal with conflicts over family formation. I take into account access to financial, health, and information resources. Finally, I look at how lesbians exploring the possibility of parenthood first enter the world of biomedicine.

When a lesbian woman or couple commits to the goal of parenthood, the decision making has just begun. In chapter 3 I describe a crucial decision: choosing a donor. As the interviews reveal, the women are highly concerned with risk management. As they consider whether to use anonymous or known donors, whether to use frozen or fresh semen, the respondents report reflecting — and sometimes agonizing — about strategies for minimizing not only biological and genetic risks but also social and legal risks. Legal policies are central to their strategies and shape the ways many of these respondents actively negotiate heteronorms on their route to pregnancy.

In chapter 4 I focus on the "how," beginning (as many interviewees do) with low-tech forms of self-insemination, which are considered ideal. As lesbians commit to parenthood and select a reproductive strategy, they generally have in mind such ideal trajectories. But in some cases, pregnancy is achieved neither quickly nor easily, and the initial strategy gives way to one calculated to offer the best chances of success, often shifting from self-insemination to a reliance on medical services. In other cases, the preferred trajectory is not possible, so prospective mothers are catapulted directly into "infertility" medicine either by choice, by protocol, or by physician recommendation. I describe these and other trajectories lesbians traverse on the path to pregnancy, exploring in particular what happens when lesbians turn to medical services developed to remedy heterosexual childlessness. How does Fertility Inc. relate to lesbians? What happens when a social identity (lesbian) is translated into a medical diagnosis (infertile)? How do the non-intended users of Fertility Inc. understand and shape its processes?

I continue in chapter 5 to examine lesbians and biomedicine, focusing on the interviewees' experiences as consumers of more advanced, highly biomedicalized forms of assisted reproduction, however they arrived at that point. I build on the concept of trajectories, extending the concept to examine the series of decisions lesbians often make as they traverse the world of infertility medicine. Together, chapters 4 and 5 demonstrate that while some women follow given technological scripts, others create their own interpretations and meanings for the protocols and practices of high-tech infertility providers, marketers, and insurers.[14] As women are offered increasingly complex or invasive technologies, they accommodate, resist, ignore, or otherwise negotiate the normative ideals of reproduction, pregnancy, and social relations. I use the term *hybrid-technology practices* to underscore both the negotiated meanings inherent in the interactions of technologies, bodies, and identities and the ways women combine several technological components into their processes; *hybrid* signals the mixture of technologies. I focus in both chapters on what happens when low-tech procedures are supplanted with more advanced techniques (e.g., ovulation detection; frozen, washed semen from commercial sperm banks; nitroglycerin tanks; and needleless syringes).

In chapter 5 I also analyze the implications of women's increasing reliance on sperm banks as key providers of "technosperm," information, and training, and explore the use of intrauterine and more advanced technological procedures, often as first-line interventions. When low-tech options are displaced, the stakes are high: feminist health ideals may be compromised as "control" shifts from users to practitioners; access is compromised as more expensive technologies and services, often coupled with the ideology of infertility medicine, become the most widely available options; and technologies come to shape both real and imagined possibilities.[15] Overall, as advanced techniques become standardized and routinized, they come to be considered not only the "best" option but the only valid approach (Becker 2000a); other methods are no longer envisioned or available. Thus, the new options concretely structure available "choices."

In chapter 6 I examine the concept of kinship in the context of lesbian parenthood. The decisions and actions I analyze in the first five chapters relate to getting pregnant, but pregnancy is ultimately a means to an end: family formation. As they create families, lesbians find themselves reinventing what it means to be related—an undertaking aimed at gaining legitimacy in a heterosexist culture. I therefore focus on the key concepts of connection and belonging, analyzing the ways that respondents negotiate and create kinship in a culture that devalues queer lives. I introduce the notion of *affinity ties,* a kinship device that lesbians create, in the context of uncertain legal terrain, as they select sperm, assign names and significance to relationships that have no place on traditional kinship charts, and invent new family rituals. As they redefine relatedness, lesbians subvert hegemonic kinship ties based on biogenetic and legal connections; they build systems of kinship based instead on explicit commitments, shared values, social belonging, and cultural understandings of heredity.

In chapter 7 I summarize six key arguments about the implications of lesbian reproductive practices, past and present. I imagine possible futures in the realm of gay and lesbian reproductive practices. In particular, I explore the ramifications of lesbian reproduction's shift from being an alternative, low-tech practice to being an elaborate, biomedicalized process requiring the assistance of multiple actors and technologies, new information sources, and new forms of social relations. This shift, which took place gradually and circuitously, was, I argue, accompanied by an ideological shift: from compulsory heterosexuality to compulsory motherhood.

How did this shift occur? Assisted reproduction in general, and lesbian reproductive practices in particular, make strange or "queer" what is considered to be known, familiar, commonplace—the natural order of things. Lesbian reproductive practices have in common with other forms of assisted reproduction the delinking of reproduction from heterosexual intercourse. At the same time, lesbian insemination denaturalizes the assumed link between heterosexuality and parenthood. Lesbian reproduction queers reproduction by casting doubt on hegemonic foundational assumptions (about gender, the subject, knowledge, society, and history) and opening new possibilities for gender, sexual expression, intimacy, and family forms. In seeking access and claiming the right to complex biomedical interventions, lesbians have destabilized the cultural site of assisted reproduction, a site previously reserved for heterosexual "infertile" married couples. Yet lesbians do not live outside heteronormativity, and in many ways their actions both reflect and reinforce regulatory ideals of how to make sense of reproduction, family, and social life; how and when to reproduce; how to be married with children; and how to be a family.

One

From Whence We Came:
Sex without Reproduction Meets
Reproduction without Sex

IN 1994 ESTHER CALDWELL attended a Women's Action Coalition meeting and heard about a new program called "Lesbians Considering Parenthood," which would soon be offered at a San Francisco feminist health center.[1] As an out lesbian, Esther wasn't sure that children would be part of her future, but she had always wanted kids. She decided to attend the eight-week workshop as well as an instructional class on how to self-inseminate. There were eight women in the class. Each was given a small speculum and advised to hold a mirror between her legs and look inside to find her cervix. Each was then given a little syringe with water to squirt into herself as close to the cervix as possible. Esther thus learned the very simple procedure of alternative insemination. Just as important, Esther met a group of women she would see with regularity over the next ten years. After the workshop concluded, Esther immediately purchased semen from a local sperm bank and performed inseminations at home. Eight months later, she still had not gotten pregnant. Although she planned to continue trying, her plans were derailed by life events — a car accident, a change of living situation, and a break-up.

In 1998 she decided to again attempt pregnancy. This time, everything was different. She had to re-register, for a fee, at the sperm bank that she was using to purchase donor semen. In addition, the sperm bank now required all clients to have a complete "fertility work-up," as well as an intake interview and signed authorization from a designated physician. As a member of a health maintenance organization (HMO), Esther scheduled an appointment with her Ob-Gyn, who, during the exam, told her about their new "infertility clinic." Immediately referred to the clinic, Esther met with a provider who suggested she use a technology called intrauterine insemination (IUI). With IUI, Esther could not inseminate at home, as she had four years earlier, but would have to attend a clinic and have the procedure performed by a nurse.

Esther's story illuminates a key trend of recent decades. As do-it-yourself alternative insemination has evolved (unevenly, but along with women's and lesbians health movements), so, too, has Fertility Inc., a large-scale biomedical service sector so powerful that it threatens to displace the low-tech options often used by lesbians. Esther's personal experience reflects two forces examined in this book: first, the expanded sense of possibility and self-empowerment in the realm of reproduction that emerged in the last decades of the twentieth century, supported by major social movements, including the women's health, gay rights, and lesbian and feminist movements; second, the medicalization of reproduction, facilitated by the emergence of assisted-reproduction technologies. There would seem to be tension — if not outright opposition — between these forces. And yet, as Esther's story illustrates, the recent history of lesbian reproductive practice encompasses both these and a great deal of acceptance.

What explains this shift from self-empowerment and low-tech practices (self-insemination at home) to reliance on high-tech methods (requiring medical intervention in clinics and doctors offices)? To be sure, one might expect medical intervention in cases where pregnancy has been impeded by an individual's health conditions, risk factors, or age. But how did biomedical services come into play in lesbian reproductive practice despite the absence of a medical diagnosis? How can we understand lesbians' decisions to become "patients," that is, to turn to biomedical services and professionals to address a problem that is social rather than medical — a lack of access to sperm? To explore these issues, it is necessary to trace two intertwined strands of medical history: the evolving relationship between medicine and reproduction, and the evolving relationship between medicine and homosexuality.

Looking Back at Medicine and Reproduction

The practice of assisting reproduction is centuries old. It first developed as an efficient method for breeding animals. The earliest reported use of artificial insemination (AI) occurred among Arab horse-breeders in the fourteenth century (Herman 1981, 2). There were frequent and well-known experiments with AI in animals. The first documented success of AI in animals came in 1742 when Ludwig Jacobi, a German natural philosopher and fisherman, artificially fertilized salmon eggs (documented in 1765) (Poynter 1968; Finegold 1976). In 1773 Abbe Lazzaro Spallanzani, an Italian priest and professor, fertilized frog spawn, silk worms, and salamanders (Zorgniotti 1975) and was said to have produced an offspring by inseminating a female dog in 1780 (Herman 1981, 2; Poynter 1968; Guttmacher 1938).

The idea of assisting human conception appeared as early as 1550, when Bartholomeus Eustacus recommended that a husband guide his semen toward his wife's cervix with his finger to enhance the chances of conception (Rohleder 1934). However, for most of human history, sterility was viewed primarily as a social or moral issue, not as a medical problem requiring treatment. Sterility was defined as an inability to conceive due either to "natural" circumstances such as one's age and length of marriage or to more personal matters such as one's mental, moral, and sexual habits. Childlessness was often believed to denote a barren mind and body.[2] For women, external signs of masculinity, old age, and fatness were all suggestive of disordered sexual health and were considered potential causes of sterility. Idleness, abundant sensuality, eating rich food, sexualized and sexually active behaviors, depression and melancholia, drinking alcohol and/or using drugs were also considered "self-induced immorality leading to childlessness" (Pfeffer 1993). Prior to the late nineteenth century, women did not turn to medical professionals to understand, let alone solve, their inability to conceive; instead, they looked to god and the clergy.[3]

Medicalizing Infertility

Over the course of the eighteenth and nineteenth centuries, childlessness was recast as biological pathology, rather than as moral degeneracy. The context was significant. The sciences, including biology, genetics, and medicine, developed into male-dominated academic disciplines in the eighteenth century (Schiebinger 1989, 1993). In the absence of women's voices, "men . . . increasingly tightened the reins on what was recognized as legitimate knowledge and who could produce that knowledge" (Schiebinger 1993, 142). Nineteenth-century medical practices consolidated professional jurisdiction over medical "problems" and profoundly altered where and to whom people could turn to understand and make meaning out of their bodily and social experiences (Starr 1982). Women's bodies and their reproductive processes were central sites of such medicalization (see especially Riessman 1983).

Not until the late nineteenth century was a medical classification, sterility, assigned to those unable to conceive or carry a pregnancy to viability. Women's bodies were placed under the medical gaze for "treatment" and "cure." The speculum, a diagnostic tool introduced in the early nineteenth century, allowed doctors to survey the internal landscape of women's genitalia and create new bases for theorizing the biological causes of childlessness. The "abnormal" size, appearance, and disposition of women's internal genitalia all became factors thought to contribute to sterility (Pfeffer 1993).[4] By the late nineteenth century, surgeons were performing surgeries to "restore fertility." To be sure, over the course of the eighteenth and nineteenth centuries, medical science produced new insights into male and female reproductive processes and their mutual contribution to fertility (e.g., the spermatozoon theory of reproduction, or the meeting of the egg and sperm) (Zorgniotti 1975). However, this new knowledge did little to dispel the belief in character as the key to fertility, and most medical practitioners continued to view "barrenness" as primarily a malady of women and largely an expression of women's moral condition (May 1995). The continuing focus on women's moral fiber was exemplified by Francis Galton, the founder of eugenics (the use of scientific knowledge to influence genetics), who believed childlessness to be a result of degeneracy, a failing race, or the deleterious influences of civilization (Kevles 1985).[5] This moralistic interpretation of childlessness continued into the nineteenth century but was soon joined by biological models.

At the beginning of the twentieth century, concomitant with ongoing moral inflections, advances in biology, medicine, and agriculture began to consolidate (Clarke 1998), leading to new, "scientifically based" approaches to assisted reproduction.[6] The first reported "cure" for sterility appeared in 1909, as reported by the physician Addison Davis Hard, who had witnessed an experiment that William Pancoast, a prominent Philadelphia physician, conducted while treating a sterile couple. In his examination of the woman Pancoast found no known physical abnormality.[7] He then inspected the husband's ejaculate under a microscope and found no signs of spermatozoon (sperm).[8] After several months of using the husband's semen without achieving results, Pancoast selected the "best looking member of the [medical] class" to provide semen for the experiment. (It has been suggested that it may have been Hard himself who donated the sperm.) While the woman was under anesthesia, he inseminated her with the donor sperm using a needleless syringe. She conceived, and it is alleged that neither Pancoast nor her husband informed her that a donor had been used. This experiment was groundbreaking, not only expanding the focus of sterility research and treatment from women to men but also initiating the use of sperm donors in assisted reproduction (Hard 1909).[9]

Hard's report unleashed controversy over the practice of "artificial impregnation" (May 1995), its consequences for the sanctity and naturalness of reproduction coming into question. Critics expressed alarm, concerned that the practice would harm the nation by destabilizing the presumed naturalness of heterosexual married intercourse as the foundation of moral social life and American kinship. They warned that the use of donated sperm might disrupt the bonds between husband, wife, and children as legally sanctioned and secured by heterosexual sex and the biological link of parents to children. Other opponents argued that artificial impregnation would lead to the "bastardization" and "illegitimacy" of children and, by extension, the stigmatization of the entire social (family) unit. In short, some objected to its presumed unnaturalness, others to its assumed anti-natalism (in not promoting biological reproduction), and others to its eugenic implications.[10]

Expanding "Scientific" Medical Authority

Early objections to donor insemination are central to understanding the gradual legitimacy of assisted reproduction for most women and men. One strongly held belief was that having another man's semen in a woman's vagina was, even when inserted by artificial means, akin to adultery. Marital intercourse was not only constructed as natural but also granted the power (symbolic and legal) to bind together man, woman, and child (Pfeffer 1993). Heterosexual intercourse that resulted in conception was considered a measure of a man's potency and masculinity, an assurance of his biological fatherhood, a preservation of "true" fatherhood (privileging the biological definition of fatherhood), and an escape from any signs of unnaturalness or immorality associated with infertility. These constructions signaled a necessity to create a rhetoric whereby medical treatments for sterility would be understood as "assistance" of the "natural," and therefore not as "intervention" into the "unnatural" or pathological.

Despite ongoing resistance to assisted reproduction as expressed in these controversial perspectives, "scientific medicine" continued to expand its understanding of human reproduction and to devise new technologies for overcoming obstacles to conception as well as unwanted childlessness. Beyond basic knowledge of fertilization, the most significant scientific developments for assisted-reproduction technologies occurred in three areas that together led to a new specialty — infertility medicine — and its associated technical and pharmaceutical innovations.[11]

The first area was the study of the menstrual cycle.[12] Understanding the menstrual cycle and hormonal changes in women's fertility allowed doctors and women themselves to track ovulation through various means.[13] Charting the menstrual cycle was and remains an important development for infertility medicine.[14] Ovulation prediction has long been in existence as a method to both prevent and assist conception. In its most simple form, women simply chart their menstrual cycle based on experiential knowledge about their bodies: changes in vaginal mucus, skin and mood changes, timing of menstruation, and so on.[15]

Charting basal body temperature in order to predict the timing of ovulation produced the knowledge needed to diagnose anovulation (infertility based on an inability to ovulate) and set the groundwork for the medical "treatment" of this new disease classification.[16] Resulting from this knowledge were pharmaceutical therapies for anovulation — the second area of technoscientific discovery that contributed to infertility medicine as a large-scale specialty.

In the 1960s clomiphene citrate was introduced and was found to be a convenient and effective treatment for ovulation "problems."[17] In 1966, ten years after its initial development and following six years of clinical trials, clomiphene citrate received approval from the Food and Drug Administration, was released under the brand name Clomid by the pharmaceutical company Merrell (Gruhn and Kazer 1989), and became widely available as a treatment option for infertile women diagnosed with anovulation (Pfeffer 1993). The development of clomiphene citrate facilitated the now close relationship between pharmaceutical companies that develop, manufacture, and market hormonal treatments for infertility and the doctors who prescribe them. This association was made possible by laboratory science, by the mass-production of drugs, and by the placement of these drugs in doctor's hands not only as patient-treatment options but also as justifications for what became a large-scale procreative service delivery system.

The third area that helped launch infertility as a medical specialty was the study of spermatozoa, including semen storage, semen analysis, and cryo-preservation (freezing and thawing sperm).[18] The development of tech-niques for cryopreservation of human sperm specifically for use in human reproduction is attributed to Jerome K. Sherman's and Raymond G. Bunge's work during the mid-1950s (Sherman 1954; Bunge and Sherman 1954).[19] Medical cryopreservation was first used for helping men with low sperm counts to consolidate sperm in their semen and for banking small supplies of donor sperm to facilitate the coordination of artificial insemination by do-nor.[20] Cryopreservation, which most commonly involves the immersion of semen in liquid nitrogen, was developed in the 1950s and for a decade or more was practiced on a small scale by private physicians, often as "fertility insurance" for men who were to undergo a vasectomy but might later desire to have a child. In the last decades of the twentieth century these advances drove the formation of a large-scale commercial sperm-bank industry. To make this procedure commercially viable, scientists had to develop methods for washing, concentrating, freezing, storing, and transporting sperm, as well as techniques for delivering sperm into the female body.

Knowing how to time insemination was crucial. Cryopreservation signifi-cantly reduces the amount of time sperm can survive in vivo.[21] While fresh sperm can live four to five days in fertile vaginal mucous, "post-thaw" sperm live for only twelve to twenty-four hours. This narrow interval decreases the likelihood of fertilization, requires careful timing of insemination, and in-creases the need for advanced technologies that can deposit sperm cells closer to the egg. The realities of cryopreservation profoundly shape the considerations of women with medical infertility and/or the social need for sperm donation.

With this knowledge in place, cryobanks — laboratories for the screening, preparation, storage, and distribution of frozen sperm — began to open. Cryobanking (for both research and clinical applications) was at first lim-ited primarily to university-based banks. The first commercial semen bank opened in 1972, and others followed with the expectation of serving men undergoing vasectomies (Sherman 1979). Cryobanking researchers also developed procedures for "disease washing and testing" of semen in order to ensure maximum health (Bunge, Keettel, and Sherman 1954). Cryo-banking has developed into a large-scale industry that not only stores prod-uct but also procures, screens, and manipulates it. These procedures, along with the management of information and risk, contribute to the present contours of lesbian reproduction.

   The emergence of this new specialty — infertility medicine — and its associated organizational, technical, and pharmaceutical innovations exemplifies the process of medicalization, which, among other things, tends to
assign diseases and their related "problems" a medical categorization (Conrad and Schneider 1980; Zola 1972). Medicalization therefore involves constructing boundaries of normalcy and deviance, often with rigid alignments
to an idealized normal and its associated other. The medical classification of
infertility has replaced that of sterility and thus destigmatized the state of
being childless by shifting it from the realm of personal character to the
realm of the biophysical. This shift has given jurisdiction for treatment to
medical professionals. Yet medicalization, never total or unchallenged, also
allows for ambiguities and resistances.[22] Becoming infertile first requires
one to try to become pregnant and to want to overcome childlessness.
Infertility is at once a disease classification and a designated state of procreative limbo (i.e., not yet pregnant) (Pfeffer 1993). The term constructs a
legitimate issue for medical treatment and a symbolic liminal space between
not-pregnant and soon-to-be-pregnant.[23]

   Interestingly, infertility became an official disease category only in 1993
when it first appeared in the *International Classification of Diseases,* published
by the World Health Organization, as a category requiring medical intervention. As a clinical term and basis for insurance coverage, infertility is
used to define a state in which a conception does not occur after one year of
regular, unprotected, presumably heterosexual intercourse.[24] The classification of infertility privileges the identity category of heterosexual, thereby
creating a moral order around reproduction. Lesbians in many places continue to be beyond the pale of recognition.

From Treating Infertility to Assisting Conception
   By the late 1960s biological explanations for fertility and its associated
problems were firmly in place. Ovulation aids became big business as a
treatment for unwanted childlessness. Such hormonal treatments were
widely prescribed by physicians and extremely profitable for pharmaceutical
companies, some of which entered the market with both ovulation-inhibit-
ing and ovulation-stimulating preparations.[25] Throughout the 1970s, ovula-
tion-induction technologies flooded the market and revolutionized the field
of reproductive endocrinology with new tests, procedures, and stimulation
techniques (Chen and Wallach 1994).[26]

As infertility medicine developed, its technical aspects turned out to be more complicated and challenging than anticipated. The gonadotrophin-based follicle stimulators of the early 1960s were found to carry many risks, including overstimulation of the ovaries, which led to multiple eggs and births (Gruhn and Kazer 1989).[27] Despite known risks, doctors continued to conduct studies on human-gonadotrophin stimulants, research that was largely funded by transferring high costs to wealthy, mostly white patients who were able and willing to pay to remedy their childlessness. In the 1960s and 1970s, these studies and other factors combined to lead to a revolution in medical interventions that facilitated fertility and treated the myriad problems that appeared under the reconstructed category of infertility.

In 1978 came an event that shook the world of reproductive medicine and made headlines around the world. Following a decade of research by the gynecologist Robert Steptoe and the Cambridge physiologist Robert Edwards, Louise Brown, the first "test-tube" baby, was born as a result of in vitro fertilization (IVF). This breakthrough fully launched a new biomedical industrial sector (Marsh and Ronner 1996). It also fit into already articulated feminist fantasies about reordering the gendered world of reproduction and parenting (see especially Firestone 1970). Within the medical world, it helped firmly establish the subspecialty of endocrinology-infertility, whose expanding range of assistive reproductive strategies, including IVF, created a market for those procedures and services. Getting pregnant became big business (Scritchfield 1989). As rates of those labeled infertile increased, so, too, did media coverage and subsequent awareness of infertility treatment.[28] This awareness shaped both the demand and the growth of infertility medicine itself.

Through the 1980s, the number of commercial IVF clinics and reproductive-health specialists exploded. Clomiphene citrate was the blockbuster drug of infertility. Alongside pharmaceutical therapies were "advanced assisted reproductive technologies" developed to further help natural fertility; these included procedures such as IVF, intracytoplasmic sperm injection, and gamete intrafallopian tube transfer.

As reproductive technologies evolved and their success rates improved, education about these technologies became widespread and an increasing number of people sought medical evaluation and treatment for unwanted childlessness. Although the advances came from the laboratory, the media often cited "miracles" and "blessings" in reference to births among infertile heterosexuals who could not reproduce "naturally." Furthermore, these stories of extraordinary technologies were accompanied by images of white heterosexual couples who could afford them. Reproduction for all was not (yet) the message. The media made this implicit social code clear by featuring primarily white, wealthy women in their stories about miracle births.

The cultural representations and material practices of infertility correspond with the stratification of reproduction across the twentieth century: wealthy (white) women receive support in order to reproduce and are able to access infertility services, while poor women and women of color do not receive such support. Although white women are depicted as having higher rates of infertility, perhaps due to the fact that many can better afford infertility services and thus account for the majority of infertility patients, it has also been shown that black women have higher rates of infertility (Scritchfield 1989; Aral and Cates 1983).[29]

The implication was that infertility services and techniques were expanding in response to an existing and growing need among white women. In fact, the incidence of female infertility among all women is largely unknown and unknowable. After all, not all women want to or try to become pregnant. Yet common discourses around unwanted childlessness define it through the prism of infertility — the inability to conceive after one year of timely, unprotected intercourse or to carry a live pregnancy to birth (Aronson 2000). Using this definition, infertility is understood as a health issue that affects approximately five million American women (ibid.). Yet to be infertile one must also be engaging in heterosexual intercourse; the fertility or infertility of those who have not tried to conceive is unknown.

This medical story is produced and shaped within and alongside cultural trends. Beginning in the mid-1960s, the baby boom ended and the civil-rights, feminist, gay- and lesbian-rights, and other social movements altered the social landscape. Activists worked to end involuntary sterilization practices, institutional race and class discrimination, and to secure equal access to healthcare services for poor and low-income girls and women of color. Reproductive rights was one agenda item shared across many activist movements. Large numbers of middle to upper-class women gained access to education and "white-collar" employment. Making use of newly available contraceptives, many women also "delayed" childbirth, and others chose not to have children. Still others, for the first time able to support themselves without husbands, were free to lead lesbian lives. Of course, these increased reproductive options were and remain unavailable to some women.

In the 1960s and 1970s there was a decreased demand for obstetrical services, and childbirth and delivery specialists faced a decreasing volume of patients. To fill gaps in work and income, many such specialists embraced the emergent subspecialty of endocrinology-infertility (Aral and Cates 1983).[30] The profits associated with such specialties allowed physicians to fund their research and market their services to additional clients.

Advances in reproductive services and technologies are not the outcome of advances in basic science and medical practice alone; they are also largely shaped within and through political-economic, social, and cultural forces. These include the large-scale expansion of the "biomedical technoservice complex" and the stratifications this for-profit healthcare system perpetuates.[31] As the numbers of "patients" with fertility difficulties — and financial resources — increases, their demand for infertility services shapes the big-business expansion of the industry. This leads to increased competition for patients (Kolata 2002), increased investor ownership of medical services (McKinlay and Stoeckle 1988; Starr 1982), and advances in technologies that together shape the growing for-profit healthcare industry.[32]

Further, the presumed demand for infertility services is shaped within social and cultural forces. The depiction of infertility as an illness facing large numbers of women and curable only by means of medical treatment was challenged by 1970s and 1980s feminism. Some feminists argued that infertility practices represented another variant of pronatalism and constituted a backlash to women's social, economic, and political advances.[33] Infertility was interpreted as a consequence of a social imperative that encourages women to want children and to seek medical help to have them. Arguments against infertility medicine suggest that women choose infertility treatments to satisfy patriarchal mandates (Corea 1985; Franklin 1990) — women "want" children and "want" conceptive technologies because they are socialized to want them — and that having children reproduces sex inequalities (Lorber 1989). Following this line of reasoning, the rhetoric of choice that now surrounds the discourse of reproductive technologies can be read as a reflection of the normalization tendencies which control and manage the population (Clarke 1995).

Placing normalcy and health, instead of deviance and illness, under the medical gaze is not new, yet its increasing importance and emphasis is characteristic of biomedicalization.[34] Today's biomedicalization of fertility effaces the social by technoscientifically defining and intervening in a growing number of aspects of people's lives (Clarke et al. 2000, 2003). For example, in 1999 the American Society for Reproductive Medicine launched its "Protect Your Fertility!" campaign, a series of public-service announcements that targeted men and women in their twenties and early thirties, encouraging them to recognize the connections between their decisions now and their ability to have children in the future. The campaign focused on fertility risk factors such as smoking, sexually transmitted infections, unhealthy body weight, and advancing age. Another campaign featured a baby's bottle in the shape of an hourglass with the headline "Advancing age decreases your ability to have children." And additional text stated, "While women and their partners must be the ones to decide when (and if) to have children, women in their twenties and thirties are most likely to conceive." These advertisements perpetuated the ideology and fear that certain women, especially those who spend time gaining an education and developing a career, may delay childbearing too long to join their peers in familyland. Overall, the campaign constructs as a social problem women unwilling to fulfill their "natural" imperative to reproduce or unable to do so due to delayed pregnancies. Surprisingly, the ad campaign chose to use the word *partner*, which signaled a possible decline in homophobia and in the invisibility of lesbians as procreative, a signal in direct contrast to the long history of medicalizing homosexuality in general and of constructing lesbian sexuality in contrast to "normal," procreative women. Yet it nevertheless pointed to compulsory reproduction for lesbians and heterosexual women and everyone in between.

Over the course of the twentieth century, "scientific" medicine advanced the field of assisted reproduction to the current status it now holds: a legitimate means of overcoming unwanted childlessness. While assisting reproduction can be read as a means of promoting childbearing at any cost and thereby strengthening the heteronormative family form, these technologies also challenge conventional notions of family formation and extend the field of possible procreators beyond the heterosexual married couple.

Looking Back at Medicine and Homosexuality

Just as sterility and childlessness were associated with deviance and medical pathology, "sexual inversion" in women was portrayed as both disease (pathology) and moral corruption (degeneracy). Foucault (1980a) argued that sexuality was put into discourse in the nineteenth century. Sexuality, he asserted, is not merely a means to reproduce the species, the family, and the individual; sexuality and its bodily practices are also constituted and contained through a variety of medical, social, and juridical discourses that regulate and monitor proper expressions. Such discourses, he continued, construct normative forms of conduct, expression, and embodiment.

In the nineteenth century the medical classification of sexual attributes joined earlier, intertwined classification systems based on race and sex.[35] Deviance versus normalcy formed the epistemological foundation on which was constructed the idea that homosexuals were distinct and inferior types of human beings. The new taxonomy of sexual behaviors included homosexual, deviant behaviors predicated on the presumed existence of normative heterosexuality.[36] It also deemed normal those sexual behaviors that led to reproduction and transgressive those sexual acts that occurred outside of marriage and/or for purposes other than reproduction (e.g., pleasure) (D'Emilio and Freedman 1988). Lesbians did not escape the repercussions of this trend, and contemporary lesbian cultures are constituted within this discourse.[37]

Medicalizing Homosexuality

Concurrent with the classification and medicalization of infertility was the classification and medicalization of homosexuality. Then, as now, discourses of sexual, racial, class, and other difference influenced one another. In the late nineteenth century same-sex desires and acts were no longer cast as sins or crimes, but were instead assigned medical and scientific terms and associated with particular types of people (Foucault 1980a). This coincided with the reframing of childlessness from moral degeneracy to biological pathology.[38] The medicalization of sexuality gained momentum from about 1870 onward in Britain, Europe, and North America with the emergence of the science of sexology (ca. 1850–1930), the scientific study of sexual behaviors, identities, and relations, including sexual anatomy and physiology (Irvine 1995).[39]

Throughout the nineteenth and early twentieth centuries, gender-conforming and gender-transgressive behaviors were placed under the medical gaze. Women who exhibited same-sex sexual desires and/or participated in same-sex sexual activity were medically understood as having a "condition" that required the attention of a physician. Rather than being approached as "normal" human variation, or as a social problem needing the intervention of priests or judges, lesbian behavior was instead addressed by psychiatrists and physicians. Lesbians were caught in an ideological netherworld between immorality and madness. Insanity in women was constructed as "manifested by, and dependent upon, sexual 'deviance' and discernible physical anomalies" (Ordover 2003, 101). Confinement in asylums was often employed to contain lesbians' and gays' "moral insanity" and to protect society from their degenerate ways (Vicinus 1989).

By 1910, the science of endocrinology had explained the anomaly of same-sex desire in hormonal terms and had created a discourse around homosexuality as a condition to be cured by medical intervention.[40] Physicians began treating homosexuals with sex-appropriate hormones to make them heterosexual (Oudshoorn 1995). Medicalization has often been thought to reduce stigma by providing scientific justification for a person's anomalous behaviors; for example, some advocates for gay tolerance used inversion theories strategically to promote homosexuals as innocent victims of biological factors.[41]

Fascination with hierarchical classifications of human types in the early twentieth century led in 1935 to the launching of the Committee for the Study of Sex Variants by the gynecologist Robert Latou Dickinson. This "scientific" study of homosexuality was based on gynecological exams in which Dickinson contrasted the physically discernable genitals of sex variants with those of normal women. Although no control group of normal woman was actually used, Dickinson described lesbians' genitals as being of extraordinary size and distinctively different than normal women. Despite the purported largeness assigned to the lesbian vulva, labia, prepuce, and clitoris, the uterus was defined as unusually small and as therefore affecting their reproductive capacities. Lesbians were described as possessing multiple masculine attributes, including narrow hips and underdeveloped breasts, that were in opposition to symbols of fertility. Overall, the terms used to describe lesbians' genitals and body types "marked the subjects as pathological" relative to normal, unmarked women (Terry 1999, 205).[42] The search for the cause and "proof" of homosexuality as pathology focused on physical characteristics, often the shape and size of genitalia. Yet even the psychoanalyst Sigmund Freud (1920) and others asserting an acquired model of sexual difference could find no visible differences between lesbian and heterosexual women.

These early efforts to differentiate and classify normal from deviant bodies by virtue of their sex organs and sexual desires are indicative of the centrality of medical discourse in the making of the modern lesbian subject. Furthermore, the search to locate physical deviations may be an early indication of the construction of lesbians as nonprocreative as a result of their "condition."

Lesbians stood in contrast to the ideal fertile woman who possessed the normal-sized uterus, large breasts, and wide hips necessary for childbearing and breastfeeding. Further, Dickinson's study concluded that homosexuals were "unable to adjust to modern society's high standards requiring adults to establish and maintain a home proper for raising children" (George Henry quoted in Terry 1999, 211). Siobhan Somerville (2000) described similar examinations of an African "Bush Woman." The myth of the extra-large clitoris was one of the most consistent medical classifications used to construct black and lesbian women's genitalia as "abnormal" (Somerville 2000).[43] Identifying and measuring physical features as part of the organization of human beings into discrete sexes, genders, races, and sexual systems has a long and ongoing history in which those positioned as other, based on the assumption of their inherent difference (or perversion), became objects of the medical gaze. Although the categories were discrete, each took on racial, sexed, and colonial meanings.

In the early part of the twentieth century in the United States, lesbianism and the criminalization of lesbians were defined in racialized terms (Somerville 2000; Freedman 1996). In this discursive frame, conceptions of race and of sexuality are clearly articulated. In the white imagination, the so-called aggressive female was associated with African American women, who contaminated normal, feminine (mostly white) women. This paralleled other eugenic and anti-miscegenistic anxieties and penal laws that existed at the time. After World War II, what had been the criminalization primarily of black lesbians began to include white, working-class women as well, thereby establishing a classed (as well as raced) version of female homosexuality (Freedman 1996). The white discourse of race suicide reemerged, with white lesbians being seen as rejecting heterosexuality, thereby threatening true womanhood and its synonymous reproduction of the white race. Mannish women were seen as posing a danger to normal (white, heterosexual, feminine) women and a threat to the procreative order by their capacity to seduce normal women away from men.

As medicalization shifts discourses of sins and crimes to pathology, the cultural ideas behind these assertions often remain in circulation. In the case of female sexuality, deviations from natural female instincts (desire for men, maternal tendencies) continued to be viewed as moral perversions: women who did not have children inside married heterosexual unions were considered violators of their own maternal instincts or thought to be lacking such instincts. Scientific and social discourses constructed lesbian sexuality as a betrayal of the "natural order" of the sexes as well as of the procreative order of society. The mannish lesbian preyed on weak-willed normal girls or "womanly women" who lacked the strength to resist seduction and, in some cases, the fitness for childbearing (Terry 1999, 65). Like other normal women, these women were naturally seduced by masculinity, whether the seducers were "normal men" or inverted women. Medical discourse produced parameters of sexual normalcy along gender lines. Such interpretations demonstrated the strength of the two-sex gender model, the cultural legacy of sexology, and the co-construction of medical, legal, and cultural discourses on female sexuality.[44]

Furthermore, psychoanalysis constructed an idealized modern, Western reproductive family (Terry 1999), with homosexuality being cast as an unresolved developmental crisis, an immaturity, that posed a particular danger to the social order.[45] As Nancy Ordover (2003) demonstrates, biological and psychological discourses were not and are not mutually exclusive; rather, they work together to define and intervene in lesbian and gay bodies, psyches, and lives. The Freudian bedrock of psychoanalysis — an understanding of gender and of mature (hetero, genital) sexuality as individual psychosexual development — lost supremacy during the 1970s, and the "lesbian subject" and her resistance to her natural place in the sex-gender system emerged as a key site of analysis for feminist psychoanalytical theorists (and practitioners).[46]

Producing Lesbian Reproduction

While the medicalization of infertility has legitimated the use of assisted-reproduction technologies among heterosexuals by lending natural reproduction a helping hand, the question remains whether and to what extent lesbian reproduction has garnered such support in society at large. Within and among lesbian worlds, the emergence of self-insemination as a community-based, women-centered knowledge has led to and justified the use of assisted reproduction. How has this occurred? Medicine, as a field and a profession, has had a long history of pathologizing lesbian experiences. Allied and overlapping fields, such as psychoanalysis, have viewed the lesbian as developmentally arrested and essentially immature — not an appropriate candidate for motherhood. Taken alone, these histories would not have predicted the large numbers of lesbians who have chosen motherhood in recent decades, both outside and within the realm of biomedicine. What were some of the forces that helped give rise to the lesbian baby boom of recent decades?

Social Movements for Gay and Lesbian Rights

Homosexuality as it is variously understood and practiced today has been shaped by several social movements, including those for lesbian and gay rights and women's health. Prior to the 1969 Stonewall uprising, which marked the beginning of organized and public gay and lesbian civil-rights movements, same-sex desire was primarily understood through a lens of sexual deviance, gender anomaly, and medical pathology. This involved the construction of homosexuals as nonprocreative, which emphasized these bodies and their behaviors as profoundly deviant and "abnormal." The association of homosexuality with childlessness has only very recently begun to be supplanted, a shift that is driven by both social movements and medical technologies.

Social movements of the 1960s and 1970s in the United States actively worked to challenge and reform the hierarchical organization of U.S. society along race, class, gender, and sexuality lines, striving to expose the unequal distribution of resources and opportunities. Feminisms in the 1970s engaged in a critical examination of gender relations and protested women's unequal status in U.S. society, as well as racial and class-based inequalities. The gay- and lesbian-rights movements engaged in similar struggles to bring the unequal status of gay men and lesbians into political focus.

These post-Stonewall campaigns had both political and intellectual strands drawing inspiration from several sources. The lesbian- and gay-rights movements drew heavily from 1950s homophile movements, sex research that viewed homosexuality as nonpathological, urban subcultures that had been expanding since World War II, and the feminist movement. Lesbian- and gay-rights movements politicized the conditions of personal life and everyday culture. Some were highly critical of normative notions of masculinity and femininity and so-called proper expressions and ways of inhabiting sexed bodies. Some struggled against legal injustices, discriminatory policies in education, employment and family policy, and anti-gay harassment, stigma, and bigotry. At the same time that second-wave women's movements fought for reproductive rights such as access to contraceptives (the right to fewer pregnancies) and the prohibition against forced sterilization, sexual-liberation movements within feminisms and lesbian- and gay-rights movements struggled for freedom of sexual expression, including same-sex desires.

In 1974, in the wake of gay and lesbian social movements, homosexuality was removed as an illness from the American Psychiatric Association's Diagnostic and Statistical Manual (Kirk and Kutchins 1992). Medical classifications are socially constructed categories and therefore dynamic over time. Removing the label of "illness" from same-sex sexuality had far-reaching social and moral effects. Demedicalization affected not only how gays and lesbians were perceived and treated (both socially and medically) but also how people in general understood and gave meaning to themselves.

These movements were not monolithic. While some gay movements championed all that was positive, pleasurable, and creative in same-sex desires and behaviors, others put issues of sexual freedom and liberation aside in favor of equality.[47] Identity politics emerged throughout the 1970s, and groups (re)claimed their voices and fought for equality. In terms of sexuality "coming out of the closet" was in the 1970s one way to counter the silences and invisibility of gay life. This tactic was borrowed from feminists' "Take Back the Night" rallies, consciousness-raising groups, and other forms of giving voice to previously invisible oppressions. What had once been viewed as individual behavior and identity was reconceptualized as a phenomenon that had complex social meanings with profound effects on communities, experiences, and institutional practices (Lewin 1996, 1998a).

By the 1990s, identity-based social movements for gay and lesbian rights coexisted with fluid constructs of difference, multiplicity, and fragmentation (Lemert 1993; Seidman 1997). Instead of assuming a unified homosexual (or heterosexual) identity, some challenged the belief that the homosexual was a universal and natural occurrence in society (Seidman 1997), arguing instead that queerness was socially created. In 1990, galvanized by the AIDS epidemic and AIDS activism, a group of pro-gay activists formed Queer Nation, strategically using the term *queer* to be "confrontational-opposed to gay assimilationists and straight oppressors" and to signify all marginalized people and "a new generation of activists" (Berube and Escoffier 1991, 14).[48] Over time, these social movements and theories collectively redefined same-sex intimacies as normal expressions of human sexuality.

Writings that Document Lesbian Lives and Lesbian Motherhood

As a result of the social movements of the 1960s and 1970s, sociologists, historians, and community activists began documenting lesbian lives.[49] This vast literature was an attempt to talk with and against dominant construc-tions of those lives as deviant, perverse, and lonely, lacking the supports of family life. Since the 1969 Stonewall liberation movement, lesbian-feminist scholarship has depicted lesbian lives and desires as forms of woman-em-powerment and documented that many women occupying the newly con-structed category of "lesbian" were becoming mothers despite the ideologi-cal construction that they were unfit to do so.

A key text countering medicalization tendencies was Phyllis Lyon's and Del Martin's *Lesbian/Woman* (1972), the first book that documented les-bian lives based directly on interviews with lesbians. This text stood along-side, yet contested, biomedically inflected books that speculated about the pathologies of those classified as the "third sex," "mannish women," and "inverts" (see Terry 1999; Fausto-Sterling 2000). *Lesbian/Woman* chal-lenged the assumption that lesbianism was a malady or social deviation.

Joan Nestle's *A Restricted Country* (1987) and Elizabeth Kennedy's and Madeleine Davis's *Boots of Leather, Slippers of Gold* (1993) provide detailed portraits of how lesbian life was structured and thrived before gay- and lesbian-liberation movements, giving particular attention to the profound significance of butch-femme desire, expressions, and organization of social life.[50] Concomitant with the visibility of butch-femme desire, Kennedy and Davis break the myth of same-sex sexual desire as always separate from reproduction and parenting. In their ethnographic account, they demon-strate that most incidences of lesbian parenting from the 1930s to 1960s resulted from previous marriages, pregnancies during prostitution (sex work), or relationships with women who had previously had children in either of these settings.

Kennedy and Davis found that although most of the lesbians who had children identified as femmes and had been previously married, butch identity did not preclude the desire to raise children. Butch narrators were divided on their interests in having children; among those who wanted to raise children, social oppression was identified as the main factor for the suppression of that desire.[51] *Boots of Leather, Slippers of Gold* countered the historical erasure of lesbian mothers and the invisibility of lesbian parenting prior to 1970s gay-liberation movements. The reality of lesbian lives as inclusive of parenting talks back to the cultural work performed by the medical and social worlds that legitimated the place of heterosexual, married women as natural mothers and that thereby opened the door for the medicalization of infertile couples and the construction of heterosexual couples as appropriate users of these services.

In the 1970s and beyond, the arts—particularly music and poetry—played a crucial role in affirming lesbian identities by reflecting lesbian experiences and shaping lesbian-feminist ideologies. Concerts, music festivals, poetry readings, and theater performances brought together hundreds, sometimes thousands, of lesbians. Until the 1970s, social discourses often perpetuated the myth that lesbians posed a danger to children. Case in point: Lillian Hellman's play *The Children's Hour* (1934) depicted a lesbian love affair which generates a schoolhouse sex panic resolved only by the suicide of the lesbian protagonist. In contrast, the lesbian-feminist arts explosion of the 1970s offered positive accounts of lesbians' ties with children and portrayed lesbians' experiences in raising children (their own and those of their partners). For example, children could be heard singing with Alix Dobkin on the album *Lavender Jane Loves Women,* which Dobkin produced with Kay Gardner in 1973. This was the first album by, for, and about lesbians, and it presaged a dynamic (mostly white) women's music movement and effective distribution network. As the visibility of lesbians' relationships with children grew, debates about whether male children were welcome at women-only concerts (e.g., the Michigan Women's Music Festival) raised awareness of motherhood within some lesbian communities. Family formation emerged as an important concern and was the subject of the poet Audre Lorde's 1979 article in *Conditions* magazine, "Man Child: A Black Lesbian Feminist Response."

In addition to Lorde (1978, 1979), other prominent writers published works reflecting their experiences as lesbian mothers, including Joan Larkin (1975), Pat Parker (1985), Minnie Bruce Pratt (1989), and Adrienne Rich (1976). Some authors, like Jan Clausen (1980), wrote about co-mothering.

Still others, like Becky Birtha (1991) and Irena Klepfisz (1977), published important works on women living childfree. Many writings by lesbian mothers and about lesbian motherhood followed, and some lesbian writers, including Gloria Anzaldúa and Alexis deVeaux, wrote books for children. Many popular books on lesbian parenting appeared in the late 1980s and early 1990s (see especially Alpert 1988; Arnup 1995; Benkov 1994). While the visibility of lesbian and other queer communities has altered social practices, expectations, and lives, these changes must be read with caution. The extent of biological and psychological research into the causality and treatment of queers has only accelerated, and such discourses are traveling widely.

Lesbian Health Movements and Alternative-Insemination Practices

Lesbian reproduction was also shaped by 1970s and 1980s women's health movements, which fought for not only the right to not have children (via access to contraceptives and abortion) but also the right to choose when and under what conditions to procreate. The seminal text of the beginning of the "second-wave" feminist women's health movement was the Boston Women's Health Book Collective's *Our Bodies, Ourselves* (1971). This newspaper-style publication provided theretofore largely unavailable information on a wide range of women's health topics, including diet and nutrition, conception, childbirth, birth control, abortion. The articles were written through the subjective experiences of heterogeneous women and based on women-controlled and -designed research.

Our Bodies, Ourselves embodied several core attributes of women's health movements: it provided information about women's bodies from the perspectives of women themselves (Ruzek and Hill 1986); it educated women about their bodies and biological processes as a means to increase their control over their health in general and reproductive choices in particular (Ruzek 1978); and it served as a how-to guide to enable women to take aspects of their healthcare into their own hands (Morgen 2002). Also embodying these ideals was the opening of dozens of women-controlled health centers in the 1970s. These centers were formed as alternatives to conventional health- and medical-care delivery services; they were managed and staffed by self-trained, nonprofessional women; and they were often organized as nonhierarchical organizations, with nurses in leadership positions and with limited policy-making roles for physicians. The defining characteristic of such organizations was the inclusion of empowerment programs, self-help groups that provided women with knowledge, cervical self-exam skills, abortion services, and support groups previously unavailable to them (Ruzek 1978).[52] It was in this context that several founders of the Feminist Women's Health Centers pioneered the development of a menstrual extraction technique that gave women the power and skills to terminate pregnancies (Murphy 1999); they later disseminated and offered techniques for self-insemination.

The early edition of *Our Bodies, Ourselves* was criticized for its omission of lesbian-relevant materials and perspectives. The second edition, published in 1976, included a chapter titled "In Amerika They Call Us Dykes." This chapter, cowritten by Amber Hollibaugh and E. G. Creighton, was the first to address lesbian health and included a brief discussion of artificial insemination directed toward lesbians: "Gay women who would like to have children of their own but don't want to have sex with men or find it almost impossible [*sic*]. Artificial insemination and adoption are not permitted to open lesbians, so they are forced to be bisexual. Many lesbians are married to men" (Boston Women's Health Book Collective 1976, 96). The same chapter also included discussions of homophobia, coming out, finding community, relationships, sexual practices, and legal issues concerning lesbian marriages, medical rights, and parenthood. A later chapter, "Considering Parenthood," discussed the reasons for and against deciding to have children, but did not mention technological means of achieving pregnancy or lesbians in particular.

Combined, these efforts undermined the legitimacy of biomedicine as the sole or best provider of information and healthcare for women and as the authoritative voice on lesbian lives. By creating community-safe institutional contexts in which women could organize, share information, and/or gather support, women's health movements created foundations for alternatives to biomedical knowledge and what was considered male-centered medical healthcare services.

Throughout the late 1970s and early 1980s, feminist accounts of donor insemination began to proliferate as women's health movements organized self-help groups and healthcare organizations designed to address the reproductive health needs of women. Accompanying women's rights to choose when not to have children (contraception and abortion rights) was the right to choose when, and under what conditions, to procreate.[53] A newly articulated freedom to have children without men and/or outside of marriage led to a proliferation of materials describing artificial insemination as a simple procedure that could be performed at home by people with no medical training. These materials explained the timing of ovulation and described techniques for examining oneself or other women (to observe the position of the cervix and its opening, the os). Although originally intended to empower women in the realm of contraception, these insights and skills also helped women to self-inseminate. It was not long before some women's health centers began teaching women how to inseminate based on the theory of self-help promoted by this feminist movement.

For example, in 1984 Francie Hornstein published a personal account of her decision to try, and subsequent experience with, donor insemination, which she first tried in 1973 while working at the Feminist Women's Health Center in Los Angeles. In her short essay she also presented an unofficial history of what she termed "feminist-controlled" and "self-help donor insemination," beginning in the mid- and late 1970s. As documented by Hornstein (1984), the Feminist Women's Health Center in Los Angeles opened a donor insemination program in 1978. At the same time, the Vermont Women's Health Center and the Chelsea Health Center in New York City also assisted women in getting pregnant by donor insemination.

In the 1970s most sperm banks denied service to unmarried women, so many lesbians sought "known" donors through friendship networks. This "alternative" pathway to pregnancy among lesbians was invested with the dominant ideas of the women's health movement and second-wave feminist movements. In the spirit of women's empowerment outside male-dominated institutions, a wide array of women's self-help publications soon followed women's health services.

Emerging from these new feminist ideals, self-insemination groups formed with the intention of sharing ideas and providing support for acquiring semen and conducting insemination. The first self-insemination group was formed in 1978 (Duelli Klein 1984; Wikler and Wikler 1991). Soon, the first edition of *Lesbian Health Matters* (O'Donnell et al. 1979), a publication of the Santa Cruz Women's Health Center, devoted a full chapter to "alternative fertilization." The goal was to support and empower women in their right to decide if, when, and under what conditions they would have children, an objective that was contextualized with the assertion that "the mechanics of alternative fertilization are as easy as 1-2-3," despite the fact that "doctors mystify and try to control artificial insemination" (O'Donnell et al. 1979, 67). The chapter then discussed some of the key issues involved in alternative insemination, including finding a donor, the mechanics of insemination, timing of ovulation, and emotional issues. Each topic was covered with the explicit purpose of educating and empowering women to do it themselves.

A 2004 *New York Times Magazine* article told the story of a lesbian couple who became pregnant through alternative insemination in 1979. "Within months of falling in love, [the couple] decided to have a family together. Having heard of other women doing the same, 'these mythical, amazing stories,' [the couple] flew to San Francisco, where [one of them] was inseminated. Using a syringe, sperm donated by a gay friend of a friend and the instructions on a mimeographed pamphlet circulating in the lesbian community at the time, she became pregnant on the first try" (Dominus 2004, 3). The mimeographed instruction sheet revealed not only the underground elements of this practice, but the ways knowledge was circulated in a community context.

Throughout the 1970s and 1980s, lesbian reproduction occurred in a context in which gay men were often important players (Pies and Hornstein 1988). Prior to the development of a commercial sperm bank industry and willingness among medical practitioners to provide reproductive service to lesbian and single women, it was often men within lesbians' social networks who provided sperm. *Lesbian Health Matters* stated that finding a donor could occur through two pathways (O'Donnell et al. 1979). The first option was to contact a medical doctor who provided infertility services and thus offered limited donor services available or knew other physicians who maintained small semen banks.

The second option was "finding a donor through connections other than the traditional medical profession such as friendship ties, women's self-help groups, alternative health services, relatives, etc." (O'Donnell et al. 1979, 50). A "go-between," an individual responsible for picking up and delivering the semen donation, was suggested to ensure both parties' anonymity. The suggested course of what was termed "alternative fertilization" was to have the known donor ejaculate into a clean jar or condom, then deliver his semen into the vagina using "a turkey baster, an eye dropper, a diaphragm, or an inverted condom" (ibid., 53). The emphasis on everyday, easy-to-use technologies is central to the success of do-it-yourself methods. Although the turkey baster has disappeared from use, its symbolic power in lesbian reproduction continues.

The 1984 edition of *Our Bodies, Ourselves* represented the first published discussion of self-insemination by the Boston Women's Health Book Collective. The technique described therein is characterized as "the simplest, least invasive and most widely used of the technologies [of reproduction] . . . it doesn't require professional help, and we can do it at home" (318). The publication described in detail how to predict ovulation. It included photographic and descriptive representations of the heterogeneous cervical changes that take place throughout the menstrual cycle. The description of the donor insemination procedure itself embodied the language and ideals of 1970s self-insemination discourse from the women's health movement: "When you know from past cycles that you are about to ovulate . . . You suck the semen into a needle-less hypodermic syringe (some women use an eye dropper or turkey baster), gently insert the syringe into your vagina while lying flat on your back with your rear up on a pillow, and empty the syringe into your vagina to deposit the semen as close to your cervix as possible" (Boston Women's Health Book Collective 1984, 318).

The description makes clear that with knowledge of one's own body, insemination can be performed at home, far from the medicalizing tendencies of conventional healthcare. Alternative insemination was portrayed not as requiring advanced technologies, but as an alternative practice that existed outside of patriarchal and biomedical control: women were "doin' it for themselves." Some women continue to use this method, using sperm acquired from acquaintances or by means of privately arranged donations. However, its practice has been supplanted by the increased use of commercial sperm banks, which make semen storage, selection, and purchasing easier, albeit more expensive.

Debates over Lesbian Reproduction within Lesbian/Gay and Feminist Communities

As the lesbian and women's health movements expanded access to information about insemination and lesbian motherhood became more common, debates erupted within feminist and lesbian and gay communities.

Is Lesbian Reproduction Liberatory?

Feminism in the 1970s was informed by two divergent theoretical ideas about motherhood. One considered motherhood—like any other connection to men—to be in the service of patriarchal oppression and the continued subordination of women to men. The other viewed motherhood as a distinctive woman's experience, as well as a source and reflection of women's unique power. As lesbian parenthood became more common, these positions fueled controversies, with some lesbians viewing motherhood and parenting as conventions of heterosexuality, and others seeing them as unique expressions of alternative, chosen family forms able to transform dominant conventions of gender and sexuality.

Does Lesbian Reproduction Demonstrate Normalcy
or Mark Transgressiveness?

Some of the questions that fueled debate three decades ago continue to spark controversy, including one that concerns assimilation and resistance. Divisions in queer politics, for example, were fraught over whether or not to embrace all alternative cultural practices in an effort to ally the marginalized to resist dominant gender, sexual, and other norms. Others, however, focused their political struggles on state recognition and, thus, inclusion in civil-rights entitlements, a position that asserted that gays and lesbians were just like everyone else and should therefore be recognized as part of mainstream social and cultural life.

Does having children, and thereby demonstrating normalcy, pave the road toward equal civil rights for lesbians? Can the act of parenting and forming a family destabilize dominant constructions of gender, sexuality, and the family? In wider culture(s), pronatalism historically ebbs and flows; for lesbians, being or becoming a mother is never an obvious or easy social identity to achieve. Although resisting the dominant script of women-as-natural-mothers has long been a part of lesbian activism, the prescription to reproduce that upholds "traditional values" is not only alive and well, but in many ways it is staging a comeback. The controversy continues over whether and to what degree lesbian parenting is a consequence of normalization and the pronatalism of dominant culture and to what degree it marks a continued transgressiveness from feminisms and queer cultures.

Does Lesbian Reproduction Contribute to
the View of Women as Asexual Mothers?

A key text of lesbian feminism was Adrienne Rich's "Compulsory Heterosexuality and Lesbian Existence" (1980), a statement of woman-identified resistance to patriarchal oppression. According to Rich, the lesbian transcends history and culture in her shared association with and common link to all women who affirm themselves as activists and passionate friends. The place of sexuality in such relationships was not specified in Rich's essay, thus marginalizing women who dared to make same-sex erotic desire explicit, particularly the butch-femme communities. Similarly, Lillian Faderman, in her book *Surpassing the Love of Men: Romantic Friendship and Love between Women from the Renaissance to the Present* (1981), emphasized the historical continuity of women's passionate friendships in the middle and upper classes throughout history and gave minimal attention to explicitly sexual lesbian communities across history. Both works have been critiqued for focusing on similarities in relationships between women but ignoring the changing historical conditions that create different kinds of relationships and for valorizing nonsexual relationships (Vicinus 1989; D'Emilio and Freedman 1988).

Defining lesbianism as woman-identification contributes to an essentialized view of woman as asexual. Attempting to separate lesbians from this category, Monique Wittig (1982) argues that the term *woman* is produced by, expressive of, and perpetuates (through its continued use) an economy of heterosexual relations. Since sex serves the economic needs of heterosexuality, Wittig argues, a lesbian is not a woman, because, in refusing heterosexuality, she is no longer defined within that opposition, which necessarily produces male and female, man and woman. Wittig's argument sits on the fence between earlier work that essentialized identity and queer theories that assert multiple identities. Lesbianism could include any form of same-sex erotic desire and thus provided a conceptual foundation for theorizing "difference" within lesbian communities, as elsewhere. If a lesbian is not a woman in that she does not participate in compulsory heterosexuality, then assisted-reproduction technologies have the power to make her one by appropriating compulsory heterosexuality (Rich 1980) and repackaging it as compulsory reproduction. In other words, if the "lesbian" procreates, does she then become a woman? The emergence of self-insemination discourses within women's health movements is instrumental.

What Are the Meanings and Consequences of
Lesbians' Use of Reproductive Technologies?

Lesbian and gay identity politics of the 1980s and 1990s and queer politics and theories contributed to analyses of the meaning and potential consequences of reproductive technologies for social life. Would they lead to acceptance and integration of lesbian and gay lives into the mainstream? If so, would this remove discrimination and open an avenue for social justice? Or would lesbian use of reproductive technologies further marginalize more alternative queer lives and thus lead to further discrimination and social injustice?

Questions about the social impact of reproductive technologies are not limited to discussions of queer reproduction; scholars have repeatedly debated whether reproductive technologies are progressive, having the potential to sever the link between sexuality and reproduction for women, or regressive, representing power and a patriarchal strategy to keep women tied to motherhood.[54] In *The Dialectic of Sex* (1970), for example, Shulamith Firestone famously advocated the use of technology to free women from "the tyranny of reproduction." Patriarchy, the root of women's oppression, was about the control of women's bodies, fertility, and sexuality by men. Access to effective contraceptive and birth technologies could liberate women from that oppression: biology need not be destiny. This stance relied on a social-constructionist argument of the gendered social order and the construction of gender itself. Although a form of technological determinism, Firestone asserted, a "technological fix" (i.e., an artificial womb) would free women from the tyranny of their own biology. Not all feminists shared this viewpoint.

Throughout the 1980s, many voiced concerns about assisted-reproduction technologies as reinforcing the "cult of motherhood," pointing to the historical continuities of the ideology of motherhood. Others argued, from a radical or cultural feminist position, that such technologies were means by which men could appropriate reproductive capacities, the ultimate source of female power, from women. A powerful example was Gena Corea's (1985) image of the "mother machine," a future in which women become professional breeders — a prescient thought given the professional surrogates who work today (see also Corea 1984, 1987). By the 1980s, heterosexual donor insemination was widely accepted as a treatment for infertility, despite objections from feminists who argued that the medicalization and professionalization of fertility and childbirth were forms of male-dominated social control of women's bodies (Corea 1985; Rothman 1986).

Lesbian feminism receded in the 1980s, along with the feminist sex wars, the validation of lesbian sex as a distinctive source of pleasure as well as danger, and the recognition of butch-femme as an erotic system that fostered and shaped women's desire (see Snitow 1980; Vance 1982). But the theoretical debates regarding the consequences of assisted reproduction continued to unfold. By the 1990s, feminist theorizing by Jana Sawicki (1991) and others who examined assisted-reproduction technologies dismissed one-dimensional thinking, arguing that it failed to take into account the ways in which a practice or institution could empower some women and disempower others. Furthermore, such accounts captured neither the interplay between domination and resistance nor the ways they could coexist in the same set of practices and/or institutions.

From Turkey Baster to Biotechnological Accomplishment

Esther—the lesbian who self-inseminated without success, stopped trying, then resumed her efforts four years later—responded to a request for volunteers that I had placed in the newsletter of a nonprofit sperm bank that serves lesbians. After a phone conversation in which she agreed to participate in the research, she invited me to her home to conduct the interview.

At the time of our interview, Esther was thirty-five years old. She had begun trying to get pregnant in her late twenties. She described herself as a white, Jewish, lefty liberal at the height of her career, having recently been promoted to executive director of a nonprofit organization. Her annual income, $35,000 per year, qualified her to purchase a condominium in a housing complex with assistance from a middle-income-housing grant program in San Francisco.

In 1997, when Esther resumed her efforts to get pregnant after a four-year hiatus, she encountered a changed set of assumptions and protocols. This time around, purchasing semen from a sperm bank involved her in a full fertility work-up. After receiving the work-up, Esther purchased a box of six ovulation-predictor kits from her provider at a cost of $19.99 and went home to wait for her next cycle to begin. Nine days after the first day of her next period, Esther began using the ovulation sticks every morning to predict when she would ovulate. The day the line turned from white to blue indicated that her ovulation was imminent (and would occur in twenty-four to forty-four hours), and she knew her "best chance" of conceiving was approaching. Esther phoned the infertility clinic and scheduled an IUI for the next day.

As an HMO member, Esther was not concerned about the monthly cost of office visits for each procedure; she would be required to provide only a $5 copayment. The cost of purchasing sperm from a sperm bank—approximately $150 per insemination—would not be covered by her HMO because she did not have an official diagnosis of infertility based on the *International Classification of Diseases* or the guidelines of her HMO, but instead simply lacked a source of sperm.

When after six cycles she was still not pregnant, Esther scheduled an appointment with the infertility specialist to determine why. They discussed possible next steps, including additional technologies and pharmaceutical drugs she might try. Esther decided to continue inseminating without the use of hormone therapy for three additional cycles of IUI. If these were not successful, they would add clomiphene citrate (Clomid), an oral medication used to stimulate egg development, to her insemination routine. On the seventh cycle, before initiating the use of Clomid, Esther conceived, but she miscarried a few weeks later. The miscarriage was emotionally devastating, but after taking a few months off, Esther started again, immediately using Clomid. She also added human chorionic gonadotrophin, another ovulation stimulant and a hormone used to produce ovarian progesterone during the first trimester to protect against miscarriage. She continued to use IUI technology for the inseminations.

In our interview, Esther described these cycles as "very scientific. . . . I was doing the Clomid and they had me come in for a sonogram to get a visual on the eggs. They were doing more lab tests to see how I was reacting to the hormones and they also did some extra blood tests to rule out things that may cause miscarriages, lupus and some other stuff." Esther continued, "In the beginning, it was very important to me that I did it at home and that I lit candles on my altar. And now I could care less. It's the end; the means is not the issue anymore. Now, I am very clear with myself. There are decision changes as you get on the path. Everyone says, 'I'll never go further than this,' and then everyone ends up going further."

In addition to these biomedical interventions, Esther described other strategies she employed to enhance her fertility. "Oh, I also changed my diet a bit, less sugar, alcohol, and caffeine. I took those prenatal supplements and I started doing yoga to increase my strength and energy flow. I don't know if it will help, but I may as well try." At the end of the interview, Esther paused and said, "It's really interesting because a couple months ago they changed the name of the clinic from the infertility clinic to the fertility clinic. It's like they want to destigmatize these procedures and capture a wider market."

At the time of our interview, Esther had completed the second month of trying to conceive with the help of fertility drugs, and was not yet pregnant. Although she had been pursuing pregnancy as a single woman, she described her hopes that her new relationship might develop into a coparenting partnership. As we talked, her partner was preparing dinner in the next room.

Esther's story shares qualities with those told by the other thirty-five women I interviewed: an expectation that getting pregnant can and will be an easy, low-tech process organized mostly outside of medical worlds; a tendency to draw on both women's health resources and biomedical resources; and a nonlinear trajectory—her pregnancy plans were disrupted by life events, shaped by emotional ups and downs, and required a lot of work.

What comes across most dramatically in Esther's story is her shift from self-empowerment to patient status. What was once espoused by women's health movements as a simple procedure that any women could "control" is today often a biotechnical process requiring increased reliance on medical expertise and services. This process carries health risks, legal risks, and an assumption of technoscientific progress as measured by the continuous introduction of new technologies that promise to be more advanced and efficient.

This broader trend in medicine has shaped lesbian reproduction as well as heterosexual reproduction. Although social movements have redefined homosexuality in nonmedical terms, the medicalization of bodies and bodily processes has been uneven and complicated. At times, and under certain conditions, medicalization is an encroachment into people's social lives. At other times, it is a welcome resource for ameliorating and making sense of social lives. There are no simple analyses or one-way arrows. The lingering feminist health ideals of the 1970s and 1980s often coexist with biomedical expertise and services. Even as many social movements have resisted medicalization, individuals have turned to medical discourses and services as a matter of everyday pragmatism to meet their goals.

The Ultimate Guide to Pregnancy for Lesbians (Pepper 1999), a key self-help resource for lesbians seeking parenthood, exemplifies this unevenness. Written by a new lesbian mom, the book offers a firsthand account of "the conception roller coaster" and provides a step-by-step guide for conception, beginning with one's first ovulation kit and moving toward increasing technological sophistication. Although it in part reflects feminist health ideals, this account is ultimately a hybrid. The author first states, "The best expert is you . . . follow your OWN intuition. Because only you and your partner (if you have one) can sense how your body is responding and what feels right to you. Intuition is a powerful tool in this process. Go with it!" In describing how to get pregnant, she advises, "Make the first time special, then move on." The special first time refers to the at-home, do-it-yourself procedure; moving on refers to IUI, which usually takes place in a medical office. The latter, Pepper argues, "is more effective because it lets the sperm, which are often 'spun' to shake out the dead or less effective swimmers, bypass the long journey through the cervical mucus and the vagina, placing it closer to the egg" (ibid., 66).

In another self-help account (R. 2000) a lesbian couple and their known donor quickly learn that insemination will not be the demedicalized, legally sanctioned procedure they had hoped for. First, in order to receive legal protection, they have to enter the medical field. Second, in order to reduce expenses, the recipient has to be given a diagnosis of infertility before she receives a physical exam. And third, they have to find an Ob-Gyn who will counter standard practices by performing an insemination with "live," not frozen and tested sperm. Similar hybrid stories have appeared on feminist Web sites, in gay and lesbian magazines, and in other newspapers and media. Each and all of these images and events contribute substantially to the cultural climate in which lesbian reproduction takes place today.

Contemporary Lesbian Reproduction

By 2000, assisted reproduction in the form of vaginal insemination (often self-insemination in the context of women's health movements) and IUI techniques had fully entered the mainstream. Both are now widely viewed as legitimate, relatively low-cost procedures for achieving pregnancy when few biophysical constraints are present. Alongside low-tech, assisted-reproduction technologies exists a large-scale biomedical infertility delivery service system: Fertility Inc. (This term denotes the corporate contours of this highly profitable medical sector and all the services and products it encompasses.)

As this system has evolved, assisted-reproduction practices have become more likely to draw on Fertility Inc.'s highly commercialized and com- modified set of biomedical fertility and infertility services.[55] While self- insemination and alternative health information remain accessible, concep- tion and its information resources are most often accomplished by accessing Fertility Inc. and thereby purchasing a variety of biomedical services, infor- mation, and technologies.

Throughout the 1990s, biomedicine co-opted many of the ideals of wom- en's health activism. Women's health centers, for example, are now big business for biomedicine. In creating such centers, biomedicine has not only profited but also effectively displaced the many centers that grew out of the feminist health movement, replacing them with clinics devoid of the original feminist spirit of patient empowerment (e.g., Worcester and What- ley 1988).[56]

Advances and Resistances

In the final year of the twentieth century, a baby was born to two mothers. Fertilization took place in a petri dish, with eggs harvested from one woman and sperm from an anonymous donor. Once an embryo formed, it was placed into the uterus of the woman's partner, who carried the baby to term (Crummy 2000).[57] Neither woman received a medical diagnosis of infer- tility, yet their reproductive bodies became the objects of biomedicine.

Today, artificial insemination is a routine medical treatment and an ac- cepted form of assisted reproduction. But questions remain. Has the medi- calization of assisted reproduction and its associated discourses effectively established the legitimacy of these services *as well as* an increased need for them (Hartouni 1997, 74)? If so, for whom? The legitimacy of artificial insemination and other infertility treatments continues to rely on an im- plicit (and often explicit) heterosexual frame.

Insurance policies reflect this fact. In the United States insurance policies generally cover the costs of assisted reproduction for married couples only. In Oklahoma, for example, doctors are not allowed to provide IVF services to single women; this effectively excludes lesbians who by law are unmarried. Doctors are, however, permitted to provide IUI services to single women. Therefore, while social movements have opened up the possibility for les- bians to have children, institutional structures continue to position these same women outside the category of legitimate users. But this picture is

complicated: corporate medicine certainly wants these consumers for reasons of profit and some lesbian health organizations have transformed themselves into sperm banks and alternative-insemination service providers.

Looking Ahead

Despite the demedicalization of homosexuality in 1974, ideas of same-sex
sexuality as nonprocreative and therefore unnatural continue to shape institutional practices concerning appropriate and actual users of assisted reproduction. Of course, what and who counts as an "appropriate" user of
such services has fluctuated across the decades. What remained consistent is
the configuration of the heterosexual, married couple as normative users of
assisted-reproduction technologies. Assisted reproduction has, therefore,
secured heterosexual privilege (as well as race and class hierarchies). Contemporary practices of lesbians' achieving pregnancy have resulted from a
confluence of these discursive worlds.

In October 2005 the Indiana legislature tried to pass a law that required
"intended parents" using assisted reproduction to be married to each other,
thereby denying parenthood to single, lesbian, and gay male persons and
creating a category of "unlawful reproduction." Such legislation reflected
the political tenor of the times. The 2004 presidential elections marked a
return to "family values": eleven states passed amendments to define marriage as being between a man and a woman. Current policy actions around
marriage, domestic-partner benefits, and adoption situate lesbian mothers
and queer families on unstable ground. These policies not only threaten the
legitimacy of same-sex relationships and the bonds between parents and
children but also the ways in which people are recognizable as belonging to
families, citizenry, and social life. It is easy to regard marriage-definition
laws as strategies for both protecting and shoring up the heterosexual nuclear family. Assisted-reproduction technologies and ad hoc family formations "trouble the normal" and construct new ways of knowing about kinship, of becoming related, and of destabilizing the nature-culture divide.

Why Do Such Policies Seek to Limit Lesbians' Reproduction?

As the sociologist Amy Agigian (2004) eloquently argues, lesbians' use of
artificial insemination provokes many fears, including homophobia, fear of
losing fathers' rights, fear of combining stranger and kin, and fear of mixing

racial types. During the twentieth century, a high value was placed on maintaining the opposite-sex, two-parent family as the dominant family unit (both symbolically and in actuality) and on sustaining the sanctity of marriage and importance of paternity as key aspects of family ideology.

These attempts to maintain the gendered social order, with its reliance on heterosexuality and the nuclear family form, are not surprising given the potential of reproductive technologies to delink sexuality, procreation, parenthood, and blood ties from their seemingly natural web (Haraway 1997). Whether or not such technologies fulfill this potential and under what circumstances requires in-depth analysis. As I will argue, lesbian reproduction does not represent liberation from gender norms and the sexual and reproductive order, nor does it merely reinforce that order. Further, reproduction has always been and will continue to be stratified as groups are differentially supported and constrained in exercising their reproductive rights (Collins 1999).

Enforcing Biopower

The history of assisted reproduction is a history of the enforcement of biopower. That is, when a race, class, and gender lens is applied, it becomes clear that across the centuries, stratified reproduction has been enacted through efforts to support, impede, and otherwise control the reproduction of certain groups.

Articulations of biopower may be found both in scientific research and in its application in clinical "treatments." Such articulations affect not only research and healthcare practices but also the dissemination of knowledges and differential access to technologies. Over time, they give life new interpretations and forms, making life itself problematic. In short, assisted reproduction challenges previously held notions of "nature" and "life itself." The professional organization of infertility services and its associated discourses have constructed conceptive technologies as legitimate means to achieve pregnancy for married heterosexual couples unable to fulfill their "natural" desire to procreate (Hartouni 1997, 74). However, the use of such technologies by those not considered "appropriate" reproducers (according to dominant social ideas) is still viewed as problematic. Although this dominant discourse shapes practices of use of reproductive technologies, it does not have the power to stop their use by lesbian women.

Two

"Real Lesbians Don't Have Kids" or Do They? Getting Ready for Lesbian Motherhood

AS SHE SPOKE ABOUT HER DECISION to pursue parenthood, Roslyn, a Native American high school teacher, reflected back on her thinking as a young woman: "Real lesbians don't have kids." When she recalled this conviction, I found it surprising, and at the same time I had to acknowledge that it was all too familiar. I had grown up with lesbian mother(s). And yet my coming out was greeted by my mother's tears. Would I have children, she wondered? She expressed fear that my life would be more difficult than those of my (presumably heterosexual) brothers.

Her concerns lingered in my thoughts for many years, and I have come to realize that they shaped many of the questions that ultimately led to this research. How is it that a lesbian mother could question the procreative possibilities of lesbian subjectivity? What are the cultural, social, and political forces that shape thinking about lesbians and motherhood? How do they impinge on the decision making of individuals and couples? In what ways do prior constructions of lesbian sexuality as unnatural and nonprocreative shape the meanings and practices of becoming mothers for women who do not identify as heterosexual?

I report in this chapter on the processes lesbians go through as they decide whether to pursue parenthood, the obstacles they confront, and the forces that influence their decision making. I look at the decision-making process as experienced by individuals and couples and explore the assumptions that underlie their struggles and negotiations. The concept of "les-

bian" has been discursively produced by relying on a relational discourse of
lesbians as the nonreproductive other to normal, heterosexual women. This
construction not only forecloses linguistic possibilities for lesbian motherhood but participates in shaping lesbian subjectivity. It is therefore central
to many of the struggles and negotiations described by the respondents I
interviewed. For this reason, I look at the political framework in which
deliberations occur and examine the intersection between ideology and
individual decision making.

My research focused on women who were actively seeking pregnancies
and therefore reflects decision-making processes that moved individuals or
couples toward parenthood. It does not report on the decision-making
experiences of individuals and couples who choose not to have children or
form families. It does, however, report on individuals and couples who
decide, after long periods of trying, not to continue pursuing pregnancy.

Facing Decisions with Eyes Wide Open

The lesbian participants in this research faced pregnancy decisions and trajectories with eyes wide open. They pursued conception in conscious, self-
actualizing ways as informed, active consumers of healthcare information
and services. Accidental or "oops" pregnancies were uncommon, as lesbians
must actively choose to bring sperm into their lives and bodies. When their
best-laid plans met unexpected obstacles, women responded to uncertainty
and change in much the same way they approached their pregnancy decisions
— as active consumers. They negotiated unexpected contingencies, faced
emotional challenges, and addressed financial and biophysical obstacles.

These are stories of affirmation and determination, and yet they are often
embedded in personal accounts of emotional pain: struggles with self, family, and partners, as well as a wide array of political, legal, and social concerns.
For each woman, the decision to pursue parenthood required a convergence
of identities that may seem, at times, irreconcilable. What would it mean to
be a lesbian and a mother? Or, for women who identify differently, to be
queer and a mother, or a dyke and a mother, or transgendered and a mother-
father-parent? How feminine do you have to be to be motherly? What would
it mean to be a lesbian mother in partnership with another woman who was
making a different choice? What would it be like to find oneself interacting
with medical providers in a new way? What about the legal implications? As a

pregnant woman or parent, would one be regarded differently at work or in the community? What kinds of negotiation awaited?

Although each woman's story was different, reflecting the unique and personal processes she created for herself, these were common questions and concerns. The narratives of soul searching and active decision making I heard certainly contrasted with the romanticized cultural discourses so often associated with heterosexual reproduction: diving into the adventure of parenthood, dispensing with birth control, playfully hinting at or disclosing plans to friends and families, joyously anticipating pregnancy and the arrival of a baby. Of course, this script shapes heterosexual actions as well. For most, it effaces the complications and "real" struggles of living in the world. Economic hardships, work-family balance struggles, difficulty conceiving, miscarriages, and other issues are absent in this script yet variously present in lived lives.

Struggling with Sexual Identities

The women who participated in this research reported their sexual identities in many ways. While twenty-one participants — more than half — self-identified as lesbian, five identified as queer, four as gay, two as dyke, one as bisexual, one as transgendered lesbian, and one as alternative. That fourteen women did not align themselves with the category "lesbian" demonstrates tensions in feminism, queer theory, and cultural politics over the very meaning of sexual identity and the use of identity categories. As I grapple with the term *lesbian,* so do the respondents I interviewed.

Whatever their preferred self-identification, many of the participants struggled to reconcile the idea of motherhood with a deeply held self-concept. They were not immune to cultural and social constructions — found in medical knowledge, popular culture(s), and liberation politics — that questioned whether "mother" and "lesbian" were compatible notions. Like Roslyn (and my mother), several participants wondered whether real lesbians have children. Such wonderings indicated struggles between loyalties to liberation politics and lesbian communities and loyalties to "maternal instincts," children, and "womanhood" itself (see Lewin 1990). As Marie, Roslyn's partner, said, "I was thinking that being a lesbian and a parent were incompatible with one another. That's how I felt and that's the message that I got very clearly: a lesbian was a terrible thing to be." It was lesbianism and its connection with motherhood, not parenthood itself, that was marked as deviance. Marie articulated the seamless connection between being a "normal" girl and becoming a mother.

Discussing the decision to pursue parenthood, Roslyn and other participants reflected the power of the "heterosexual matrix," what Judith Butler (1990) defines as a complex of assumptions and assertions reinforcing the idea that real boys and girls grow up to be real men and women whose realness is realized by their natural desire for members of the opposite sex: their expressions of (hetero)sex leads to their parenthood. The power of this seamless connection between sex (male/female), gender (becoming boys and girls), and sexuality (how one directs one's desire) was central to the often agonizing work done by the respondents as they got ready for lesbian motherhood.

Speaking to the complexity of these constructions, Janella said, "I remember that one thing that kept coming up was that I would love to have a kid but I was really worried about it. One thing I was worried about was that I wasn't really feminine or motherly and people wouldn't view me as motherly, they would be really shocked at the idea, and they wouldn't accept me in the role of mother. I feel it was connected to being a lesbian. It definitely had to do with being a lesbian and the self-image of not being feminine and therefore not being maternal." Beatrice explained the difficulty she had with the idea of becoming a mother: "For me, being a lesbian, I never really considered parenting. I've only been in one other long-term relationship and she didn't express the desire either. I've been trying to think about it, whether that's because we're lesbians and you just don't even go there or if it is something else."

Another participant, Dana, said, "One of the things that my mother said was she thought it was really sad that I wasn't going to have a family. I remember saying to her at the time, 'This is no reason why I can't,' and she said, 'No! Lesbians don't have children.' When I said I could adopt, she said it wasn't the same. Which I found really offensive." Dana had always wanted parenthood, but she believed that as a lesbian she would never be able to parent and implied that it was her sexuality that would prevent her from participating in the social identity and experience of motherhood. She continued, "Once you get to the point where you want to have a baby, I think that is kind of obvious, and I have always wanted to have kids as long as I can remember. It is something I have always known but I have always believed that I would never be able to because I am gay." As Lewin (1990) argues, choosing motherhood reaffirms many lesbians' gender identity.

Identity Issues and Generational Differences

To be sure, whether to have a child is a deeply personal decision. And yet such decisions are shaped within a larger cultural context — and that context may hold special power when the decision-maker belongs to a socially embattled group. As cultural contexts change over time, individual decision making may therefore reflect generational experiences.

As Arlene Stein (1997) has demonstrated, lesbians' attitudes toward parenthood reflect generational experiences.[1] Younger women (born in the 1970s and later) came of age in an era that gave greater credence to the notion that all women could reproduce. This notion has expanded to encompass the possibility that any man can be a parent. In a 2004 *San Francisco Chronicle* report on the "gay-by" boom in the Bay Area, Brian Misson, a thirty-two-year-old copywriter, was quoted as saying, "One of the first things my mom was saying when I first came out 14 years ago was, 'I'm not going to have any grandchildren.'" Nowadays, he said, a mother might be disappointed to learn her son is gay, but she can comfort herself with the knowledge that he can still get married and have kids (Shreve 2004). A *New York Times* article titled "O.K., You're Gay. So? Where's My Grandchild?" made this clear as well; in the article gays and lesbians described their parents' repeated claims that "You would make good parents," claims perceived as supporting the position that gays and lesbians could be parents, too (Leland 2000).

In contrast, older generations (born in the 1960s and earlier) have a greater tendency to see lesbianism and motherhood as mutually exclusive. When partnerships bring together women with different assumptions or different levels of commitment to parenthood, struggle and compromise often follow.

Formulating the Desire to Parent

Some participants described becoming a parent as something they "always wanted," but found it difficult to trace or fully describe these desires. All of their stories are marked with a sense of childbearing as problematic. Carla captured this well: "It is hard to think of it as something I decided. . . . I remember thinking, I really don't want to have children of my own. . . . I even investigated being a surrogate parent for a while . . . then something shifted and I started trying to pursue having a child on my own and keeping it and raising it on my own."

Diane identified several life-course moments when she thought seriously about whether or not to have a child: "When I was nineteen, I remember having thoughts that maybe my boyfriend could father a child for me . . . so way back I was already thinking how I might become a parent. Around twenty-one it started hitting me that I really did want a child, but I knew I wasn't ready. I think I just knew then that no matter what, I really wanted to have a child. And I was going to have a child somehow. And I was fantasizing, well, the sperm of who could I use and all this kind of stuff started way back. I guess I knew I was bisexual and would probably want to do this alone or with a woman."

Leslie, who adopted a child after two years of trying to conceive, put it this way: "I have always wanted to have a child. It is just something that I have been putting off for many years because I would find myself in a situation with a partner who was not interested. I kept waiting for the right person and the right time." Her comment highlights the fact that many lesbians do not assume that having or raising children will be part of their futures, nor do they want to be parents. Although Leslie "always" wanted to have a child, several of her partners did not.

For many of the women I interviewed, the quest for pregnancy was, at least at one time or another, a clear and explicit desire. Bonnie described how this desire increased over time: "I felt as though I had to have a child or I would somehow wither into oblivion. I was about to burst." Marilyn, a single lesbian, had always wanted to have a child, and her narrative reflected a presumption of future parenthood that endured throughout her life-course and at times affected her decisions: "I've always sort of had that picture [of wanting to be a parent] in my life. I also knew it wasn't going to be in my twenties because I was definitely going to be Marlo Thomas in *That Girl*—a professional single woman. When I got into my thirties, I thought, yeah, I really want to do it soon before it is too late. So it has always been what I wanted to do."

Parenthood as a Shared Goal . . . or Not

While many of the women I interviewed reported a clear, unwavering desire to have a child, others said that their quest for parenthood emerged after a process of reassessing their personal desires, relationship needs, and general plans for the future. All participants who described a turnaround — from not wanting children to planning a family — had found themselves at odds with their partners over the issue of becoming parents, and both partners had had to rethink their assumptions and preconceived ideas about becoming parents.

Many of the lesbians I interviewed said that, before their relationships began, their partners had already decided not to become parents; thus, the interviewees' decisions to conceive disrupted their partners' desires and plans. Some described their partners as acquiescing to or grudgingly going along with the plan to have a baby. Leslie said of her partner, "She didn't want to be a part of it. She didn't want to have children. . . . She felt in her heart that she was not ready or willing to have a child and this was not part of her long-term plans." Diane made a similar point about her own partner: "She decided she was not going to have a child a long time ago and that there just wouldn't be a child in her life."

For many women, support groups, one-on-one therapy, and just a lot of discussion helped to bring about the adjustments needed to overcome the contradictions in their relationships.[2] Some women's adjustments were more overt than others. Leslie, for example, described her partner as only reluctantly acquiescing to her plans to have a baby: "[My partner] was not really supportive from the start about this. She was not sure if she was going to be staying in there for the duration. . . . When I stopped inseminating, I was grieving by myself. [My partner] was happy. It was hard for her not to show her relief. . . . Later she reluctantly accepted my plans to adopt, but was negative." Such acceptance coupled with negativity illuminates the tension and difficulties that relationships must endure when individual plans don't match. When Leslie successfully adopted a little girl, she said, "[It was] a miracle. . . . [My partner] was completely transformed . . . and all of a sudden it became this magical thing that we were both doing together."

Rachel described her experience of trying to have a child as one of isolation, despite the fact that she was in a relationship. While her partner was willing to have a child with her, Rachel felt pressure to be the sole facilitator: "I must say that there were several times in my life when I almost attempted to do it on my own. It came to a point in 1995 that I discussed it with my partner and said that this is what I am doing pretty much, despite her lack of enthusiasm. I just decided that this was it. I was turning thirty-five and I thought this was it, I was going to try to have a child before I turned thirty-five. I think age was finally the last catalyst. I knew I had to make it happen if it was going to work out. She would be there, but I was in charge."

Similarly, Renee felt that in her relationship she was the primary force behind the idea of parenting. She and her partner worked on the issue for months before they started trying to get pregnant. For many of these months, Renee downplayed her "readiness" in an effort to provide space for her partner to choose if and when she wanted to begin the process. "I waited for her to bring it up. Of course, I was ready. Once she said she wanted to do it, I said, 'Sure I want to do it, too.' I always have. We really didn't know how we would. We were from the south bay and while there are some [gay parents] down there, it's not talked about. There wasn't really a lot of exposure. We were really clueless and had no idea how to do it."

As some women described, when their partners acquiesced or grudgingly went along with the plans to have babies, the decision put stress on their relationships. Renee and Rachel both spoke at length about difficult and painful discussions with their partners. Similarly, Leslie described undergoing a tense process with her current partner, with whom she has stayed together: "We talked about it all the time to see if one of us could imagine what the other wanted. It was really hard. . . . Eventually a point in time arrived when I said, 'You know, if I have to do this by myself I will. I feel really strong about this.'"

Despite variations in coming to the decision to become mothers, once these women shifted their focus from "maybe baby" toward achieving pregnancy, they began gathering information and resources, finding support, and gaining financial and emotional stabilities. These processes, like the decisions to become parents, were variously shaped by feminist health and biomedical knowledges.

Gaining Stability in the Face of Profound Uncertainty

Once the women I interviewed felt "ready" to embark on the material aspects of the achieving-pregnancy trajectory, they attempted to gain (relationship, emotional, and financial) stability and to find the information, knowledge, and social support they felt necessary to become parents, all of which they discussed with me at length. Once women moved from the frame of "maybe baby" to that of potential motherhood, their narratives centered on actively working on their selves, their relationships, and their careers and finances to prepare for pregnancy and parenthood. Alongside the profound intentionality that infused this process, and all aspects of lesbian trajectories of achieving pregnancy, was a conscious desire to create a sense of stability prior to embarking on parenthood. This stability was often gained through accessing a variety of knowledge sources on pregnancy, parenthood, and queer communities of support.

Lesbians did not turn to the large-scale biomedical infertility industry to gain stability and gather information. They instead sought community-specific institutional contexts with roots in women's health and/or queer community services, a phenomenon that may not be specific to women with pregnancy goals or to queer society. The proliferation of community network Internet sites fostering all sorts of social connections indicate that the yearning for alternatives is widely shared. The grass-roots healthcare activism and ample lesbian, gay, bisexual, transgender, queer, and intersex (LGBTQI) resources of the San Francisco Bay Area are central to shaping how and where lesbians in the area turn for information.[3] The turn to community resources may also be indicative of a more profound salience of nonbiomedical worlds in what is today a highly biomedicalized culture of health, pregnancy, and reproduction.

Getting Relationships Ready for Parenthood

Getting relationships ready for parenthood—finding them, stabilizing them, and feeling secure in them—emerged as an important early step toward achieving pregnancy. The women I interviewed took conscious actions toward achieving the relational stability they perceived to be crucial to parenthood, continuously negotiating, planning, and acting toward the goal of having children. Their intentional, eyes-wide-open approach constituted a prioritizing of stability over personal goals, over the means of achieving them, and even over the uncertainties involved in becoming further marginalized as lesbian mothers and gay families.

One strategy was to attend individual therapy, couple's therapy, and support groups, therapeutic venues constructed as the means through which women gained stability and security in their lives and relationships. As they attended support groups, they also collected information about the legal, social, and medical issues involved in becoming parents and developed support networks for their eventual needs as parents.

For the couples who found themselves in agreement over parenting, gaining stability became the next step toward motherhood. Heather, in describing how she and her partner stabilized their life together, mentioned that her partner had ended a previous relationship with another woman because the other woman did not want to parent. "We both have always wanted kids. Once we got together and got the relationship on its feet, we talked about that. It had been a real sticking point in Judith's past relationship that she had left. Her [previous] partner didn't really want kids. She said Judith could have them if she wanted and she'd kind of help, but that she would not go into parenting with equal intent or intent to be an equal partner. Once Judith and I got together, it was great that we both definitely wanted children. That part was easy." Judith agreed, describing how, soon after they first met and started dating, they had discussed wanting to have children. Once they decided to become parents, Judith explained, they took the next important step—getting ready. "It was always understood that we both wanted children, and we always talked about that and I felt like I finally met the person who would be the perfect person who I would parent with. And I finally had the green light and we talked about it a lot more. It's a real choice for us. Then we had to talk about whether we were ready for it. Was it time? One of the considerations was my age. At this point I would be about thirty-five years old, so that made us begin to move on trying."

Focusing on Personal Finances

Financial stability was also frequently a preoccupation. Many of the women I interviewed discussed their fears of not having enough money or clear plans for gaining financial security. Bonnie and Audrey stated that sometimes women, including themselves, did not start the pregnancy process until they felt economically ready. In describing how they prepared their finances, they commented that their experience may have been overly rational and controlled. Speaking to her partner, Audrey said, "You were afraid . . . you didn't have the economic stability. You were by yourself and everything." Bonnie responded, "Thinking now, I really sort of regret that. That I wasn't thinking more recklessly about my life and just said, 'Let's just do it, whatever happens.' But I kept planning for the future and that overtook the need to have it right away."

Later in the interview, Audrey reflected, "But I was also very scared of all the responsibility that comes with being a parent. And then the strength of our relationship. . . ."

When they met, Audrey already wanted to have a child and was aware of time passing; she was in her late thirties and felt that her age increasingly influenced her pregnancy plans. She and Bonnie decided to go to couples' therapy to develop the relational readiness they perceived to be necessary for parenthood. As Bonnie said, "[The therapist] made us go through premarital counseling." Both women wanted to have a relationship and, once together, they worked on stabilizing their commitment to each other and to their partnership before trying to get pregnant.

Chloe described the "work" of preparation as an encounter with personal growth: "It is such a conscious process and so consciously initiated and perpetuated that there have been some conscious opportunities, too. Like the thing about me having to ask some guy for sperm. It's like me overcoming this whole thing that I can ask for what I want in the world. It is an opportunity for personal growth . . . an opportunity to do some work. I am ambiguous about how I feel about that because it is so contrived and so conscious."

Dana described wanting to strengthen her finances and sense of maturity before getting pregnant. Once she achieved this, she encountered multiple fertility issues that prevented her from becoming pregnant. "I planned, I worked up to it for a long time and I went to therapy because I was really scared to do it alone. So, I went to therapy for a long time and really worked on that, what it would be and what I would need to prepare myself, and I waited until I was really secure in being a teacher and everything and by then I wasn't very fertile anymore. So, I really waited to get secure in my job and finances and it took me a really long time to grow up and get stable." Age as a social category that indicates maturity emerged as an important factor in women's sense of readiness. It is also a familiar cultural discourse: when one is too young, one is immature and thus not ready for parenthood; but if one waits until one is mature and ready, one's body may no longer be able to naturally conceive and carry a pregnancy to term. Such developmental narratives represent a normative logic of reproductive time ruled by biological clocks and strict rules of lifecourse timing of marriage and family (Halberstam 2005). Normativity thus remains intact.

Confronting Barriers to Family Formation

In addition to discussing struggles regarding individual identity, participants talked about the obstacles facing them as they contemplated forming families with their partners and children — existing and future. Speaking at length about social discourses of heterosexual privilege and how they influenced her personal life, Dana identified several social structures as barriers to procreation and family formation among gay men and lesbians. For her, those obstacles included state and federal laws that dictated adoption and second-parent adoption policies, prejudiced social workers assigned to second-parent adoption cases, and the fact that "biologically tied family members," rather than self-identified gay parents, were often awarded custody.

Second parent adoption is the primary way for lesbian co-parents to secure parenthood for the nonbiological mother. Legally, a second-parent adoption, or "independent adoption," requires the state to investigate the adoptive parent and the adoptive parent's home and family before approving the adoption. Depending on the state, the investigation can include a two-hour, at-home interview and a fee of $2,000–$3,000. Anticipating the home visits of the social worker, Arlene stated, "Neither of us pass [for heterosexual] anymore, and you need to [for second-parent adoptions], although we may get lucky. We may get a social worker who is different. . . . I get upset and cry a lot. You know, it is the world and how you are treated if you're queer, never mind being female. . . . You have to do things to fit in, in order to obtain some of the benefits in society."

Passing, the ability to be recognized by others as someone different from "who you are," becomes central not only to achieving one's parenting goals but also to obtaining recognition, in this case state recognition, of belonging. Arlene and her partner, Chloe, understand not only the policies but also the ways these have the power to produce their intended family's recognition as legitimate. Legible gender and (hetero)sexual performances must be enacted to secure this belonging.

Financial Barriers to Assisted Reproduction

Both economic and racial inequalities play a central role in shaping lesbian reproduction. Financial stability is increasingly significant in the U.S. for-profit healthcare system, particularly in the infertility system with its technological imperative, which swiftly moves patients up the ladder of high-tech (and expensive) services. Today even the most noninvasive methods of assisted reproduction are costly. Medical expenses, in combination with legal expenditures, create even higher financial demands.

Table 2 lists the average fees associated with many of the medical services

Table 2   Description of Fees for Assisted Reproductive Services and Technologies*

TECHNOLOGY / SERVICE	COST**	DESCRIPTION
Ovulation Prediction		
Manual mucus assessment	Free	Self-prediction
Basal body temperature	$15.00	Charting bodily changes
Detection kits	$30–$50 (6–9 cycles)	Measure LH surge
Insemination Procedures		
Self-insemination (at-home vaginal insemination)	Free	Syringe or other device
Intrauterine Insemination (IUI)	$250–$350	Catheter is passed through cervix into uterus where IUI-ready semen are released
Sperm Types		
Fresh	Unavailable	There are no fresh-sperm clinics in the U.S.
Unwashed	$185–$205 per 1.0 ml	Unwashed, whole, frozen semen
Screened and tested	$215 per 0.5–1.0 ml	Washed, frozen, screened semen
IUI-ready sample	$185–$200	Washed, frozen, reduced semen
Donor Profiles		
Template	Free	Classification grid comparing all donors
Long profile	$15–$25	Donor answers questions (usually by hand)
Donor photo	$35	A picture of the donor
Donor photo-matching service	$40–$45	Donor appearance matched with recipient(s)
Donor medical chart	$15	Multigeneration questionnaire
30 min. donor-selection consultation	$50	Meeting with sperm bank staff
60 min. donor-selection consultation	$85	Meeting with sperm bank staff
Donor sperm-count research	$40	Test performed to test sperm count
Other Technologies		
Hormone Therapy	$200–$3,000 per month	Drugs that act on the ovaries to enhance egg development and induce ovulation by causing the pituitary gland to secrete an increased amount of follicle-stimulating hormone. The most common drug prescribed is clomiphene citrate (sold under the trade name Clomid).

Table 2   continued

TECHNOLOGY/SERVICE	COST**	DESCRIPTION
Assisted Reproductive Technologies -In Vitro Fertilization -Intracytoplasmic Sperm Injection -Gamete (Intra)Fallopian Transfer	$8,000–$13,000 per cycle	Procedures used outside the body to bring sperm and egg directly together
Surgical Intervention	$10,000–$15,000	Procedures used to correct problems — such as blocked fallopian tubes, fibroids, or endometriosis — that may be interfering with conception

* This is not an exhaustive list. Many other services are offered, including shipping and storage of sperm, fertility consultation, transvaginal and other sonogram tests, and so on.
** Averages are based on information gathered in October 2004.

and technologies accessed along trajectories of achieving pregnancy. When donated sperm is used, each at-home vaginal insemination costs $500–$1,000 for the first menstrual cycle and $300–$700 for each additional cycle thereafter. Recipients who use semen from a known donor usually have the sperm tested and screened for a variety of genetic and transmitted diseases; each test carries additional costs.

Despite the high costs, health-insurance companies are mandated to cover infertility services in only ten U.S. states and mandated to offer them in only three. Table 3 illustrates the most recent legislative policies concerning insurance coverage of infertility treatments. Despite these policies, many lesbians with insurance but without an infertility diagnosis fall outside all mandates for coverage. This leads to extra costs for lesbian couples, costs that vary by state, insurance status, and diagnostic category. Furthermore, reproductive-healthcare specialists do not provide services equally across populations. Until the mid-1980s, for example, physicians regularly refused to provide insemination to unmarried women; some physicians deny such services to this day (National Center for Lesbian Rights 2004).

Many physicians provide services exclusively to women diagnosed with in/fertility and/or to women in heterosexual partnerships. And, since infertility services are not covered by most health-insurance plans, most specialists provide services only to those with the financial resources to pay in advance. For those who are either unable to obtain such services or choose not

Table 3 Fertility-Insurance Legislative Policies

STATE	DATE	MANDATE TO COVER*	MANDATE TO OFFER**	IVF COVERAGE	IVF EXCLUDED	IVF ONLY
Arkansas	1987	X				X
California	1989		X		X	
Connecticut	2005	X		X		
Hawaii	1987	X				X
Illinois	1991	X		X		
Louisiana	2001				X	
Maryland	1985	X				X
Massachusetts	1987	X		X		
Montana	1987	X				
New Jersey	2001	X		X		
New York	2002			X		
Ohio	1991	X				
Rhode Island	1989	X		X		
Texas	1987		X			X
West Virginia	2001	X				

* A law requiring that health-insurance companies provide coverage of infertility treatment as a benefit included in every policy. A policy premium would include the cost of infertility-treatment coverage.

** A law requiring that health-insurance companies make available for purchase a policy that offers coverage of infertility treatment. The law does not require employers to pay for the infertility-treatment coverage.

Source: Resolve: The National Infertility Association, 2007.

to use them, commercial sperm banks and private healthcare providers may offer insemination services. Thus, access to reproductive technologies in the United States is from the outset a class-based and sexuality-based phenomenon, and the institutional organization of these services enacts the reproduction of class and sexuality hierarchies by assuring the survival and ongoing proportionality of middle-class (usually white) heterosexual families.[4]

By weaving together medical and social justifications for decisions concerning who will be provided services (Cussins 1998; Bateman-Novaes 1998) and who will not, biomedicine itself structures inequalities. The ideological message is that some people have a greater right to reproduce than do others, and entitlements are often provided to those possessing the "correct" relationship and sexuality status. Nonetheless, in terms of relationship and sexuality status, access to assisted reproduction is not universally or tightly enforced, so multiple pathways to information, resources, and services open up. Technological practices have the power to produce specific cultural effects on bodies and to construct certain "truth effects" about users (Balsamo 1996, 105), and in the case of reproductive technologies these practices not only enact truth effects but also enact disciplining consequences on the bodies of users, real and implicated actors.

The services and technologies listed in table 2 as "access points" are by and large professionally regulated. That is, there are few state or federal regulations concerning the use of these services, and decisions regarding use are made professionally (not governmentally). Nonetheless, ability to pay and insurance status have profound implications for access to these services.

There is no federal law requiring insurance coverage for infertility treatment; however, as of 2007, fifteen states have enacted some type of infertility-insurance-coverage law, which can be described as mandate-to-cover or mandate-to-offer insurance. A mandate to cover requires that insurance companies provide coverage of infertility services, including the cost of treatment, as a benefit in every policy. The states with mandate-to-cover laws include Arkansas, Connecticut, Hawaii, Illinois, Maryland, Massachusetts, Montana, New Jersey, New York, Ohio, Rhode Island, and West Virginia. However, what exact procedures are covered, what conditions and definitional requirements must be met before they are covered, and how many procedures are covered varies in each state. In contrast, mandate-to-offer coverage requires that companies make available for purchase an insurance policy that covers treatment, but it does not require employers to pay for this coverage. Three states have such policies: California, Texas, and, to a lesser degree, Louisiana, where insurers are only required to treat correctable medical conditions that result in infertility and where coverage is not offered for fertility drugs, IVF, or any other assisted-reproduction technique (Resolve 2007).

Access to assisted-reproduction technologies vis-à-vis lesbians is highly complex. One complication involves the fact that in the United States same-sex partnerships are not legally recognized. Due to this discrimination (and the U.S. system that attaches healthcare to employment), lesbian couples are not able to provide health insurance to their partners. Unless both members of the couple are employed in full-time jobs that provide health insurance, access to infertility services covered under an insurance plan is extremely limited. In addition, even in those situations wherein women have insurance, most insurance policies only cover infertility treatments

when a physician's diagnosis has been made. In the absence of heterosexual intercourse a diagnosis of infertility is difficult to obtain. Lesbians continue to be referred to infertility specialists, however, where they pay for the cost of their care on a fee-for-service basis. Even when a diagnosis is given, either from a "flexible" physician or due to a clinical infertility condition, only the cost of services are covered; "products" are not. Sperm is a product that is always categorized by insurance guidelines as an "elective" healthcare service. And in most cases physicians do not allow the use of "directed" (known) donors unless those donors are legally married to the women receiving care.[5]

Accumulating Cultural Health Capital

Given the limited legal and financial access to assisted reproduction, it is not surprising that the participants interviewed for this research are women stratified "up" the ladder: that is, they are often wealthy and usually highly educated. They possess what Janet Shim (2006) calls cultural health capital, "the repertoire of cultural skills, verbal and non-verbal competencies, and interactional styles that can influence healthcare interactions" (3).

Shim borrows from the French social theorist Pierre Bourdieu (1984), who used the term *cultural capital* in his discussion of the reproduction of social classes; cultural capital refers to the access to educational and social resources often necessary to reach a desired goal. Cultural *health* capital includes elements of social status such as verbal skills and educational attainment; ability to acquire and consume scientific and biomedical information; facility in interacting with biomedical "experts"; capacity to be proactive in acquiring self-knowledge; and potential for self-transformation (Shim 2001). Cultural health capital is related to social and cultural capital in that it constitutes a nonmonetary set of resources critical to the accumulation and exercise of power and the struggle for social distinction. Specifically, it encompasses a broad set of attitudes, practices, knowledges, and competencies that enable individuals not only to heed health-promotion prescriptions but also to negotiate them as well.

Economic capital, among the women I interviewed, clearly shaped decision making. For many who did not have disposable income, the cost of getting pregnant was burdensome, but they were able to access information necessary to minimize the financial costs and make decisions that would allow them to pursue pregnancy nevertheless. Thus, while class differences may have been evident in whether women chose to use known donors (free) or anonymous donors (a commodity for a fee), even the women who selected known donors to minimize costs possessed the cultural capital necessary to know about and perform self-insemination. All the women I interviewed possessed knowledge that enabled them to access either reproductive-health services or to access the information necessary to perform the inseminations themselves. For example, Chloe said, "I can't afford to walk in [to a sperm bank]. . . . It is about two hundred dollars a vial and you use two vials each month. So it really adds up." For Chloe, using a known donor and doing the inseminations at home meant that getting pregnant would be more affordable. "We decided to talk to our friends and find someone willing to donate his sperm. We knew it would require more legal maneuverings, but it felt right to us." The legal knowledge necessary was another form of cultural capital that many of these women possessed.

To participate in this research study, women were required to be actively seeking pregnancy via reproductive technology. As a result, my findings are biased toward those with cultural health capital. Lesbians who desired to have children via reproductive technology but who did not possess sufficient economic or cultural capital are invisible in this research; however, their presence and significance is included in my analysis. Of course, women who want to become pregnant are always already constrained or enabled by their economic and cultural capital, as well as by their social positions and biophysical attributes. The use of assisted reproduction takes place within a biomedical context that is heavily commodified whether or not users try to minimize their contact with biomedicine. As such, the participants present in this research possess some form of cultural capital inherent in their abilities to negotiate the cost of medically mediated assisted reproduction, legal maneuverings, and/or second-parent adoption.

It is precisely due to the need for cultural capital that resource readiness — that is, gathering information and resources — emerged as another aspect of gaining stability in the face of uncertainty. Chloe described her preparation as a process of becoming a "responsible adult" wherein becoming an adult was attached to getting her finances and health insurance in order: "Over the past couple of years, I have really structured my life with this being the goal. . . . I was doing my own finances and paying off my bills . . . trying to pull work, money, and health insurance together and trying to do the 'I am a responsible adult' thing." In all, I interpret what reads as a hyperplanning for pregnancy and parenthood as a means to minimize uncertainties and enhance a sense of stability. While many participants discussed the difficult decision of whether or not to pursue pregnancy and parenthood as a personal journey, the uncertainties that shaped these decisions may have more to do with the place of queer parenting and queer families in an increasingly heteronormative society. I read intentionality as a means to control (or, at least, to create an illusion of control) over an action (getting pregnant) and a set of identities (becoming a queer parent and gay family) that are marginalized at best and actively resisted in a culture dominated by conservative views of faith, values, and family that include legislating against same-sex marriage and gay adoptions. Furthermore, proactive and intentional negotiations are often class tactics used by well-educated, middle-class actors to maneuver within systems and maximize their results.[6]

Gathering Information and Resources

Reducing uncertainty was achieved in part through the information sources participants turned to in their quest for pregnancy. Despite the existence of a large-scale biomedical infertility industry, lesbian participants clearly sought community-safe institutional contexts from which to gather information and receive support. Although all participants appeared knowledgeable about biomedical resources and had adequate health insurance and medical providers, they did not turn to these sources as a first line of information gathering. This is indicative of the ongoing influence and activities of women's health movements as well as a persistently heteronormative culture.

In response to marginalization and exclusion, women's health movements of the 1970s focused on developing knowledge by women for women, with an organized consciousness-raising component, to empower women to learn about their own bodies. Consciousness-raising groups were informal support, information, and political theorizing groups held in women's homes and community organizations. While the term *consciousness-raising group* has gone out of use, participants in this research nevertheless accessed current versions of feminist information and support groups. Many attended groups to learn about insemination, to make connections with other lesbian parents-to-be, and to theorize the personal and social ramifications of their childrearing plans. These activities at once created stability and readiness and reduced uncertainty in a stratified culture that continuously transformed queer people, communities, and choices into outlaws—people who threatened the perceived fabric and stability of "American life."

The women I interviewed gathered information about how to get pregnant from a host of sources, including support groups, informal social networks, books, the Internet, and other media. That this research was located in the San Francisco Bay Area was significant: most women found that all the information they needed was very close at hand, in local newspapers, informal networks, and formal organizational resources. The Bay Area has one of the largest and most ethnically diverse gay and lesbian populations in the United States and is home to a vast network of alternative political, professional, and community-based health organizations serving LGBTQI communities. This progressive environment in some way influenced all of the respondents I interviewed. Participants described gathering information from local, queer-friendly newspapers; the Lesbian, Gay, Transgender Pride Parade; the International Lesbian and Gay Film Festival; local feminist and gay bookstores; local healthcare providers; organizations serving the queer community; and informal support and information networks organized by gay community members. Heather described the importance of location to resource readiness: "It certainly helps living in an extremely gay-friendly area. We have tons of resources, support, and medical practitioners, specifically gay groups for everything you can imagine. It's easy here."

Another resource available to Bay Area lesbians is the broad selection of events and activities that take place during Lesbian and Gay Pride Month (celebrated in June to commemorate the Stonewall uprisings of June 1969). While many cities across the United States hold queer pride activities in this month, San Francisco's pride offerings are especially elaborate, varied, and daily. Activities during this month often served as primary access points to information. Paula described a specific film series at the International Lesbian and Gay Film Festival, held as part of San Francisco's queer pride month: "One film was a profile of two different couples, two men and two women who were foster parents and then adopted kids. Really neat stories. . . . And then the third one was about . . . these two women who go as a couple, the older woman was going to be the first to carry the child. And it was a friend of theirs who was donating the sperm. And just the trials and tribulations she went through because she wasn't getting pregnant. So three short films. It was great." Regardless of the source of information, women in the Bay Area found it easy to obtain the knowledges they felt necessary to prepare for pregnancy.

Like relational readiness, information gathering reflects intentionality, the legacy of women's health movements, and the proliferation of biomedical knowledges and resources. In the current era acquiring health information has become a "patient's" responsibility in the United States, whereas in the past nonprofessionals' access to biomedical information was severely limited, constrained by what amounted to a professional monopoly on access per se, as such information dwelled almost exclusively in medical libraries and schools that were firmly closed to the public. Popularized "lay" health information was also rare. Not until the 1970s and the interventions of the women's health and consumer-health movements did self-help health books enter the mainstream. Health sections in bookstores were once rare and limited in their offerings (Clarke et al. 2003). This has changed rapidly as biomedicine has expanded its reach into daily life. Literatures on health and illness proliferate in all kinds of media: in newspapers, on the Internet, through direct-to-consumer prescriptions, and via over-the-counter-drug advertising. Moreover, individuals are increasingly held responsible for acquiring relevant biomedical knowledge and for managing their own health.

A cross-over between biomedical and "lay" discourses around health has emerged: current healthcare materials resonate with self-help language, and self-help materials rely heavily on healthcare knowledges to make their claims. As the line between the literatures of healthcare and self-help blurs, each invites readers into a medicalized subjectivity, and readers respond variously. Many of the resources gathered by the women I interviewed were indicative of this blurring. Furthermore, within medicine, the acquisition and consumption of biomedical and other health knowledge are no longer seen as the privilege of the few, but rather as a mandate for the masses. Individuals are being transformed from passive, lay patients to active consumers increasingly responsible for their own biomedical destinies (Lupton 1997).[7]

Participants in my research frequently accessed three community-based healthcare organizations: Lyon Martin Health Services; Maia Midwifery and Preconception Services; and Prospective Queer Parents, organized by the Rainbow Flag Sperm Bank. The Lyon Martin clinic, a San Francisco–based feminist health center, was founded in 1971 and served as a major center for women's healthcare throughout the 1970s and 1980s. In the 1990s the clinic ran a series of workshops titled "Considering Parenthood." Maia Midwifery, which opened in 1995, provided midwifery and preconception services — including education, counseling, support, and consultations — to the lesbian community of the Bay Area. Prospective Queer Parents formed in 1991 with the express purpose of providing a forum for the exchange of information and a social gathering space for members of the LGBTQI community who were interested in child raising and parenting. Monthly meetings, held in people's homes, were designed as an opportunity for queer people interested in parenting to encounter new friends and potential parenting partners. Many of the people I interviewed had at one time made use of the services provided by these organizations.

Michelle described the usefulness of a support group that she and her partner, Janella, attended at Lyon Martin.

> At first we didn't know anything about alternative insemination. We joined this group. That was the main thing. We discussed everything there. "Lesbian Prospective Parents." That was really helpful. I remember when we first went there . . . we didn't know anything about how we would go about getting pregnant. We hadn't even decided that was what we were going to do. Then things went really quickly. We got loads of information from them. We came back from the first night thinking, "Wow this is really possible. I think we will do it." We went in not knowing anything but a vague idea, and then we started going every month and they were telling us everything we needed to know: what the sperm banks are, how to go about it, what the costs are, what legal information we need, just all these different things. After that we moved really quickly. A lot of people had been trying for a while. That group made a BIG difference.

The self-insemination spirit was also represented in Esther's story, in her description of the Lyon Martin workshop she attended. Having learned how to find her cervix and perform an insemination at the workshop, she decided to join several others in ongoing meetings. "We all started meeting informally and talking about our lives and thoughts about becoming parents. For some of us it has worked out and others decided to do other things. It's been really nice, it's been years and we just keep meeting once in a while."

People found out about these groups through flyers at bookstores, in the local gay newspaper, and though friends. Esther, for example, described standing up at an activist meeting and announcing to the crowd that she wanted to have a baby and that if others wanted to get together to talk, she would like that. The next day somebody called and asked if she wanted to attend the Lyon Martin group with her. "[The caller said she] just saw in the paper that there's a thing this weekend at Lyon Martin, a day-long conference on considering parenthood. . . . [We went and] it was really informative. It got me really excited about it. It answered a lot of questions and opened a whole new slew of questions that I hadn't thought about. I think it really started me on the path."

Many women reported finding these groups so helpful that they continued to attend the groups long after the workshops ended. Kim described how she and her partner went to a group that met for years: "A couple of concrete things we did that were pretty helpful were we went to a 'Considering Parenthood' workshop. It was a six-week workshop at Lyon Martin, maybe eight weeks. That was good. We still meet as a group, there are four of us. One woman had a baby last week and two of the other people are still trying. That's been pretty good."

While some women found the groups instrumental, others felt they didn't meet their specific needs. For example, Dana participated in the Lyon Martin group but did not feel that the group sufficiently addressed her concerns as a single woman. She started a single-woman's insemination group by placing an ad in the local newspaper: "In terms of support, before I even started [inseminating], I started a lesbian support group. And before that I went to a support group at the Lyon Martin Groups and sometimes I just felt, everyone was couples except me and this other woman. And sometimes I just felt there was some discrimination. They ran around and said, 'What are you guys going to name your baby?' and when they came to the single people, they just skipped us, like we didn't count. And that's why I started this other group for single women."

The existence of community-based groups demonstrates that women's health activities continue to provide resources and knowledges to lesbian lives. The success of the women's health movement is further evident in the proliferation of self-help books by and for women. Both the self-help literature and woman-centered services are central to lesbian experiences of getting ready and gathering resources.

The women I interviewed had no trouble locating self-help books on the topics of both lesbian parenting and pregnancy through technical means.

The books most frequently mentioned include *Challenging Conceptions: Planning a Family by Self-Insemination* (1994) by Lisa Saffron; *Considering Parenthood* (1988) by Cheri Pies; and *Having Your Child by Donor Insemination* (1988) by Elizabeth Noble. These resources perform some of the emotional work necessary to support lesbian reproduction, support that is absent from mainstream culture and mainstream biomedicine. These books also participate in creating the emergent lesbian script of what it means to "get ready," gather information, find sperm, and achieve pregnancy.

For women who lived outside of San Francisco proper, but within the larger Bay Area, support groups were easily accessible. Flyers describing groups were posted at bookstores, and advertisements for groups appeared in the *Bay Times* or *Bay Area Reporter,* two newspapers serving the Bay Area's queer populations. Renee and her partner attended a group after seeing a flyer in a feminist bookstore located in their town. Renee described the group: "There is a woman's bookstore in the next town over. We saw on their newsletter that they had a group for prospective parents . . . for lesbians that were thinking about having kids. It was a group of people getting together to say, 'What are the options?' 'Do I want to do this or don't I?' It was great for us."

In many ways these actions resonate with the discourses of the women's health movement and enable women to gain agency in their own healthcare practices, to refuse to be passive objects of the medical gaze. Biomedical marketing frequently co-opts and claims as its own organizational strategies brought about by women's health movements and other grassroots social movements such as disability rights, AIDS activism, and other disease-specific movements (e.g., Belkin 1996; Worcester and Whatley 1988). Organizations that provide services to lesbians are not immune from such tendencies. The creation of self-help groups designed to support lesbian pregnancies and families, for example, may be a testament to the sustained efforts and influence of women's health movements. While many of these resources are community driven and mobilized, the utilization by lesbians of institutionally based support groups may also be indicative of biomedicine's cooptation of women's health and the alteration of feminist health principles by feminist health organizations themselves. Contemporary biomedicine has proved particularly adept at cooptation of earlier feminist interventions, shearing the outward forms and rhetoric of their feminist roots and epistemological and ontological processes (Clarke and Olesen 1999).

Many of the women I interviewed also discussed learning things from friends and co-workers. Marilyn gathered information from her future roommate: "At the time I had just met my roommate. She had answered an ad in the *Bay Times* that I posted in which I was looking for a romantic partner. When we started talking, it turned out she had inseminated with a known donor a number of times a few years ago and wasn't able to get pregnant. When we met, I had an appointment for the next month. So she answered a lot of my questions and provided a lot of support for me to have the strength and information I needed to keep going. I met her at the perfect time."

Shari described herself as a skilled networker who talked with everyone she could think of who might have knowledge about the process of getting pregnant. She relied on friends to help her locate and choose a sperm bank. "I just started talking to my friends that were getting pregnant. There were so many. I quickly learned that there is a sperm bank here that many people use. I also have a really good friend who used to work there and she also gave me a lot of information. It was very easy to learn that many of our friends had used this same sperm bank. I just picked their brains for information from them on everything they did. And then I was off."

In addition to gathering information, respondents also gathered the inspiration they needed to move forward. Raquel described this well: "We learned originally from a lesbian couple who had gotten pregnant very quickly, the second try, in fact. Just at home, using vaginal insemination. That was inspiring! They had a big, fat folder full of stuff about everything: basal body temperature, charts, sperm banks, the everyday stuff they came across. They stuck it all in the folder. What a resource! They had photocopied things about lesbian parenting from books, essays, testimonials from people about their different experiences with the process. It gave us a lot of ideas."

The women I interviewed mentioned finding support groups and information on the San Francisco–based Harvey Milk Center and Alternative Family Project. Although both organizations drew heavily on the spirit of the women's health movement, they were developed by and for gay men and lesbians, a result of the gay and lesbian activism of the 1970s, 1980s, and 1990s.

Once having decided to inseminate, participants searched for information online, accessing Web sites and locating pertinent online communities for discussion and support. A July 1998 headline on CNN's site read "Surfing for Sperm: Reproduction in Cyberspace." The author states that "cyberspace is rapidly becoming a lucrative place for sperm banks to advertise" and that lesbians are increasingly becoming those who "shop for sperm on the web" (Dornin 1998). The three local sperm banks in the Bay Area each have a Web site for marketing their services, technologies, and "products."[8] The Web sites also serve as information resources on how to inseminate.

Beatrice described deciding to start the process: "Finally we just said if we're going to do it, let's do it. And boom we went online and did our research and found the sperm bank to use." Joyce also used the Internet: "I remembered the Feminist Women's Health Center from the 1970s. I knew or at least I was fairly certain they didn't exist any more, so I went online to do research. I found the Sperm Bank and some other ones, too. . . . As I was reading about the Sperm Bank, I realized that's what happened to the Feminist Women's Health Center. They're now this sperm bank. So it was great, I knew I wanted to go there."

Thus, while knowledge sources proliferate, they do so with complications. Although the Internet purportedly democratizes access to knowledge, a priority is often placed on the political-economic (i.e., corporate) interests of the "Biomedical TechnoService Complex" (Clarke et al. 2003). That is, information technologies like the World Wide Web may be transformative in their broad dissemination of medical and health information and resources and in the heterogeneity of "expertise" among those who contribute content in terms of gay or feminist identification, but profit motives are also ever present. As people log on to informational resources, sometimes at a cost, they are barraged with advertisements and other marketing strategies. Moreover, do-it-yourself sites are less common and less likely to be hot-linked (Moore and Clarke 2001).

Information in a Biomedical Age

The material practices of seeking resources and the types of information available provide entrance into understanding lesbian reproduction as a highly biomedicalized practice. Biomedicalization involves a shift from medical "control over" to biomedical "transformation of" particular processes and properties of the human, the nonhuman, and the hybrid (Clarke 1995).[9] While expanded professional medical jurisdiction and control is

sustained, its accomplishment is achieved through technoscientifically organized innovations (Clarke et al. 2003). With regard to gathering information and resources, biomedicalization processes are significant for their influence on not only mainstream organizations but alternative ones as well.
Biomedicalization involves an increased reliance on information technologies that facilitate access to health information. The women I interviewed,
for example, often gathered information online and found support by accessing online communities.

Thus, while biomedicalization processes continue to seek control over
access to conventional medical and healthcare-related information, the ways
in which it does so are not monolithic, all-encompassing, or centrally located. Agencies and constraints coexist, as do sources of information and
services indicating hybridity associated with lesbian practices. For example,
the women in this research drew on various Internet resources (medial, lay,
self-help, and others) for their own purposes, as they gathered information
to help them achieve pregnancy. Their acquisition of information and
knowledge reflected a deeper sense of purpose: to gain control, ensure
stability, and reduce uncertainty. Their work also indicated a temporal and
geographic mix as women cobbled together ideas from multiple places and
spaces — thereby disrupting absolute control of information from biomedical sources.

Reproductive rights have long been central to women's movements, and
these rights include the right to choose when and if to reproduce. Lesbian
feminism responded to this right by creating a vast network of lesbian-
centered consciousness-raising groups and services organized for lesbian
mothers. The original intents of self-insemination as empowering and
women-controlled remain salient, despite biomedicine's cooptation of reproductive healthcare and women's health in general. Further, the establish-
ment of a few niche-market sperm banks targeting queer clientele to some
extent reflects biomedical tendencies of transformation, but also must be
interpreted as a response to increased control (i.e., medicalization) tendencies, complete with the stratification of reproduction wherein the reproduction of some women is legally, financially, and culturally supported, and that
of other women is not. The de facto exclusion of lesbians and single women
by medical providers provoked such niche-market services to open their
doors, and while many of these services profit right along with their biomedical peers, their feminist intent persists. These organizations firmly re-

sist the ideological construction of lesbians and single woman as nonprocre-ative and the stratification of reproduction that supports the procreation of mostly wealthy, white, heterosexual couples (thereby reproducing the strat-ification of society). Thus, while the biomedical healthcare system has con-structed intended users of assisted reproduction as heterosexual, married couples (temporarily) unable to fulfill their natural procreative desires, dis-rupting these embedded cultural scripts is not only possible but has been taking place for at least thirty years, as lesbians and other queer actors have selectively challenged technoscientific identities while pursuing pregnancy.

Although biomedical knowledges and services are increasingly central to lesbian processes of gaining readiness and stability, they are neither straight-forward nor universal. Women's knowledges about conception processes include both biomedical and self help information resources, some of which are more "alternative" and grassroots than others. While this may point to biomedicalization's tendency to infiltrate social life, it is also evi-dence of the strengths and continuities of women's health movements. Groups designed to help lesbians navigate the complex biological, social, and legal issues of parenthood are thriving throughout the nation. Such groups offer services including seminars, support groups, model legal docu-ments and advocacy, and informational resources on how to get pregnant, how to seek belonging, and how to live as a queer person and family in heteronormative social structures, social interactions, and cultural norms.

The proliferation of these services and their online content both indicates the mainstreaming of queer America and expands the ways in which one can gain stability in uncertain and highly heteronormative terrain. That is, these groups simultaneously reflect the mainstream and serve as pragmatic sources though which to resist normative cultural discourses that dictate marriage, reproduction, and family along strict and exclusionary lines. Biomedicaliza-tion is thus both controlling and transforming. Furthermore, stratifications and social positions matter in negotiating resources and services.

Many of these organizations and online resources are outgrowths of community-based women's health and gay and lesbian movements that specifically address lesbian actors. These social-movement groups are adept at negotiating marginalization and fighting for equalities.

Three

Choosing a Donor:
Gaining, Securing,
and Seeking Legitimacy

MARIE AND ROSLYN LIVE IN THE EASTERN SUBURBS of San Francisco with their newborn, Kyle. When I arrived on a sunny Saturday afternoon at their small arts-and-crafts cottage in the hills, Marie greeted me at the door and invited me inside for some tea. While Kyle napped in the living room and Roslyn read beside him, Marie and I sat at the dining-room table and talked. Marie appeared relaxed and, like many of the women I interviewed, was looking forward to telling me her story and finding out what I had learned from others.

Marie is thirty-one years old and a physical therapist. Roslyn, whom I later interviewed, described herself as a mother, a lesbian, Native American, and a high-school math teacher. Marie and Roslyn had been together for five years and had two teenage children — Michael and Scott, from Roslyn's previous heterosexual marriage — when they decided to conceive. Marie described having wanted children since her own childhood. Roslyn, too, wanted to have another child, but was past her childbearing years. They discussed children and parenting on their first date, and by the time they became partners, they knew they would pursue parenthood and that Marie would be the one who would try to become pregnant. When they moved in together, they first spent some time getting used to being a family, then moved from San Francisco to the eastern suburbs with the boys. Eventually, Marie and Roslyn inseminated using sperm purchased from a local sperm bank, having decided, Marie said, that using an anonymous donor was their best option; neither had a close male friend who would be a willing or appropriate donor.

Further conversation revealed a more complicated picture. Marie mentioned that at one point in the process, when they were having a hard time getting pregnant, a friend offered to be a sperm donor. He attended their church, a small congregation where everybody knew each other. Although Marie and Roslyn thought seriously about the offer and met their friend several times, they ultimately decided that their church was so small that members might learn the donor's identity: "We didn't want people thinking that it was his kid and my kid as opposed to Roslyn and I being the moms." Moreover, they did not want to "take the risk" that the donor would change his mind about his role and seek parental rights. Having undergone a difficult, lengthy, and expensive custody battle with her ex-husband, Roslyn was clear that she did not want to create a situation that could lead to another custody battle. For all of these reasons, they decided to use an anonymous sperm donor.

Recognition and Belonging: Choosing a Donor

The decision to create a family together threw Marie and Rosalyn into an arduous decision-making process — one based on the particularities of their histories and lives. Finding a path to pregnancy often requires an individual or couple to confront questions that heterosexuals are less likely to encounter. Who will be involved in the reproductive process that creates this family? In selecting a donor, which criteria matter most? Do individual donor characteristics matter most, or should the donor's extended family be considered? How are health issues factored in? Who will the baby look like — and how much does that matter? What about race, ethnicity, or religious affiliation?

Issues about donor characteristics may be easier to resolve than questions about roles and relationships. Will the donor be known or anonymous? How will understandings about roles be negotiated? Is trust a reasonable basis for proceeding, or should legal contracts be drawn up? Who will know about that process, and what will they know? What information will the child have? If so, when? What about other children in the family? How are they connected? What will everyone call each other? And to whom will the baby belong — in every sense of that word?

Belonging goes to the heart of the matter. Belonging is an intersubjective process involving the recognition of ties between oneself and others (see Butler 2004, chap. 6). It is also a social process, encompassing cumulative interactions among self, other, and larger social structures. Lesbian reproductive practices reflect anxieties about social connection and shed light on belonging in each of these senses. My research closely examines donor-selection practices and the ways that lesbians imagine kinship and belonging — with an emphasis on potential children. How and in what ways does one belong to families, communities, and social and political worlds? In what ways does one seek such belonging, and in what ways does one recognize oneself and others as part of or outside of such social formations?

Getting-to-pregnant is a self-project that involves complex and varied demands for recognition and belonging. Seeking recognition includes the intersubjective process of recognizing oneself as a parent, but it also includes being recognized by self and others as belonging to or connected with a child; as part of a family; as legible (and thereby legitimate) mothers, parents, and families in social interactions; as full citizens, via state benefits and entitlement; and as full participants in the polity or sociality. These self-projects are, thus, demands for respectability and normalcy.

Lesbians use reproductive technologies to produce new and old forms of belonging and recognition. As a result they are instances of queering as well as instances of securing normativity. Much of the normative-cultural work lesbians perform in achieving pregnancy is constituted by intersubjective desires and the political necessities of securing social legitimacy. In their efforts to secure social legitimacy, lesbians respond to a culture that not only assumes but privileges heterosexuality and builds these assumptions into institutional, social, and cultural practices. Lesbian reproductive practices can both subvert these ideologies and create new norms. That is, they both "trouble the normal" and produce new normativities (Warner 1999; see also Butler 2000). Beyond who and what makes a family, what are the broader issues of sociality and the ways subjectivities and social relations are constituted in discursive practices?

Whose "Family Values"?

The framework of social forces that have shaped the early years of the twenty-first century include a return to traditional "family values" at the government and policy levels and an explosion in the diversity of family forms, including gay and lesbian households, reconstituted families, and an array of ad hoc domestic arrangements.

While official and legal definitions of what constitutes a family vary in the United States (Minow 1998), the privatized nuclear family holds a sacred place in the American psyche and is embedded in most major social and legal institutions.[1] As Mary Bernstein and Renate Reimann (2001) argue, "As an ideal type, *The Family* consists of a legally married (biologically male) husband and a (biologically female) wife" and their children. One legal ramification of this is that the nonbirthing parent in a lesbian couple has *no* automatic parental legal rights of parenthood (J. S. Murphy 2001).

The stories that follow represent attempts to secure legitimacy and recognition of belonging in the face of overt discrimination. While Marie's and Roslyn's family mirrors the many blended step-parent families created by divorce, separation, a spouse's death, and single-parenthood, their household nevertheless exists outside of dominant ideas of what and who make a family. Yet the 2000 Census reported that some 150,000 same-sex couples in the United States are raising approximately 250,000 children in their homes — these families are indeed part of American culture (Sears, Gates, and Rubenstein 2005). Lesbian and gay mothers and fathers and same-sex-couple families queer the hegemonic view, with its assumption of heterosexual family forms. Whereas for its first three decades the gay-rights movement focused on sexual freedom and acceptance, in future decades the movement seems destined to continue its current battle for the right to marry and, by extension, to parent (Dominus 2004).

Kinship and Reproductive Technologies

Like same-sex sexuality, reproductive technologies challenge and denaturalize idealized kinship, while at times reinforcing it. Assisted reproduction enacts the "dispersement" of kinship through the presence of multiple procreators defined by their participation in the acts of conception (Strathern 1992, 1995).

Figure 1, a cartoon from the *New Yorker,* depicts the potential for the dispersal of the field of procreators. The children gathered outside the heterosexual couple's window signal the man's presumed procreative link to each of them, which challenges the reader to consider another link: the sibling relationships among those who hold the banner. The banner reads "Happy Father's Day," which privileges biology over nurture by position-

1   "I thought that sperm-bank donors remained anonymous." Nick Downes, *New Yorker*
(21 June 1999): 212. © 1999 by The New Yorker Collection, Nick Downes, from www.cartoonbank.com.
All rights reserved. Reprinted with permission.

ing the man as father and not donor. Contrast this image with figures 2 and
3, which appeared along with the title story, "A New Kind of Family," in the
April 2005 issue of *Health*. Figure 2 draws the gaze of readers to a dominant
two-parent family form. This image, however, is supplanted by figure 3, in
which a lesbian couple appears with one father. Such an image extends the
field of procreators from two to three and queers the dominant logic of two
opposite-sex parents.

In a similar depiction, *Rolling Stone* ran a cover photo with the headline
"The Name of the Father and the Making of the New American Family"
(figure 4). The image was taken from the now infamous case of Melissa
Etheridge and her then partner Julie Cypher and the "mystery" surrounding
the birth of their children. The image "outs" David Crosby not only as the
donor but as the father. The declaration that these three adults and their two
children are "the New American Family" asserts a "queering" of the family

Today's reproductive technology is invasive and complicated. The result is the most natural thing in the world.

BY MEREDITH MARAN

PHOTOGRAPHY BY JAMES SALZANO

a new kind of family

In 1975, a year into marriage and well into a campaign to get pregnant, I sat with my then-husband in the office of a Berkeley urologist we'll call Dr. Nuts. Having run a battery of what seemed to us impossibly sophisticated tests—sperm count, sperm motility, compatibility of sperm and egg—the physician delivered our dismal results: My husband was unlikely to father a child. Then he made a suggestion that I found startling, even as a 24-year-old, even

APRIL 2005 | Health 143

2   *Health* (April 2005): 141. Photo by James Salzano. Reprinted with permission.

3   *Health* (April 2005): 142. Photo by James Salzano. Reprinted with permission.

and an extension of the field of procreators. A paradox arises: while dispersed kinship forms have the power to extend kinship, they also have the potential to re-entrench the nuclear family by tightening the two-parent hold on normative family tropes and thereby securing the nuclear family's social legitimacy and replication. That is, they provide the other by which the norm is maintained. Yet, in a queering move, all of these images illustrate three parents and thereby destabilize the nuclear family form.

Lesbian reproduction has profound consequences for kinship, a core concept of anthropology that refers to the pattern of relationships that define people's connections to one another. Kinship has long been understood to vary enormously across cultures, geographic locations, and historical moments. With the poststructural turn, issues of structure and the social stability of cultures via structural arrangement gave way to issues of practice and then, with the cultural turn, to issues of discourse. Sociological work on the family has not kept up.

Kinship extends far beyond nuclear families to encompass social, cultural, and institutional practices; "blood ties" are not always and only what count as relatedness (Schneider 1964, 1968).[2] The concept of "social ties" is used to denaturalize kinship on the premise that relatedness is a culturally produced and understood notion and that it produces inequalities.[3] Historically, kinship (see especially Franklin and McKinnon 2001) denotes how individuals and groups are socially connected through biological relationships (consanguineous ties) and social relationships of marriage (nonsanguineous ties). Kinship is both a theoretical concept explaining structures of social organization through which relationships are classified and ordered, and a means of organizing knowledge about the world in general.

Reproduction has always been a fundamental organizing principle in kinship studies; it reveals the ways biogenetic and legal-social ties are naturalized through culture (i.e., in the ways they produce kin relations). Kin relations are understood in both biological and social terms (as described by Carsten 2000), and the social arrangements contained by kinship do not only imitate but are based on and deploy "processes of biological reproduction" (Strathern 1992, 3). In other words, if biological reproduction is the taken-for-granted kinship signifier in Western culture, assisted-reproduction technologies offer one intervention into this biological foundation. As Marilyn Strathern (1992) argues, what was once taken to be natural has become a matter of choice: nature has been "enterprised-up" (30). That is,

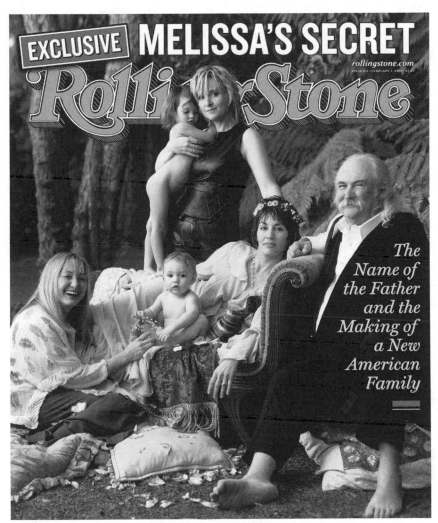

EXCLUSIVE MELISSA'S SECRET

Rolling Stone

rollingstone.com
ISSUE 835 · FEBRUARY 3, 2000 · $3.95

The
Name of
the Father
and the
Making of
a New
American
Family

4   Cover of *Rolling Stone* (3 February 2000). © 2000 by Rolling Stone LLC. All rights reserved.
Reprinted with permission.

reproductive technologies have enabled people to choose to reproduce when they might not have otherwise been able to. The more nature is assisted by technology, and the more the social recognition of parenthood is circumscribed by legislation, the more difficult it becomes to think of nature as "independent of social intervention" (ibid., 30).

Strathern's (1992) argument emphasizes shifts in knowledge as productive of social change. Assisted reproductive technologies and the "choices" they produce alter the very ways we *think about* kinship. In the process of altering knowledge itself, previous cultural assumptions about kinship are destabilized.[4] Strathern (1995) uses the concept of "dispersed kinship" to signal the field of procreators who are defined by their participation in the acts of conception, not by their participation in the family. She emphasizes that while kinship includes new participants (sperm donors), it continues to rely on biogenetic and legal ties for its meaning and enforcement. She argues that while kinship was once predicated on the "facts of life," reproductive technologies have given rise to new objects of popular knowledge for conceptualizing persons. Instead of kinship, she argues, there is genetic destiny; genetic health, genetic origins, and genetic histories become the salient facts (Strathern 1992). Genetic thinking is enabled through biology, which has traditionally been the frame through which people link themselves to others and distinguish themselves from others — that is, biology has long been a source of identification and affiliation. Therefore, it is according to biology that belonging, as identity and membership, has been understood and made to work in certain ways. Human reproduction is thus not only about making persons, parents, and social relations; it is also about making oneself recognizable as a person or parent, then demanding recognition of one's inclusion.

Queering Kinship

Research on lesbian family formation has also theorized kinship relations. Kath Weston (1991) argues that lesbian families created through alternative insemination are at once similar to those formed in heterosexual unions (as biogenetic connections), yet also in opposition to those biological relations. The opposition can be found in the formation of new kinship ties forged on the basis of choice and love: a distinctive feature of lesbian alternative insemination, she argues, is its "technique for acquiring children that challenges conventional understandings of biological offspring as the visible outcome of a gendered difference grounded in the symbolics of anatomy"

(169). According to Weston, biological ties are displaced and distinctiveness (based on sexual difference) created. In this formulation, queer definitions of family do not rely on a heterosexual norm for meaning; instead, these "chosen" families are free from dominant definitional and institutional norms. These families are pluralistic; they combine people and forms of social connection in a variety of ways.

Ellen Lewin (1993) argues instead that "motherhood" in American culture overrides most of the distinctiveness which differences of sexuality create. Lesbian mothers therefore exemplify traditional American social and gender accounts, which does not allow room for alternative constructions of a sense of self, family, or kinship. In Lewin's account biological ties remain central and sexual differences lose their relevance. What remains in her account are dominant institutional and definitional norms of family based on gender and blood and legal ties.

Resolving this difference, Corinne Hayden (1995) argues that biology is not displaced but appears in the explicit mobilization of biological ties by lesbian families; that is, it is used as a cultural device to signal biological connection. Hayden suggests that lesbian mothers who conceive through the use of donor insemination simultaneously affirm the importance of biogenetic ties as symbolic of kinship and challenge the idea that biology is a self-evident fact on which kinship is based (56). Thus, the American blood-love symbolic hierarchy is ruptured by lesbian and gay families' negotiations of biogenetic connections. Instead of being a prerequisite for relatedness, biology is transformed into a mere signpost of parenthood.

Similarly, the anthropologist Sara Franklin (1993) analyzed the AIDS crisis and the emergence of reproductive technologies and argued that what could have eroded heterosexual privilege actually led to its reinforcement. She demonstrated that although the AIDS crisis of the 1980s opened an opportunity for increased acceptance of homosexuality, the convergence of AIDS and assisted reproduction led to a renewed and vigorous homophobic backlash. In the realm of reproductive technologies there occurred a strengthening of convictions that asserted the "naturalness" of the nuclear family and of heterosexual marriage. By arguing the "unnaturalness" of gay or lesbian parenthood, ideological arguments concerning heterosexuality and homosexuality were revamped and applied to the "configured users" of new reproductive technologies.

Challenging Heteronormativity, Queering Reproduction

In the case of lesbian reproduction, same-sex parents and single lesbian mothers challenge many of U.S. society's most taken-for-granted assumptions about the family and gender relations. In *Baby Steps: How Lesbian Insemination Is Changing the World* (2004) the sociologist Amy Agigian explores the ways in which heteronormative discourses underpin family institutions, law, biomedicine, and economic and social policies. She argues that "secrecy has been the accepted medical protocol and near universal norm of artificial insemination" (5). In the biomedical context the husband's infertility, if present, is masked by the secrecy of using a donor and the legally married couple is helped to "achieve the state sanctioned hetero-patriarchal family" (Agigian 1998, 8). The legally sanctioned medical event of artificial insemination, Agigian argues, maintains the illusion of biomedicine and the family as seamlessly united. However, despite the cloak of secrecy and the protection of heteronormativity, lesbians have been getting pregnant outside of heterosexual unions and without biomedical intervention for decades.

Two social processes are central in lesbian reproduction: where and how lesbians find sperm and legal issues shaping queer families. Part of "finding" sperm is attributing meaning to it. Lesbians construct sperm as a necessary biomaterial that is either separate from or part of men's bodies and selves. The complex meanings they apply to sperm informs their construction of relatedness as well. Do they understand sperm, and all that sperm embodies, as a means to link themselves and potential children with donors (i.e., to construct social relationships)? Or do they depersonalize sperm from the (male) body in which it was produced? Or are their meanings something in between and/or beyond these two options? The meanings lesbians apply to sperm and to the situations involved in finding sperm are consequential for the meanings they assign to kinship, relatedness, and belonging. Therefore, it is important to analyze the social and legal issues involved in selecting what "type" of sperm and sperm donor to consider. It is also important to understand how lesbians mobilize biological, genetic, and social discourses in making sense of their reproductive practices. Who is included in the family and who "drops out" are shaped by patterns of sociality and senses of alliance and affiliation that are not determined by the crude criteria of blood connection (Edwards 2000).

The Lesbian Sperm Hunt:
Extending the Field of Procreators

Where and how to obtain sperm for reproduction are central issues and questions lesbians face when embarking on pregnancy plans. For all the women I interviewed, the one indisputable known factor was that the sperm would not originate from their primary partners. Of course, heterosexual women and their husbands often use donor sperm when male infertility is present, but their quest for pregnancy very rarely begins with this option. Moreover, they usually prefer to use sperm from an anonymous donor who closely resembles the "father" (Becker 1990).[5]

In contrast, for queer people, processes of obtaining sperm are varied, and each "choice" brings with it different possibilities of transformation or accommodation. As Weston (1991) described so well, for gay and lesbian people, families are more about choice than about sanctioned legal and blood ties. This queering, a (sub)cultural narrative of choice, is both influential and overshadowed by dominant heterosexual norms and biomedicalization processes. Once women decide to pursue pregnancy through technical means, regulatory ideals such as those enacted by cultural discourses of social norms, by legal and public policies, and by biomedical services organized around infertility shape their practices. Yet women were enterprising in the strategies they used to find sperm, just as they had been in gathering information and resources.

The process of locating and, if necessary, purchasing donor sperm includes negotiating heteronormative assumptions embedded in cultural ideas of kinship (i.e., relatedness) and political-economic constraints around sperm and fertility and infertility services. The women I interviewed had explored multiple possibilities based on the unique circumstances that differentially constrained their "choices." These women largely selected between two main types of donors: unknown donors drawn from sperm banks, and known donors, often termed "directed donors," drawn from the women's own social networks. Sperm-bank donors can either remain anonymous or specify that they are "willing-to-be-known" to a child once he or she turns eighteen; the latter are often termed "identity release" or "yes" donors and are in high demand among lesbian consumers of sperm-bank services. In contrast, a known donor can fulfill a range of potential constructions of relatedness to the parent(s) and child(ren): from acknowledgment as the donor to full co-parent status. This choice to use a known donor is influenced by a host of factors that often require negotiation. For example, thinking through the degree to which known donors will or will not participate in potential children's and mother(s') lives is commonplace: will the donor's identity be the only part he plays beyond conception, that is, as someone who the parent(s) can describe to the child? Will he become an "uncle" figure, or will he perform as both a biological and social father and co-parent the child-(ren)? In known-donor arrangements, the relatedness of a donor to the potential parent(s) and child(ren) is negotiated outside of sperm banks and can take many forms.

In general, the process of finding sperm from a known donor includes negotiating the type of relatedness one desires. It requires considering whether one wants an active father, an inactive father, or no father. If one uses a known donor, one must decide whether to use already known friends or relatives or to find new acquaintances for sperm donation. If using an anonymous donor, one must select a sperm bank and criteria by which to choose a donor. One must negotiate emotions, legal issues, interactions, and other profoundly social issues. Similar to other aspects of the journey toward pregnancy, the quest for sperm can alternately involve intentionality, fluidity and revision, and constant negotiation.

Defining the Situation: The Meanings of (Sperm) Donors

In negotiating possible parameters of social connection among the donors, parents, and offspring, the women I interviewed asked themselves multiple questions about legal implications, parental "rights," and the contours of desired social relationships. Their decisions to use a known or unknown donor were variously influenced by cultural trends, legal issues, and social norms, as well as by complex feelings regarding biology, connectedness, and parenting. At times, they were also influenced by perceived and "real" feelings of multiple other actors: the living partner (if there was one), friends, and family members; the known donor and his relatives; the unknown donor; and even the child.

The first consideration that many of the women I interviewed took into account was their feelings and concerns regarding the future involvement, and therefore future connection, of a donor in parenting. This included the meaning and place of the "father" in the child's life. This issue implicates the processes of constructing relatedness that are embedded in practices of achieving pregnancy. Among the women I interviewed, constructing the "name" and parameters of social connection (i.e., the extent of the relationship) that a donor would or would not have with the child was an early and highly consequential step in constructing social and familial ties. It was also an early step in the degree of queering the woman or women would undertake. For Chloe, an essential criterion was "a donor and not a parent." Speaking of a man her sister had introduced to her, she said, "I don't think he meets my basic criterion, which is of a level of maturity where they know the difference between donation and parenting."

The main factors that differentially influenced the women's practices were cost of reproductive technologies and relationship to biomedical institutions, age and physical health, and perception of emotional and legal entanglements. For women who were financially unable to, or chose not to, access biomedical services, known donors provided sperm. Women over thirty-five or with an infertility diagnosis tended to use technologically advanced treatment protocols that required the use of frozen sperm and thus precluded the use of fresh sperm from a known donor.

Perceptions of emotional and legal entanglements were part of every woman's story. The women were quite aware of and informed about their legal vulnerabilities as lesbian mothers and the importance of biological and legal ties with children. It was with regard to such entanglements that the choice to select a gay man to be a known, unknown, or willing-to-be-known donor emerged.

Arlene and her partner, Chloe, lived in a flat in the mission district of San Francisco. Their apartment was full of paintings, photographs, and sculptures. Both women were longtime residents who had moved to the city when they were young, socially active, and engaged in various political and social issues. They both identified as white, working-class dykes, and both had at one time been actively involved in leather communities. When I met Arlene and Chloe they were looking for a sperm donor and had not yet started to inseminate. Arlene described part of their decision concerning sperm donors: "We have talked about anonymous and known donors and we have considered having a co-parent. [We decided] anonymous would be easier [for us] legally and difficult for the child. Children want to know things. I had a lover that was adopted and didn't know her parents; it drove her nuts not knowing her birth parents. Although I know it doesn't do that for everyone, I would want the child to be able to say, 'Okay, fine, who was the donor?' So those are the things that are important to me. How is it going to impact the child?"

When I asked Chloe to describe where she and her partner are in the process, she replied, "We are right at the point of the great American sperm hunt. We are looking for a donor, going through our lists of friends and friends of friends and their friends, and going to groups." For women who had chosen to find known donors, but who did not yet have anyone in mind, the hunt for sperm infused everyday life. For example, when I asked Arlene the same question, she paused, stared, and asked me, "Well, do *you* have any friends?" Feeling suddenly implicated as another key actor in her process, I laughed awkwardly. She then said, "It is this hunt for sperm . . . it is finding the people, making connections and making decisions about wanting to have a known parent or a donor, anonymous or known. It is also expensive to purchase sperm. That is one reason why we need a known donor."

The process of finding sperm was not easy for Arlene and Chloe. At the time of the interview they were charting Chloe's menstrual cycle and looking for a known donor. They had decided to find a gay man by attending a local support group, Prospective Queer Parents (PQP). Describing the donor factors she was considering, Arlene said,

> It's interesting because [my partner] has been asking all of her women friends if they know anyone. And I say, "We have to ask." She says, "I have been asking." And I said, "No we need to ask the men." We are going through our closest circle and asking them if they know anyone. And then there are things that are criteria for the people we ask. They have to know they want to be donors and not co-parents. Most of the men we meet at PQP want to be co-parents. If they don't want to be a known donor that is a problem. And people change over time and I worry about those changes over time. So I think it is really, really important for us that the donor know they want to be a known donor and what that means. For us it means at some point in time when the child asks, "Who is my daddy?" we can say that you have two mommies but your donor is so and so and then they can choose what they want to do about that. The child may want to make a parent out of that person, depending on the culture, and there is no way to know what the child is going to want to do. Children tend to have personalities all on their own. I am pretty loose on other criteria.

Describing the thought process she and her partner had gone through, Shari said, "We wanted to keep it as simple as possible and we wanted to be the primary parents, without any complications." A desire to avoid complications and to keep things "simple" was common among the women I interviewed. As Judith put it, "There is enough difficulty in getting consensus between two people, let alone four. So we didn't want a nice couple of gentlemen being co-parents with us. We wanted to keep our family, and our decisions, simple, with just the two of us being moms."

Dana also voiced concern about the influence a known donor might have on her decisions and the potential child. For her, the importance of having a long-term, positive relationship with a man before entering into a co-parenting agreement was essential. "I feel like if you are going to raise a kid with someone you should really know them well. It's not just like just gee, I think I will pick that man and do it with him. Who knows? This person is going to influence your child and you don't know what his psyche is like. You better know that person well and know that you are going to have a long relationship with him. Since I didn't know any men like that, who it was perfect with, I decided to go to a sperm bank."

Choosing unknown donors thus minimizes both legal and social risks. The social risks entail the complications and complexities involved with finding and then negotiating parenting decisions with a known donor. The legal risks concern custody battles if those negotiations fail.

The Power of Choosing: Knowing a Known Donor

When women choose to engage a known donor, they must select from three possible donor pools: relatives of the nonbiological mother, long-term friends, and new acquaintances. A few of the women I interviewed considered using relatives of the "non-bio mom" to be a possible donor solution, but no one had actually secured this type of arrangement. Kaye described her and her partner Alison's process.

> Alison's brother's name is Ray. At first I thought it would be very nice if Ray was willing to help us out because I felt that Alison's family would feel more like the child was actually part of their family. But when he said no, he didn't say flat out no. He said, "I have some issues around this. I think I'd rather not. If it's really, really important to you, let's talk about it some more." And Alison decided that she didn't want to pursue it with him. I mean I really think if we were going to use someone who wasn't anonymous, at least in my mind, that was the strongest contender because at least there was a reason why you'd confront all those issues.

The importance of biological connection was central to Kaye's narrative; had that pathway been pursued, both women would have been biologically related to the child (i.e., by blood and genetics). Even more interesting was the construction that that relationship would create "better," or more comfortable, connections for all family members. Also influential was the cultural script of relatedness as biologically mediated. Kaye's description points to the complex emotion-work involved in making donor decisions. A key theme, emotion-work (Hochschild 1979, 1983, 1997) results from fears of emotional and legal entanglements, and it is indicative of negotiations that occur between real and perceived social actors. In Kaye's and Alison's case, family members emerged as significant actors in the negotiations.

For some lesbians, having a known donor is not only preferable but is an essential element in their family formation. These women want the donors to be known to the children and part of their lives, albeit with different preferred degrees of involvement. Having a known donor was not an element that the women would revise, although the types of agreements and extent of relationships with the donors were more flexible. When Carla began pursuing insemination, she wanted to form a co-parenting agreement with a close male friend. Early in our interview, she talked about a close friend whom she had met in a therapy group. They had decided to co-parent together, but after two years of trying, he changed his mind. Despite this, Carla remained committed to the idea of her child knowing the father: "That's been the struggle part for me. It's interesting because I really wanted to have that. . . . I feel like I am going to cry. [She cried silently for a minute or more, then, still crying, continued.] I really wanted to have a situation where I knew the father and the child knew the father, because of my own background where I didn't know my father." Her biography — the absence of her own father — informed her nonnegotiable criterion: finding a donor who would be willing to be known to the child. Her more flexible criteria included the father being gay, being known to her, and being interested in co-parenting.

As time progressed and Carla developed a committed relationship with a female partner, these flexible criteria were constantly renegotiated and reconfigured. Despite Carla's acknowledgment that there were "a lot of options," the essential criterion of having the donor be known to the child remained stable. Although she originally preferred to find a father whom she knew and with whom she had a long history, she revised her plans to include a donor whom she had just met, and she genuinely hoped this person would become the potential child's father. "I'm being more open. I'm sort of, I mean, I was going through this whole thing of not knowing who my biological parent was and feeling like I had to have it a certain way and now I am not feeling so attached to that. There are still things I am attached to like the child knowing who the biological father is even if he is not in the child's life that much. . . . It's just something that I really want to try to think about before I start getting engaged in all these discussions. . . . I know I want someone to co-parent. But that may change."

Carla attended a group for adoptees, which influenced her decisions regarding the potential role of the donor in her and her child's life. She discussed the importance to her of knowing one's biological origin by referencing a popular lesbian children's book, *Heather Has Two Mommies* (Newman 1989).[6] "I went through this whole sort of counseling group and it was really interesting 'cause there was this one lesbian mom, everyone in the group was a lesbian . . . we all had the same opinion which was, you know the *Heather Has Two Mommies* book, what a bunch of shit! . . . That's not what kids care about. We had all been adopted, I had been adopted by my stepfather, I didn't know I had a different father. . . . It's amazing, you know, wanting to know where you come from."

Chloe and Arlene also wanted to use a known donor, but they did not want a co-parent. Chloe said, "We decided to go the known donor over the unknown yet not sperm bank route. It just seemed too ridiculously complicated and another hoop to go through to have an intermediary. We know there is a history, in women's groups, of having one person as an intermediary between the women and the donor to protect anonymity. That just seemed so complicated. So this is what we are going through now." According to Chloe and Arlene, the selection of known donors included certain elements, some more flexible than others, including ethnicity, health, and body awareness. Arlene said, "I am pretty loose on other criteria. I would like the donor to have some ethnic background and to have a healthy background. However, [if those aren't there] I am willing to say, okay, fine." When asked to elaborate on her meaning of healthy, Chloe said, "An awareness of your body . . . what is your HIV infection, do you have other transmittable and/or genetic diseases. . . . It is just an awareness. It isn't something I would decide to not use their sperm, but I think family history is important." The contemporary understanding of heredity is invoked here as the transmission of genetic disease (e.g., carrying the breast-cancer gene).

In selecting the type of donor, plans are frequently revised. Because these processes take place in a specific time and place, they are contingent and negotiable. For example, although Chloe admitted that two years before our interview she hadn't been "known donorish," she no longer felt uncomfortable with the idea of using a donor who the child-to-be might know or at least be able to know. The criteria for choosing donors includes both negotiable and nonnegotiable elements.

With regard to using new acquaintances as sperm donors, finding a suitable donor often begins with making a list of everyone — male and female — in one's social network, in order to broadcast that one is looking for a sperm donor. In the 1970s and early 1980s lesbians turned primarily to gay men as sperm donors, either asking their friends directly or remaining anonymous by asking mutual friends to serve as go-betweens. The go-between would ask a man to be the donor, and only she would know the identities of the donor and recipients. It would be the go-between's role to secure agreements by all parties for how they would construct the relationship. Most often the donor would be asked to relinquish all parental rights and to remain anonymous. The go-between would transport his sperm to the recipient to ensure confidentiality at each insemination, and she (or he) would be responsible for maintaining the anonymity of all parties. These measures lent an increased sense of legal and emotional security vis-à-vis the intended confidentiality of the transaction (Kendell 1996). In less formal arrangements, friends were simply asked to find a male from their social networks who would be willing to provide his sperm and to discuss with the mother(s)-to-be his future role in the child's life.

Several legal and health issues were involved in using known donors. For example, a known donor could legally challenge for custody. Medically speaking, his sperm would not necessarily be screened for HIV or other sexually transmitted diseases; therefore, the health of the sperm and potential children might be compromised.

Enter "Techno-Semen": Sperm Banks and Known Donors

As sperm banks have evolved, they have added technologies for screening and testing sperm at the time of donation and after a six-month quarantine. Issues of health safety using a known donor are often addressed by directed-donor programs, which are offered at sperm banks, and by known-donor questionnaires developed by legal scholars. In recipient-donor programs, a donor (selected by the intended mom or a go-between) deposits his sperm at a sperm bank for routine screening and testing. His sperm is then used by the designated recipient. Matthew Schmidt and Lisa Moore (1998) have dubbed technologically advanced donor sperm "techno-semen." In so doing they focus on the increased ways sperm is tested, screened, procured, and ultimately "managed" using technologies such as cryopreservation, measurement of sperm morphology and motility, semen analysis under a microscope, and sperm washing to separate sperm from the seminal fluid. It is these technoscientific "advances" that signal a shift from lesbian alternative insemination to the biomedicalization of fertility.

Deborah wanted to use sperm from a close friend, yet still receive the same level of "security" she would have if buying anonymous techno-sperm. She said, "I knew we could test and freeze his sperm to make sure it was the safest it could be," referring to a new acquaintance with whom she hoped to develop a friendship. Deborah had met this man when she traveled to the Midwest to visit a close gay male friend who was dying of AIDS.[7] During the visit, she became friends with one of his caregivers. Later, attending the funeral for her friend with AIDS, Deborah and the caregiver began talking about their sadness, loss, and their desire to add life to the world. She told him she wanted to be a mother and that she had hoped their mutual friend could have lived to be a father to her child. When the caregiver asked if he could do this with her, she was thrilled, but she knew she was not willing to co-parent with him. "Unfortunately, when it came time to write the contract, he backed out. Mostly because I was firm that I wanted to be the sole parent." Deborah returned to California. "I had some neighbors at the time who were watching my cats. I came back disappointed and told them what had happened. A couple of days later they came back over. They are a heterosexual unmarried couple. The guy said, 'Well, if you would have me, I would be willing to be the donor if you really want to do this.' I was surprised. I was really happy because he is a really sweet guy. He is the donor, and it wasn't easy. He has been through a lot to be the donor. At the time I said, 'Let me think about it and let me ask a lot of really very personal questions' that I really had no business asking. But we got through it." The personal questions concerned his health and sexual history as well as the histories of his previous partners. Such questions, she told me, were necessary to ensure the safety of his sperm. She also asked him about his willingness to surrender his biological rights to parenthood in an effort to ensure the security of her parental rights.

HIV remains a central health and political issue for gay communities, as well as for global health and healthcare in general. For lesbians selecting semen donors, the issue of HIV presented itself in numerous ways. Arlene described HIV-infected men as undesirable donors, saying, "We know some men who are absolutely wonderful and would be fabulous as donor and/or co-parents, but they are positive." Many respondents said that HIV influenced their decisions. Although the conflation of HIV and gay men did not occur in Arlene's statement, it is represented in sperm-bank practices. As presented by the Centers for Disease Control and American Society for Reproductive Medicine, current guidelines for sperm donation state that men who have had sex with men in the past five years are not to be approved as sperm donors. This discriminatory policy assumes that gay sex equals unsafe sex and that heterosexual sex equals safe sex. While existing technology can remove HIV from semen samples, or at least reduce it to undetectable levels, this technology is not used in the United States. The issue of HIV transmission in alternative insemination involves the construction of a presumed link between gay men, HIV, and "fit" parenthood. Most commercial sperm banks continue to discriminate against gay men by conflating sexual behavior (same-sex sexual practices) with HIV risk. By prohibiting sexually active gay men from becoming sperm donors, sperm banks perpetuate the cultural conflation of queer and diseased.

As lesbians continue to seek donors from personal networks, considerations of HIV and sexual orientation remain significant to their decisions. Chloe described this position: "What we did is we went through a list of all of our friends and acquaintances in our own life. Most of our close male friends are HIV positive and are very supportive but have their own out there. The next thing we did was talk to our heterosexual women friends about friends or acquaintances they know who would be appropriate donors. We asked them to look through your friends for possibilities. So we got some possibilities out of that." In the discussion that followed, Chloe described her wish that U.S. sperm banks would offer the sperm washing techniques available elsewhere, making it possible for her gay male friends who are HIV positive to donate sperm.

In addition to using personal networks, lesbians and gay men who want to parent frequently advertise in gay newspapers and on gay Web sites. For example, on Craig's List, an online bulletin-board, personals placed by lesbians seeking gay men to serve as sperm donors were fairly common during the years I conducted this research.

Legal issues often structure the decision between a known or unknown donor. The founder of the PQP information-exchange forum explained to me the legacy of legal concerns for lesbian parents: "What's true in the lesbian community is that there's this long history of lesbians losing their children to their former heterosexual spouses and even their parents as grandparents. Even as the [Sharon] Bottoms case in Virginia. So there's this paranoia that has very significant justification, roots, real roots in the lesbian community that I think is deeply rooted in the lesbian parenting psyche. But when the donor is queer also, it's totally different. It becomes a very different picture."

In 1996 I attended PQP as a recruitment site for interviewees and met three of the women interviewed for this research. Arlene, Chloe's partner, described the influence of the group.

> PQP has been an eye opener, especially around men and seeing what gay men want and how they want to create something and what kinds of commitments can be made and held. Especially the organizers and what they have done, I'm just flabbergasted. It really gives me hope that something like this can be done, it gives me hope. And where before for me it was like, no, you can't trust them, I don't care if they are gay or straight, they are still men. I think the most important thing about groups is to see other people's process and to see the patterns, the patterns that women have around getting pregnant and what they do and what they have done.

The development of informal community networks designed to introduce gay men and lesbians who desire parenthood represents not only a return (if the practice ever diminished) but also an organized, alternative "queer" practice or script. Arlene, for example, also described the group as providing her with the opportunity to "practice" asking men if they would become sperm donors: "The support group is good for checking men out, and it has been good for the actual talking to men and getting some practice."

Carla also attended PQP. She described her desire to have a gay male friend as a known sperm donor: "I've asked all my friends. . . . I say what I want, someone to co-parent. That may change now. I have one friend who says you are never going to get that. This is a gay man who, he's like, that's ridiculous, you are never going to get that. And then I know other gay men that say, 'Yeah, there must be, are you kidding, there's got to be people out there that want that.' So, I am going to that Prospective Queer Parent thing, 'cause I have some friends who just met someone through that and they are on their way." Carla, who felt strongly about having a gay man as a known donor, discussed a new technology developed in Italy: "The other thing I have investigated which I think is interesting about your topic is this friend of mine who has AIDS. He and I have once again started talking about doing the insemination. And so we have gone on the Internet and started to find out about sperm washing for HIV and [learned] that there are some things trying to be done with heterosexual couples. So, he and I have sort of been looking into this because it is something that he would love and it's something that I would love. I know his family, I know what there is to know about the guy and, you know, it would be ideal for me." After the interview, Carla and her new partner met a gay male couple at PQP and had one child by alternative insemination. To secure legitimacy and recognition, the four parents and child share a chosen last name and live in very close proximity.

Whether choosing a known donor who is a relative, a friend, or a new acquaintance, lesbians must negotiate with donors with regard to the type of relationship. Those women who choose and locate specific known donors to be either co-parents or donors describe often elaborate negotiations, which sometimes involve creating some form of contract between the parties. Once known-donor arrangements are in place, contractual (legal or verbal) arrangements are usually formalized. Carla described the process of reaching such an agreement as a four-year pursuit.

> I have been working with the same person trying to figure this out. He's a friend of mine. I brought it up in a little sort of therapy group. It wasn't a therapy group, it was a group of people who got together to talk about stuff going on in their life and, you know, what their goals were for life and that kind of thing. And, um, I said that I had decided to do this and I was really gonna start pursuing it because I had just been out of a relationship for a few years with a woman and I decided I really want to do this thing. And I really need to start moving on it even though I am not in a relationship because, um . . . [pause, then she starts to cry] because I thought I would, I would be in a relationship and then I would be able to decide to do it [her crying intensifies] I'm sorry. . . . [pause] I mean I wanted it to be, [her crying continues, more quietly] I wanted it to be a gay man that I knew. And the person I had talked to a long time ago in the beginning has AIDS so that became not possible.

My interview with Carla was the first in which I heard a story that was both fraught with difficult emotions and closely linked with HIV/AIDS and gay men. The link between community and family formation within gay communities was clear in her desire for the donor to be a gay man. Deborah, too, described an initial conversation she had with a man who agreed to be a donor.

He is a totally open guy. He assured me he was monogamous and had had an AIDS test in the last year and it had been negative. He had a history with alcohol and drug use problems and I asked him when was the last time he used. It had been a couple of years since he had a drink and he hadn't used any drugs in five years. And I said he had to make sure not to fuck up in those areas. And it was a really laid back conversation, it was serious, but by then I had lived here a year or so and he and his partner were probably my best friends. We were both a little uncomfortable because these are really personal questions. It turned out the things I was concerned about were okay . . . And I told him that I wanted to be the sole parent and I wasn't going to ask for anything except for his sperm and I don't want you to consider yourself a parent. I am never going to call you a father. But, I did want, and he agreed to this, that I wanted contact, and I wanted the child to be able to make contact with him at any time he wants. So he has to be a known donor but with no rights or responsibilities. And he said, "Good because if you wanted a parent, I never would do it." So that is how that worked. So he is the donor.

Deborah's comments resemble those of other respondents who chose to use a known donor and required him to assume limited or no parental rights.

At some point after informal agreements have been reached, more formal written contracts become necessary. All the women who negotiated known-donor contracts utilized "sample contracts" from either queer books, local organizations, or queer Web sites: they did not turn to biomedical resources or mainstream legal services. Once they found samples, they modified them to fit their own needs. As Diane said, "For a long time there was an informal agreement that I thought we would keep. But then I drew up a formal contract I found in this handbook from the National Center for Lesbian Rights. I just copied it, pretty much verbatim, and changed a few things. Then I gave it to [the donor], and he signed it and I signed it. That was it. So, we have that. It states that he has no rights or responsibilities for the child. So I can't ask him for money and he can't take the kid. I don't think it's legal, it's not binding, in the state of California's eye." Deborah described it this way: "The next steps were to call around and find out what contracts looked like because I didn't want to start without a contract. I read a little bit standing in bookstores. The Women's Health Center had a sample of a contract and they let me Xerox it, and I wrote up my own based on that. I changed it to say that he would be known. That was the only difference. So we signed the contract, we had a witness, and we had it notarized. He has a copy, and I have the original and a copy." When the field of procreators is expanded in assisted reproduction, such agreements become necessary. While it is possible for a child to have up to five legal parents (a sperm donor, an egg donor, a gestational mom, and the adoptive parents), that number can be expanded to include social kin and chosen parents and family. While such numbers are uncommon, assisted-reproduction technologies do create such possibilities.

Similar to activities involved in gaining stability (getting ready, gathering resources), obtaining sperm involved conscious planning and negotiations and was often fraught with complex negotiations, the outcomes of which took multiple forms depending on the decisions and medical fertility issues encountered (e.g., whether or not an egg donor is involved).

Choosing an Unknown Donor: Fears of Legal and
Emotional Entanglements

The California Family Code section 7613(b) states that "the donor of semen provided to a licensed physician and surgeon for use in artificial insemination of a woman other than the donor's wife is treated in law as if he were not the natural father of a child thereby conceived" (*California Family Code* 2001). The law is designed to protect married heterosexuals who use donor insemination as a result of male infertility. In this case, the woman's husband is legally regarded as the father. Thus, embedded in the law are parameters for who has legal jurisdiction over insemination (a licensed physician and surgeon). Also implicit in that law is the assumption that women who are recipients of donor semen are legally married. Unless lesbians (and unmarried heterosexual women) choose to inseminate via sperm banks or through a licensed physician, the California Family Code legislates parental rights based on biological and marital ties. It does not secure parental rights over and against those of a donor when insemination takes place outside of medically assisted contexts, and it privileges paternal ties, thus reinforcing sexism.

The lesbians I interviewed were familiar with these laws, which influenced their decisions regarding whether to use a known or unknown donor. Concomitant with these legal issues were the emotional stresses that might accompany a legal battle. Rachel expressed concerns with regard to known donors: "I had some male friends who offered, and that's when [my partner] and I both decided that it would be better to be anonymous because there are too many emotional issues that could become a problem. I think that you can never underestimate a biological bond even if the individual says they have no interests. I think once they see the child, it is a different story and that, um, pretty much propelled me to go the anonymous route." If a woman uses a known donor's sperm without the assistance or intermediary of a sperm bank or licensed physician, then the donor can be granted legal parental rights. If, however, a donor gives his sperm to a physician who then hands it to the woman to be inseminated, even if she inseminates herself, the donor is not the legal father. Thus, in practice, clinics and professionals stand in for "paternity," highlighting the close coupling of biomedicalization and the legal parameters of stratified reproduction. Institutionalized heterosexism and the professional authority of physicians are both embedded in jurisprudence and biomedicine.

The women I interviewed were all keenly aware of this policy and frequently considered the importance of having a state-sanctioned go-between for legal protection. For example, Heather said, "We decided on a provider rather than a private arrangement. . . . There were lots of gay couples having kids and there was all kinds of legal problems emerging. We didn't want that. The law seemed behind. We were very clear that we didn't want a co-parenting situation, and that we just wanted the two of us, and that we didn't want the donor involved at all. The clearest legal path to that was going through [getting] the anonymous sperm donor through a provider."

Although Dana also chose this route, she wished that it could be different: "I talked with a friend. You know, it was more of a fantasy. He was a straight black man, and I just thought, if this ever went to court, who would win? And how involved would he be? . . . And, you know, I really decided I wanted to go to a sperm bank because I didn't want the legal implications of someone coming back and saying, 'Gee, I'm straight and I'm going to win you in court.'" Legal concerns frequently emerged as women discussed contemporary social and cultural forces regulating lesbian and gay legal rights. These concerns generated complex negotiations regarding sperm donors.

Due to a history of court cases involving child custody, the women I interviewed took into account not only "real" actors but also "imagined" actors: the anonymous donor, as well as family members of the donor who, by law, often have more custodial "rights" over the offspring than does the mother who does not have a biological connection to the child. In one case a deceased donor's parents sued for custody of a child born through known-donor insemination. Several participants based their practices on the "folk-lore" that in at least one case the donor's parents were declared the "legal grandparents" based on their biogenetic ties to the offspring. It was asserted by my respondents that the donor's parents were subsequently granted custody.[8] Carmen and Angela described how this story influenced their decisions: "We did not want there to be any chance that somebody would come along [with] paternity suits, and, and want to share the parenting. Because we wanted to do all the parenting ourselves, so we could not, you know, we never even explored using [a known donor]. . . . I didn't want to ask anybody and we didn't want to have to deal with it."

A general concern with security and protecting their family infused these interviews. Esther was not only aware of such cases in general but also of the case in which the grandparents were granted custody of the child born through donated semen. Esther invoked the long history of custody cases involving lesbian mothers, cases that most often end with the lesbian mother losing custody.[9] She described her fear of not only legal and emotional entanglements but also of being unable to protect her family: "I don't want anyone else to have any legal rights over my child. I think that's just 'cause I've seen horrible custody stuff. I have real fears. You hear the horror stories of the donor who comes back. Or the donor who died and his parents sued for custody and they were totally against the whole gay thing. And, blah blah, their son was dead. I just think I am not taking any risks. I don't want anybody involved. I used to say that all the time: 'I don't want anyone else to have any legal rights over my child.'" Esther, however, also described going to a meeting where gay men and lesbians were introduced in an effort to create co-parenting agreements: "I did at one point go to the Egg and Sperm Mixer. It's where they have a lot [of people] who are interested in parenting and being donors and co-parenting. . . . So I went to that once or twice and then I actually met this guy. We got together for coffee. And then I thought, 'Oh My God! I don't even know this guy!' So I decided not to pursue it."

During their journeys toward pregnancy, the women I interviewed frequently revised their plans as new information, resources, and factors emerged. Each relationship seemed complex in its own right and became even more so through constant engagement in a flow of negotiations that often included multiple others, real and imagined or implicated social actors.

(Re)Configuring the Social via Legal Discourses: Marriage and Adoption

The law represents one avenue through which the institution of the family is regulated. Because gay and lesbians have never been able to marry legally, their relationships are outside the scope of family law. However, there exist two primary ways that lesbian and gay parents secure legal rights over children outside of marriage: joint biological production of a child and adoption.

Lynda became pregnant after four years of trying. She conceived using an egg donated by her partner, Elsie, which was successfully implanted into Lynda's uterus after IVF using an unknown donor. After their son, Max, was born, Lynda and Elsie began to negotiate the legal system in an attempt for both mothers to be granted legal recognition of parental status. The couple had had the law in mind throughout their route to pregnancy, and they intentionally navigated legal policies to secure what they perceived as their rights and to minimize the risks associated with the legal denial of parenthood to the nonbiological mother, which is possible until the (legally recognized) second-parent adoption takes place. Once IVF became their route to pregnancy, Lynda and Elsie knew they would fight to have a judge decree co-parent status rather than go through second-parent adoption.

Lynda and Elsie had done their research, and they knew that a legal precedent existed. In a case similar to their own—one woman was the gestational mother, the other woman was the biological mother—the judge had decided that the two women were both mothers, so no second-parent adoption was necessary, and he had decreed them co-parents. Lynda and Elsie, with a lawyer from the National Center for Lesbian Rights (NCLR), took their case to court to secure their own rights and to present a test case for the new idea of a decree.[10] Their case went to court locally under Judge Donna Hitchens, who was well known for her support of second-parent adoption among lesbian co-parents. Judge Hitchens granted Lynda and Elsie status as Max's legal moms.

When I last contacted them, Lynda and Elsie were continuing to work closely with the NCLR. Max was nine months old, and they were still fighting the state offices to obtain a birth certificate. Standard birth certificates have spaces for "mother's name" and "father's name," so the couple is fighting to have Max's birth certificate list them both as "parents," rather than listing a gendered mother and a gendered father. Although more couples are following Elsie's and Lynda's route to pregnancy and parenthood, using IVF to secure parenthood has many problems. It is not a routine technology, it is highly interventionist, and it is beyond the financial reach of most individuals and couples.

The U.S. adoption system, following heteronormative assumptions, is structured around the needs of two populations: married (heterosexual) couples filing for joint adoptions and single individuals filing for single-parent adoptions. The law, however, does not account for gay and lesbian couples who press for access to joint adoptions without the benefit of marriage. Analyzing the U.S. system of adoption as it affects gay and lesbian actors, the sociologist Susan Dalton (2000) identifies what she sees as the core assumption of U.S. family law: that families consist of married heterosexual adults and their biological offspring. In contrast to this "natural" family, adoptions are human-made; they are created and regulated through state-legal and institutional policies. In Dalton's analysis state adoption policies are defined by a three-tiered hierarchy of the family (see table 4).

In the first tier of the hierarchy, automatic fathers are created when wives reproduce children, whether conception occurs through heterosexual sex or assisted reproduction. The second tier represents step-parent adoptions, created when men and women legally marry partners who have children from previous relationships. In most states the investigation is relatively brief and nonintrusive, primarily used to check for criminal or violent histories of the adopting parent. The third tier, independent adoption, is the most relevant for gay and lesbian couples. Independent adoptions represent the one avenue through which people can adopt children outside their immediate families. It is therefore the course that gay and lesbian parents-to-be must often traverse in order to secure legal protections of their families.

Table 4 Adoption Hierarchies

I. SUMMARY ADOPTION
    (PRESUMED FATHER AND ASSISTED REPRODUCTION STATUTES)
    – Retention of parental right by birth mother
    – Extension of parental rights to birth mother's husband
    – No state investigation of the adopting parent
    – Marital requirement
    – No financial cost

II. STEPPARENT ADOPTION
    – Retention of parental rights by custodial parent
    – Extension of parental rights to custodial parent's spouse
    – Limited state investigation of the adopting parents
    – Marital requirement
    – Relatively low financial cost

III. INDEPENDENT ADOPTION
    – Relinquishment of parental rights by all existing legal parents
    – Acquisition of parental rights by individuals formerly unrelated to the child
    – Detailed state investigation of the adopting family
    – Relatively high financial cost

Source: Dalton 2000, 207.

The third tier, independent adoption, is different from the other two in the degree and cost of state involvement and in the relationship between the custodial biological parent(s) and their children following the adoption. States are highly involved in independent adoptions, conducting in-depth investigations into the adopting adult's home and family lives. Subject to investigation are the home; medical, financial, and employment status; previous relationships; previous and current use of drugs and alcohol; parents' opinions on discipline and childrearing; relationships with parents and siblings; religion and faith; and criminal and sexual-abuse records. All of this is accompanied by a two-hour home visit, an office interview, and a cost of $2,000–$6,000. Finally, and perhaps most important, in independent adoptions birth parents must relinquish all of their parental rights as their children are transferred from one family to another family.

The three tiers are inherently problematic for lesbian (and gay) parents. They do not allow unmarried couples to adopt a child jointly, and in independent adoptions they require birth parents to relinquish ties to their children before the adoption can be completed. A lesbian biological mom would therefore have to relinquish her parental rights before her partner could adopt her child; it is thus legally impossible to assign parenthood to two moms (or two dads). To address this problem, a fourth tier, second-parent adoption, was created by the NCLR in the mid-1980s, when the first such adoptions were granted in San Francisco.

In second-parent adoption, the custodial parent retains parental rights, the custodial parent's partner receives parental rights, a detailed state investigation of the adopting family is required, marriage is not required, and the cost is relatively high. Over the past two decades, second-parent adoptions have been granted in a steadily growing number of state and county jurisdictions. Currently, second-parent adoptions are available by statute or appellate-court decision in California, Connecticut, the District of Columbia, Illinois, Indiana, Massachusetts, New York, New Jersey, Pennsylvania, and Vermont. Only four states have expressly resisted the trend of judicial decisions elsewhere; appellate courts in Colorado, Nebraska, Ohio, and Wisconsin have held that second-parent adoptions are not permissible under their respective adoption statutes (National Center for Lesbian Rights 2004). In 2001 Utah and Mississippi passed laws that effectively prohibit queer adoptions. Moreover, private adoption agencies can almost always exclude gay parents at their discretion (Minot 2000).

Of course, even without the benefit of legal protection, gay men and women have been raising children for long enough and in numbers large enough that they have become an acknowledged part of many communities. Despite such progress, the law has in many ways served to maintain the two-parent family as heterosexual, thereby disadvantaging women who co-mother (Dalton 2000). For example, the continued assertion of "best interest of the child" as the foundational question through which adoptions are granted in practice means that the best interest of the child is up to each judge hearing a case. And the fact that gay parents are granted no legal connection to each other limits the benefits they receive from second-parent adoptions, especially compared to those enjoyed by heterosexual couples who adopt through marriage. Only one state, Massachusetts, permits same-sex couples to marry. Therefore, gay and lesbian couples are co-parents without legal ties to one another.[11]

The participants in this research were keenly aware of both the specifics of adoption laws in California, where this research was conducted, and the influence of marriage and family policies in general. Speaking about marriage policies, Chloe said,

> I don't know how this fits, but I have also thought a lot about gay marriage differently. I am really against marriage as a social institution. But the more I see family service laws and family child-protection laws that are geared toward married couples, the more I am in favor of marriage equality. The fact that a second-parent adoption for gay couples costs between two thousand and three thousand dollars, and for a step-parent to get married to a person with children and adopt their kids is two hundred bucks. It makes you think. So I have taken a look at some of those issues. Before I thought marriage is so stupid; it is such an institution. But now, I think, how do you keep some sort of semblance of steady adults in a kid's life unless the parents have some recognized relationship to each other? . . . When you have a contract and it is acknowledged by a federal or state government, all of a sudden you have rights.

Chloe's comments reflect not only an articulate and reasoned response to unequal policies but also the ways such policies include social recognition (and mis-recognition) by the state. Chloe understands marriage as both legally and symbolically important in that it provides a means through which persons are recognized as citizens by state entities and are recognizable as legitimate members of a group — in this case, a family. Marriage, then, not only secures a relationship between two persons but also serves to recognize, and thereby culturally legitimize, individuals as related to their children.

Many of the participants desired such recognition, yet also found the possibility to be a source of great tension. In my interview with Raquel and her partner, June, Raquel said, "When we first started the process June had a lot of reservations. She wondered if we were just hopping on the breeder bandwagon. Why do we have to be like everybody else? . . . Since I've been pregnant, I feel like I don't necessarily want us to be pigeonholed into the lesbian and gay parents thing either. But, on the other hand, I want us to feel like we have a community. . . . Yeah, I still want to feel like I have my identity as a bisexual woman, separate from being a parent. I'm afraid that being a parent cancels [my lesbian identity] out. I know being pregnant and walking down the street does." June added,

> It's like a lot of things about being a lesbian in this world. Choosing to have a commitment ceremony has the same feeling to me. There was nothing about it that was prescribed. A lawyer said to me, "You know, because we have no legal

status, we're, our marriages have no legal status, it also gives us the opportunity to sort of define what it is we want [muffled comment] in the world.
Do you want to be just, treated just like a husband and wife, or do you want to
really carve out something different?" That's always the question for me related to being a lesbian. It's difficult not to have some of the legal rights or the
tax breaks or the health insurance, but we do get to decide in a proactive way
what parts of convention we want, what of these institutions we want to
participate in and what we want to create and what don't we want.

Raquel and June were not alone in their consideration of what reproduction means for one's identity and for the larger distinctiveness of queer
communities. The tension they identified was about larger questions of
assimilation and resistance, or what I have posed in terms of normativity
and queering. Reflecting on this issue, Esther said, "Being gay and creating
family is a hard thing to do. There's this system set up and it doesn't include
us. I have a couple of straight friends and they get married and all of sudden,
bang, they have families and kids make it nuclear. Most gay and lesbians
were cut off from their nuclear families, so they created their own family.
Then when they start having children they aren't recognized by the state.
The good part is they have chosen families, too. I just wonder what all this
procreation will do to chosen families."

Esther articulated the connection she saw between marriage and cultural
recognition. She questioned what would happen to the distinction of queer
identities and communities from heterosexuality. While she identified the
state as exercising the power of recognition, she asserted that persons also
hold the power to recognize (and thereby legitimate) each other. It is
apparent that power — in this case, as recognition — operates laterally as well
as hierarchically. Everyone participates in knowing who is and who is not
recognized as belonging. Belonging is profoundly social; it is given form
and meaning in everyday interactions and through state policies and family
law. One turns this recognition on oneself as well as on others. Esther
continued this line of thought in considering what it would mean when and
if she had a child: "In some ways I think I am going to feel more complete
[when I have a child]. I want a partner and a baby. [Laugh.] You know, I'm
okay if there's no white picket fence, but I want a family, too. I do consider
my friends family, I call them my family. But I want to add a child or
children in my life, too. I think that will make me feel more complete. I
know my mom will think so. And I know everyone else will, too."

Esther's discussion reveals the ways state policies and cultural understandings are co-constitutive. Although Esther's life includes the families she created by choice, they are not socially perceived as making her complete. This is another place of continuity for all people who choose both to live childfree and to expand their families through love, not biology or law. Yet, embedded in many U.S. institutions and cultural norms is a recognizable family form, the nuclear family, and this form often accomplishes (and forecloses) certain forms of recognition and belonging. That is, there are many ways to seek cultural recognition, an intersubjective process, but there are established ways in which the state grants citizenship rights and benefits. These are both present in lesbian articulations and actions.

Heather wanted to create an ad hoc family form outside the bounds of normativity, but was unable to escape cultural ideals of who and what makes a family and the ways norms are consolidated each time these ideals are reproduced. Her comments reflected the constraining effects of normativity: "I think you define family as a group of people who love each other; it is love, not that we are all necessarily biologically or legally related. Families can take any form, there is no 'right' way that things have to be. . . . A while ago I was living with two women who were partners, one was my ex. We talked about raising a child together. I was going to be a single parent, but they could co-parent with me." Although the field of parents would be expanded to three, Heather would remain a single parent, which would reinforce the hegemonic ideal that there can be only one parent of each gender. While the social form of her family may queer belonging, the logic of family law remains firm.

The power of the state in shaping family legitimacy emerged primarily when the women I interviewed discussed birth certificates and second-parent adoptions. In describing the birth of her child, Renee said,

> When I gave birth, I don't know if it was the nurse or what, but when they came in to get the name of the parent, they were really weird. It was strange to me because my doctor does that. I mean he does artificial insemination. . . . Then when she came in to ask me who was the father, I said, "There is no father. It was a donor. I used artificial insemination." She said, "Well, what do you want to put on here? Do you want unknown put on here?" And I said, "No!" I don't want my daughter to grow up thinking that her mom went out with some guy and didn't know who he was and got pregnant. I want her to know that I chose this way to have her — artificial insemination. I want that

put on her birth certificate. And she said, "Well, I don't know if I could do that." She had to go ask her manager. They eventually did it. But they also told me, I don't know why, that we could not use my partner's last name. We wanted to hyphenate [our last names]. They told us we couldn't, so we didn't on her birth certificate. Now we have to legally go change her name. The hyphenation is her name. And that's what she knows it as. Nobody else can tell her any different. She's very strong in that. So, I don't want her to see her birth certificate and not have it on there.

Lynda and Elsie continued to fight family law policies for nine months after Max was born. Lynda said:

The second-parent adoption process is expensive, cumbersome, invasive. It just stinks from start to finish. The California Protective Services, or CPS, comes to your home. They do an extensive search. They talk to your neighbors, your job. They look through your bank proceeds. And it's incredibly invasive. And then, even if all of their write-up says that you are the best parents they've ever laid eyes on, best thing since sliced bread, they have to at the very end say, "But we do not recommend this adoption because they are two parents of the same gender." They have to. And then the judge looks through it. He or she reads the pros and says, "Yeah, these are going to be great parents." Stamp: they can be parents. But it's an expensive, lengthy and invasive process. . . . One thing that they [NCLR] were really looking at was doing a judge's decree for co-parent status without going through the adoption process. At the time, there was one case that had been done in San Francisco. It was the same idea as ours, where one mom was the gestational mom and one was the genetic mom and they brought it up for second-parent adoption. When the judge looked at it, he said, "I don't need to grant an adoption because you're both clearly already mothers. So I will just decree that you're both mothers and we can just skip the adoption process." . . . So, we talked with a lawyer who was working with the NCLR about being kind of a test case for this new idea of a decree. And in fact it went here to the family court of Donna Hitchens and she passed it. So, from the time our child was born, he was legally both of ours.

Tina and Elizabeth, in contrast, had to go through the second-parent adoption procedures. When Elizabeth described the process, she expressed her anger and outrage:

From my perspective, the fact that we had an attorney up in San Francisco who had modified all of the forms to say 'giving up sole custody' was important. I mean, the forms read like I'm some unwed sixteen-year-old who's giving up the baby to some unknown agency. And it doesn't even accommodate the fact that I'm granting joint custody to somebody of my choosing. So, you know, when you get through it all and you put it behind you it's fine, but the process doesn't reflect what's really going on. You are actually cobbling together some very disparate systems. And it feels that way, too.

Judith and her partner, Heather, had recently adopted a child. Their adoption was unique in that a friend knew a young woman who had gotten pregnant and wanted to find a lesbian couple to adopt the child. The friend knew that Heather and Judith had been trying to get pregnant for years, so she told the young woman, who then phoned the couple to ask if they wanted to adopt the child she was carrying. At the time of my interview with them, they had been parenting Jason for several months. Judith described the legal case in which they appealed the second-parent-adoption policy that compelled automatic denial to unmarried (and, by extension, same-sex) parents.

We had the home study from the department of social services, as all adoptions need to, whether they are private or public. It costs you twelve hundred dollars, and at the end of the beautiful description of the home study, the last line says, "We do not recommend that the child be placed in the home because of section this and this code and that and that . . . two people have to be married to adopt a child together." If we were doing this single-parent adoption, however, we would've been having to appeal on the basis that a child could not have two parents of the same sex. So, either way they get you. But we were setting more precedence by appealing this particular part of the law. We had a gay family lawyer who really knew the risks. She also knew that our county, which is San Mateo County, was fairly liberal. She knew some of the judges and felt that it would go through, and it did, without any problems, even though it was a conservative judge. We won on the basis that the birth mother was looking for lesbian parents. It was a miracle. . . . It's not an automatic for us. Since we don't get married, it is not assumed that we are responsible people. When heterosexuals get married legally, both are considered responsible people for possible adoptees automatically. That is not automatic with us. We had to make it clear before we even started.

Such women are certainly making headway in terms of challenging hetero-normativity; they clearly assert that lesbians are part of America's institution of the family.[12] Yet, a diversity of family forms exist even among these respondents. I asked women who had previously adopted or birthed children to talk about the ways in which their lives had changed. Many respondents mentioned the meaning of family. For example, Rachel, who had tried to get pregnant for several years, had recently adopted a girl from China. In our interview, she said,

> I still consider family the same. But I have to admit that I feel more as though I fit into my family. For example, I just returned from holidays with my folks in Florida and my three brothers were all there, and two of them have children of their own, two of them have little girls who are within a year of [my daughter]. So, the three little girls together was quite a scene. And, I was mommy; I wasn't just their daughter. I was mommy and this was their grandchild and they were very, very proud of her as their grandchild. They had just made a 360-degree turn on this. . . . I was more a part of the family, rather than an outsider, because now I had a family of my own and they legitimized that family. In some respects, I guess they have legitimized my partner more as well. As best they can anyway, although she did not join me for that celebration.

Rachel's consideration of family reveals the ways others figure centrally in family recognition: recognition is not just about state or government entitlements, but about how one is treated socially. Rachel's daughter has made Rachel a recognizable and legitimate person. As a mom, Rachel is, presumably, no longer the unrecognizable lesbian daughter. Her partner's absence may suggest that her partner does not feel or perceive the same sense of recognition and belonging.

Lynda also talked about social recognition. The mother of nine-month-old Max, Lynda described her family's outings: "People invariably when they see two women and a stroller say, 'Oh who's the mother?' And we usually say, 'Oh, we both are.' And after people kind of gag for a second, they say, 'What a lucky child to have two mothers. That's wonderful!' And these are not people in the Castro, these are people in West Portal or Pacific Heights. So it's really interesting. I think society recognizes that two moms are phenomenal. I just hope two dads are treated as phenomenal, too." For Lynda, two mothers allow a queering of reproduction among people outside the Castro (a reference to people who are more embedded in a culture of heteronormativity). Furthermore she sees two mothers as a queering of the normative assumptions of opposite-sex parents.

Undoing and Redoing Gender: "Dads," "Donors," and "Mothers Who Father"

So, in what ways do lesbian reproductive practices queer reproduction and kinship and in what ways do they create new norms? To fully examine this issue, it is important to consider not only lesbians' practices but also the impact of these practices on the social categories of mother and father — and on how gender figures into these categories.

Reproductive technologies separate what was previously regarded as a natural and necessary link between fatherhood and motherhood and between the (hetero)sexual act and conception. Fatherhood is no longer a requisite to family formation.[13] Dualistic gender is potentially displaced, as are hegemonic definitions of the family. What may be undone, then, are normative conceptions of gender, sexuality, and ways of being related.

Lesbian reproductive practices have subverted the logic of the heterosexual matrix in part by delinking gender and parenthood. More specifically, if masculinity-fatherhood and femininity-motherhood are delinked, gender is reconfigured, revealing the ways gender is something done or performed. The lesbian-headed family allowed by reproductive technologies represents only one of many emergent and diverse family forms. Same-sex two-parent families and multiple-parent families also disrupt the psychoanalytic narrative of gender acquisition.[14]

The practice of using assisted-reproduction technologies remains controversial within the field of reproductive medicine. Lesbian mothers offer their children a familial context, which differs in a number of important characteristics from the traditional heterosexual family; in lesbian-headed families, for example, the father is often absent from the start, and the child is raised by one or two mothers. Such a reconfiguration of family destabilizes gendered power in its queering of masculine domination. Lesbian families and other queer family arrangements are part of the new postmodern family forms.[15] That is, such forms, in their plurality and capacity to alter hierarchies and power relations, constitute postmodernity.

It has been argued that lesbian mothers undermine traditional notions of the family and the heterosexual monopoly of reproduction by revealing the cultural foundations of these positions (Sullivan 1996, 2001). But gender categories have nothing to do with characteristics associated with mothering and fathering: gender categories are socially produced. Furthermore, the same-sex context coupled with collaboration with donors supports a refashioning of kinship relationships (Dunne 2000).

Lesbian mothers and mothers-to-be who use donor insemination are engaged in practices of cultural production in which new logics of gender and the family are enabled. Lesbians often draw a distinction between father, donor, and parent in ways that push meaning in new directions. The queering of parenthood through the expansion of kinship to include donors can, however, also be read as reinforcing the normativity of the two-parent structure. In a recent study (McNair et al. 2002), for example, it was found that 83 percent of prospective lesbian mothers anticipated that the child's parents would be the biological mother and her same-sex partner. Therefore, while the field of procreators could have been expanded, in most cases it was not. The content and performance of "father" or "donor" is frequently imagined as separate from a notion of "parenthood" (where parenthood is defined as day-to-day decision making, care, and residency of the children), the two-parent nuclear structure is maintained.

In a qualitative study Rosanna Hertz (2002) finds that the efforts of mothers and children to transform anonymous or known sperm donors into "dads" offers a window on the ways in which blood kinship is mobilized to create families (see also Hood 2002). In her comparative case study of twenty-five sperm-donor-assisted families, Hertz uses powerful metaphors and images to guide the reader through an interactionist analysis of the genetic, psychological, and social boundaries of "family" and "kinship." Hertz's comparison of anonymous- and known-donor families offers many insights into the use of genetics as a means to "instill in their children and identity that assumes two parents are necessary to create (though not always raise) a child" (3). For example, with regard to anonymous-donor families, she describes how "absence forms a presence," how the "gift of gametes . . . becomes a token of the child's identity and self," and how mothers create "ghostlike" fathers to help their children develop looking-glass selves by imagining how their absent fathers might think of them (17). Although known donors provide more information for the crafting of looking-glass selves, they remain in the shadows while the mothers vigilantly guard the boundaries between genetic and social parenthood (Hood 2002).

Hertz's policy is to push for known donors so that the construction of the imaginary father can be replaced with actual information about one's donor. The right to know is important, she argues. Anonymous donors are fantasy men, reconstructed by the mother-child dyad in the search to give meaning to the donor. In contrast, known donors have a genealogical-genetic history for the mother-child, but they live on the outskirts so the mother can control who has the knowledge of the father.

In discussing the power of the two-parent-family ideology, which emphasizes the importance of fathers and marriage, Hertz finds that lesbian mothers attribute to imagined fathers the unexplained characteristics of their children. For heterosexual single women who used donor insemination, Hertz concludes, the ideology of fatherhood serves a different purpose. Instead of explaining children's characteristics, it functions to maintain the fantasy of men coming along, marrying them, and adopting the children.

Although children may be created without men as physically present "dads," men are nonetheless commodified, the donor is abstracted into the traits provided on donor profile materials and made readily available for rematerialization by recipients and their children. In doing so, women decontextualize the donors that allowed them to become mothers by privileging the presumed ways that blood kinship creates families. Recipients ultimately reaffirm genetic traits and certain kinds of kinship, rather than challenge them (Hertz 2002).

Yet in separating parenthood from partnership, lesbians do create new family forms in which men may be involved but not as traditional fathers. Mothers who use anonymous donors craft imagined fathers as their children become "looking glasses" into the men they will probably never meet. These children must rely on the mothers' imaginations to create a sense of how their fathers view them (the children). While known donors are not "dads" either, mothers who use known donors can help their children imagine positive fathers, often through more concrete, personal knowledge, and these fathers often do know the children, albeit from a distance (Hertz 2002). It is the mother's construction of "fathers" and relatedness that matters and enables queering to be realized or not. The commodification of donor sperm and the men who donate the sperm may be obscured, but the commodification is central to constructing parenthood.

Deborah discussed her conceptualization of a potential donor.

The donor will never be the father. Ever! I'll never use that word to describe him. When the child is old enough to ask about fathering, because at some point it will I'm sure . . . then I sort of have my rap figured out that I'll talk about a "dear friend" who helped me give life to you and he's your donor. I just won't use that word father. I'm not willing to. The idea of being a lesbian mother to me is an exciting idea. And I'm not the only lesbian mother I know. I knew lesbian mothers in Chicago, as well as a couple out here. So it's not a shocking thing to me at all. And I actually forget that people get surprised by it. I'm proud to be a lesbian because it's just who I am. A lot of women go back and forth and they're not sure and maybe they're bi- and maybe they're lesbian. I just . . . when I figured it out, I didn't have any of those issues at all. It was such a relief to have a name to it. I imagine that might be a little problematic for the baby, but I don't think it's going to be any more problematic than being Jewish. I'm much more concerned about being a single parent than a lesbian parent, because there's no one I can hand it off to when I'm ready to scream. To me, it's just an of course, of course I'm a lesbian mom. It goes along with who you are.

Lesbian motherhood, in the above quote, precludes the presence of a father and therefore is given meaning without its relational other. Such practices displace the gendered order and hegemonic family narratives. While such a queering destabilizes the heterosexual matrix, lesbian practices of assisted reproduction must be placed within the context of recent LGBTQI desires to marry and have children, desires that have largely been put into discourse with the advent of the women's, gay and lesbian, and queer social movements since the 1970s. Such desires and practices can be understood as processes by which lesbians and gays enter heteronormativity, allowing them to be recognized as belonging to and participating in cultural norms. Marriage comes with financial and legal security for one's relationship and family.

While demands for marriage rights push the bounds of legible family life by emphasizing shared affect — claiming that lesbians and gays desire monogamy and nuclear families just as heterosexuals do — how do these demands influence the contours of normativity itself? That is, it is anatomical restriction (being with a member of the same sex) alone that prevents lesbians and gays from entering the contract of marriage and from having a nuclear family (due to lack of sperm or another "biological incapacity"). As the politics of queer inclusion in marriage demonstrate, sexuality and the family continue to be sites of rigorous regulation, and normative values that seek to mitigate potential irregularities may create heterosexual marriage's own instability by highlighting it. Same-sex desires, sexual practices, and ways of organizing one's family do not fall within the usual restrictive "normative range" of sexuality, and however "normal" they appear, they continue to be rendered illegitimate. Seeking recognition and belonging through marriage undoes gender dualism and queers hegemonic notions of the family even it if simultaneously reinforces reproduction and a temporal lifecourse logic. Perhaps the question that remains is, what is the cost of cultural intelligibility?

Four

Negotiating Conception: Lesbians' Hybrid-Technology Practices

I MET DEBORAH THIRTY MILES OUTSIDE of San Francisco in a small town where she was attending graduate school. We talked in her home, a small, one-bedroom apartment close to campus. She answered the door with her three-month-old son, Mason, bundled in a sling. After brief introductions and a moment for Deborah to sign the consent form, I turned on the tape-recorder and began to explain the purpose of my research. I told her that I had been surprised to learn that for the lesbians I had interviewed, getting pregnant had been far more complicated than I or they had anticipated. Deborah laughed and said, "Well, let me tell you a story."

Hybrid Technologies

The story Deborah told me had much in common with those of the other thirty-five women I interviewed. Many of them said that they had imagined an "ideal" trajectory—a linear progression that would begin with tracking one's cycle to predict ovulation, move to detecting ovulation in order to time insemination, and wind up with insemination via the method that would offer the "best chances" of success given one's biomedical characteristics (such as age and physical abilities), finances, and other social and economic factors.

For many, the path turned out to be far from this ideal. Instead, it was highly variable, complicated, circular, and required steps not previously envisioned. I found that each narrative had to be read not as a linear trajectory, but as a flexible and varied set of day-to-day practices. The technologies used ranged from the simple (donors masturbating into a jar, women self-inseminating using turkey-baster technology), to more "medical" (syringe technology), to advanced (intrauterine insemination, in vitro fertilization). When the women moved from one kind of technology to another, it was not always in the expected sequence.

The women inseminated in a variety of settings — including homes and clinics — using a variety of tools and devices. Some consulted no health professionals; others drew on a wide range of biomedical services, professionals, and resources. Their experiences did not fit neatly into simple political categories: women saw themselves as neither separatist agents of women's empowerment nor the reluctant subjects of patriarchal medical control. Such dichotomies did not encompass the complex negotiations and meanings that characterized these women's pathways to pregnancy. Instead, women often sustained the intent, content, and meaning of women's health discourse while also pragmatically negotiating biomedical assumptions and interventions.

In short, the cultural-technical practices of lesbians seeking pregnancy are varied and complex, and making meaning about them requires considerable interpretation and negotiation. What emerges from the interviews are lesbians willing to use whatever biomedicine offers to meet their pregnancy goals (see Lock and Kaufert 1998; Lewin 1998b). I therefore use the term *hybrid technologies* to account for the variations and complexities of lesbians' practices and for the multiplicity of cultural contexts and constraints in which they are situated. *Hybrid technology* characterizes practices that reconstruct or recombine practices that have generally been seen as mutually exclusive: either simple, do-it-yourself methods or advanced reproductive technologies. The women I interviewed, for example, were actively combining several technological components and variously assigning meaning to those components as they journeyed toward pregnancy. *Hybrid* signals the mixture of technologies, discourses, and practices, highlighting the complexity obscured by more binary terms (high-tech/low-tech, routine/advanced, expert/lay, medical/nonmedical).

Following Foucault's assertion that people are able to select among available discourses and practices and reflect on them, I analyzed the interviews with attention to the exact ways the women engaged in such reflections and negotiations. These women did not always accept anything medicine had to offer (although at times they did); instead they navigated biomedical discourses and services in ways that fit their goals and ideas. Their hybrid technology trajectories took into account the need to negotiate and make sense of the historical discourses of natural reproduction and natural gender that are built into Fertility Inc. These trajectories, in particular, show that behaviors are not calibrated either to follow or subvert institutional or cultural ideals; rather, actions reflect strategic navigations.

Lesbians as Implicated Users of Fertility Inc.

At the same time that same-sex desires and behaviors were being constructed as nonprocreative and therefore deviant, a healthcare specialty developed with the aim of curing (heterosexual) childlessness. This specialty went by many names — most often, infertility medicine. The "ideal" user of this healthcare sector was not usually specified, but its approaches and protocols reflected the assumption that the goal would be "natural" reproduction as the outcome of heterosexual intercourse. Medical protocols have largely been built around assumptions of conjugal sexual intercourse (and laws are similarly designed to protect these conjugal actors). By classifying childlessness as pathology, medicine constructs "natural" womanhood as synonymous with procreation. Childless heterosexuals — the ideal users of assisted reproduction — would be helped to overcome their unwelcome condition. In this way, assisted-reproduction technologies would reproduce not only human beings, but also natural women and natural families.

Heterosexual women (and men) have long been the legitimate users of the infertility medicine's interventions, in contrast to their associated "other" — lesbians and single women — whose use of assisted-reproduction technologies was thought to raise ethical dilemmas. This reflected medicine's power to define what is normal by defining what is natural (see Cussins 1998).[1] In this framework, medicine uses technology to render natural a condition once considered unnatural (the incapacity to reproduce by means of heterosexual intercourse). If the couples who benefit are heterosexual, the result is a natural family. But other users of assistive technologies continue to be viewed as unnatural, as are, by extension, the families they produce. In this construction, assisted reproduction is forever artificial when it is an unnatural (homosexual) woman or man who is in need of technology. An unnatural person who uses reproductive technology is not considered to be giving nature a helping hand, but rather to be bypassing nature altogether, thereby consolidating unnatural sexuality as nonprocreative (and raising ethical dilemmas).

This contrast is reflected in the different languages used to describe the same technologies depending on whether users are perceived as natural or unnatural. When the interventions are used to help heterosexuals reproduce, references to *artificial* and *technical* tend to be deemphasized; when applied to lesbians and single women, assistance is constructed as artificial, and stigmatizing terms are more likely to be used. Desperate infertile heterosexual couples are given a "helping hand" to solve their (temporary) inability to meet their adult expectation of parenthood and their inner drive to reproduce. The naturalness of their reproductive capacity will be realigned.

Terms that surround assistive technologies can, and often do, carry messages about the identities of appropriate users. For example, the word *treatment* connotes a legitimate dysfunction or abnormality that must be fixed. Infertility treatments are thus reserved for those with infertility—a diagnosis given to those who are unable to become pregnant naturally. This language of treatment for a "problem" undermines access and use by nonheterosexual couples: lesbians and single women. Women in these categories are not expected to reproduce, nor are they natural reproducers—therefore their inability to get pregnant is not (primarily) due to a medical condition, and their infertility thus becomes a social condition without cause for treatment.

Yet in medical practice the social category of being a lesbian or a single woman is transformed into a biomedical infertility classification, triggering referral to infertility and fertility services. When lesbians pursue pregnancy, their social category (lesbian) is transformed into an infertility status, thereby assigning *all* such women a biomedical classification and directing them to biomedical services.[2]

The language, of course, is inadequate. Lesbians and single women are frequently labeled as having a "medical condition," largely in order to make them eligible for a treatment protocol. It is difficult to ascertain whether services are differentially provided to lesbians and single women based on possession of medical classifications or social ones (lack of sperm, egg or uterus in partner). Regardless of the problematics associated with categorization of in/fertility, lesbians often need to negotiate such labeling and get diagnosed as infertile in order to pursue high-tech options (which are increasingly the most available ones). Lesbians may seek biomedical classification, but only because the biomedical in/fertility framework is well institutionalized as the key access point and structure for reproductive assistance. Thus, it may be that for lesbians who want to conceive, infertility medicine is becoming an "obligatory point of passage" (see Collon 1986).

Of course, the social category of lesbian does not in and of itself indicate biophysical infertility (although some individuals within this social group may indeed have fertility issues). Nevertheless, when lesbians seek assisted reproduction within biomedicine to achieve their goals they must negotiate the labels-diagnoses associated with biophysical infertility and the service systems associated with them. For many lesbians, this raises an interesting dilemma in terms of identity. In order to access the high-tech world, one needs to either identify with the technological category or to strategically align one's identity to fit the model.[3]

"Male-Factor Infertility": Negotiating a Biomedical Label

The issue of taking on a medical label was not lost on the participants I interviewed. One participant, Audrey, said, "The infertility concept is a tough one. I guess, on the one hand, we have male-factor infertility in that we lack sperm. But on the other hand, we're healthy, so why should we be treated like we're sick? Then again, we are 'sick' because we're missing this thing we need to get pregnant. And we need to find the best way to do that." According to Lynda, "As lesbians, there aren't good diagnostic criteria for when to say, 'You're infertile,' which there are with straight people. If you have twelve months of unprotected, well-timed intercourse and don't get pregnant, you're infertile, and they jump in with a big work-up. With us, we don't have a definition. We don't have sperm exposure all the time." Expressing an alternative perspective, Arlene said, "The interesting thing is that if we were a straight couple, it would have taken us a *longer* time to get to the infertility clinic and receive the services that ultimately helped us get pregnant. When you're lesbian it's like, you just jump right in there." Dana summarized it this way: "It's obstacles that you have to overcome. That's really parallel. Being a lesbian in this culture, you get used to being outside of inner circles, whether it's because I'm a lesbian, an artist, a woman of color, or a radical. I don't know. I mean I'm always swimming upstream."

While these descriptions exemplify the profound significance classification holds for lived experience, they also demonstrate the ways medicalization can be pragmatically taken on to meet one's goals. Although many lesbians do gain access to the infertility system and interact with the cultural discourses surrounding it, they are not the "configured" users of these technologies. Yet the construction of lesbians as nonprocreative carries forward as a potent and historically continuous cultural script and finds an ongoing place in emergent technoscientific infertility practices, discourses, and services.

Further, the medical label "infertility" produces technoscientific identities, as women first are defined in medical terms, but then interact with infertility treatments and discourses. The identification is produced through the application of technologies and sciences.[4] This new identity genre is inscribed on lesbians, often whether they like it or not, as happened for the lesbians who were automatically routed to the infertility clinic. What is significant is that people in fact negotiate the meanings of such identities, and do so in flexible, heterogeneous ways. Technoscientific identities are selectively taken. While some may resist such classifications, others may accept and take on such identities because doing so brings meanings to their social experience and mediates access to "medical miracles." Those who selectively reject such classification may do so because they understand those labels to be stigmatizing or damaging. In all, the meanings people bring to a diagnostic label such as "infertility" shape their experiences. Infertility, for example, can be read as a failure to achieve natural womanhood or as a necessary code for insurance coverage.

Today, as Esther described, many people once labeled medically infertile have been (re)defined as having fertility problems, a shift that emphasizes wellness and normalcy over disease and pathology. This opens space for the potential, given the absence of pathology, of conceiving a child (Becker 2000b). In medical terms, these medical subjects, like all women without children, are in a state of (one hopes, temporary) limbo between being childless and being with child.[5] While all women have fertility issues to varying degrees, it is *certain women* — those located within heterosexual couples — who are "configured" (Woolgar 1991) as appropriate users of biomedical fertility services because they fall neatly into accepted infertility classifications. Those outside these signifiers are "implicated actors" or users (Clarke and Montini 1993).

Over the course of the twentieth century, heterosexuality was normalized through its discursive opposition to a deviant other. Once the category "lesbian" appeared in biomedical and social worlds, her "deviance" was constructed in nonprocreative terms.[6] Therefore, while lesbians were seemingly absent from the history of the medicalization of assisted reproduction, they were *implicated* in the construction of assisted reproduction as a legitimate means through which (heterosexual) women could reproduce.[7] As social movements of the late 1960s and early 1970s took hold, the landscape began to shift, and single women and gay and lesbian actors began to "talk back" to medical discourse and create social lives on their own terms.

This raises some questions: what are the implications when the users of assisted reproduction are not the heterosexual couples envisioned and built in by scientists, designers, and institutions? How do nonintended users understand and shape their material trajectories of achieving pregnancy within this context?[8]

"More Complicated than I Had Imagined"

Before accessing fertility clinic services, Deborah had spent eight months doing vaginal inseminations at home. When she turned to a fertility clinic in her attempt to get pregnant, the first thing she learned was that the nurse preferred that she did not discuss her lesbian identity. "We had talked about it and I told her I was a lesbian. I told her the donor was not my partner and she said, 'You have to lie about that, don't tell me that, I can't do it if you are not partners.' And I said, 'Okay we are partners then. We are certainly partners in this project.' So she knew I was a lesbian all the way through but that dropped out of the conversation right there. She said [it was] for insurance reasons. . . . I didn't investigate further because what do I care, why do I care what a doctor thinks about my identity. But as I proceeded, I realized my identity precluded me from getting reimbursed for many of the services I used." Over the next six months, Deborah and the nurse clashed on many more issues than Deborah's sexual identity.

It took Deborah two years to become pregnant: "It was certainly longer and more complicated than I had imagined." She described a single insemination to illustrate how complex and stressful each cycle had become.

[The nurse] made me do ovulation kits. And what would happen is she asked me to call her when the kit said I was ovulating. Then she would make me an appointment for the day after or the day after that. And this is one of the reasons I was really mad at her because research had shown that if you inseminate the day after it doesn't work. So, this one cycle, it was on the weekend. He [the donor] agreed to rush. He had moved up into the mountains. When we first started doing this he lived nearby, but he had broken up with his girlfriend and moved thirty-five miles away. He had a car at this time, which he usually didn't have, so he agreed to rush from his home to the doctor's office. This way I wouldn't have to go all the way up there and get him. The friend who went with me had a van. The donor agreed that he would just jerk off in the van in the parking lot. It was all a big rush because of the nurse who was doing the insemination. Oh, I was doing IUI. The nurse would only give us a small window to get everyone and everything there. I can't even tell you how upset I was at this time because the nurse was giving me less and less time to arrange everything. And this time she had given me an hour. The donor lives far away, forty-five minutes. . . . So he came in his little car, went in to the van, jerked off, and gave me the sample. We went inside and did the insemination. It was just totally horrible. I can't even tell you. The nurse was all upset she had to come in on the weekend. I had ovulated on Friday and we could have done it then. But she couldn't; I was really upset about that, too. So she wanted to do it on Saturday. I already paid all this money for the Clomid and whatever other else they had wanted to do. It was around five hundred dollars. In hindsight, the procedures were just to find out my ovaries were fine. This is a lot of money to just waste. So I had to do the insemination that cycle. Not to mention that I had been on these hormones and that I had already missed an entire month of insemination opportunity to have the tests they wanted me to. So that was the last time I did intrauterine insemination at all. So I spent almost five thousand dollars and I didn't get pregnant that way.

Deborah's account of what must have been a stressful few months is fraught with tension. Her descriptions of medical tests, reactions to synthetic hormones, and complex scheduling arrangements echo the stories of many respondents. For her, Clomid, an oral hormone pill, felt like an unnecessary intervention.

After describing the IUI and scheduling difficulties with the clinic, she said, "Now, let me tell you what the inseminations were like before I went to the clinic."

Figuring out when you ovulate is interesting. The clinic wants you to use those kits and I had also tried doing the temperature thing. I was real bad at taking my temperature at the same time everyday. My periods are like clock-work, so I can tell you not only what day I ovulate but the time of day I am going to have my period. So it seemed like a waste of time using all those methods to figure it out. I would just count fourteen days and read my body and know. This is really funny actually . . . when I was ovulating, he [the donor] would use a little jelly jar. And then when one of the cats was sick, my vet had given me a long syringe to force feed her if she wouldn't eat. So I boiled the syringe and the jar and I gave him the jar. He lived next door, so I walked over and told him, "It's time." We would make the arrangements that he would come over and pick up the jelly jar and bring it back to me right away. And he would keep it out of the sun if it was the daytime, but warm. Then he would leave and I would lay down on my bed with my legs propped up and a towel underneath me and pull out the semen from the jelly jar with the syringe, insert the syringe and squirt. I would just lie there with my hips elevated for about an hour and did my homework and graded papers and all that other fun, nonromantic stuff. And we did that for eight tries, eight months, and I didn't get pregnant.

Deborah then contacted the Lesbian Insemination Group and heard from a woman that IUI had worked for her.

There was only one place in town that would do intrauterine insemination with fresh sperm. I really wanted to use fresh because I had a donor and why pay to freeze it, it just seemed simpler. That's how I met that mean nurse. The funny thing is, after doing that for six to eight months and having a ton of medical tests including a D&C and a hysterostomy to remove uterine lumps, and after spending (well, charging to my credit cards) over five thousand dollars, more money than I would have for many years, I ended up quitting the IUI and the drugs and that clinic and went back to vaginal inseminations. I used a cervical cap and after four tries, finally, I got pregnant.

She then added, "Really, most women who have any kind of health insur-ance can get birth control and a cervical cap is considered birth control, so I tell everyone I know, 'You should try this method. Just tell them you need birth control [not assisted reproduction].'" A cervical cap is a small rub-ber cylinder and a medical technology most often used as a contraceptive method to prevent the movement of sperm into the cervical os. For pur-poses of self-insemination, it is used in reverse, as a device to hold sperm near the cervical os and thus to enhance chances of conception.

Deborah was one of two women I interviewed who used fresh sperm and who returned to doing vaginal, at-home inseminations after using IUI methods and fertility drugs. As Deborah said, the decision to use fresh sperm was an economic one: "Why pay for all that testing and freezing when you don't have to?" She acknowledged that using fresh sperm was less convenient in one respect. Women who used frozen sperm did not have to consider the donor's schedule each month. They were able to take the donor himself — though not his biomaterial — out of the insemination process.

Deborah's trajectory took place over the course of two years. For Deborah, getting pregnant required complex negotiations of biomedical knowledges and resources. She needed to construct a set of practices that made sense for her given her resources, and using a known donor, fresh semen, and performing vaginal self-inseminations were part of this negotiation. Through such processes of negotiation, she also confronted the visibility of her sexual identity as a lesbian.

Deborah's story exemplifies the ways financial and cultural constraints shape practices. Her level of education and use of credit cards enabled her to overcome her own financial obstacles. When we completed the interview, I asked her what, if anything, she was most concerned about. "Well, I'm not too worried about how I'm going to support the kid because I'm not afraid of being poor. When have I not been! I mean, at some point I would like to achieve middle-class status and have a middle-class life, which is why I'm in graduate school now."

Unlike Deborah, most of the women I interviewed did not encounter overt forms of institutional discrimination. If fact, they often noted the ease with which they were able to access healthcare providers and fertility services. They described their own willingness to move through the experience, which they did with relatively little reflection. What drove their actions was a profound commitment to having a child. They were willing to go into deep debt, engage in emotionally fraught conversations with potential donors, risk their own health, and even break up with their partners to achieve this goal. As it became clear that it was the goal of pregnancy that was most pressing in the minds of these lesbians, I became aware of the necessity for my analysis to focus on the complexities and meanings of each step women encountered along their pathways to parenthood.

The quest for pregnancy usually brings lesbians into contact with biomedical services at some point — even if only in the form of a sperm bank. While the settings vary, lesbian reproduction can thus be understood as situated either directly or implicitly within the biomedical technoservice complex. Into this realm comes a body; the corporeal aspects of reproductive practices figure prominently in most accounts. Lesbian reproduction is an example of "pastpresents," the historical discourses and practices around infertility and lesbian sexualities that are present today and part of current practices, knowledges, and services. The interviews reflect the complex ways that reproductive technologies — as "technologies of power" (Foucault 1980b) — tend to enact control and surveillance. Analyzing the scripts of medical technologies and knowledges moves away from conceptualizing power as a top-down hierarchy with overt discrimination to instead include more subtle ways that power relations are embedded in medical practice. One way power is manifested is through objectification and subjectification tendencies.

The content of the interviews reveals the ways lesbians seeking pregnancy negotiate shifting control loci. It is in the day-to-day material practices that resistance and accommodations to medical definitions, legal policies, insurance regulations, and other power dynamics are made visible. I conceptualize lesbian reproduction as a largely hybrid process to highlight the simultaneity of control and resistance through these everyday negotiations.

Trajectories of Achieving Pregnancy

As a trajectory, getting pregnant is not linear or straightforward; nor is it immune from cultural and social interactions (Strauss 1993). Several features are characteristic of lesbian routes to pregnancy.

First, achieving pregnancy is a lengthy process that involves numerous social actors, multiple sources of information, resources, and services, and a variety of technologies, drugs, and expertise. Each and all are part of the practices that unfold.

Second, achieving pregnancy is a conscious process, wherein women actively and intentionally work toward the goal of having a child.

Third, achieving pregnancy is a revisional process, one that constantly changes form. While there appears to be a general trajectory, women do not follow it uniformly, in a linear fashion, or without revisions.

Fourth, achieving pregnancy is a contingent process, structured by economic, cultural, and political conditions that require negotiations.

In combination, these characteristics reveal that getting-to-pregnant practices are hybrid technologies that variously reconstruct or recombine approaches often understood as mutually exclusive: either simple, do-it-yourself methods or advanced reproductive technologies. Together, these features construct a concept of trajectory that embraces interactions among multiple actors, contingencies (unanticipated and not entirely manageable), and complexities (it is not necessarily rational, planned, and worked out). As courses of action, trajectories of achieving pregnancy can be directed at managing an evolving set of problems that are unanticipated, difficult, and even "fateful." When women first set out to become mothers, many engage in processes largely directed through their own agency. They plan, they work, they are keenly aware of their choices. However, as time passes and energy diminishes, their plans can give way to a more chaotic and less-controlled sequence of events. Unexpected stress, strains, and new social actors influence the shapes of their trajectories.

I now discuss the trajectories of all thirty-six participants in this study, from ovulation detection to at-home insemination to complicated medical procedures (see chap. 5, table 5). My data on actual inseminations is based on thirty-four respondents: Chloe and Arlene had not yet started inseminating. The examples I present highlight the knowledges, technologies, and resources participants drew on in negotiating various control loci as they pragmatically sought pregnancy.

Ovulation Prediction and Detection

The technical process of predicting ovulation often goes unnoticed in popular depictions of getting pregnant, yet it is a particularly important step in assisted conception and an increasingly important technique when using frozen sperm.[9] While "fresh" sperm cells live for up to five days in fertile vaginal mucus, frozen sperm lives for only twelve to twenty-four hours. This narrows the window for fertilization, necessitating precise timing of insemination to coincide with or occur immediately before ovulation. Furthermore, since women can only purchase a finite quantity of sperm from sperm banks (sperm is sold in 1–2 cc vials), the importance of "getting it right" the first time cannot be understated. As timing is critical for all women who use frozen sperm to achieve pregnancy, it is therefore a basic social process in infertility in general.

Timing insemination requires knowledge of one's menstrual cycle. Developing this knowledge occurs through multiple forms, from scientific tests to recorded observations of one's bodily changes. Historically, women simply tracked their menstrual cycles based on experiential knowledge about their bodies: timing of menstruation, observed changes in body temperature, tactile changes in vaginal mucus and/or cervical opening, perceived changes in physical and emotional well-being, and so on. This process included either a formal chart or informal mental or written notes. As it has been integrated into biomedical services, charting the menstrual cycle has been transformed into a medical technology with standard procedures and devices, including the basal-body-temperature thermometer and formal charting templates. Using these devices, women predict ovulation by "scientifically" measuring body temperature at the same time each day and recording this information appropriately to ensure replication and comparability. Along with tracking temperature, women are, at times, encouraged to systematically measure and record bodily changes. Other "natural" fertility signs (e.g., cervical position and openness, quality of cervical mucus) can also be recorded in the formal chart. Women's health organizations and self-help books for conception often include a sample menstrual-cycle chart that women can use when they are ready to begin the conception process. When Deborah discussed trying to take her temperature at the same time each day, she was relying on women's health discourse and the long history of charting one's cycle.

Chloe described how she and her partner tracked her menstrual cycle each month and the devices (thermometer, charts) they used for this practice. "In just the past few months, I have been able to tell when I have ovulated. Not because of the chart, but because I have been consciously paying attention to my body. I have gotten down to 'Oh, this is about day thirteen and, look, the past few months every day thirteen my skin changes and I am grouchy this day or I don't feel good.' I am getting more in tune. I think it is the attention, you start paying attention and you recognize the patterns." Her perceptual sense of her body, alongside the knowledge told through the thermometer and charts, influenced her knowledge about her cycle.

For Chloe, ovulation prediction thus included interacting with and understanding her own body. The somatic, material experiences of mood changes and skin alterations shaped her understanding and direct experience of assisted reproduction. Despite the technologies involved, she primarily consulted her own perceived understandings of her body's patterns for information. For her, ovulation detection was an embodied technical process that involved interaction with body signs that she had begun to notice taking place during her menstrual cycle. This process also included her partner, Arlene, which indicated the interactive nature of the technological work: insemination was not just between herself and the technology; it was a process between her, other social actors, and technologies.

> It was such a big move. It was ridiculous. Arlene sets the alarm clock, wakes first, and immediately places the thermometer in my mouth. She then retrieves the menstrual-cycle chart from the bedside table and records my temperature. We have really been aware of the things that [Arlene] can do. She wakes up and says, "I got the thermometer!" We have been really aware of sharing the process so that Arlene has as much participation as possible. The thermometer was her thing. She is the one who takes my temperature every morning and she writes it on the chart. . . . We are talking about all the signs, too. We know that it usually takes a few months, if you do your basal temperature, to start realizing your own patterns and paying attention to them. And once you pay attention, you start noticing patterns. Not only are you able to read them, but they become more clear.

Chloe and Arlene were co-participants in their pregnancy plans. They shared and negotiated responsibilities. The practice of menstrual-cycle tracking also signaled the highly intentional construction of shared parenthood that took place even prior to conception for the women I interviewed.

Once women begin insemination, their shared and intentional work does not change. However, it is at this point that perceptual clues and basal-body-temperature charts are often replaced with ovulation-prediction kits. Ovulation detection is today an example of the biomedical transformation of a low-tech body technology into a hybrid-technology practice. Some very sophisticated science has gone into the making of detection technologies. Since the 1960s, medical research has promoted a range of ovulation-detection tools that "scientize" other forms of knowing the body (changes in mucus, skin, body temperature). Today, the ovulation-detection kit is regarded among medical providers as the most "effective" form of ovulation detection (no longer prediction). Pharmaceutically packaged kits, computer-software applications, ultrasound technologies, and other biomedical devices have become the suggested standards of care for achieving pregnancy.[10]

OvuQuick is the most widely used and provider recommended ovulation-detection kit.[11] The OvuQuick One-Step Ovulation Predictor brand was developed and distributed in 1986 by Quidel Corporation.[12] OvuQuick and similar products enact a significant discursive and technoscientific shift — from *prediction,* a mathematical estimate, to *detection,* a medical certainty. That is, ovulation-detection kits "scientifically" detect the fertility "surge" via the pre-ovulatory release of follicle-stimulating hormone (FSH) and luteinizing hormone (LH), termed the LH surge. The LH surge signals the high point of fertility and, thus, the best day to inseminate. Like a pregnancy test, it works by detecting hormonal changes in urine that are recorded on a litmus-test stick.

The resulting message is that women no longer need rely on their own body knowledge (termed "subjective" experience by biomedicine), but can safely rely on "objective" measures delivered through scientific means. The biomedicalization of ovulation differentially impacts lesbians who use frozen sperm and are therefore particularly reliant on "accurate" timing to achieve pregnancy. That is, due to the short window of frozen-sperm viability once it has been thawed for insemination, timing is critical.

The women I interviewed understood the increasing importance of ovulation detection and planned their actions accordingly, although with constant and pragmatic negotiations. For example, while their use of ovulation-prediction kits confirmed a replacement of personal awareness with technological knowledge to a certain degree, their awareness of their own bodies and bodily sensations (Anspach 1993) could and, at times, did supplant scientific knowledges. The women continued to rely on embodied knowledge in their conception practices, rather than universally accept science over subjectivity. They chose to negotiate various knowledge sources in ways that made sense for their personal practices and for helping them achieve their goals.

Joyce described integrating the importance of the ovulation-prediction test into her knowledge of her cycle. "Really, I can't understand how we ever did it without those. [Laughs.] It's so hard to know exactly when [you are ovulating], and you have a very short window." For Joyce, the detection kit provided essential knowledge; without it, she would not know when the time was right. Therefore, the kit both simplified the procedures and maximized the possibility for success. Surprisingly, however, Joyce later described detection kits as mediating between technical knowledge and embodied knowledge: "The ovulation predictor kit says once you get a positive reading, wait twelve hours. It's telling you [that] you have a hormone surge and it's still going to be a while before you ovulate. I think it means that you're going to ovulate somewhere between twenty and thirty-six hours later. Of course, once you've ovulated, forget it! So you want to [inseminate] before you ovulate and the changes are over."

Joyce captured the complexity of ovulation prediction well. While she ascribed certainty to the test, she continued, "What I do is I wait for the ovulation predictor kit to tell me that there's been a surge. If it doesn't tell me, I'm going to go ahead and inseminate when I think it's the right time. Chances are that I'm going to have to go back to the doctor and he's going to have to do an ultrasound to make sure that I am ovulating. So, if the stick doesn't tell me, I decide and go to the doctor." As her narrative progressed, her reliance on the accuracy of ovulation-predictor tests diminished, replaced with her own observations and the certainty provided by ultrasound technology. Joyce navigated between a belief in the knowledge gained from technology and a belief in the knowledge gained from felt and perceived changes in her body. Such negotiations of knowledge sources took place wherever bodies and technologies met along trajectories of achieving pregnancy.

Thus, despite biomedicalization, or perhaps because of biomedicalization tendencies, the women integrated perceptual and scientific knowledges to ascertain the "right time" to do it. Kim also described this process: "My cycles were pretty irregular . . . they were long so we weren't figuring out exactly when I was ovulating. I couldn't feel it. I had some changes that would help me know, like cervical mucus and this and that and my temperature, but it was hard to get a good read on it. We used the ovulation-predictor kit. It didn't always work for us. By the end, we were getting more sophisticated. Each month we had a better sense, and we would try to do the insemination earlier and earlier. The time I got pregnant, it seemed like the weirdest cycle." Kim did not implicitly trust the scientific ovulation kit, but she did use it as one tool in figuring out her ovulation and the best time to inseminate. She relied on multiple strategies and perceptual cues to gain knowledge and predict her ovulation.

Raquel also negotiated among many knowledge sources.

We dutifully did the ovulation-predictor thing, and it was getting like day fifteen and I still wasn't surging. And June said, "We should just do it. We should just go." And I thought maybe it's a waste of money. And so we bickered about it. Finally, we decided to just go do it. I was going to ovulate somewhere around then. It just feels like such an unbelievable crapshoot. . . . So we went in [to the clinic]. And the nurse who was there to do the procedure said, "And what day did you surge?" And I said, "Well, I haven't yet."

She said, "Okay. And so you decided to come in today because . . . ?" She was not supportive, but we asked to be inseminated anyway. And that's how it happened. It worked! I guess it was not supposed to happen according to OvuQuick—*we* decided.

Many of the participants told stories similar to those told by Joyce, Raquel, and Kim. While technologies factor in, women draw on various personal knowledges to shape their conception practices. A complex interplay of social interactions, social actors, and nonhuman actants influence the process of achieving pregnancy. This high degree of negotiation saturates reproductive practices beyond the step of predicting ovulation.

All along their achieving-pregnancy trajectories, participants drew on multiple knowledges and a range of technological tools (devices and drugs), encountered a variety of social actors, and wound up in many settings. Women cobbled these together in different ways to shape their own conception practices and move toward their goal of pregnancy.

Performing Insemination, Constructing Hybrid Practices

Two primary insemination technologies are used to achieve conception: intravaginal and intrauterine. Intravaginal insemination can be performed using any delivery mechanism that is inserted into the vagina (e.g., a needleless syringe, an eye dropper, a cervical cap). Intrauterine insemination involves a catheter delivery system, in which a catheter is inserted into the vagina, through the cervical opening, and into the uterus. These technologies require different sperm processing. For intravaginal insemination, fresh, unwashed semen or frozen sperm can be used. For intrauterine insemination, "IUI ready" sperm must be used.[13] This sperm undergoes a process to remove prostaglandin, a substance found in semen that if placed into the uterus can cause cramping and increase miscarriage risks, and to reduce the quantity of semen for easy passage through a catheter small enough to be inserted through a woman's cervical os.[14]

The participant stories have thus far revealed that women's health organizations and discourses have played a central role in shaping ideas about becoming lesbian mothers, in gathering the necessary information and resources to do so, and in making sense of ovulation and the right time to inseminate. Discourses of women's health are present in insemination narratives and practices as well. For example, a 1970s depiction of alternative insemination reads: "Find a donor through connections other than the traditional medical profession such as friendship ties, women's self-help groups, alternative health services, relatives, etc. . . . Once the known donor ejaculates into a clean jar or condom, deliver his semen into the vagina using 'a turkey-baster, an eye dropper, a diaphragm, or an inverted condom'" (O'Donnell et al. 1979, 50, 53).

When lesbians discussed what they regarded as the most simple and ideal form of insemination, they described a vaginal insemination performed at home. It is defined as a nonmedical procedure that relies on common household devices (e.g., kitchen jars, eyedroppers, cervical caps, and turkey basters) and includes tropes of romance such as music, candles, pillows, and, at times, sexual intimacy. In many ways, this "romantic" insemination mirrors the method promoted by *Our Bodies, Ourselves* (Boston Women's Health Book Collective 1984).

My interviews reveal that while the demedicalized, alternative-insemination ideals of the 1970s hold firm, actual practices differ in several ways. The women now tend to use devices and technologies of greater sophistication, although, at times, they do return to using common household devices. For vaginal home insemination, most women use a needleless syringe; the usual collection apparatus is, instead of a jelly jar, a vial with purchased frozen sperm surrounded by dry ice in a cooler or nitrogen tank. Insemination may take place at home or in a clinic, but whatever the actual setting may be, the contours of the environment draw on tropes of both home and clinic. For example, it is not unusual to hear about romance and intimacy in the context of an office-based insemination, nor is it uncommon to hear the terms *medical* and *high-tech* when women describe home inseminations. The term *hybrid technologies* highlights these practices in which forms of technologies, settings, and meanings are combined in ways that often disrupt usual binaries.

Carla's description of her insemination practices, for example, conjured images of alternative insemination: "In the very beginning, I had this typical delusion that it would happen suddenly, without much trying. I had the idea that it might work that way for us. . . . So we started off at home. The process was different than we thought, there was no turkey baster, but it was a lot like I had imagined. We were in the same house. And he would go upstairs and masturbate into a jar. And then he would call me and I would come up. And with a syringe I would draw it up and put it inside of me." Lesbian health discourse characterized lesbian insemination as a nonmedicalized, romantic process that included technologies, but was nevertheless profoundly low-tech. In many cases, however, this narrative was diminished by the use of medically provided technologies and services (e.g., frozen sperm, sperm-bank experts, ovulation-detection kits, and dry ice), as well as professional advice. Raquel's practice illustrated this well.

> [At home we were] using frozen sperm. It was really great, very exciting, and seemed surreal. [My partner] was using an ovulation predictor. We were checking her basal body temperature. It seemed to at once be all over the place and, at the same time, it seemed like she was ovulating. There was some change in the middle of the cycle. We would drive over to [the sperm bank] with a cooler. They would pack it with dry ice and all the stuff that we needed — the syringe and everything, directions. And then, we'd bring it home. And when she was going to have time to lie down for a while, we would prop her up on pillows, put music on, light candles and everything. Meanwhile, the little vial would be sitting in a bowl of lukewarm water and thawing. I would draw the stuff up into the syringe and inject, slowly of course. And we would say, "Go spermies!"

For Raquel, insemination was a fairly simple and routine procedure. My interviews indicated that this was a usual early-stage practice of achieving pregnancy. While Raquel's insemination story, with its romantic, interpersonal setting, mirrored the 1970s turkey-baster scenario, it also included many features of contemporary medical practices, including basal-body-temperature charting, ovulation-detection kits, consultation with fertility experts, and accessing biomedical providers. While the turkey-baster narrative is alive and well, in material practice today's lesbian inseminations differ as new products and technologies are utilized.

As Raquel finished describing her partner's inseminations, she added, "She would just lie there for a while with her butt in the air. The doctor always said that, you know, orgasm was good for getting the fallopian tubes to do their thing." This statement exemplified the ways cultural ideas and scientific facts mutually shape subjects and objects (i.e., social relations). Science does not merely reflect cultural understandings, but its ideas and practices are shaped by culture and in turn constitute cultural understandings. In other words, the centrality of orgasm in conception shapes the subjects as sexually connected, continuing the narrative of romance and "natural" reproduction. The cultural narrative of orgasm, as it moves into the lesbian-insemination script, holds the potential to construct its own object and subjects.

Returning to the hybridity of insemination practices, Diane stated, "It was a nice process. [The donor and his partner] came over, they produced. And my other friend, she's obviously a doctor, came over and handed it to me. Then I went and put it in using a needleless syringe. The four of us went out to dinner. You know [small laugh], it was really nice." In Diane's insemination story, the intermediary physician ensured that legal risks were "managed." Diane was not only aware of California law (i.e., a known semen donor is considered the father of the child except "where sperm is provided to a licensed physician and surgeon for purposes of insemination in a woman not his wife"), but she actively negotiated its parameters. The presence of the "professional" actor in an otherwise nonprofessional setting exemplified pragmatic negotiations of low-tech and high-tech in an effort to guarantee legality, manage potential legal risks, and negotiate stratification issues.

Diane described the cycle in which she conceived.

> Our friends were there for my art exhibit at my home. It was the time, so we had to take a break and inseminate [laugh]. We had a ceremony around it. People were still here looking at the paintings. He [the semen donor] was about to leave, so he donated. Somebody was watching the people downstairs. [My partner's] family was here, her whole family. We were getting ready to put on barbecue. My friend pretended that I was really tired and needed to go lie down for a while. So I was lying in the bedroom and [my partner] put it [the semen] in with a 3 cc syringe without the needle on it. And she left. And then she went into the kitchen and saw her sister-in-laws; both have young children and were breastfeeding at the time. She told them about the insemination and they both started doing this dance in the kitchen. They called it a fertility dance. Then they came into the bedroom and they danced for me. And they squirted milk on me for good luck. It was pretty funny!

Such playfulness appears in many stories of early insemination. It is also characteristic of at-home inseminations and exemplifies an alternative, de-medicalized script. Yet, despite intentions to maintain such ease, lesbian conception is often marked by chaos associated with timing and scheduling. In Diane's narrative, for example, coordinating the donor's presence was not difficult for that particular cycle, as he was there to view her open-studio exhibit, but the concomitant presence of family, friends, and strangers necessitated some strategic maneuvering.

The women I interviewed demonstrated the construction of hybrid-technology practices through their material practices and the meanings they applied to them. It was not only the devices used, but also the confluence of emotions, bodies, and technologies that participated in shaping the meanings of material practices that signaled a hybrid practice. Although the degree and form of emotional experience varied, all participants described a roller coaster of emotions driven by the cyclical excitement of insemination and the disappointment of menstruation. Diane concluded a story of insemination by stating, "And then I didn't get pregnant! I found that to be very devastating and I got pretty depressed. So we stopped for a few months." Aside from the one woman who got pregnant on her first insemination and the two women who had not yet inseminated, all thirty-three of the other respondents described similarly intense emotional ups and downs.

Raquel described the cyclical waiting time and how anxiety producing it was.

> I would just wait. The waiting is the most irritating part of the process. Each month we would go through a similar cycle. It was hard not to be excited. We would just grit our teeth and wait. And then she would get her period! It was awful! We would still be testing her temperature. We knew it had dropped drastically—that doesn't necessarily mean that she's about to get her period, but boom, within twenty-four hours, she would get her period. We'd be really bummed out. And then we would have to immediately call [the sperm bank] and tell them you got your period and when you expect you will pick up [sperm] next month. It was very hard and very difficult to just bounce right back from this crash and say, "Okay, next try!" I think it's hard for everybody.

Emotional ups and down on their own do not exemplify hybrid-technology trajectories, but they are a central aspect of achieving pregnancy and often instigate additional actions. Diane's emotions, for example, led her to seek additional knowledge sources: "I started going to an acupuncturist. That helped me in terms of calming me and working a little bit on my fertility, which really is the issue. I hadn't had any problem with that, but it was really emotional." The new forms of action included drawing on additional technologies, knowledge, and changes in practice driven by the emotional contours of not getting pregnant.

June described her first-step insemination as marked by scheduling difficulties, charged emotions, and the process of amassing complex knowledges about thawing semen, performing inseminations, and using syringes. Performing insemination for her involved both low-tech and high-tech procedures.

> Twenty-four hours later [after ovulation detection], we were inseminating at home. There was a lot of running around, back and forth to the [doctor] and to the [sperm bank] to pick up the sperm. Sometimes we had to go to the store to get dry ice. There was so much craziness that went along with that. [We used] a needleless syringe. And just bringing the little vials home and warming them up and trying to make it as cozy an experience as possible was a lot of work. I think we moved into the bedroom [laugh] . . . and played music. I think we tried to elevate my butt, I wouldn't stand on my head [laugh]. I tried to do some things to encourage gravity to help us out. So all that running about and doing it at home lasted just a couple of months.

In describing her and Raquel's practice as "work," June clearly pointed to the intentional and complicated actions necessary to perform inseminations. Her use of the terms "cozy," "bedroom," and "music" reflected their attempts to displace the medical and technical aspects of getting pregnant and to insert romance and the comforts of home. Like other respondents, June and Raquel eventually altered their insemination practices to maximize their chances of conception.

Marie's story captured the shift from at-home to clinical conceptions that characterized many narratives.

> When it was at home it was nicer. It was more romantic and we were so excited about it. There were times when we'd have lots of difficulties, especially when we were going away for the weekend. But we would pack up the cooler in the car and we'd cover it over with other things. It was actually fun! Once we went to her parents and we were afraid they would not be supportive of our efforts, so we sort of snuck around there. It had this element of excitement in that it was forbidden or semi-forbidden. There was romance and thrill involved. But, after a while, it wasn't so romantic anymore. I was just feeling so depressed about it not working. And it was sad to give all of the excitement up and go to the office procedure. Once we did, it became a medical procedure instead of just us, two people trying to get pregnant and to share our love by creating another being. But, over time, we found ways to mix it up and bring some of our excitement back into the process.

Marie's description infused at-home inseminations with a "good old days" feel. The at-home insemination, for Marie and many others, was perceived as a shared and intimate practice and was important to many of the participants for its distance from advanced, assisted-reproduction technologies. Yet it was also clear that at-home insemination was no longer the simple, do-it-yourself procedure of the 1970s feminist health movements. It had undergone significant changes in terms of where, how, and at what cost sperm was accessed and in terms of the devices and information sources gathered to perform inseminations.

Users negotiate, shape, and give meaning to insemination practices in ways that make sense for them and meet their own needs. Meanings of technologies are flexible and subject to interpretation (Bijker 1987). For example, IUI is not regarded by fertility clinicians as an advanced reproductive technology. Although IUI is relatively easy to use, biomedical experts maintain jurisdiction over the technique by asserting that it requires some medical training (i.e., the ability to thread a catheter through the os into the uterus). Therefore recommended for use only in clinical offices, IUI insemination demarcates the home from office-based practices.[15] Nonetheless, participants in this research often regarded IUI as a practice amenable to negotiation. That is, some perceived it to be a high-tech procedure, while others considered it a simple device that should and could be performed at home.

Heather and her partner, Judith, as well as three other participants, used IUI methods at home, which indicated that women were drawing on biomedical knowledge and techniques, but taking them into their own hands for their own purposes. Heather, a hospital nurse, discussed her and her partner's insemination.

> I'm starting to take issue with the sperm bank we're using right now. Apparently we're the first couple in this practice to do IUI at home. The actual process is really easy: it's learning how to use a speculum that can be kind of tricky, how to find the os, and then getting the catheter in there. You do have to be careful. Then you have to use sperm that has been specially processed, spun down to just 1 cc volume because the uterus apparently only holds .8, .9 cc's. You would never guess it. All this seminal fluid has to be washed off because it contains prostaglandin, which causes uterine contractions. It can also cause really uncomfortable cramping that, apparently, in some cases can lead to anaphylaxis. Anyway, it isn't that difficult to do this if you learn how.

Although IUI is medically regarded as an advanced technology, Heather felt that it was a method one could use at home after some training, that it was relatively "easy" despite its technical requirements. Heather explained her understanding of the "scientific" reasons behind the suggested office-based use of this technology as well as the biomedical organizational constraints involved in her and her partner's decision to use IUI at home: "This whole intrauterine insemination thing has really been treated like a procedure. I had it done twice in the office, to the tune of something like a hundred and eighty dollars. The whole thing takes five minutes. In my case, we're not afraid of syringes and catheters. We know where all the little holes go. I don't have a tipped uterus in any direction. Of course, it helps that we are nurses. IUI was also really easy for me, for my body that is. I didn't have any big cramping. I didn't have any big allergic reactions. It was easy to get into my cervix and I didn't have any reactions. It was no big deal."

As nurses, Heather and Judith have a familiar, everyday connection with medical technologies, have experience using these technologies, and have been trained to think of bodies as objects. For those without such training, such a technique would not be possible or imaginable. Heather admitted the need for some knowledge and training to perform IUI, but she also demonstrated that the meaning of a technology is interpretable. While IUI is often understood as an advanced, albeit relatively easy-to-use technique, it can also and has been understood as a teachable technique that can be performed at home by lay social actors.

Heather's conception practices, similar to those of other participants, included elements of advanced and simple procedures in different combinations and for different reasons. Offering another example of hybrid-technology practices and the interpretable meaning and negotiation of insemination practices, Shari described the education and training she received at a sperm bank: "At one of the intake visits, a nurse sat with me for a long time and instructed me on how you use all the equipment available. She told me to chart my ovulation, but that what really matters is that I buy the [ovulation-prediction] test kits, which I did. Then she told me that I should just follow the directions included in the package when I pick up the sperm after I ovulate. I looked at the materials, but it was ridiculous. I mean you just draw the sperm up and squirt it in, right? It's not a big deal." In this case, a sperm-bank professional (health educator, nurse, or physician) provided training in ovulation prediction via the basal-body-temperature thermometer and chart; in ovulation detection using medical-detection kits; in insemination using a speculum and flashlight for accurate placement of the semen near the cervix; and in achieving optimal semen delivery by using a 3–5 ml needleless syringe. Professional "expertise" thus entered realms previously regarded as low-tech, thereby extending professional jurisdiction and control over these procedures.

Many of the participants in this research were told by their providers to consider procedures more advanced than IUI (e.g., hormone therapies, IVF) as possible "next steps" to getting pregnant. Many women turned to such methods to meet their goals whether they became pregnant or not. As Marie's story made clear, the use of advanced reproductive technologies introduced more scheduling difficulties and a variety of additional social actors, but the actors themselves continued to negotiate and shape the meanings of those technologies.

> We would have to bring the sperm to his office beforehand. We'd make two trips to San Francisco, which made me even crazier around the insemination. We would go in the day after the [ovulation-detection] test was positive; the doctor did an ultrasound to see if there were eggs and if they were ready. That was kind of exciting because he showed us on the screen. At that point, I decided that I needed my partner with me every time. I had gone twice to the other doctor by myself. It felt really sad. It wasn't supposed to be just me doing this medical thing. Ultrasound felt really medical, a big deal. We would then go together to the office for the insemination. The doctor would do the ultrasound and show us. It was an exciting part. Then he would just put the sperm in with one of those long intrauterine syringes, and she would hold my hand. Now I say, "She got me pregnant by holding my hand." At least we were connected at the time. And we did it three times that way and the third time I got pregnant. It's a good thing, too, because we were running out of money. It had become a six-hundred-dollars-a-month operation. Not to mention the time lost, not lost, but having to switch everything around at work and take sick leave.

In Marie's experience culture collided with science. She associated intimacy with conception, assigning agency to her partner's hand holding, yet she experienced IUI as a "medical thing," as sad, as generating a sense of being alone and powerless. In the end, her conception experience was a fluid process that changed shape and setting.

Dana similarly described insemination as a medical procedure. Her conception efforts also took place over a long period of time and included two years of inseminating. Her trajectory changed shape, moving from home to a clinical setting in which IUI methods were used, and the two years were marked by emotional ups and downs.

> I did eleven tries over a two-year period. It was really hard. I would have to take days off work to lay there with my pelvis in the air. I got that special procedure. What's it called when they put the sperm directly inside? IUI? It took a really long time and was difficult and *really* painful. Toward the end I was crying and saying, "Please, just get it in and let's get out." . . . At the end, I did two rounds of fertility drugs, Pergonal and I don't remember the other drug's name. I went to [a specialist] for a couple of tries. I have polycystic ovaries, which probably didn't help things too much, probably not at all. So, the first time they gave me a full dose of fertility drugs. I grew like twenty-four eggs. They stopped counting around twenty-four and they said, "We can't use this cycle." So I did another cycle. The second time there were two really good eggs so I used that one [cycle]. It was really weird, I got my period really soon, about eleven days after I should have ovulated. I thought, I wondered [if the insemination was done at the wrong time] . . . because I found out later that you can ovulate earlier, before the twenty-four hours after the LH surge. If you take the shot and then you inseminate twenty-four hours later you've missed it. And [the eggs] were so big by then that I could have ovulated before then. I was so upset at that point, I just gave up.

Dana experienced fertility difficulties, and her experience with advanced conception was emotionally difficult. This mirrored what was true for many other participants: when pregnancy did not occur quickly, the process became fraught with intense emotions, led to the use of additional technologies, and took new forms. The contours of this trajectory may be similar to any woman with fertility difficulties.

Shari also struggled with the process: "I was lying there. And afterwards, [my partner] came around and was touching me. I kind of reacted badly to it. I thought she wanted to be sexual. I was not sexual right then. We sort of had a big issue about that. I realize that she wanted to be part of it, to feel connected to it. And it felt just *so clinical* to me. It was difficult." Shari and her partner, Robyn, described the "clinical insemination" as at once exciting and cool, as well as difficult and emotional.

> *Robyn:* I got to push the plunger. So that was pretty cool . . .
> *Shari:* It's just like going to a pap smear or something. You get into the

stirrups. And then she puts a speculum in and they find the uterus and the opening. Then they use this thing, they call it a catheter, but it looks almost like a little long straw. And they put it up inside there and once they get it in place, they just push it in. And then they leave the room . . .

Robyn: They take the catheter out. And then the speculum was removed. . . . And they put the center of the table up, so she's kind of leaning back.

Shari: With my hips in the air.

Robyn: Yeah, her hips are up and she's kind of, like, leaning back. And they leave the room. They say, "Take your time, you can stay a while." Then we stay for fifteen minutes and whatever and try to feel close. They say it's mostly psychological. Anyway, they say you don't really have to do that because it's going right into the uterus and so it's pretty direct.

Despite its clinical setting, this clinical procedure took on some low-tech characteristics; strategies to include intimacies and partner participation are more typical of low-tech, at-home inseminations. Despite aspects of cross-over, the clinical experience is marked by emotional difficulties, embodied experiences of being prodded and poked, and the discomforts of medical spaces.

Tina and Elizabeth also described moving from at-home to clinical inseminations, in their case following a surgical procedure to flush Elizabeth's fallopian tubes. Tina began, "I remember trying it at home. The first few times it was fun. Like, 'Oh, isn't this exciting.' And it was sort of a big romantic moment. It was just playful. And then, as time went on and the difficulties started, it lost the fun. It really became a stressful thing. All this other stuff started bothering me. And then it became a lot more pressured. It was also the logistics of leaving my office and going to get my cooler to pick up the stuff, take it home on the train. Then I had a haunting feeling. I was spending a lot of money and not knowing if this is going to work. I worried about having any more surgery. So then I started getting depressed." Elizabeth entered the interview, saying,

In order to be able to use the reproductive services, you have to have the whole health check by your O.B. So, I've done that. I explained to her what was going on. I got the whole health check. We checked our ovulation and we called whenever it was the right time. We would tell them the donor number and ask them to get it ready. Then we made the appointment for IUI. We met with the nurse. She was great! She chatted with us about all these different things. It doesn't take very long. She said, "There'll be a twinge and it'll feel like a pap smear" and "Oh dear, you have a tiny uterus. Just a minute, let me back out. I'll try again." And then she said, "The proverbial psychological tilt: put your legs up. It doesn't do anything, but everybody wants to do it. So go ahead." [Laugh.] Logistically speaking, it was not always all that easy to get two appointments in a row at the times that they had. Essentially you just say, "Okay, those two days are shot." Sometimes Tina had to take the day off. It was the time that we ended up getting pregnant. It was funny. We always say, "This kid is just going to have a hectic life!" [Tina] had to take the day off because I had a meeting in Napa. And she drove with me to the meeting. She brought a book and waited outside. And, at a certain point in the meeting, I said, "I just have to go." And we had to fly from Napa all the way up to the city for the insemination. But I got pregnant.

For Tina and Elizabeth several obstacles required active negotiations, from the most routine (scheduling) to the most extraordinary (surgery). At the end of the interview, Tina added, "The real reason I was there was so we could drive in the car pool lane. [Laugh]. It was that tight!" While scheduling may seem mundane, it was among many complexities that required negotiation along the path to getting pregnant.

Understanding Hybrid-Technology Practices

Hybrid-technology practices work through lesbian users' appreciation and exploitation of the actual low-techness of advanced devices and procedures, as well as taking advantage of the sophistication of simple procedures. For example, while vaginal insemination is frequently regarded as the most simple, low-tech procedure, it requires refined knowledges about ovulation, fertilization, and techniques of insemination. Furthermore, it can require complicated drug regimens and an array of technical devices (e.g., sonograms). Similarly, procedures that are generally regarded as advanced and therefore placed within the jurisdiction of biomedicine often include routine procedures or take low-tech forms. Such procedures can take place outside clinical settings, be used by lay social actors, and incorporate fairly simple technologies. Among the women I interviewed, this was exemplified by the emergent at-home use of IUI technology by non-fertility experts, although the women who did so had medical or nursing training in other fields.

Close interactions among emotions, bodies, and technologies exist and shape trajectories of achieving pregnancy among lesbians; this intertwining occurs at all points along the way. Many respondents characterized their trajectories as "an emotional roller coaster," and many attended support groups, therapy groups, or individual therapy to help them weather the ups and downs. Achieving pregnancy often entailed unexpected social pressures that required negotiation, and some women described feelings of isolation and relationship difficulties.

These practices raise questions regarding the parameters and sources of social change. It may be that the construction of hybrid-technology experiences by lesbians in their attempts to achieve pregnancy will be consequential for infertility practice in general. While lesbians create women-centered assisted-conception experiences that borrow from biomedicine, they do not rely solely on biomedical settings, professionals, knowledges, or interpretations of why procedures work. They are thus enacting new possibilities for all infertility actors.

As they predicted ovulation and performed insemination, lesbian participants negotiated conception with eyes wide open. As healthcare consumers, they maneuvered through biomedical landscapes with intentionality and deliberation. Their practices were marked by complexities, multiple knowledge sources, and stratification along economic lines. Their practices were also marked by pragmatic approaches to issues of power that encompassed both resistance and accommodation. Technologies are rarely applied to women's bodies without the women's knowledge or participation; indeed, they are often taken into a woman's own hands. "Technologies of the self" permit individuals to self-effect operations on their bodies, minds, and ways of being. They may do so in ways that are transforming, allowing them to attain certain states of "happiness, purity, wisdom, perfection, or immortality" (Foucault 1988b, 18). Social practices of assisted reproduction are theorized throughout this book as having controlling *and* transforming potential.

Bodily cultural practices, such as reproduction, enact a means through which negotiations and resistances to processes of normalization can take place. While my study of lesbian reproductive practices reports few instances of active resistance, it does illustrate the subtle ways women negotiate biomedicalization to meet their own goals by interacting pragmatically with the shifting control loci of fertility and infertility services.

Five

Going High-Tech:
Infertility Expertise and Lesbian
Reproductive Practices

LYNDA IS AN OBSTETRICS and gynecological physician and researcher at a prestigious northern California medical center. She identified as white and was thirty-eight years old when we met to discuss her attempts to get pregnant. When I walked into her office, the first things I noticed were several photographs of an infant. I asked, "Is this your child?" She told me his name was Max and that he was six months old. Smiling, she said, "I was the gestational mom. I carried Max. But it was my partner Elsie's embryo. She is the genetic mom. . . . When we started, we were thinking, 'God wouldn't that be terrific if we could do that!' And then it turned out that our doctors actually recommended that we do it that way, and it worked."

Lynda and Elsie had always known that they wanted to have children together. When they began trying to get pregnant, they were very optimistic. Lynda described their feelings:

> We didn't care too much who the gestational mom would be. We were both fine with carrying a baby, but we didn't feel we absolutely had to do so to be complete in our lives. We started with Elsie because she was a year older than I am. We were both reasonably young when we started [Lynda was thirty-three, Elsie thirty-four], and we thought, "Oh, great! We have two completely healthy female reproductive tracts. We have unlimited sperm. This should be a piece of cake." . . . But then we ended up with problem after problem after problem. . . . After a few months, I started trying to get pregnant and then we

tried with Elsie again and for a while we would rotate each month. It took four-and-a-half years and several IVF cycles to finally have Max.

Lynda and Elsie are not alone. While the strategy they adopted was unique, their experiences echoed that of many women I interviewed who had turned to advanced technologies to achieve the goal of pregnancy. Lesbians negotiate power relations in many ways, and their pathways to pregnancy are variable and complex. The best-laid plans do not always come to fruition. This chapter therefore enters the world of infertility treatment and lesbians' experiences as consumers of highly biomedicalized assisted-reproduction interventions.

In recent decades, the world of assisted reproduction has become increasingly specialized and technological. Even in this context, women negotiate biomedical interactions to shape their conception experiences. In the biomedical territory traversed by the women I interviewed, I highlight the ways many draw "lines in the sand" (Blumer 1958) — construct boundaries that they will and will not cross, and the ways they then negotiate these lines. I ask: how exactly are specialized knowledges in the realm of assisted reproduction transforming lesbian reproductive practices? How can one understand assisted reproduction's capacity to regulate private and public life (see Foucault 1991)?

Infertility, as a specialized knowledge, labels bodily states, behaviors, and desires in its own terms and places them under the regulation and control of experts for "cure" and/or "normalization." Those who do not fit within normalized categories are ready targets for the intervention of expert knowledge, as was true for the so-called barren women who became objects of early-twentieth-century scientific and medical discourse as a result of their "deviations" from normal reproductive women.

The concept of normative social regulations is central to Foucault's formulation of discipline and frames a key research question: who are the normative users of biomedical fertility and infertility services? Biomedicine and the application of biomedical knowledges are key sites in the regulation of sexuality and reproduction. Assisted reproduction and its associated discourses shape both dominant understandings of social life and people's subjective understanding of who they are as sexual beings. What "counts" as appropriate sexuality? Who is included in reproductive "appropriateness"? Who is constructed as the "normative" consumer of medical technologies?[1] Human actors are constituted by and negotiate dominant regulatory ideals.

Normalization processes occur within infertility medicine in several ways: by classifying the normative infertility-service user as heterosexual; by constructing "normal" treatment options; and by applying a standard technological trajectory or protocol of care. These processes, in turn, privilege heterosexuality, the biological family, and specific notions of gender and sexuality. For example, infertility medicine results in normalization when it constructs a standard trajectory by defining infertility as a failure to conceive after twelve months of unprotected heterosexual sex. This definition leads at best to a step-by-step trajectory in which technologies are added one at a time, increasing the degree of intervention each time, and, at worst, to a bobsled ride directly into "high-tech" infertility services. Lesbians become patients who move from technology to technology, progressing up the ladder of care from low-tech to high-tech. Even IUI requires frozen technosperm, but getting pregnant with frozen sperm is not the same, nor does it hold the same "success rate," as getting pregnant with fresh sperm. Furthermore, only a limited amount of frozen sperm can be used, which is not the case with fresh sperm. As a result, assisted insemination inherently holds decreased likelihood of success, and, as a result, requires more precise timing and technique to maximize effectiveness.

For the lesbians I interviewed, a standard and ideal trajectory toward pregnancy may have existed discursively, but not in actual practice; their paths were marked by frequent and pragmatic negotiations (Lock and Kaufert 1998). I outline a basic social process of achieving pregnancy within clinical biomedicine: a highly negotiated and revisional set of starting points (the recommended first course of "treatment"), decision points (when new protocols are suggested), and stopping points (when women elect to stop treatment). This basic social process reveals the ways biomedical classification, probabilities, and norms shape pregnancy-achievement practices, as well as the ways the practices and meanings of "patients" interact with these structural processes. Highlighting such things as the visible points of change—places where women "move the line in the sand"—I uncover the diverse meanings women attach to their conception practices and the place of emotions and embodiment in these practices, in order to demonstrate both the complexity and the cobbling of agency and the objectification of clinical biomedical encounters.

In a 1996 examination of the "routine" procedures used in infertility clinics (e.g., pelvic exam, ultrasound, diagnostic surgery, and the manipulation of gametes and embryos in the lab), Charis Cussins finds that (heterosexual) infertility patients exercise agency and that, at times, agency is expressed by actively participating in one's own medical objectification. She argues that objectification and agency are co-constitutive, not distinct, social processes. Women undergoing IVF in her research objectify their own infertility so that they may move through medical diagnoses and treatments in a way that brings about desired changes in social identity: as pregnant or as mother. In Cussins's research, objectification of the body occurs at several sites (medical operationalization, naturalization of the patient, bureaucratization of the patient, and epistemic disciplining of the patient as subject), but within each of these there also exists an associated form of agency (Cussins 1996). She asserts that a coordinated action, or choreography, occurs to bring about a long-range self.

Cussins's emphasis on choreography illustrates the negotiations lesbians employ as they seek pregnancies, as I will explore by looking at insemination practices located firmly within an infertility delivery system.[2]

The Escalation of Medical Interventions

Lynda and Elsie clearly coordinated their actions to bring about an identity change to mothers. During the two hours we spent together, Lynda described the intense escalation of medical intervention they experienced over the years: "We progressed through cervical-cap inseminations with no ovarian stimulation to Clomid with intrauterine insemination to Pergonal or FSH injectibles with either cervical cap or intrauterine insemination and eventually to IVF." At each point they were faced with a new set of decisions. Lynda described the years of trying as emotionally daunting.

> It's so devastating. It was very draining. We put pretty much everything else on hold. We worked like crazy. We couldn't travel much because we almost always needed to be here for some kind of procedure. It was just an incredibly stressful, difficult time. We just persevered because we really, really wanted it to happen. . . . Cycle after cycle we just kept going. It even got to the point where we really didn't have hope, we just couldn't afford to think, "Maybe it'll work this time." . . . And the feelings were made worse by the drugs. One of the big problems you also have once you start doing hormonal manipulation is that

your body is just raging with all sorts of stuff. So your responses aren't really your baseline response. And everything's quite exaggerated. You're overly happy and you're overly sad and you're overly tearful. And everything is just magnified. Your body feels different: your breasts are bigger and heavier. And you have water retention. You're just different, and you're not sure how much is you and how much is the hormones. The first time I had a Clomid cycle, I was just depressed. I spent like a week feeling upset. I didn't have that much energy. I was just totally blah. I just thought life absolutely stinks. It was just awful. Elsie was just at her wit's end. . . . And, it's expensive. We put out thousands—tens of thousands—of dollars for this stuff. So when it didn't work, it's not only emotionally devastating, but financially you're just thinking, "Okay, I've got these limited resources and I just can't go anymore." So you're always wondering when to stop.

Lynda's description illustrates a coordinated action taken with the explicit purpose of attaining pregnancy and motherhood. She and Elsie put things on hold, "worked at" becoming pregnant, and persevered to reach their goal despite financial and bodily difficulties. The couple's questions about when to stop led them to an IVF specialist. A friend who worked with a reproductive-endocrinology group volunteered to look at their charts and recommended they try IVF using Elsie's eggs and Lynda's uterus. This, they believed, might help them bypass the fertility difficulties they were experiencing. Another specialist, however, recommended that even though the numbers did not look good that Elsie should try at least one cycle of IVF. The decision to progress to IVF involved both financial and personal consideration on their part. Until that point, most of the expenses beyond the cost of the sperm itself had been paid by Lynda's health insurance. IVF, however, would not be covered under her plan at all. Luckily, they had friends in the medical field who were able to provide "some favors and some things were made easier for us." Emotionally, however, moving to IVF was scary.

Over the previous three years they had always found some reassurance and comfort in the fact that there was always something else to try, that IVF could be used if they were unable to get pregnant using other techniques. Once invested in the goal to achieve pregnancy, Elsie was devastated by not being able to conceive and carry a pregnancy to term. Many lesbians I interviewed felt similarly: while they started along the path to pregnancy with an understanding of multiple outcomes, somewhere along the way their drive and desire for a child grew stronger.

Elsie and Lynda never fully expected they would try (and pay for) five cycles of IVF. In the first cycle they used Elsie's eggs and uterus, but performed the conception outside her body. After consulting additional fertility experts, the couple decided that Elsie would harvest her eggs, and the fertilized embryos would be implanted in Lynda's uterus. On Lynda's fourth try—the couple's fifth IVF attempt—Lynda became pregnant with their child, who would be the legal, biological child of Elsie and the gestational child of Lynda. Lynda bore Max, a healthy baby boy, some nine months later.

Reflecting Cussins's finding, Lynda told me that she would advise other lesbians who are trying to get pregnant to be aggressive and proactive: "Because of the problem in identifying infertility in lesbians, you really need to be aggressive. Also, most of our friends are older when they start to have kids, so again, you have to be pretty aggressive. People often go into it saying, 'You know, I don't want drugs. And I don't want this. And I don't want that.' And that's really fine as long as you realize that the trade-off is you may not have a kid. So you really have to be realistic about what you would like and what the reality is of how to get there. So those are kind of the big things." Identifying infertility in lesbians is a problem because the medical classification is defined in heterosexual terms. The definition could be extended to lesbians by referring to twelve cycles of intravaginal insemination rather than twelve months of unprotected heterosex, but this shift has not taken place. Instead, either lesbians are immediately routed toward infertility medicine due to the obvious absence of sperm, or their pregnancy attempts take place outside of biomedicine. In many ways, the starting place of lesbians' trajectories depend on what they think and feel about biomedicine, advanced technology, and natural reproduction, as well as what they know about women's health movements and their connections with alternative insemination. Of course, in the United States, access to healthcare and health-insurance coverage can factor even more decisively into decision making.

Lynda and Elsie's practices were inherently pragmatic actions used to strengthen existing personal strategies and make statements about who they were as persons. As medical professionals, they were aggressive yet compliant in the face of expertise offered by other medical professionals. They followed the recommendations of their doctors, believing that these were the most efficient and effective. The objective of getting-to-pregnant drove their decision making and proved more powerful than any impulse to resist or accommodate biomedicalization tendencies. Their maneuvers were ways to minimize risks to achieving pregnancy, even if such maneuvering resulted in objectification. Lynda said, "We usually went with whatever the protocols were for the doctors we had. We agreed to each next step. We tried to use as little sperm as we could, just because we bought twenty vials from the guy we decided to use. And [we] wanted to spread it out and hopefully have more than one kid with it. So we wanted to be as sparing as we could. Be prudent, but sparing."

In what ways are agency and objectification simultaneously present? In what ways and under what conditions do these users negotiate biomedical encounters?[3] Answering these questions became most possible when I looked at routine decision-making points. In analyzing starting, revision, and stopping points, I paid attention to what the women I interviewed said they would do in a given interaction and what they actually did.

Negotiations between agency and objectification were most clearly visible in clinical encounters — especially at junctures where decisions had to be made to begin, alter, or stop a clinical practice. As Lynda explained, agency could mean both acting aggressively and going along passively with standards of care; there may be times when women choose or would be willing to experience objectification of their bodies in order to achieve their goals. The division between object and subject is not clearly bound; instead, negotiations take place.

Women construct emergent and fluid biomedical trajectories. They maneuver the biomedical trajectory in ways that mimic, borrow, and supplant normalization tendencies. The forces of biomedicalization can thus be furthered, resisted, and ignored in various ways as actors respond to their constraints and make their own pragmatic adjustments to what is desired or demanded by the rules governing the institutions and contexts in which they act (Lock and Gordon 1988; Clarke et al. 2003).

Constructing a Standard Technological Trajectory

Biomedical trajectories include a host of conditions that shape or determine starting points, decision points, and stopping points. These are constrained and enabled by cultural capital. As Lynda asserted, "Money was not a deterrent. When it got right down to it this was more important than anything in our lives. So we weren't going to go absolutely broke, but I was moonlighting like crazy to be able to pay for reproductive technology. And Elsie's mother died so we had a little bit of money from that." Although biomedical trajectories are structured in specific ways (i.e., by medical protocols and standards of care), they are fluid in their enactment. Women negotiate trajectories to meet their own needs, variously interpreting the complex interactions among bodies, technologies, and emotions that emerge throughout biomedicalized conception experiences. There is no single pathway to conception; there are no uniform starting points. Instead, there are heterogeneous beginnings and multiple decision points as women navigate and make meaning of their clinical conception practices.

Although most of the women I interviewed had originally envisioned an ideal trajectory of achieving pregnancy — track ovulation, perform home insemination, seek fertility expertise and apply advanced technologies only if necessary, become pregnant — in practice their pathways varied greatly, influenced by economic, political, and institutional power, and other social interactions. Many did follow the ideal model, but their material practices suggest that even this was highly variable in its contours and meanings.

Indeed, the initial step of performing at-home insemination appears to be slowly disappearing. Table 5 diagrams the technological trajectories taken by the respondents I interviewed. The diagram demonstrates not only the pathways to pregnancy but also the multiple decision points that arose along the way. Of the thirty-six respondents I interviewed, twenty-eight had embarked on trying to get pregnant themselves, six were partners, and two, Chloe and Arlene, had not yet started trying to inseminate. As the diagram illustrates, eighteen lesbians started with at-home, vaginal insemination. Of these, twelve at some point decided to try IUI. Of these, eight also used some method of hormonal intervention to assist ovulation. Of these eight women, one chose IVF as the next step, three continued trying IUI, one chose to stop trying altogether, and three chose to start "achieving adoption."

While participant trajectories differed, each shared certain components: they were usually "progressive" in their development; they were always described as routine and matter-of-fact; each step made sense as a means through which to increase chances of achieving pregnancy; and each step was understood as holding out hope (see also Becker 2000b). Yet, despite having elements in common, the participants' material practices with technoscientific biomedicine did not follow a standard trajectory. That is, rather

Table 5   Respondent Technology Trajectories

FIRST METHOD	ADDITIONAL PROCEDURES		OUTCOMES*
			Pregnant
Vaginal Insemination (n=18) → n=12	Intra-Uterine Insemination → n=8	With Hormonal Assistance	2 with Vaginal 3 with IUI 5 with IUI + Hormonal Assistance
		n=1 ↓	
			Pregnant
Intra-Uterine Insemination (n=9) → n=5	Intra-Uterine Insemination With Hormonal Assistance → n=1	In-Vitro Fertilization →	4 with IUI 1 with IUI + Hormonal Assistance
			Pregnant
In-Vitro Fertilization (n=1) ——————————————→			1 with IVF

* Eight respondents were in the process of trying to get pregnant during our interviews and four had stopped their efforts.

than describe an identifiable ladder of care or intervention, a step-by-step sequence, participants described complicated, uncertain, and rarely methodical moves.

During the interviews, women were ready to discuss the moments in which they altered their planned path to pregnancy and did so with clarity. Their stories illustrate the ways in which emotional, embodied, and technological processes converge in divergent ways to uniquely structure the experiences of achieving pregnancy as a lesbian. Rachel's trajectory, for example, represented a multidirectional technological model that appeared to follow a classic ladder-of-care script: "You start out by doing the inseminations that are just intravaginal. And if that doesn't work, you progress into intrauterine insemination. And if that doesn't work you move into having the eggs removed and having the ovum implanted as well as the sperm." Rachel identified a clear and expected technological trajectory that was "progressive" and methodical. It was also void of emotional or other forms of complications. I read this description as a cultural script: a standard protocol or normal trajectory that respondents know and are able to narrate. Its significance emerges as participants describe the social practices of getting pregnant and the ways this script bends and shifts. Like other participants, Rachel used the word *you* to signal a cultural ideal of an "appropriate" user — a conventional infertility-service user who enters with some form of biophysical infertility. Many of the women I interviewed told similar stories in similar language.

As they recounted their social practices, however, it became evident that their material actions deviated from the protocol. Having described her expectations of the standard model, Rachel then said, "I never got that far. I only got to the intrauterine inseminations. And [it] went on for about nine months, not very long. . . . [I stopped] because I was so disgusted and depressed by the whole process. I would go in with great expectations and end up in despair. I think the hormonal treatments I was taking were just messing with my psyche. I just couldn't handle it. Another month lost. I was spending my savings." In a matter of moments, Rachel's description of the standard trajectory was complicated by the emotional toll of achieving pregnancy. Expectations turned to despair. Her embodied sensations with hormones contributed to these emotional ups and downs. She described a final attempt to get pregnant: "I truly, absolutely thought I was going to get pregnant. I had gotten the shot the previous day to cause me to ovulate. I went in and I had an ultrasound, I saw the egg. It was there. Ready to go. I got the shot to release the egg and I went in the next day for the IUI insemination. So I thought, 'I am psyched, this is it, we are golden, this is going to be the one.' I was also just getting to the end of my rope. Each month heaping hope onto hope; each month I came crashing down. Anyway, I had the insemination and I left. And three weeks later I got my period. And that's when I quit. I never contacted them again. That was the last straw. I couldn't take it anymore." For Rachel, the trajectory of achieving pregnancy did not follow the script she had imagined. It was instead shaped and complicated by emotions, embodied experiences, and clinical interventions. Getting pregnant did not come easily, as she and others had hoped it would.

Similarly, Kim described her trajectory as a process of discovering a series of "problems." She said, "You find out as you go along that there are things that can go wrong with your body." After two years of inseminating she stopped trying. She accepted the specialists' opinion of why "she failed to get pregnant": she was not ovulating. Kim had maximized the dosage of ovula-tion-enhancement therapies, which caused her to produce over forty eggs each cycle. She said, "Using drugs helped my body naturally grow more eggs, but it exaggerated my body's natural ability, too. I mean, I produced more eggs than is normal." In her interpretation, technology merely lent a helping hand to the natural body — an explanation that clearly illustrated the ways in which nature and culture are considered co-constitutive.

When complications emerged, the progressive, normative model collapsed and became a technoscientific, clinical trajectory. Sometimes the moves to include additional therapies were visible decision points, and sometimes they were minor incremental changes that went unnoticed. Renee described a standard insemination trajectory that was transformed as she and her provider made decisions about increasing technological involvement. Such decisions, however, were not necessarily visible turning points. Throughout my interviews, for example, women noted when they moved from insemination technologies to IVF or from not using drugs to using hormonal stimulants. However, they did not note dosage changes or additional ultrasounds. It was the more obvious and profoundly physical and emotional changes that were described during our interviews. It was in connection with these changes that interviewees discussed experiences of subjectivity and objectification. Renee explained, "You start your period and then they go five days. On the fifth day they start you on the fertility pill. You take that for five days. Then you finish it. And then five days later they have you come in for an [ultrasound] scan. They actually look at your ovaries. . . . And then he watches them until they get to a certain size. Then he gives you a shot to make you release them. And they know you'll release it within twelve to twenty-four hours. And then the day after that is when they do the IUI insemination." Renee began her narrative with a sense of subjectification and agency, referring to her own actions of taking the pills. Simultaneously, however, technoscientific interventions such as scans, hormones, and IUI insemination figured centrally. Very quickly the meanings she ascribed to these social practices came to include a sense of objectification and disembodiment: "they" were doing things to her and her body. Renee continued, "They check to make sure the follicles burst and then they do the insemination. And sometimes you do like two or three. Especially when you're on fertilities, that's why a lot of the women end up having, like, twins or triplets or whatever, because of that. I never did. And I think it was because my periods were never normal. So maybe I didn't always ovulate. They upped me pretty high on it, on the fertility pills."

The seeming invisibility of some decisions, such as hormonal dose changes, led me to ask: what conditions shaped starting points? When did women renegotiate the interventions? And under what conditions did women stop a particular trajectory or choose to stop the technoscientific trajectory altogether? How did they decide to go down certain pathways? Why did they start where they did? Was there a "natural" pathway suggested by clinicians? I found that medical classifications, probabilities, and norms structure starting points and continue to shape each phase of the trajectory.

Classification

Medical definitions assign meaning, shape protocols of care, and are used for insurance coverage. Infertility has long been the standard classification necessary to access medical fertility services. Since the definition of infertility relies on heterosexual intercourse for meaning, it privileges some points of view while silencing others, creating an order of ideal users and other users.[4] The process of classification, however, is also inherently ambiguous (Bowker and Star 1999). Infertility is no exception and allows no clear-cut, simple, or singular categorization (Becker and Nachtigall 1992). For example, the lines between reproductive capacity and incapacity, between health and disease, and between normality and deviance have always been obscure, hinging on individual reproductive choice, social circumstance, and cultural norms (Pfeffer 1993, 10). The term *infertility* itself suggests a contradictory system of classification, designating a medically and socially liminal state of capacity, health, and normality.

Nonetheless, infertility medicine uses the clinical classification in ways that place lesbians outside the realm of health and normalcy. It relies on cultural prescriptions that view reproduction as part of the natural design of the human species and of a woman's life-course. The classification of infertility asks questions of identification, and the identity category of heterosexuality functions as an optic (how, what, who gets seen) that enables and constrains one's sense of morality, conduct, and selves.[5] In this case, homosexuality is silenced, and homosexuals become the implicated actors (see also Clarke 2005; Clarke and Montini 1993) of infertility services.

Alongside sexual identification exist classifications of age, biomedical diagnoses, medical history (endometriosis, infertility), and financial capital (see Fosket 2004 for the ways these are embedded in practice). Together, these both stratify users and shape probabilities and norms used in biomedical protocols. Each category has a normative "best-chances-of-achieving-pregnancy" story linked to the range of decision points that follows. Movement is facilitated (or prevented) by efforts to maximize best chances, perceptions of increased interventions as a total gamble, and built-up lines of coordinated action.

As my interview data indicates, cultural and material factors such as financial resources, race or ethnicity, and age shape women's assisted-reproduction experiences. The most obvious factor was financial stability. With enough resources, most women negotiate "best chances." In other words, for women who can afford the technology, experiences become a series of "choices." For others who may be able to afford some but not all technologies, experiences become a series of choices contingent on resources. In many ways, financial resources symbolically stand in for parental "appropriateness." It is those with money who are constructed as legitimate users and receive institutional and cultural support. This signals the importance of cultural health capital (Shim 2006) in practices of achieving pregnancy.

For example, for Deborah the cost associated with this process was paramount; limited financial resources structured her decisions. This situation was common for most interviewees, including Michelle, whose trajectory was also determined by her financial circumstances. She described her experience as "playing the odds" and weighing her "best chances." While the suggested protocol included doing two IUI inseminations per cycle, she and her partner were only able to do one clinic-based IUI and one home-based vaginal insemination. "We started to feel it would never happen. We will never get pregnant. So we did two [vaginal] inseminations at home. After a while we started doing one IUI at the office and one [vaginal] at home. Just to up the chances, you know. I guess they recommended it. Doing two IUIs would up chances more, but the cost was too high. We charged it all. We had no cash. So that was the best we could do."

Michelle also described her age as contributing to her biomedical experience: "No [drugs], very low-tech. I was very prepared to do that because [my doctor] told me he would have a very low threshold for failure. And we would move into high-tech very fast, considering my age." June likewise stated, "As she [the doctor] heard my age, and I guess at that point I was thirty-seven, you could see [her change]. Then she went into this whole older woman rap [laugh]. And suddenly, I realized I was in this category that I hadn't [laugh] really been fully aware of before. [It's] more difficult and [they] expect it to take longer." Age was used as a means though which to categorize, stratify, and, ultimately, to structure the experiences and trajectories of achieving pregnancy. This was true not only for "older" women but also for younger women. Beatrice was thirty-one when she started trying to achieve pregnancy: "Actually, when we walked in there we were ready to do it [IUI] a lot sooner. But after talking to her, she said, 'No, no, no! The average is five to seven tries. You're young. You're probably very fertile.' So that stepped us back. 'Okay,' we said, 'we'll give it at least four tries.'" Age — in this case, her relatively young age — structured her selection of insemination as the first step. The biomedicalization of aging was closely coupled with medical categorization, as many diagnosis categories are age-related.[6] Within assisted reproduction, aging emerged as a medical problem consequential for infertility (Estes and Binney 1989; see also Joyce and Mamo 2006).

Similar to age, the starting point assigned and movements made along the technological trajectory are dependent on medical categorizations that classify people as being at increased "risk" (e.g., having endometriosis, previous miscarriages). At-risk designations also exemplify the social construction of "what counts" as low-tech and high-tech. Life experiences, including biomedical ones, shape different understandings and definitions of technologies. Health categories, such as endometriosis and age, are constructed as biomedical entities. These, in turn, structure experiences in different ways, thus rupturing dichotomies of low-tech/high-tech and natural/artificial. Despite this ambiguity, organizations that support the use of insemination technologies construct normative standards.

Some lesbians' reproductive experiences were defined by a relationship with biomedicine that began when difficulties in achieving or maintaining a pregnancy emerged. Carmen's and Angela's path was shaped by two miscarriages and by the managed-healthcare organization to which they then turned. Carmen described their experience: "We were immediately referred to the fertility clinic. All of these [procedures] took a lot longer than we expected. I thought that they would be faster. We had these ovulation-predictor kits, they worked, and I thought once the LH surge was shown we would get pregnant. But I was deemed high risk because of all of the problems I had. I had lost the two [had two miscarriages]. So that moved me into a different category. All of a sudden you get a lot more attention and more interventions."

Marilyn began IUI after receiving a diagnosis of endometriosis. She emphasized her interpretation of such clinical inseminations as low-tech by virtue of not using ovulation-stimulant hormones. "You walk in and they are ready for you. You don't even have to sit in the waiting room. They put their tiny little catheter in, it hurt maybe a tiny little bit, like a Pap smear, and it was over in less than five minutes. It was kind of cool. There was nothing to it, nothing compared to the women that have all kinds of very technical interventions and have to take a lot of drugs. I didn't even really have much in the way of testing because they already knew I had endometriosis. I had some blood work just to identify that my eggs weren't too old. They did estrogen-level testing and something else I can't remember. . . . And that's all I had done. Very low-tech." For Marilyn, endometriosis (not her social lesbianism) led to the infertility diagnosis required for advanced biomedical treatments.

Marilyn's description of her relations with medical providers and the meanings she attached to them indicated that her route to pregnancy had less to do with resisting or accommodating biomedicalization and more to do with achieving pregnancy. To meet this objective she navigated the constraints of her age and medical condition. Other participants had to also negotiate the probabilities involved in achieving pregnancy.

Negotiating Probabilities and Norms

Constructing statistical probability is a common feature of the biomedical script and is a means through which biomedicalization processes occur. At several points along the trajectory, women and their healthcare providers perform a "dance" in which they consider and weigh the odds of achieving pregnancy. This dance determines subsequent practices. In describing and understanding their own trajectories, lesbians routinely use a rhetoric of statistical science, including biomedical classifications such as age and health status. These classifications establish starting points and decision points (e.g., length of time a particular woman should use a given technology). A woman's circumstances, with their associated norms and probabilities, thus help shape her trajectory. For example, whether or not a woman began with IUI was structured by her age. Because fertility is statistically less likely, and achieving pregnancy more difficult, among women thirty-five or older, women over thirty-five are frequently advised to use IUI immediately, while those under thirty-five are advised to begin with "regular" inseminations. The number of cycles in which one uses a given technological intervention varies according to statistical probabilities that depend on other factors. However deployed, biomedical solutions seem to be an inevitable part of the sociocultural story of lesbian reproduction because the statistical probabilities associated with pregnancy success "make sense" (Porter 1995). As the women in this study demonstrate, trajectories of achieving pregnancy are shaped by the construction of "best chances" for pregnancy success.

The biomedical stories narrated by participants included an interplay among best-chances rhetoric, biomedicalization as uncertainty, and a standard technoscientific trajectory. The narratives shared cultural and biomedical space despite their variety and seemingly incongruous meanings. How can the notion of a standard trajectory share space with the reality of assisted reproduction as uncertain or a "gamble"? Several of the respondents pointed to this discrepancy. Ray, for example, described a standard trajectory that she moved along step by step. She acknowledged that although each rung up the ladder of care to a more advanced intervention was undesirable, it was also unavoidable. Ray said, "Although I was still within the average attempt, I knew I would get help soon." The phrase "average attempt" signaled the normative biomedical trajectory and illustrated that biomedical scripts were also culturally meaningful (Akrich 1992). Ray used the rhetoric of science and applied it to her cultural standard of the processes toward pregnancy, which demonstrated the power of biomedicalization and the ease with which people accepted clinical authority. Even though, according to evidence-based medicine, Ray's chances of success were diminished, her actions and hopes signaled a continued belief that she remained part of the norm.

Paula, however, complicated statistical probability with best-chances rhetoric. She also followed a standard model of technological intervention. She began with IUI, a decision that was determined by her age. Her age also created the condition under which increasing the degree of intervention was perceived as both statistically ideal and inevitable. "I did two inseminations per cycle. I just figured if I'm going to do it, I'm going to give myself all the best chance that I can. I understand percentages. It's just about averages. Somebody might have tried once [using] intrauterine and once at home. That lowers your [chances]. I figure since they showed us a little diagram and it said the best chances are with IUI, I figured, well, we're so damn close, you know? And if I'm taking the kit, the test, and it's testing positive, then I'm ovulating. Chances are pretty good. And I had full-blown medical tests before to make sure that everything is okay. . . . Then I do the IUI." Paula's description revealed a belief that technologies provide accurate information and a means to play the odds and maximize the best chances for pregnancy.

Deborah's trajectory was marked by the use of advanced technologies, and her experience was fraught with unknowns, ambiguities, and learning that "things had gone wrong." Even though she perceived biotechnology as "horrible" and "awful," she nevertheless chose this route to pregnancy as an effort to secure best chances. Deborah's practice revealed that technological best chances can and do coexist with technological uncertainty. She said, "It just seemed like I never knew what the procedure was going to be, and it was different every time. And my current doctor [said], 'There is no indication for you to be on those hormones.' My estrogen level was a little high because I am heavy. And heavy women often have higher estrogen levels. But, according to my current doctor, not high enough that I should have been on hormonal treatment. And the Clomid, the doctor assumed I wasn't ovulating regularly. And maybe I wasn't, I don't really know. Sometimes, when I was using the ovulation kit, sometimes it looked as though I was and sometimes it looked as though I wasn't. So maybe I wasn't. I don't really know that."

Similarly, Carmen described the "mystery" associated with the technological interventions: "Who knows if Clomid helped me get pregnant or not? No one knows." The juxtaposition between a routinized, methodical technological progression for increasing chances (or odds) and a mysterious, unknown, ambiguous process exemplifies the power of biomedical authority and the willingness of consumers to negotiate biomedical parameters to secure their own best chances. Participants both negotiate and accept professional knowledge. For example, although Carmen embraced technological advances and decided to do IUI with Clomid, she did not fully accept that the procedures helped her to achieve pregnancy: "I said to my doctor, 'There's got to be another way. How can we increase our odds here?' I did intrauterine ones at that time. I just went once a month, and the dot turned blue, the ovulation kit worked. . . . I did Clomid a few times. I may have only taken it for two months. And I got pregnant. Who knows if that's what triggered it and got things going. Nobody knows and nobody will. It's just one of those things. Who knows if I would've gotten pregnant at that time anyway without them?"

Janella also experienced a coupling of technological best chances with technological uncertainty. She and her partner attempted insemination without "scientific" knowledge of the procedure. "It just feels like such an unbelievable crapshoot," she said, describing her negotiation and management of "unknown" variables. This mirrored other respondents who described a form of "playing the averages" that was structured by emotions, embodied sensations, and other factors, such as finances. Janella said,

> We just couldn't believe it didn't work. We talked to them again. And they said, "Look, you know it's frozen. And there's an average. It takes nine months on average. You just got to keep trying it." They said we should try it a few times and change something. Change one of the factors. Then try a couple of times, and if it's not working, change another thing. So we also thought, "Well, it's cheaper probably to do IUI in the long run, rather than going month to month to month like this." Once it became so medical, we thought, "Whatever," we just wanted to put an end to this whole waiting thing and give it another chance. So that's why we decided to do IUI and we tried four times and then, the last time we tried with Clomid, too, because we had done three without success and they said to change something. So we did Clomid. We [didn't] want it to be drugs. And then you realize that you have this frozen sperm. It's so lame. You know what I mean? And then, it's also they give you half the amount than the normal dose. So the odds just aren't good. You just need to give it a boost. We were like, "God! We tried three different people so we knew it wasn't that all of them weren't fertile." So we went along and made changes as things didn't work.

Janella managed all the variables and permutations that came her way. She played the averages according to given certain statistics (e.g., the nine-months average).

Technological certainty, therefore, is disrupted by agency, and biomedicalization is not the tsunami it appears to be. Women negotiate biomedical trajectories in ways that increase their odds of achieving pregnancy and meet their desired goals. But they also do so in ways that accept the ambiguities of lived bodies and that thus do not fully "buy in" to the biomedical script. The language of biomedicine and infertility that women negotiate includes both uncertainty and probability. The navigation of agency and objectification is also clearly highlighted by the complex ways women approach decision points to start, alter, or stop an intervention.

Moving Lines in the Sand

As the women I interviewed proceeded toward potential pregnancies, many visible decision points revealed the ways that they managed particular parameters of the technoscientific trajectory to fit their unique goals and needs. The most visible occurred when a seemingly normalized script or technology was not followed and/or when a "leap" from one technology to another took place. In addition to constructing stopping points or drawing lines in the sand, women redrew certain lines, which made negotiations evident. In general, I found that women's perceptions of high-tech and low-tech, natural and unnatural, reason and unreason shaped their practices, and that these discourses were cultural discourses.

Raquel articulated how she and other women selected, revised, and maneuvered through these complicated processes in ways they could not have anticipated. They were enterprising in their actions.

> It's interesting, because at the beginning we decided we wanted no drugs. And then we found out she had polycystic ovaries. And it was like the worst thing in the world. And after a week or so we thought, "Okay, we could do with some drugs." So we did the "Clomid challenge" which was supposed to be for three months. And we knew at the time that we didn't want to go any stronger with the medications. But it wasn't working and we were bummed. It was the worst thing in the world for a while. Then, okay, we could get a little stronger because the doctor was recommending Fertinex, which was the next thing. And that was something I had to inject her with, which I was not thrilled about at all. I'm glad I have this new skill, but. . . .

Raquel and her partner had drawn the line at using hormonal stimulants, but it wasn't long before they were using oral Clomid, then self-injecting hormones at home. Their decision to redraw the line emerged from multiple factors, including embodied sensations and emotional and structural experiences. It was also a pragmatic way to achieve their objective of pregnancy.

A close reading of the respondents' stories reveals a tension between "controlling" every step toward pregnancy and "going along for the ride." In the highly visible and conscious decision points along the trajectory, women were explicitly called on to decide whether and how to proceed. These moments included the shift from vaginal to intrauterine inseminations and the shift from inseminations to IVF or other methods that require surgical egg retrieval. The less visible (yet still apparent) moments occurred more frequently and included incremental steps such as hormone use, increased hormone dosage, the incorporation of ultrasound technology or a fertility work-up, and more advanced insemination methods. It is in such incremental steps that much of biomedicalization takes place. It is also where women must deal with biomedical labels and pathways.

The lesbians I interviewed did not always proceed through every step agentically, but instead attempted to negotiate the trajectory as needed. Gradations and complications emerged, obscuring the differences between controlling and going along with assisted reproduction. Furthermore, those who used language like "they did this" and "they did that" seemed to remove themselves, and their personal agency, from the process. They described objectifications, yet continued negotiations. Raquel's narrative illustrated that no single biomedical script shaped her pregnancy-achievement practices. The ability to remain agentic even as one's control is diminished may explain why many women seem willing to go along with professional recommendations, even if that requires that they modify their original plans.

Judith's description of the point at which her physician suggested IVF reveals how she tightly linked technologies, bodies, and emotions.

> It ended up, after fifteen tries, they did a laparoscopy [a surgical procedure and visual evaluation of the pelvic organs] and they found so many adhesions that my ovaries were wrapped in. And there was no communication between my ovaries and my fallopian tubes. They said the only way that I could get pregnant was through in vitro fertilization. So I had to think about that. And in vitro fertilization is no little jump because it's massive hormones and it's physically uncomfortable, which is something I could deal with. I could handle that fairly well. [My partner's] a great support. Emotionally you get weird because of the hormones. At this point, the desire to get pregnant is all encompassing. I am a very practical person, but I was not reasonable anymore. This was not a matter of reason, this quest for pregnancy is unreasonable, and the hormones make it and you more unreasonable.

Although Judith described her body in a personalized way, the language of modern industrialism characterized her body as a "broken" machine: the communication lines between her ovaries and fallopian tubes had failed. Characterizing IVF as "no little jump" and hormones as "physically uncomfortable," she demonstrated the embodied experiences of biomedicine and the ways they shape women's decisions. Closely linked with technological progression is the "unreason" that is literally produced by hormone treatments.

Judith explained that finances were an important factor as well: "On top of the monthly costs, the cost of IVF would be huge. . . . We're talking about thousands of dollars that we put into this, for the in vitro fertilization. And not only that, but a lot of the tries. We're talking about anywhere from three hundred to four hundred dollars a month. It's been a long time and that's a lot of money when you add it up." The shift from at-home vaginal insemination to clinical IUI visibly moved the line in the sand. Although the move between at-home insemination and IUI was fraught for the women I interviewed, it was also a step they were prepared to take once they had "unsuccessfully" sought a conception at home. Nonetheless, the at-home versus clinical distinction is not a clear one.

Sara described her decision to shift to IUI performed in a clinic setting. In a well-thought-out manner, she and her partner had chosen to begin with at-home vaginal insemination, and their move to IUI was an emotional step. It represented both an undesired medicalization and a change from personal to professional control.

> We both were taking it into our own hands rather than going in and doing it intrauterine. And even though we're really comfortable with medical stuff, I think there was something off-putting and nerve racking [about it]. There was something pretty unappealing about doing it in such a medicalized way, about doing it intrauterine. So we continued at home and we ended up doing nine cycles total. So, six with the first donor and three [with the second], which you can imagine was very expensive. And then, after much thought and discomfort, [we] decided to do it intrauterine. . . . At that point, we were definitely ready for it to work. And we were definitely over worrying about whether it was really romantic or anything. And definitely ready to try and do whatever, to up the chances. Short of chemicals. Because I didn't feel like every single month I ovulated. I would buy the kit, and I didn't really think that it was all that likely at thirty-four, when I was ovulating nine months in a row, documented every time, that it was that likely that I wasn't ovulating. So I wasn't ready to go to, like, IVF or even drugs.[7]

Once Sara decided to do IUI, she found a specialist who would be covered under her health-insurance plan. Some healthcare insurers will pay for "infertility" procedures but will not pay for semen unless male infertility is present. Thus, the cost of the procedure was covered, but Sara and her partner had to pay for semen. While not all sperm banks offer insemination services, the one they chose did. Should they use the sperm-bank providers or other medical providers? Their decision involved consideration of insurance coverage, but it also included financial rather than medical considerations. "They seem to do all these extras. Each little thing costs extra. It wasn't clear what was based on science and what was based on money. We were turned off by that." Yet Sara selected to move to IUI when she was "ready to try and do whatever to up the chances . . . short of chemicals." As she moved up the ladder, she continued to manage her decisions and actions.

Esther, too, articulated the ways in which her line in the sand moved. Although Esther began by doing at-home inseminations, which was very important for her at the time, she eventually turned to clinical inseminations and in some ways embraced the change. She described clinical procedures as providing her with control over a process that seemed uncertain. After conceiving through vaginal insemination, but miscarrying, Esther did six months of clinic-based IUI with no success. For her seventh IUI, she added the therapeutic use of Clomid. She did get pregnant again, but again she miscarried. At the time of our interview, Esther was again trying to conceive with IUI inseminations and Clomid. "I could care less what the environment is like. The means is not the issue anymore. It's the end," she said.

In reflecting on this process and her decisions to use increasingly sophisticated technologies over time, Esther described her experience as hopeful and proactive. She approached each new intervention with pragmatic agency. What had once been a line in the sand became revisional, and the technologies themselves became a source of personal empowerment and control: "I felt kind of excited. And I think one of the things that give you the sense of having some control over the situation is the technology. In many ways, I feel like I am taking action. I'm doing something to make it better, to make it work this time. So there's something actually I can do and this feels good. It makes me feel more positive."

Esther had not anticipated taking the technological route to pregnancy, but once pregnancy proved elusive, she saw accessing medical professionals and biomedicine as a means to an end. When individuals choose or require advanced technologies, medical experts play important roles in redrawing the lines. Two stories illustrate the role of medical personnel in moving the technologies in either direction. In Kaye's case, the provider was adamant that things move forward: "Well, for the first year, I just was doing vaginal inseminations at home. And it didn't work. I had yet another annual appointment with my Ob-Gyn. She basically said, 'What! Not pregnant yet? Still doing that home vaginal inseminations? What are you crazy?' She really read me the riot act and said, 'It's time for you to go IUI. I don't want to see you back here next year. If that doesn't work in four times, then I want to see you back here and we'll figure something else out.'" The Ob-Gyn believed that technologies should be stepped up to increase odds of pregnancy. Kaye followed her advice and became pregnant using IUI. In Marilyn's story, on the other hand, the provider advised a low-tech approach. Marilyn, a nurse, said, "We were prepared and knowledgeable about IUI and other more high-tech procedures. [We] saw it rationally and even wanted to move up for expediency, but we were advised that it wasn't necessary."

Renee also began with more simple procedures and progressed to advanced technologies. She, however, eventually reversed course and became pregnant via vaginal insemination at home.

> She put me on progesterone suppositories and Clomid. So, some months I had to come in for a vaginal ultrasound and some months I didn't have to. It just seemed like I never knew what the procedure was going to be, it was different every time. . . . And after I didn't get pregnant the first three times, she recommended that I go in for a hysterosalpingogram. That is where they flush this stuff through my tubes. They want to make sure your tubes are clear. And my tubes were clear. But they discovered three lumps in my uterus, three reasonably large lumps. So, she said, "Before we do any other inseminations, you have to have those lumps taken care of." At our follow-up meeting, after she'd done the surgery, she said to me, "If that's the problem, then we should go back to low tech." I didn't even ask her about intrauterine [she had done IUI before]. But she said we should go back to the low-tech kind for at least a little bit because it's silly to spend all that money and do that invasive procedure when I might be able to get pregnant without it. And I did.

Renee's healthcare provider took her health status into account and encouraged the shift "back to low-tech." A new, clean bill of health allowed Renee to return to low-tech strategies. Yet her narrative does not indicate conscious decision points; she seemed instead to merely go along with the professional's recommendations. This is quite different from more visible moves such as her move from insemination to IVF, when she actively decided to make the change. Thus, Renee's "unique" experience of returning to low-tech was in fact based on the traditional biomedical script of infertility. Overall, these stories highlight how not only women but also healthcare providers are key actors in shaping the pathways toward pregnancy.

Stopping Points

Another significant decision point is when women stop seeking to achieve pregnancy, opting out of the costs, pain, and difficulties associated with continued efforts. These women continue to desire children, but for various reasons they "choose" to or are forced to discontinue assisted reproduction.

The technological imperative in biomedicine assumes that people will continue to increase medical interventions as long as new or additional technologies are available to help them achieve their goals. But women do not always do so. Advanced technologies are more costly, carry increased health risks, require uncomfortable bodily interventions, and add complications that some deem unnecessary. Decisions to stop attempting to get pregnant, or to not move forward with more advanced technology, are webbed together with experiences that are emotionally, and at times physically, painful. Financial considerations may also be significant.

Under what conditions do women stop trying to achieve pregnancy? Among the women I interviewed a confluence of factors affected the decision, including structural and discursive contingencies and emotional and embodied experiences. Dana described what led her to end the technological interventions: "You get the scans and then go back for when they inseminate you. Then, you have to wait two weeks—the frustration of waiting and thinking you are [pregnant]. But you're not sure. And then finding out you're not, it's hard. It's really emotionally hard. And you get to the point of, 'When are we going to decide that it's not going to work and stop?' . . . You get your hopes up. And then they are sort of lost. And then there is always next month. I was so upset at that point, I just gave up . . . financially it was nine thousand to ten thousand dollars. I stopped a year ago." The point where Dana "got off" the technological trajectory was marked by frustration, high financial cost, and the difficulty of high-tech interventions. The effects of fertility drugs on her body and the emotions she experienced from month to month were simply too disruptive.

Rachel, who also decided to stop, talked about the deep frustration, emotional fluctuations, and financial burdens associated with her interactions with reproductive-health specialists and sperm banks. She recalled feeling troubled from the start: "I must say, I had a really creepy feeling about going to the sperm banks. The [specialist] was very expensive and they were all out of pocket. And there is no proof that what they are giving you is sperm. . . . I had a lot of doubts about doing the fertility drugs in the first place, because they are linked with ovarian cancer. . . . I was really afraid of taking the Clomid because I had heard of a lot of women having a lot of depression and anger." Before we concluded the interview, I asked her if she had anything else she would like to add. She sighed and said, "I still have some sperm stored up until I have a baby in my arms," which suggested not only her deep pain but also that her movement off the pregnancy trajectory might not be permanent.

Both Dana and Rachel described very emotional experiences, and their accounts were often accompanied by tears. The manner in which they told their stories reflected an underlying ambivalence. For example, Dana said, "I was not as intent on having my own baby from my own body. . . . I was more ambivalent about that . . . and I wasn't as intent as other people who do that." Rachel said, "Psychologically, my head wasn't all one hundred percent on this getting pregnant through artificial insemination." For them, the stopping point was not only marked by emotions, including ambivalence, but also shaped by the embodied experience of technical intervention. Their narratives illustrate the confluence of biomedicalization, emotions, embodiment, and financial resources that shape achievement processes.

In these stories, the cultural script of women as ideal procreators and as naturally able to achieve pregnancy shapes biomedical technological trajectories, the pathways taken, and how women understand the steps taken. Of interest here is whether lesbians who are actively pursuing pregnancy understand the technological trajectories as consistent with a "norm" that "normal" people go through, despite their own practices, which often contradict their ideal of a normative model. In other words, to what extent do their contrary experiences undermine the norm?

Lynda and her partner tried to get pregnant in alternating months following a standard technological protocol: "We progressed through cervical-cap inseminations with no ovarian stimulation to Clomid with intrauterine insemination to Pergonal or FSH injectables with either a cervical cap or intrauterine insemination and eventually to IVF." Lynda's description was matter-of-fact. The ways in which lesbians' contrary experiences undermined norms emerged when trajectories were understood as fluid, multidirectional, and complex, and not as a biomedically constructed standard, ideal trajectory. The confluence of emotions, bodies, and technologies was central to the displacement of the standard biomedical model. The interplay of these components was at work at the most visible points in the process.[8]

The various decision points, both visible and hidden, reveal the complex ways women negotiate trajectories of achieving pregnancy by moving the line in the sand and revising their original intents. Revisions do not indicate passive acceptance, but instead reflect pragmatic negotiations. Revisions further demonstrate that lines are fluid and contingent on many factors including financial, biophysical, emotional, and embodied elements.

"The Girls Are Having Each Other's Babies": Constructing New Cultural Scripts

In 1998 the *Advocate,* a high-gloss gay and lesbian magazine, ran a leading story with the headline "High-Tech Pregnancies" (see fig. 5). The story ran with the tagline "The girls are having each other's babies" (Bennett 1998).

Girls having each other's babies certainly represents a queering of reproduction and a queering brought forward through technoscience: achieving this sort of pregnancy requires using the advanced technology of in vitro fertilization to implant the eggs from one partner into the uterus of another. Lesbian IVF is preceded by the more obvious queer ability and, at times, necessity to confront whose body will undergo intervention to become pregnant. This is not an easy decision, nor is always available; age or disinterest or other factors may preclude the option. Among the women I interviewed, when one partner could or would not conceive, the couple shifted their efforts to the body of the other partner.

This practice surfaced in three of the interviews I conducted.[9] Heather and Judith, for example, switched from one partner to another after Judith underwent one round of IVF and did not become pregnant. They had begun with at-home vaginal inseminations without the use of pharmaceutical therapies. Judith then had surgery for blocked fallopian tubes, and after the surgery she began taking Clomid.

I met Heather at a major university health center, where she worked and

was enrolled in a degree program. Heather hoped to study same-sex parenting when she completed her degree. She described the process she and
Judith had been through: "We had been trying to get Judith pregnant for
like two years prior. We went through many, many cycles of artificial insemination with her and then found out, during pre-surgery, that she had
blocked fallopian tubes. So we tried one cycle of IVF. It didn't work. . . . It
was awful. We were very depressed and upset about it. Also, we couldn't do
it again immediately because we didn't have the money. My lord, it was all
out-of-pocket. . . . And then we decided to try with me getting pregnant."
When I asked her if she was trying to get pregnant using the same technologies and procedures as they had used with Judith, she said, "Oh no,
actually we're not! We are doing interuterine for me, which we didn't do
with Judith. We skipped trying to do intravaginal at home. The advantage
with IUI is apparently that the vaginal environment is really hostile to
sperm and you can bypass this. . . . So we started doing intrauterine with me
because apparently each individual try increases chances of pregnancy. And

we want to get pregnant." For Heather and Judith, the round of IVF was a final step in Judith's attempts to become pregnant, but it was also a first step in choosing to switch to Heather's body.

June and Raquel also chose to switch after June did not become pregnant. Their stopping point occurred after a few months of hormonal injections to increase June's egg production. June said, "After a year the doctors wanted to step up the medical interventions. I said, 'Wait a minute, we have another option.' We were hating it. I was miserable. Raquel was having to administer drugs to me and all this stuff. So we decided, we have another option here. Let's not do this anymore. Especially since they started talking about the risks of ovarian cancer increasing with the use of hormones. They said there's uncertainty about the connection between some of these higher hormone medications. So we put a stop to it." Raquel and June's decision to switch came after considering both the risks involved with taking hormones and the emotional toll of continuing to proceed with hormone shots. Raquel said of the hormonal injections, "It just felt like a big, risky medical experiment that I was performing on her. It just freaked me out. It just seemed like we hadn't even tried to get me pregnant."

I interviewed Raquel and June separately. Both women described the ways in which their second attempt at achieving pregnancy, once they had switched from June to Raquel, was different than the first. Again, their previous experiences and the knowledge gained from them shaped the switch, its contours and meanings. The past became a resource, a knowledge base that women drew on in understanding and making decisions. For example, when couples switched partners in an effort to achieve pregnancy, starting points often changed as well. June's starting point was vaginal insemination, while for Raquel it was IUI.

Pregnancy trajectories vary, and their pathways do not follow stepwise progressions with consistent starting and stopping points. Tina moved from performing at-home insemination to using a variety of clinic-based procedures: "It was kind of overwhelming," "a lot of intervention," and the specialist thought "in vitro was next." Tina and her partner, Elizabeth, decided not to progress to IVF because of the cost and high-tech nature of the procedure. They instead switched partners to Elizabeth, who previously had not wanted to be pregnant. Early in our interview, Elizabeth discussed her ambivalence about the relationship between lesbianism and motherhood in American culture. However, she and Tina did want to become mothers, so after Tina was unable to conceive, Elizabeth somewhat reluctantly began trying to get pregnant herself. This time, however, the couple decided to go directly to performing clinical IUI inseminations.

For many of the women I interviewed, their lesbian subjectivity required hard thinking about the cultural and historical meaning of motherhood and womanhood. The larger cultural script that linked womanhood and motherhood in a natural bond was destabilized by their lesbian identification. Elizabeth, for example, spoke at length about both the pragmatics of whether lesbians should become parents and what this might mean for gay and lesbian politics and also larger cultural ideas that define womanhood in terms of motherhood. She said, "I guess there was always this undercurrent of wondering, 'Was I really womanly in the same way as my heterosexual friends are?' I certainly think I am different in some ways. I never wanted to be pregnant. I never thought of myself as passive, selfless, and nurturing in the way I think people speak about other women. It was surprising to find myself not just reconciling the fact that I would be a mom, but that I was trying to get pregnant."

In many ways lesbian conception practices are removed from the cultural script of natural motherhood. But is this due to the technological assistance often used to achieve pregnancy, or is it due to their refusal to participate in heterosexual sex? All technological conceptions occur outside of heterosexual intercourse, yet for lesbians technologies do not necessarily symbolically disrupt their subjectivities as women. This subjectivity has already been on shaky ground. The literature on infertility and heterosexual women demonstrates that biomedically assisted reproduction can disrupt gender for heterosexual women, who may not have previously questioned or even recognized the existence of a cultural conflation of womanhood and motherhood. As a result, the cultural script of infertility differs for lesbians and heterosexuals. For many heterosexual women, the cultural script of infertility includes stigma and distress. While the two may share emotional distress associated with the clinical gaze, they do not always share a stigma associated with lack of procreation.

The women I interviewed did not discuss stigma, failure, or shame with regard to unsuccessful attempts at conception. Queer subjectivity may offer some protection: compared with heterosexuals, lesbians appear to rely less heavily for meaning on dominant constructions of femininity. As a result, when technologies must be employed in the service of reproduction, the social location of being outside dominant norms of womanhood and motherhood protects lesbians against stigma. Again, queer users do not conform to the characteristics of the standard "infertility" actor envisioned by biomedical services and providers. Although clinical encounters may cause objectification, this objectification does not unbalance lesbian subjectivities in the same way as it might for those heterosexuals whose femininity has been linked to their status as "not-yet" mothers and, therefore, as appropriate reproducers. Achieving the socially desired identity of motherhood requires medical operationalization and naturalization. The biomedical subjectivities formed can either be in the service of biomedical objectification, when stigma arises, or in negotiation with biomedicine, when pragmatic action arises. Whether these differing positions represent agency or merely the act of "going along with" is arguable.

Perhaps what is most significant is the variety of meanings queer users employ to understand and describe their achieving-pregnancy experiences. As the narratives demonstrate, the cultural dichotomies of low-tech/high-tech and natural/artificial are dominant. Low-tech/high-tech is a cultural distinction that people draw on as they make meaning out of their experiences. For example, for some queer users, ambiguity and uncertainty in the process led them to rely on the heteronormative cultural narrative of "woman equals mother." Paula describes this well: "It felt like there was something wrong with her. She's defective. Women are supposed to be able to get pregnant." Associating womanhood with fertility and pregnancy is a longstanding cultural script. "Women are built for it and she can't do it. . . . [Fertility difficulties were] very upsetting when we were in the midst of it. It was upsetting because things were going wrong. We felt defective," Paula said.

Although the emotional experience of "technological failure" emerged as salient for lesbians, it was not merely a script of stigmatization but also one of agentic resourcefulness—which contrasts with what the literature has shown about heterosexual infertility, which is often coupled with feelings of shame and stigma. This is changing, however. While lesbians do not expect the "failure" of the body, neither do they expect that conception will come "naturally" and "with ease." That is, they know that conscious effort must occur. While they often construct high-tech procedures as devastating, lesbians do not frequently view such procedures as stigmatizing. This was clear in the case of Lynda and Elsie, who decided to use IVF technologies to have one's eggs implanted into the other's uterus. Lynda described the experience.

The results for [Elsie] were really devastating because they basically said, "Forget it. There's no chance." And it meant more to [Elsie] than to me to have a genetic baby. So, for her, that was really devastating. The man who's the lab director here, who's an embryologist, is a friend of ours. He's a scientist. So we decided that we would talk with him and just run some things by him. And he really convinced us that even if the numbers were bad, we should go ahead and give [IVF] a try with [Elsie] and see what happens. So we actually had previously done one cycle of IVF with me and had embryos from that. At the same time, we were doing a cycle of IVF with her eggs. We were planning on freezing the embryos because [Elsie] had a big fibroid. They figured, if they had a choice, they'd rather use my uterus. So [Elsie] went through IVF, froze all the embryos. I went through an additional IVF cycle and I didn't get pregnant. And then we started putting [her] embryos back in me. And we had two straws of embryos. We actually had four straws. We put them in, in two different batches, and the first cycle didn't work. And the second cycle — voila! — thank God, finally we got pregnant.

In Lynda's narration the heterosexual cultural narrative of distress is absent. In contrast, Esther constructs her experience as a controlled, efficient, and methodical "scientific" process, equating high-tech with science. For her, technology created agency, not stigma.

This cycle is, like, very scientific. I'm doing the Clomid. So, because [of] the Clomid, they had me do a sonogram. Well they're doing more lab tests to follow how I'm reacting to it. They also said, "Let's go ahead and do some extra blood tests to rule out some things that sometimes cause miscarriages, since you've had two now." Basically, they said, "Let's do the things that are noninvasive and not those that are going to be harmful in any way." So we did some blood tests. "Let's just rule out the easy stuff." They're having me take a baby aspirin every day which will thin the blood a little. For some women, they have small blood clots, which in your everyday life is not a problem, but when you're trying to get blood and oxygen to the baby, that could be an issue. She [the practitioner] told me if you're pregnant you can take baby aspirin. So I'm doing stuff to make it better next time.

Esther later said, "We were taking it into our own hands."

Embedded within lesbian experiences of achieving pregnancy lies an emergent cultural narrative of conception that is consequential for the shape of assisted-reproduction practices and discourses in general. In contrast to the distress and stigma that are central to heterosexual infertility, the emergent lesbian sociocultural narrative is marked by agentic resourcefulness. In negotiating technological scripts based on their own interpretations and meanings, queer users subvert the expectations and scripts of the developers, marketers, and services organized around the technologies.

(Re)Considering Normalization

While the ideals of feminist health and women's movements shape lesbian practices to some extent, the highly intentional and proactive means through which lesbians seek pregnancy reflect pragmatic approaches to becoming mothers, rather than attempts to challenge biomedical values. To be sure, lesbian subjectivity is central to these participants' reflections on their decisions to seek pregnancies and parenthood, but encounters with biomedicine seem to reflect a false universally experienced women's gendered subjectivity with one's "right," as women, to mother.[10]

Although interactions among reproductive technologies and lesbian subjectivities are difficult to unravel, the intentional goal of creating "alternative" family forms and achieving pregnancies without heterosexual sex signal at least a destabilization of normative family conventions. Of course, reproductive technology opens possibilities for differently configured cultural relations no matter the subjectivity of the user (whether an older parent, single parent, multiple parents, or same-sex parents). Reproductive technologies continue to shore up heterosexual families and define procreation as the normative activity of heterosexual couples.

Yet the rhetoric of choice that now plays such a large role in the discourse of reproductive technologies can be read as a part of the rationalization and normalization tendencies which control and manage the population. Reading lesbian pregnancies as being based only on volition and choice misses the political-economic and cultural context. In the biomedical era there is no choice but to always exercise choice. Doing so may appear to allow freedoms, but in fact only further enacts the usual stratifications, conventions, and norms.

While normalization and control are ever apparent, what can one make of Lynda and Elsie, who intentionally used IVF to challenge the law and cultural ideal that there must be a "mother" and "father"? Their act directly confronts the hegemony of the two-parent, opposite-sex family as the natural procreative unit. As a result, these actions not only serve their pragmatic interests but also demonstrate transformative possibilities. Are Lynda and Elsie merely reinforcing dominant cultural ideals, or do their practices reveal complexities previously unimagined?

If a goal of reproductive technologies in the era of biomedicalization includes a "re/de/sign and transformation of reproductive bodies and processes" (Clarke 1995, 140) then where and under what conditions does this take place? The participants in this research negotiate biomedicine in complex ways: while their encounters with biomedicine are pragmatic and shaped by their cultural capital, one cannot dismiss the resulting creation of what remains an unconventional family form, even if it is achieved through a conventional practice (pregnancy).

Transformative possibilities exist when new subjectivities seek bodily transcendence as a means to achieve fulfillment. This is the case as lesbians continue knocking at the door of healthcare delivery services. While the intersection of queer bodies and subjectivities with reproductive technologies may not fully erase the "sexed" hierarchy of knowledges and is often complicit with hierarchical organizations based on sex, gender, and sexuality, there may be room for resistance and other alternative positions. If one follows Foucault's never fully developed point that where there is power there is resistance, one could argue that reproductive technologies are changing the categories on which theories of sex and gender have been built.

Six

Affinity Ties as Kinship Device

SARA, A THIRTY-EIGHT-YEAR-OLD white healthcare provider, is in a partnered relationship with Sue, a Korean American physician. They have two children by donor insemination. Sara began her description of the donor-selection process by noting their challenges as an interracial couple. After describing their ongoing discussion of stigma, race, and racism in the United States, she said, "There was absolutely no question in my partner's mind that she wanted our children to be mixed in the same way as her sisters' [children] are. We had a lot of discussion about race. She feels that if we have an all-Korean child who is a girl, she would only be valued for being very beautiful. She felt like whether a boy or girl, an all-Korean child would experience different kinds of racism, if purely something. So she wanted both of our children to be [racially] mixed." In Sara's story Koreanness was an important characteristic for herself, her partner, and their potential child, but it was also something to moderate according to Sue's experiences and the couple's discussions. As a result, the choices Sara and Sue made were based on a desire to "match" the potential child not with themselves, but with other members of their family—in particular, with Sara's nieces and nephews.

In heterosexual assisted reproduction, matching donor characteristics with those of the "nonbiological" father has long been practiced to suggest a connection between the child and the acting father. Heterosexual couples thus have the option of concealing their use of assisted reproduction. While such secrecy is not an option for and, according to my findings, not desired by lesbians, they, too, practice donor matching. For lesbians, matching has two central purposes: to match one's own appearance and/or ancestry to those of the child; and to match the characteristics of the child with those of extended family members. These practices are pragmatic negotiations in which lesbians ask two questions: will the child be accepted as mine? And will the child be similar enough to me and my family to be accepted as ours?

As Sue and Sara illustrate, lesbians selecting a sperm donor often rely on ideas of biology and heredity to imagine shared ancestry, thereby producing familial similarities. A Korean donor, for example, will enable Sue's and Sara's potential child to look like his or her cousins. However, the selection also acknowledges racism, as it attempts to help the newborn avoid the cultural stigma attached to "all-Asian" children. Sue's biographical and profoundly personal experiences of stigma determined what was important and what was unimportant to her in selecting a sperm donor.

As lesbians described their selection processes, it became clear that their interactions with sperm-bank materials included speculating about what was "known" and "unknown" regarding the role of genes and other biological markers in heredity and human development. Their interactions were filtered through their own cultural understandings of genes, genetics, and heredity. During her discussion of selecting donors, Sara said,

> I think our primary concern was genetic. I change all the time on how much I think is genetic and how much is environment, but our general feeling then, which has changed now that we *actually have* kids, then we thought that we know so much about mental illness and genetics and even a lot of personality traits. . . . We had the belief and it's often true that a lot of personality traits are influenced by genetics. Our feeling was that we would stack the deck as much as we can. Even though every single pregnancy and every single combination of genes is different, it's a total crap shoot. With our understanding of medicine and genetics and personalities, we thought that we would stack the deck as much as possible in favor of having someone who was flexible, creative, would cope well in life, and would be happy. Our family is fairly prone to depression, so we thought we could avoid that. No major mental illnesses, no suicidality, no episodes of clinical depression.

Sara attested to the uncertainties inherent in genetic explanations of human development, yet she and Sue entered into a selection strategy understood as a means of predicting the future. Her description reflected a general conflation of biological markers with personality development. For example, she associated with genes such personality characteristics as creativity, flexibility, or the capacity to cope well. Eliminating donors with histories of depression was one way to deploy her prediction, but in her imagination the absence of this history promised much more. Sara and Sue engaged in strategies of both enhancing identities (making flexible, happy babies) and reducing perceived potential risks (limiting possibilities for developing "genetic" depression). Their attempts to "stack the deck" were enabled by both the commodification of sperm and a vision of the future that relied on a cultural metaphor of DNA as predictive.

In this chapter I examine the meanings and practices of lesbian sperm-donor selection for their implications for theorizing kinship and technoscience. I focus on the ways lesbians mobilize genetics and heredity to make meaning of human development and to imagine and craft future relationships. Four questions guide this chapter: what is the significance of sperm as a culturally relevant object and biomaterial? In what ways do sperm banks, a technoscientific institution and set of practices, constitute kinship choices? In what ways do lesbian recipients select sperm for reproduction? What implications do these practices hold for meanings of kinship in general and queer reproduction in particular?

Imaging Futures of Relatedness: Kinship and the Genetic Imaginary

In her book *After Kinship* Janet Carsten (2004) asked what repercussions developments in reproductive technologies might have for everyday concepts and practices of relatedness. I offer an analysis of some ways in which ordinary people — in this case ordinary lesbians — pick and choose what to consider as "natural," "genetic," and biosocially "shared." Nature, or the "facts of life," is today biologized and geneticized. The conception narrative, which describes the origin of life, is webbed together with two other narratives: the kinship narrative, which explains the ties that make a family, and the genetic narrative, which explains individuals and their connections to the past and future.

In its simplest form, kinship signifies the ways in which individuals and groups are socially connected. The term has largely been used to signal social connection based on biological relationships (consanguineous ties) among parents and children, biological ties among siblings, and "legal" ties between marital partners. As this definition attests, persons recognized as kin primarily divide into those related by blood and those related by marriage. However, this conceptualization is being profoundly destabilized in the twenty-first century: social connections are far broader than such a definition allows. As a result, the concept of kinship has been a rich area of analysis for sociologists and anthropologists studying reproductive technologies and diverse family forms.

The use of assisted reproduction challenges many taken-for-granted assumptions about gender, kinship, and social relations. Reproduction no longer relies on heterosexuality, and, with donor-sperm reproduction, the family is no longer bound by paternity. Same-sex parents' further challenge the idea that anatomical sexual difference is necessary for the reproduction of society. That is, some believe that gender and gender differences are a necessary precondition for the development of imaginary and symbolic difference, and thus of all social difference. Opposite-sex parents, the theory goes, transmit to their children, by virtue of their very configuration, an ability to recognize (gendered) difference and thereby maintain this social form; by the same logic, same-sex parents do not transmit an understanding of difference to their children. As the argument goes, two mothers, two fathers, mothers who father, and fathers who mother disrupt gender norms, thereby altering the basis of gender and harming children's ability to make sense of and operate well in the social world. This script naturalizes heterosexual reproduction and pathologizes other forms of parenting. It further reinforces kinship as a legal bond produced through heterosexual sex and the heterogeneous mixing of eggs and sperm.

As the field of procreators expands, and as possible parents therefore multiply, the traditional kinship narrative (at least in the West) is shown to have cultural and not natural underpinnings. Same-sex parents and other "queer" parenting forms have the power to alter the ways people understand and make meaning out of social connections that go beyond the nuclear family to include new (and old) forms of belonging, connection, identity, and relatedness. So the question emerges: do lesbian parents disrupt and/or stabilize dominant forms of gender and kinship?

Genetic Imaginary and a New Lamarckism

Biology today is increasingly geneticized and individualized, and genes have become an iconic vocabulary. One now hears of genetic mothers, genetic fathers, genetic ancestors, genetic risks, genetic responsibilities, and genetic ancestry. Genes are perceived to have the power to explain who one is, what one will become, how one is connected to others, and what might happen to one in the future. Molecular genomics and biotechnology are cultural resources shaping and transforming definitions of "life itself" (see Franklin 2000).

In my analysis of lesbian reproduction, the power of genetics is omnipresent as sperm selections are made and futures are imagined. As lesbians imagine these futures they employ affinity ties, negotiations of relatedness enabled through hybrid assemblages of meanings of blood, genes, and social and cultural connection. The ways natures and cultures are assembled in these narratives conjure a return to Lamarckism, the theory of evolution posited by Jean-Baptiste Lamarck, the eighteenth century's leading thinker on the transmission of characteristics from generation to generation. Lamarckism asserted that all life forms had arisen through a continuous process of gradual modification throughout time. This idea was based on the generally accepted theory of acquired characteristics, a belief that new traits in any organism developed to meet environmental demands and were transmitted to its offspring. While it has been displaced "scientifically," Lamarck's theory of the transmission of acquired characteristics has in many ways returned through cultural understandings of geneticization (Lippman 1992), as a growing number of human traits are understood to be the result of genetics.[1] This neo-Lamarckist narrative is constituted within biomedicalization, wherein life itself becomes an object of continuous manipulation offered by the convergence of molecular biology and computer-information sciences.

Biomedicalization and Sperm Selection

Lesbian practices of selecting donor sperm take place within and are profoundly shaped by contemporary biomedicalization and its emphasis on transforming and manipulating life itself. As part of postmodernity, biomedicalization includes and often relies on historical discourses. Histories of the cultural understandings of genes, heredity, and genetics, as well as their technoscientific applications, shape donor-sperm selection practices.

That is, contemporary practices of selecting sperm donors are entangled with complicated histories of genetic explanations of self, sociability, and relatedness as well as eugenic practices of controlling who and under what conditions persons are supported and constrained in their reproduction. This includes governing what and who makes a family.

Sperm Banks and Governmentality

The widespread availability of commercialized sperm banks over the past twenty years has certainly altered public understandings of procreation as the "natural" product of heterosex; the emergence of donor sperm as a consumer market for lesbians is more recent. While the social problem of infertility (inability to conceive through heterosexual sex) was medicalized long ago, lesbian infertility is most often the result of an absence of sperm in sexual activity; donor sperm is always a required biomaterial for its solution. While lesbians have always become mothers in a variety of ways, it is only recently that a large-scale commercial industry and a plethora of technoscientific practices have emerged as a solution. This does not make lesbian motherhood a new practice, but it does produce new meanings. Biomedicalization processes have shifted what was once a low-cost, relatively simple procedure of donor insemination into a highly commodified, complex, and elaborate process.

*The first commercial sperm bank opened in 1972 (Sherman 1979) as a laboratory that ensured the screening, preparation, storage, and distribution of frozen sperm.[2] At that time, additional procedures for "disease washing and testing" of sperm were designed to ensure maximum health. As of 1992, the last year that the government sponsored the collection of data on this industry, commercial sperm banking was a $164 million per year industry. In 1995, sperm banks operated in all fifty states, and by 1998 it was estimated that between fifty and one hundred fifty sperm banks existed in the United States (Daniels 2006, 90). A large proportion of those accessing fertility services turn to these banks, whether for screening, testing, or storage of known-donor sperm, or as a commercial site for purchasing anonymous sperm.

Regardless of the targeted recipient, sperm banks share similar marketing strategies. They offer a range of print and online sperm catalogs to assist their recipients in choosing sperm for reproduction (see table 6). The biomaterial sperm and services such as reproduction, which formerly were

Table 6   Sperm-Bank-Donor Characteristics

DONOR #	ETHNICITY	HAIR; EYES	HEIGHT; WEIGHT	COMPLEXION; FACE
201 *Limited supply available*	French Canadian/ Italian	Brown, thin; Brown	5'11"; 165 lbs.	Medium; Rounded, nice looking, European features
205	German/ English/ Norwegian	Brown, straight; Blue	5'8"; 165 lbs.	Medium; Pleasant features, attractive eyes
253 *Limited supply available*	African American/ Irish	Reddish brown; Brown	5'6"; 143 lbs.	Light brown; Strong jaw, freckled, boyish
296	Japanese	Black, thick, straight; Brown	5'7"; 125 lbs.	Medium; Soft eyes, high cheekbones

excluded from the marketplace, are now suddenly omnipresent as objects for consumption. Since the consumer base of sperm banks is not very elastic, these services must profit either by increasing "unit" costs or by somehow expanding their consumer base, especially as heterosexual couples shift away from using donor sperm and toward using advanced reproductive services such as IVF with intracytoplasmic sperm injection to maximize their chances of "biological" relatedness.[3]

In 1999 the *San Francisco Chronicle* ran a mock sperm-bank advertisement for the Sperm Bank of California.[4] The hand-drawn image depicted two women dressed fashionably in colorful, sleek skirts, blouses, and high heels.

BODY BUILD; BLOOD TYPE	MEDICAL HISTORY; FAMILY MEDICAL HISTORY	EDUCATION; WORK	PERSONALITY; HOBBIES
Tall, medium build; O+	Excellent health; M-migraines	B.A. in psychology, M.A. in sociology; Production manager	Amicable and outgoing; Gardening, biking
Medium frame, compact; A-	Mild seasonal hay fever, excellent health; F-high blood pressure, PGF/MGF-heart problems in old age, MGM-breast cancer	B.S. in design; Marketing, hospitality services	Strong, self motivated, adventurous; Reading, drumming, skiing, mountain biking
Small, trim, muscular; A+	Excellent health; M-alcoholic	B.A. in child psychology; Behavioral therapist, professional boxer	Friendly, energetic, sensitive; Athletics, outdoors, literature, cooking
Small, strong, compact; B+	Childhood asthma, allergies, glasses; s-Down syndrome (donor has been tested and is not a carrier)	B.A. in film, M.A. in education; Retail management	Thoughtful, conscientious, empathetic; Outdoor sports, reading, film, motorcycle

M = mother, MGF = maternal grandfather, MGM = maternal grandmother
P = father, PGF = paternal grandfather, PGM = paternal grandmother, s = sibling

The women stand in front of a cosmetics counter and shop for products as a saleswoman, dressed in what resembles a nurse's uniform, assists them from behind the counter. Each woman holds a differently colored tube selected from a case of tubes near the counter. The bold-face tagline accompanying the image reads "Maximum Return," and is followed by text stating that single women and lesbians no longer have to feel marginal or secretive when buying sperm. Such services are not only available to these populations, but are marketed directly to them. The tagline "Maximum Return" is particularly meaningful for its reference to capital investment, which equates sperm-bank "investing" with other forms of consumer purchasing that are accompanied with a promise for the future. The message is also one of self-empowerment and self-choice, with women gathering around a counter to pick and choose.

Self-empowerment as a message appeals to women who have grown up taking for granted many of the social changes fought for by previous generations of feminists. Self-empowerment offers an image of womanhood that is about possibility, limitless potential, and the promise of control over the future. Embedded in the image is the sense that motherhood is within reach of women who learn the skills and/or have the characteristics necessary for continual self-invention. The constraints of age, physiology, class, race, and sexual desire on this bright future are effaced by the idea that individuals can overcome all with the right attitude, knowledge, and drive—that is, with agency. American preoccupations with individualism, self-improvement, free enterprise, and high-tech medicine combined and are productive of a culture of biomedicalization in which one is able—indeed, expected—to employ (consume) medical technologies to alter one's self and one's anatomy to make them more socially advantageous.

In the biomedicalization era, sperm banks commodify sperm and sperm donors and market them to potential consumers. As institutions, sperm banks evoke ideas of commodity exchange, altruism, and future capital investment. Sperm banks offer a technologization of nature when they "sell" biomaterials that can produce social relations through technological interventions, thereby challenging fundamental assumptions about the "facts of life" and kinship (Carsten 2004, 163).

Sperm banks and their associated products and services are consumer products in which, as Marilyn Strathern so eloquently argued, nature has been "enterprised-up": "What was once taken to be natural has become a matter of choice" (1992, 30; see also Strathern 1995). The more technology influences nature, and the more legislation circumscribes the social recognition of parenthood, the more difficult it becomes to think of nature as independent of social intervention. The social arrangements that inhere in kinship relations are "not just imitating but based on and literally deploying processes of biological reproduction" (Strathern 1992, 3).

Natural facts are revealed as social constructions (as described by Carsten 2000, 2004) and through technoscience, a new object of popular knowledge includes conceptualizing persons and relatedness, using terms such as *genetic destiny, genetic health,* and *genetic origins* (Strathern 1992; see also Franklin

2000). According to Strathern (1992) nature and technology are deployed interchangeably: just as nature helps improve the "effectiveness" of technology, nature itself is improved by technology. This conceptualization both reveals the construction of the "natural facts of life" and reinforces the power of science and technology to transform those "facts" into desired outcomes.

Regulating Donation

Until the 1980s, screening of sperm donors was primarily limited to self-reporting of medical history. After transmission of AIDS became a known risk, sperm was tested for HIV, frozen, quarantined for six months, then retested. U.S. guidelines (not legal regulations) for anonymous-sperm-banking practices were established by a professional association, the American Society for Reproductive Medicine (1997). The guidelines both for commercial sperm banks and for private sperm banks located in physician offices do not merely protect recipients and their potential children but also regulate the donation of sperm and, thus, the reproduction of several types of men. Professional guidelines recommend excluding men as sperm donors if they have ever engaged in sex work, had sex with men, and injected drugs, or gotten acupuncture, tattoos, or body piercing. In sharp contrast, standards concerning who is an appropriate recipient of insemination services are professionally regulated on a de facto basis; medical professionals, physicians, and sperm-bank administrators are granted the freedom to decide to whom they will provide services.

Sperm banks in the United Stated typically enforce the standard guidelines for donors and routinely ask for additional information. For example, the New England Cryogenic Center requires a family-health history dating back three generations, a résumé, college-board scores and grade-point average, and a three-page questionnaire on life-goals, hobbies, television and movie preferences, even favorite colors and flavors of ice cream. Frontal and profile photos, similar to mug shots, also are required. In 1988 the U.S. Food and Drug Administration (FDA) and the Centers for Disease Control (CDC) recommended that all sperm be frozen and quarantined for six months. In 1995 the FDA began a process of developing regulations for donated tissues and cells, including sperm.

Sperm-banks regulations were finalized in 2004 under the "Eligibility Determination for Donors of Human Cells, Tissues, and Cellular and Tissue-Based Products" (Food and Drug Administration 2004). These guidelines divide reproductive donors into three categories: an anonymous donor, a repeat anonymous donor, and a directed donor. Each category has a different set of eligibility requirements. An anonymous sperm donor must meet all requirements, and his sperm must be quarantined for six months and then retested before it qualifies. Repeated anonymous donors must be tested every six months. Directed donors (those known to recipients) only have to be tested once and do not have to meet all requirements, although the recipient has to be made aware of the risks associated with decreased screening.

The requirements for donor screening include a medical-history interview, a physical exam, and a review of relevant medical records. Donors cannot have certain diseases and disease agents, including chlamydia, syphilis, gonorrhea, HIV-1, HIV-2, hepatitis B, hepatitis C, HBV, HCV, HTLV-I, HTLV-II, sepsis, vaccinia (agent in the smallpox vaccine), Treponema pallidum, cytomegalovirus, Creutzfeldt-Jakob disease, severe acute respiratory syndrome, West Nile virus, and disease risks associated with xenotransplantation (see, for example, the American Society for Reproductive Medicine and Food and Drug Administration Web sites). In addition, certain men, including men who have had sex with men in the past five years, are currently barred from anonymous sperm donation via licensed sperm banks. This is an overt discrimination against gay men cloaked in the form of behavioral (not identity) guidelines.

What are not explicitly evident are the heteronormative assumptions built in to these regulations. First, sexually intimate partners are excluded from regulations. This implies that knowing and sleeping with a heterosexual man makes him less risky. It also results in a lower cost of "doing business" than if you use an anonymous or directed donor. Second, while directed donors and those not sexually intimate with recipients are eligible, they must undergo more screening than do intimate partners. Third, sperm banks often require that directed-donor sperm undergo the same screening, freezing, and storage processes required of anonymous sperm, which thereby increases the disparities. Finally, before men are selected to become sperm donors, many are disqualified for being "too fat, too short, too gay, the wrong color, or with the wrong educational credentials"; they must first meet the presumed cultural standard of socially valued and desired masculinity (Daniel 2006, 104).

Sperm Bank Practices

Today, with cryopreservation and the development of a large-scale sperm-bank industry, recipients are able to choose from among a far greater number of donors, and donor characteristics, than they could when fresh sperm was the standard. Donor sperm is represented to prospective recipients using various classification grids compiled into a donor catalog. There are two primary types of donors available at most sperm banks: identity-release or "yes" donors, who agree to let the child learn his identity (usually when the child is eighteen years old), and unknown or "no" donors, who seek to remain anonymous. There are usually many more no donors available at mainstream sperm banks and more yes donors at gay-friendly sperm banks. All sperm banks provide similar, short catalogs that report donor characteristics in an easy-to-read manner. The most common characteristics provided are race or ethnicity, height, weight, eye color, hair color, body build, complexion, and health history of the donor and his immediate family (see table 6).

Along with donor sperm are a full menu of services available on a fee-for-service basis, including screening procedures and technologies such as "testing" sperm count and motility; infectious-disease screening; sperm quarantine; sperm washing; and sperm analysis. Sperm samples are prepared to accommodate either vaginal or intrauterine inseminations. IUI sperm must undergo additional preparations to remove prostaglandin, which is pre-ejaculate. Finally, in-depth profiles of donors are often available for a fee.

The cost table, which lists the standard procedures and materials and costs provided by sperm banks, illustrates the imperatives of corporate bio-medicine that have infused all aspects of sperm-bank institutions (see chap. 3, table 2).While it may not be surprising that for-profit sperm banks are profiting from this growth-oriented market, nonprofit organizations are also maximizing their fees. Feminist organizations, like other nonprofit groups, face fiscal difficulties for a variety of reasons, and when funding and charitable giving are down, these organizations often secure monies through fees for services rendered. Thus, they have increased rates not to profit, but to secure survival. However, the shift from drop-in support groups to a fee-for-service model is also part of a corporate trend, as marketability and profitability are constantly expanded.

Corporatization has occurred not only among feminist organizations but also among sperm banks, which need to expand their markets to remain profitable. Cyberspace is rapidly becoming a lucrative place for sperm banks to advertise and extend their client base (Dornin 1998). The move of corporate biomedicine as a culture into feminist health is indicative of the biomedical, political, and economic context of health care. That is, feminist health organizations find themselves in a highly competitive market as Fertility Inc. continuously expands. There exists only one non-profit sperm bank in the United States, the Sperm Bank of California (previously known as the Oakland Feminist Health Center). This sperm bank, as well as a few others, survives in the competitive marketplace through the use of "niche marketing" to "non-traditional families" (Daniels 2006). As a commodity, sperm is marketed and sold to consumers within the context of a biomedical-industrial complex (i.e., the commercial sperm-bank industry), and as customers seeking services, lesbians respond. Although they are not the imagined or state-legitimated producers of "families," lesbian parents use sperm banks to produce kin and thus challenge the state's denial of queer citizens' right to produce families.

Meanings and practices of selecting sperm are situated within this medical context as well as within a shifting legal terrain that is organized state by state. Legal issues profoundly shape lesbian reproductive practices. Under California law, a known sperm donor is considered the father of the child except "where sperm is provided to a licensed physician and surgeon for purposes of insemination in a woman not his wife."[5] The phrase "licensed physician and surgeon" eliminates most family practitioners and internists who are not surgeons and all nurse-practitioners who are not licensed physicians from providing this service in such a way that maximizes legal protection for the recipient and donor. Thus, although directed donors are still involved today, it is increasingly difficult. When directed donors are used, many women nevertheless turn to a doctor for assistance, in an effort to assure legal protection. Further, an infertility diagnosis is often required to assure private health coverage of these services. Receiving an infertility diagnosis remains difficult for lesbians; the definition of infertility includes an inability to conceive after twelve months of intercourse. This has since been shortened to six months, a signal that infertility is expanding its jurisdiction.

Imagining Futures of Relatedness

A primary mechanism for consumer choices of donor sperm is the donor catalog. Most of these catalogs use a variety of classification grids that visually display information. Donor characteristics are placed in a grid structure, which allows (and encourages) recipients to quickly compare donors and select "the right sperm for the job" (Clarke and Fujimura 1992). In-depth donor profiles, available for purchase, go into more detail; in them, donors respond to a series of open-ended questions such as "Describe your hobbies and interests," "Why are you becoming a sperm donor?" and "What are your goals in life?"[6]

Sperm banks highlight cultural beliefs about sperm, race, heredity, social desirability, and power, beliefs that women draw on when making their selection choices. The lesbian recipients of donor sperm in this study interpreted these catalogs in ways that show how sperm banks market sperm differences and thus provide an opportunity to rematerialize, reconstitute, and reproduce the body of the donor. Recipients mobilized late-twentieth-century cultural understandings of human life, genetics, heredity, and notions of relatedness in making their choices meaningful. The organizational structure of sperm banks transforms a lack of sperm into an opportunity to pick a winner (Schmidt and Moore 1998). As Cynthia R. Daniels (2006) argues, such a winner reflects predictable social values of masculinity, from weight and height to hobbies and educational attainment.

The women I interviewed clearly understood that lesbians represented an emergent consumer market for sperm banks. "I'm sure you know or have heard stories about how odd it is to go shopping for a donor in those catalogs and online," Dana stated. Similarly, Esther said, "It feels really weird to walk in off the street and pick up a bottle of sperm and pay for it. . . . I feel like lesbians trying to get pregnant is a whole market. Every time prices go up, I get so mad. . . . We really feel like, 'Oh! Here's a market that doesn't have a lot of options, so, we [can] jack the price up and they'll still come.'" It is not only sperm that is commodified, but also the biological and social differences of donors themselves. The marketing of difference supports anthropological claims that blood ties are not what counts as relatedness, nor are they what holds society together. Instead, social and cultural difference can and does stand in for kinship and becomes a marker for not only social connection and belonging but also for social power.

Selecting Desirable Donor Characteristics

Purchasing sperm involves selecting desirable donor traits. In presenting the physical and social attributes of the donors, sperm banks inscribe sperm with difference and imply that all characteristics may be inheritable. The product stored and invested at these sperm banks is not a neutral biomaterial available for purchase, but is imbued with certain qualities that affect its value. As Diane Tober (2001) argues, banks place an emphasis on altruism in an effort to redefine the commodity quality of sperm as a gift and thereby imbue it with higher emotional and moral value. Sperm is then marketed and read as a biomaterial that holds future possibilities.

In turn, women mobilize cultural understandings of genes and relatedness in the context of this highly commodified biomedical arena in ways that reinforce yet challenge the nature-culture divide: they employ the ambiguities already present in ideas about genes, generation, and heredity for their own purposes. This raises questions concerning which traits are socially desirable and for whom. In my interviews, I asked, "What were the factors and donor characteristics you considered as important when choosing a sperm donor?" Respondents first named the elements they considered to be most important, among them, although not in any particular order, whether or not a donor was willing to be known to offspring, the donor's health status and family health history, the donor's racial or ethnic background and religious ancestry, and the donor's social and cultural characteristics. Presented with the opportunity to choose sperm (and whatever else sperm embodies), however, the women constructed more elaborate criteria with which to make selections. Recipients described a process in which they first balanced and prioritized all the characteristics provided in the short-catalog scripts, from which they selected between one and four "top pick" donors, whose long profiles they then purchased for additional information. The women I interviewed frequently referred to the long forms, which provided information beyond basic donor characteristics, including such attributes as clarity of handwriting, articulateness, and perceived empathy and generosity.

Users read the catalog scripts in a manner that rematerializes or reimagines the characteristics and attributes of the donor himself. A social connection with potential children is imagined through shared social, cultural, and ancestral histories as enabled through biogenetics, not learning. Characteristics once considered as belonging to the donor are expected to appear in the children. While not always explicit, the lesbians' stories of selecting donor sperm were also stories of imagining future children, future familial connections, and future social interactions.

Users select sperm in three ways: by physical "matching," by maximizing health and reducing risk, and by mobilizing genes and generations in ways that maximize social affinities with imagined children. Many of the lesbians I interviewed privileged issues of biological identity, drawing conclusions about a donor's genetic health history and considering social subjectivities. Imagining affinity connections with donors and future children thus became a kinship device employed when selecting sperm. Lesbians constructed liminal spaces between biogenetic and social ties as markers for future relatedness.

I use the concept of affinity ties to signal the tendency of a recipient to select a donor who appears to have a likeness to the mother or mothers to be; likeness, however, is often not described as physical resemblance, but includes an imagined future connection forged through shared ancestry, hobbies, and other more cultural attributes. The concept of affinity ties complicates the distinctions made in gay and lesbian kinship theories between ties created by blood and ties created by choice or love. Affinity ties are a kinship device in which "naturecultures" are put together and mobilized in context. The context is usually one of uncertain legal rights and social legitimacy. The concept emerged as women explained the ways they considered biological, genetic, and social attributes of sperm donors as they were listed by sperm banks. As recipients made donor selections, they imagined and constructed kinship with potential children, and did so as a means to secure legitimacy in the face of a heteronormative culture.[7]

"It's kind of like buying a husband," Kaye stated, revealing that while a sperm donor is clearly not a husband, recipients often rematerialize and imagine the donor as a means to imagine offspring. Kaye not only understood donor selection as a consumer practice, as was evident in her use of the term *buying,* but also acknowledged that by listing donor characteristics, sperm banks shape selection in much the same way that dating services do; that is, they list a range of biological, cultural, and social options for recipients to select. Kaye continued.

My partner and I were overwhelmed with the choices. At first, we did not know what to choose. We were a bit surprised by all the options. But then we decided we felt we should choose somebody tall. That was important. And I felt we should be making a choice based on health, that if it at all possible [we should] give the child the gift of good health. [That] was something that was worth something. And we both thought athletic and smartness was important. And then the whole ethnicity discussion came out. And that's a whole difficult discussion even to have. . . . [My partner] felt it was going to be difficult enough for our child to be the child of lesbian parents, that to raise a child of mixed ethnicity who was also the child of white lesbian parents was just basically too much. So we chose a white donor.

These are not only practices of selecting sperm: they are ways of imagining future connections and social relationships, relationships that are given meaning through shared biological *and* social characteristics. Specifically, affinity ties are elaborated through the construction of sperm as possessing an ethnic origin, a health history, and a range of social and personality characteristics that when imagined by recipients are variously understood through terms of genetics and heredity.

Recipients implicitly rely on cultural understandings of inheritance when imagining their potential child's development. That is, they rely less on conceptions of their own nurturing as parents than they do on cultural understandings of heredity and genetics. This practice serves as a kinship device in that it mobilizes the nature-culture divide in ways that give meaning to future families (real or imagined). In other words, while ambiguities and uncertainties exist with regard to the relative influences of nature and nurture, recipients select sperm in ways that privilege nature. The cultural and physical traits of the donors are rematerialized into the imagined offspring. This serves as a kinship device in that it enables the recipients to envision their own social connections to the imagined children. Kinship becomes relational: potential mothers select donor characteristics they might share with — that is, have in common with — potential offspring. These attributes are not only physical but also social and cultural.

Affinity ties are also central to imagining future relationships outside the family as providing potential social legitimacy. This was most clear in racial-ethnic decisions to select a donor who "matched" both mothers when they were of the same ethnicity or to select based on the ethnicity of the "non-biological" mother-to-be. In terms of social legitimacy, the women I interviewed grappled with idealized kinship forms and wondering where they fit in. What type of families would they create? Assisted-reproduction tech-

nologies and sperm banks provide the institutional and technical knowledges and tools necessary to bypass social conventions of the heterosexual
family, but they do not necessarily bypass cultural and social ideals of what
and who make a family. Affinity ties, therefore, provide legitimacy in the
context of uncertain legal rights and in the context of everyday interactions
with heteronormative society.

In this context, technoscientific practices of selecting sperm through
sperm banks constitute "true" familyhood. That is, looking like and being
like someone accomplishes social legitimacy and erases the stigma that often
accompanies apparent differences. As Chloe said in discussing the meaning
of family, "Who am I? I mean, where do I fit in? The societal message is that
there is one unit model of the mother and the father, you know." Audrey
understood family as both biology and choice.

> I have a couple of straight friends and they get married and they have families
> and it becomes nuclear. And most gays and lesbians, for so long the nuclear
> family was lost or separated. So we created our own families. And now, we
> have other [extended] families in place, and when we started having children,
> the other family's already there, so by adding children we make different types
> of families beyond the nuclear kind. . . . The importance of defining a family
> should be a group of people who love each other, not who are all biologically
> related. Families can take any form. There is no "right" way that things have to
> be. We have to be careful not to overcompensate, not to make the mistake of
> going the other way and freak out about not having "daddies" as if that *really*
> means something.

On the other hand, some respondents interpreted their actions as reinforcing heteronormativity: "It was like a fairly conventional — you know, heterosexual marriage — way in which we saw ourselves building a family, and
how we portrayed it to our families that we would build a family. So, it just
seemed natural in that way," exclaimed Robyn.

As the medical anthropologist Gay Becker (2000a) argued, one goal of
donor insemination was to create an "as if" family, one in which the children appeared to be biological offspring of the husband and wife. Practices
of matching and anonymity facilitated this heteronormative goal (Agigian
2004). In my research, while yes donors may be more desirable to lesbian
consumers, the genetic choices are not used to physically match appearance
in the hope of creating a perception of "natural" relatedness. Nonetheless,

the biological family, whether an illusion or not, is a very powerful ideal that, even when revealed to be an operation of power, does not cease to hold power over social interactions. A desire to maximize connections, therefore, exists for lesbians as well.

Affinity ties are a kinship device used to create social and cultural legitimacy. Sperm banks market sperm using donor traits; consumers select a donor by drawing on contemporary discourses of genetics, despite the ambiguity in the connection between genes and human development.

Physical Matching

Many recipients want their offspring to resemble either the biological mother or the nonbiological mother in terms of race or ethnicity. Depending on the sperm bank, ethnic characteristics may be listed in terms of national ancestry (e.g., Dutch, German, Italian) or as racial phenotype (e.g., Caucasian, Hispanic). Matching is not a straightforward case of "let's make a baby that looks like me"; it is more accurately indicative of the mobilization of biology and culture to create shared ancestry and histories with potential offspring. Matching signals a strategy by which to maximize affinity.

Among the women I interviewed, rematerialization almost always included matching racial or ethnic donor characteristics to the nonbiological parent-to-be, and sometimes to the biological parent-to-be. However, race and ethnicity were variously constructed according either to physical similarities or to one's ancestral history and thus to one's religious, ethnic, and/or national history. "Knowing" one's identity is a potent narrative of empowerment in U.S. culture, a culture shaped by immigrant narratives emphasizing ancestral and geographic origins. Certainly, racial or ethnic or geographic identity is central to how people come to know themselves and their families and to how they situationally define groups in relation to "others." As such, knowing one's identity is a narrative that underlies sperm-selection practices, with many recipients feeling that their children must eventually be able to know their identities.

"I tried to match the men in my family: blonde, blue eyed, six feet, a hundred and eighty pounds, Irish, English, Northern European," Marilyn explained. For her, her Irish and English racial origins provided knowledge and shared characteristics. While Marilyn matched to her brothers, Judith matched to her partner, Heather, the nonbiological mother: "We looked at characteristics and phenotype. We started off romantically putting her phenotype into me." Like Marilyn and Judith, Joyce incorporated phenotype into her selection criteria as a means of mixing or blending together: "I ruled out ones that were nationalities that I wasn't interested in or ethnic backgrounds that I wasn't. I basically chose donors that were similar to me in that . . . I went for donors that I felt would have looked similar to me maybe, blue-eyed and with a light complexion."

For Shari (white) and Robyn (Latina), matching Robyn's Latina heritage was important. Shari was thirty-five and planned to be the biomother. She described a key criterion for donor selection: "He's three-quarters Spanish and a quarter Mexican, with green eyes, and that fits her most, you know. The dark hair and everything. . . . Having mixed children is social. I think that in this environment and this society it's better to not be identified one way or the other. It's my ideal world for everybody to be a blend of something. That's how people are, are learning to get along better on a social basis. We were choosing someone who was some Latino mix. Dark features and tall [laugh]. He's, like, five-eleven, a hundred and seventy pounds, nice, trim, athletic guy. He's educated. He has a big family as we do and he has no health problems." Robyn agreed and elaborated on the importance of the donor's family size: "I thought it was great that the donor came from a big family. That was something that I related to." For Robyn and Shari, matching was about both physical attributes and history and lifestyle — two issues these women could relate with and, therefore, find meaning in.

Constructions of race and ethnicity in women's narratives were by and large taken for granted; that is, while such constructions were present in recipients' choices, they appeared with little reflection. A close coupling of race and ethnicity with ancestral origin permeated these discussions. By describing racial or ethnic origin as a *social* attribute, the women I interviewed emphasized social relatedness through physical likeness, shared identity, and knowledge of one's connection to genealogical and historical pasts. In this the women drew on U.S. cultural ideas of biology, heredity, and kinship, but their practices complicated the hegemonic ideology that perpetuated the unquestioned validity of racial matching. That is, they relied on matching, but they did so in complicated ways that included strategies to maximize perceived affinity and belonging.

The practice of selecting an identity-release or yes donor, described as an important selection criterion by most respondents, was part of the logic of knowing one's roots. For example, at first Michelle did not feel strongly about the importance of knowing one's origin. She described the insistence on knowing as an American quirk: "I think it is cultural. Americans are very conscious of their roots, where they come from, identity. That is not something that is true for me . . . probably because it is so much more homogeneous in Italy. I never knew anyone who was adopted, but here in the U.S., I know a lot of people who are and I realize the importance of knowing your biological roots." This description includes shared ethnicity and genetic similarity in affinity ties as kinship (see Thompson 2001), but it goes a step farther in its mobilization of relatedness as based neither solely on biogenetic ties nor solely on social ties, but as a product of a sociality enabled through perceived genetic and biological outputs.

Right-to-know donor policies and the selection of yes donors reinforce the cultural ideal that one's identity stems from blood and ancestral knowledge (see, for example, Modell 1994). This raises the question of whether knowledge of biological ancestry is necessary to move into the future and to develop one's sense of self. Sperm banks market sperm in ways that enact the possibility for women to rematerialize sperm into ideal forms. These ideal forms mirror U.S. cultural discourses of not only masculinity, as Matthew Schmidt and Lisa Moore (1998) argue, but also kinship and relatedness. As Patricia Collins (1999) argues, in the United States biological connections are affirmed by legal, state-certified marriage, legitimated by science, and sanctioned by law. This logic constructs an ideology whereby biological connection provides "rights" in much the same way as citizenship does. Biological connection, given meanings through racial and ethnic and visual "likeness," operates as a marker of family boundaries and of natural, state-sanctioned family forms. Today, many forms of assisted reproduction are constructed as legitimate means through which heterosexual married couples unable to conceive can do so. While heterosexuality and the construction of the natural biological family are illusions reinforced culturally, they are nonetheless powerful ideals of normalcy, morality, and truth that hold power over social interactions. Thus, the practices associated with assisted reproduction, the discourses that surround them, and the institutional worlds developed support them have historically functioned to reinforce dominant heteronormative narratives of relatedness (see Haraway 1991, 1992, 1997; Hartouni 1997, 1999; Casper 1998).

Managing Health, Minimizing Risk

Sperm banks construct discourses of reproductive risk, capitalizing on consumer concerns about health hazards, risks of birth defects, and increased time to conception. Technosemen is utilized as a means to overcome sperm limitations such as uncleanliness, poor motility, low velocity, and unpredictability (Schmidt and Moore 1998). In promoting technosemen, sperm banks employ a rhetoric of risk management as they highlight screening procedures to both ensure trust in the integrity of the sperm and attest to the selectivity of men invited to participate in reproduction. Procedures advertised include sperm testing for sperm count and motility; infectious-disease screening; six-month semen quarantine, followed by retesting; semen washing (to remove seminal plasma and nonsperm cellular material, thereby reducing the risk of uterine cramping and infection); and semen analysis to measure parameters such as liquefaction, volume, viscosity, pH, motile-sperm concentration, total sperm concentration, percent motility, progression, percent abnormal morphology, and white-blood-cell concentration.

Sperm-bank practices reflect late-twentieth-century discourses of genetics. Analyzing the current meanings and practices of assisted reproduction requires confronting the (eu)genetic past. It was not long ago that cultural fears of race suicide permeated white American culture and that eugenics was a legitimate scientific practice. In a public speech delivered in 1906 President Roosevelt advocated "positive" eugenics, strategies to improve the race of the nation by increasing the reproduction of the "best stock" by encouraging reproduction among those deemed to be the cultural elite (Clarke 1998; McClaren 1990). However, "negative" eugenics — strategies to improve the race of the nation by decreasing the reproduction of the worst stock — was also considered viable and acceptable.

In the United States eugenic ideas were taken up within many segments of the political spectrum and were interwoven with campaigns for forced sterilization, population policies, and birth-control movements.[8] Eugenics societies promoted compulsory sterilization and selective breeding to improve the genetic quality of the population (Kevles 1985). These practices were early forms of "scientific" modification to the population and instances of stratified reproduction.

Contemporary lesbians' practices similarly employ cultural beliefs around genes and generation in their understandings of heredity and, by extension, social connection. While the theory of the transmission of acquired characteristics has been displaced "scientifically," in many ways it has returned through cultural understandings of geneticization (Lippman 1992). These beliefs emerge as lesbians increasingly interpret aspects of people's fate (in this case the fate of donor's and their potential offspring) to be the result of their DNA. In doing so, lesbians construct and mobilize a cultural kinship device that privileges nature over nurture. At the same time, social characteristics, such as religious affiliation and hobbies, are attributed genetic power. Lesbians imagine both what they might share with their children and what their children might inherit from donors.

The ways this inheritance is imagined takes many forms, from Mendelian genetics, in which dominant physical traits are passed from each parent, to a belief that donor characteristics may rematerialize in the potential child. Nonetheless, in assisted reproduction, conceptions of genetics do not override social understandings of identity and selfhood; that is, ideas of kinship already combine notions of individualism, biological relatedness, and sociality (see also Strathern 1995). Who is included in the family and who "drops out" are shaped by patterns of sociality and by senses of alliance and affiliation that are not determined by the crude criteria of blood connection alone (Edwards 2000); they are cultural criteria that involve complex and shifting understandings of genes, genetics, and heredity.

In sperm-selection practices cultural criteria are central to the ways women imagine future connections by rematerializing donors as objects through which genetics flow. Reflecting today's heightened scrutiny of genes as causal factors in one's health, sperm banks rely deeply on genetic discourse and knowledge in their services. Most sperm banks provide donors' health histories going back one to five generations. In selecting donors women engage processes of understanding their own health and family health history in relation to the donors.' Their decisions become a way of reducing risk for the child: if breast cancer is present in a biomother's family, for example, the recipient might choose a donor with no family history of cancer.

In selecting donor characteristics, nature is not only "enterprised-up" (Strathern 1992, 30) through the selection of positive characteristics but also enabled by the minimizing of risk through careful review of disease histories. Although dominant cultural discourses about genetics, heredity, and health were not transparent to the women I interviewed, many understood the implications. "My family and I were calling it genetic engineering," Joyce said. All of respondents thought they knew that some aspects of health are inheritable and identified certain illnesses as proof. Tina said, "It did feel like genetic engineering, though. How tall would we like him? Do we prefer a graduate student or an athlete? What about physique, intelligence, and health? Is there a history of cancer?" Tina's awareness is clear: health concerns are quickly joined by social characteristics such as intelligence and athleticism. The presumption is that these too may be transmitted from generation to generation. In terms of health, Raquel emphasized cancer and schizophrenia as genetically determined risks, Paula was concerned about alcoholism as a genetic issue, and Esther perceived good eyesight as inheritable.

> *Raquel:* We wanted to pick someone who, even though we trusted that [the sperm bank] probably wouldn't have in their catalog someone who had a huge amount of schizophrenia in the close relatives or something like that. We wanted to stay clear of people with even an appearance of some kind of cancer.
> *Paula:* I think what was a really big issue for me was people who had alcoholics in their family. I don't know that there's hard conclusive evidence, but there's a lot of [studies] that have shown that there is an inheritance of alcoholism. And I guess 'cause I've seen situations of families who've adopted kids whose parents were alcoholics and what's happened to their child. . . . And there isn't any alcoholism in my family.
> *Esther:* I think my really big issues are health and then eyesight. I've really gotten stuck on eyesight lately. I want to give him a chance [laugh] and figure if the donor has twenty-twenty vision, then I figure they've got a shot, you know.

In the biomedicalization era genetics have emerged as key means through which life is understood and by which, it is assumed, dis-ease will be cured. As human-genome mapping has uncovered genes for breast cancer, early-onset Alzheimer's disease, and Huntington's disease, and as the media has proclaimed the "discovery" of genes for Down syndrome, prostate cancer, and so on, cultural understandings of "health" and "illness" have become increasingly geneticized.

Today, the "new genetics" and its public discourses have profound effects on the contours of assisted-reproduction practices and debates, as well as on cultural understandings of heredity and kinship itself.[9] The new genetics is an avenue through which kinship has been biomedicalized. That is, genetic ideas are part of a continuing sociohistorical trend of understanding human evolution, development, genetics, and the resulting stratifications they enact.[10] Lesbian accounts of selecting donor sperm from sperm banks reveal just how these actors mobilize biology—in particular the meaning of genes, heredity, and genetics—in making sense of their reproductive practices. While recipients understand genetics and heredity to be extremely important to their selection choices, they draw arbitrary lines between what is and is not genetic, what environment or nurture can overcome, and what is "known" to be passed through blood and genes. The nature-nurture divide is blurred and negotiated. While genetics are important, cultural understandings of genes and heredity are mobilized in a variety of ways.

For example, sperm-bank guidelines require testing of semen for a host of diseases believed to be transmittable to mothers and fetuses or to be inheritable (genetic); if any of these conditions are found, the guidelines indicate the exclusion of the donor's semen. While these procedures do not constitute genetic engineering per se, in that they do not alter the human geneline, they do provide a means through which the genetic make-up of potential offspring can be "selectively" enhanced. Thus, contemporary "choices" concerning a sperm donor's ancestry, health history, eye color, hair color, and so on rely on cultural understandings of genetic inheritance, understandings that draw as much on historical beliefs as they do on contemporary ones.

The women I interviewed selected socially and physically dominant donors, assuming that their sperm would help "build" socially dominant offspring. At times, the women chose donors who they felt could enhance familial shortcomings (e.g., by choosing a tall donor when the biomother was short). In addition, women looked for social health (such as education, hobbies, interests) in donors. With regard to both physical and social power, the women's selection decisions mirrored dominant U.S. cultural understandings. Key indicators of physical and social power included health, height, weight, body build, athleticism, occupation, grade-point average, and years of college. As Schmidt and Moore (1998) argued, these are social indicators of one's ability to be physically and socially dominant—the ghost of eugenics reappearing as genetic selection (see also Daniels 2006).

Such selection practices inform my finding that technoscientific practices and lesbian elaborations of kinship are co-constitutive. June, for example, describes her belief that health is genetically inherited: "We were looking for someone with remarkable health that extended out to maternal, paternal grandparents and aunts and uncles, too; someone healthy without a cancer history or Alzheimer's or other things that seemed genetic. My mother said, 'You know more about this donor then I ever knew about your father when we started having kids.' But we figured, as long as we have a choice we might as well try to go for the most remarkable health stuff." Sperm, as commercial sperm banks attest, can be sick or healthy. Judith similarly linked the commodification of sperm with the ability to "buy" health: "What really affects me is how much I have to pay to get healthy sperm that can survive freezing. Sperm that has been quarantined and tested for all the diseases. I know a lot about this person in terms of health. I know what he's not carrying. If I met him at a bar or he was my best friend who didn't tell me a few things, I wouldn't know. I think it's important to know these things and it's not anything personal. It's a matter of health. It's a matter of viruses. It's a matter of self. So let's stay healthy about it. And that's one of the reasons we went to the sperm bank." Not only are women making these decisions "because they can," but they are also identifying the commodification of sperm, health, and genetic inheritance as raising the questions "What are screened sperm worth? What are 'good' genes worth?"

Sara describes the variety of qualities that came into play in choosing a donor, as well as the ambiguities of the meanings these hold for heredity.

> Health was first and then music. Intelligence wasn't really an issue because the people they recruit, at least among the Asian donors, are very intelligent already. They all had over fourteen hundred on their SAT scores and were in graduate school, or they were undergraduates and had amazing grade-point averages. They all seemed really intelligent already. If you can pick, we figured we definitely wanted someone that can do what they'd like in life, whatever they'd like to make them happy. Handwriting and creativity were also important issues. I guess it extended to include general creativity and what they seemed like, their personality. Part of this was what they thought of the women in their lives. They write opinions of their relatives and siblings and what they said gave us an idea of their personality. What is their mother like? We asked ourselves, "Do they feel really positively towards the women in their life?"

Sara clearly mobilized cultural ideas concerning genetics and heredity, which assumed that qualities, like a health condition, could be known and mapped as inheritable through blood ties. "We know how biological all this is," and "I think my primary concern was genetics," Sara said. She emphasized what she believed we "know" and "don't know" about heredity. In a move that to a certain extent discounted environmental explanations, she chose to eliminate donors with any history of mental illness and substance use in their ancestral lineage, which she considered to be health issues. She took such health issues into account in order to enhance potential offspring and reduce risk. Further, in Sara's account, social characteristics such as musical abilities, intelligence, lack of misogyny, creativity, adaptability, and strong coping skills emerged as possible hereditary attributes, despite the fact that these are more commonly construed as acquired, rather than hereditary, characteristics.

The new genetics has created a proliferation of beliefs in genetic inheritance, marked by an explosion of research in genetics and genetic inheritance (e.g., the Human Genome Project).[11] These activities are consequential for kinship and other ideas of social relatedness and can be found in multiple biomedical sites (e.g., donor selection, health screening and surveillance, illness diagnosis, etc.). These sites are key places in which people experience, interact with, and come to understand ideologies of genetic inheritance, particularly within contexts of family and kin relations. A "hegemony of the gene" draws family and kin arrangements into the biomedical domain through current understandings that diseases are genetically transmitted from generation to generation (Finkler 2000). The biomedicalization of kinship promoted by the new genetics espouses the notion that family and kin are the medium through which inheritance flows. Although eugenics may appear to be peripheral to this history, it demonstrates a strong legacy of stratified reproduction through its construction of "appropriate" reproducers and "types" of reproduction. Further stratified reproduction continues through the design and enactment of social policies and regulations that explicitly and at times implicitly assist some people's reproduction more than that of others.

The multiplicity of donor characteristics lesbians considered led me to analyze the ways women imagine relatedness more deeply, going beyond my original two questions: will the child be accepted as mine? Will the child be like me/us? The complex kinship device I call affinity ties raises a third question: how does one create "legitimate" kinship in the context of heteronormativity?

Biomedicalized Kinship through Technoscience

In addition to managing health by reducing risk, recipients construct potential relationships by selecting donors with shared histories, physicalities, and social subjectivities. The in-depth profiles provided for a fee by sperm banks allow recipients to fully rematerialize donors. As Janella commented, "It then became, like we felt, like, when we gave the guys names and stuff, 'Oh there's Juan!' Whatever nationality they were, we gave them a name and they were like novel characters or whatever. They became these people that we felt like we got really attached to." In responding to a series of open-ended questions about their hobbies, interests, preferences, life-goals, and so on, donors put their personality characteristics into discourse and prepare them for understanding in terms of genetic and heredity. Lesbians frequently referred to in-depth donor profiles and discussed the ways they took into consideration attributes such as clarity of handwriting, articulateness, and perceived empathy and generosity.

Affinity Ties as Kinship Device

As affinity ties are mobilized, they thus signal the biomedical shaping of human relatedness produced through technoscientific medical practices. The biomedicalization of kinship promoted by the new genetics espouses the notion that family and kin are the medium through which inheritance flows.

Tina and Elizabeth were thirty-three and thirty-five years old, respectively, and had one child. Elizabeth was pregnant with their second child. Both children were conceived by donor insemination using a commercial sperm bank.

> *Tina:* I remember making that first call to the sperm bank and saying, "You know, we're ready to start looking at donor profiles, but we don't know what your process is." And the woman said, "No problem, we'll send you the fall catalog." It was like, "Oh! Sears! Or J. C. Penney's." It was just such an unusual phenomenon. It was interesting. In terms of our criteria, the most important thing for us was a white donor, just because it seemed easier. The next biggest criteria was having a yes donor because we thought as parents it was important to give the child a chance of knowing, to at least leave that open to the kids just to have the option to find out who the donor was. After those two criteria it

was kind of who looked like us, I guess, who has similar hair color. We never really cared too much about anything else.

Elizabeth: It was kind of fun. I remember being really surprised when the extensive profiles came with handwritten copies. I remember just thinking, well, this is interesting. It sort of allows some handwriting analysis. If people write well or not, you know, you get some sort of sense. . . . This guy, I remember, used a lot of exclamation marks and, I can't remember if they asked if they wore boxers or briefs, but he said, "I wear briefs and proud of it!" with exclamation marks. You see a different sort of personality come through with handwriting versus typed data. That was kind of interesting. It was fun. We thought, "He has a personality, he seems vibrant."

Decisions concerning racial or ethnic origin were significant for Elizabeth and Tina. They selected white donors because they felt that being like one's parent was "easier" on both the child and the parents. The perceived affinity that shared whiteness would create served as a kinship device driven by technoscience and by views of race in a society that privileged whiteness. Affinity ties made through whiteness maximized social legitimacy and projected a normal family form ripe with shared ancestral histories.

Tina and Elizabeth felt that looking like and being like someone not only created an affinity — a connection with the donor and his characteristics as they might be rematerialized into the child — but also social legitimacy and a version of themselves that "fit" hegemonic ideals of "true" familyhood. As Elizabeth described, "Did the donor look enough like both of us that the child would look enough like both of us? That it wouldn't be a constant flag in the world that this wasn't *really* our child. I know that a lot of other people deal with that, certainly with international adoptions and interracial adoptions and it's not insurmountable, but since we had enough similar coloring ourselves, we thought a donor who also had similar coloring would make us all seem connected, you know?" With regard to how physical appearance can serve as social legitimacy, they noted their desire to minimize risk and maximize health. As Tina said, "We wanted her features. Since I'm carrying the baby, it's going to obviously have some of mine, so we looked for physical characteristics like blonde hair, blue eyes. That was what we started with. From there we looked at personality type and other physical characteristics such as weight, height. . . . We also looked for things to eliminate. Things like a sister who was schizophrenic." Elizabeth and

Tina viewed genetic ties as providing a necessary link with the ancestral past and as being in the interest of the child; this affirmed the cultural narrative that knowing one's ancestral past can facilitate the formation of one's self-hood. Further, Elizabeth and Tina interpreted the donor's personality characteristics through his handwriting, and their interpretation emerged as significant to the selections they made.

Overall, donor characteristics were mobilized in such a way that they were imagined as shared with the parent(s)-to-be. Whether the donor characteristics were personality traits, cultural ancestry, personal health status, family health history, or physical appearance, they were constructed as inheritable. If the respondents believed musical ability and athleticism to be the result of one's environment and nurture, then it is likely that their influence as parents could lead to a child's interest and, thus, abilities in sports and music. The women I interviewed did not discuss what they as parents would offer; instead, they gave credence to the belief that nature and thus biology influence musical and athletic traits. Sarah stated, "I was looking for somebody that had music as one of their interests. My partner wanted somebody with athletic interests or, or some of the same things that she shares, some of, perhaps athletic or other things." While Sara's statement certainly reflects biological determinism, a literal reading of her assertions would overdetermine the meanings they attribute to nature and culture. However, a strong desire among potential mothers to share affinities with potential offspring cannot be oversimplified. Marie's partner expressed a desire for the donor to share social characteristics with her. Janella believed that personalities were something one was born with, something inheritable, and she accordingly expressed her and her partner's desire to share subjectivities with the donor and, by extension, with the child: "Even though we didn't know the person, any sign at all about what he was like felt really important. Anybody who seemed really uptight or something, we thought [laughing] no way. I mean, they're born with a personality. You have some influence, but we thought we could try. They're kind of like an imaginary person. Their personality is imaginary. If you think the person [donor] is kind of a nice person, it's better to hope." Respondents frequently mentioned selecting donors based on personality characteristics such as "niceness" and "decency," social characteristics such as "well-educated," and physical characteristics such as "athleticism," strength, or excellent health.

In all, respondents emphasized social qualities alongside biological ones, thus expanding kinship into new conceptual spaces. For example, in describing the importance of a yes donor, she also took into consideration personality attributes that she felt would provide a window into the donor's potential response to the child if and when the eighteen year old contacted him: "I don't know if you've ever seen the list, but it's pretty extensive. They have three categories: known or never known; the ones who make the videos; and then the ones who the child gets to call. So we basically said the only option for us was the one where at least our child would get one phone [call to the sperm donor]. That was real important to us. So he had to be a nice guy who would take the call someday." A perception of "niceness" was thus important to her decision. (Notably, in her sense that one phone call would provide closure, not an opening up of possibilities, is the implication that knowing one's roots creates a form of wholeness, a means to know oneself and to close the unanswered question of who you are and where you came from.)

In practices of considering personality characteristics, too, cultural understandings of genetics and heredity were employed in ways that maximized affinity and belonging. Lynda constructed personality as genetically inheritable: "My big thing was I wanted someone who was just a nice, good human being with good sense of humor and smart. Things I would find appealing in a person. You don't really get that part from the biosketches. Since we went to our friend who knew all of the donors at the bank, we told him we really want a great guy who is light in color [Lynda was a fair-skinned Caucasian] and pale in complexion. We narrowed it down to a couple of different ones. One was really, really handsome and a great guy who was a bit darker in color and another was a super guy and cute. So we said, 'O.K. We'll take the super and cute one because he's lighter in coloring.'" Like many women I interviewed, Lynda expressed the importance of social characteristics for potential shared affinity ties and for projecting a normative idealization of herself and her family in the face of uncertain legal ties and a generally heteronormative culture. Her comments also indicated a return to Lamarckism, in which acquired characteristics are theorized as being passed from generation to generation. Lynda and her partner relied heavily on the donor's own words and own handwriting to ascertain his values, beliefs, and personality. Sperm banks sell the long profiles to recipients, thereby suggesting that personality qualities found in these responses

could be consequential for the child. Sperm is thus inscribed with the personality of the donor, and the users are given the opportunity to rematerialize these characteristics. In the case of "yes donors," personality also signals
how a donor might respond if a child contacts him in eighteen years.

Respondent descriptions indicate a desire for shared affinity with the
potential child, which points to another set of desires: for normality, legitimacy, and acceptance. The recipients mobilize social characteristics as
being, in some ways, genetically inheritable and therefore overriding nurture. Janella's comments, for example, illustrate how recipients consider a
range of factors when selecting a donor: "What were the characteristics
about the guys we picked? Somebody athletic and well-educated. Someone
who seemed nice and decent. Someone not too freaked out or type A.
Those were the biggest things." Since all of these characteristics are listed on
the sperm-bank donor profiles, it is not surprising that women prioritize
these attributes and make decisions based on them. In other words, the
donor profiles provide a script for women to make sense of sperm, affinity,
and identity. Women are not only passive recipients of this script, they are
also bring to the set menu their own interpretations and desires, thus constructing relatedness based on perceived affinity ties. Affinity ties not only
include physical appearance but also encompass social and cultural characteristics such as national origin, religious ancestry, cultural interests, hobbies, and social qualities. While these are not known to be genetically hereditary traits, their meanings are mobilized as if they are. Thus, they serve as a
kinship device for constructing not only imagined relatedness and social
connection but also social legitimacy.

Looking Ahead: From Kinship to (Biomedical) Belonging

It was over a decade ago that Sarah Franklin (1993) asserted that what
could have eroded heterosexual privilege instead led to its reinforcement.
But much has happened since 1993 in terms of access and use of commercial
and biomedical assisted reproduction. Today, lesbians are a primary niche
market for sperm banks and fertility services, and according to my study, the
market has proved more inclusive than the state.

Sperm banks and sperm-donor selections reveal that sperm is commodi-
tized and given value as an investment in the future. The kinship device of
affinity ties produces a destabilization of the nature-culture binary in an

effort to maximize social legitimacy and true-familyhood in the face of heteronormative culture. As this ethnography demonstrates, the biomedicalization of reproduction enables a distinctive biomedicalization of kinship in which aspiring parents build affinity ties to secure social legitimacy and imagine future social connections.

What started in the 1970s as an unintended convergence of sex without reproduction and reproduction without sex has produced some fundamental questions regarding intimacy: what constitutes a family? What and who is a mother, a father? How is relatedness formed and given meaning? In what ways do blood and genes signal relatedness? What of intimacies through choice, affilial, and consanguine connection? In what ways are the boundaries between heterosexual parenthood (often considered normal and natural) and queer parenthood regulated? Finally, in what ways, if any, are these questions shaped by and through the use of consumer-based medical reproductive technologies? Beyond addressing reproductive stratification, these questions are also profoundly important to issues of group-based treatment. Some of these questions are answerable by this and other ethnographic research, but many remain open. One must therefore be willing to allow complexity and multiplicity in how one conceptualizes belonging and connection.

Sperm, as a technoscientific commodity, is given cultural meanings in practices of consumption. It is invested with the potential to forge connection with offspring (and partners). In practices of selecting sperm, recipients construct relatedness in ways that draw on cultural understandings of genetics and heredity. These understandings are mobilized along with cultural ideologies of relatedness and kinship. Lesbian recipients of donor sperm create affinity ties, a kinship device employed to secure legitimacy in an uncertain legal terrain. Their cultural practices are consequential not only for lesbian reproduction but also for American constructions of kinship, family, and relatedness in general. As technoscientific innovations continue to transform the markers of kinship and as new social groups participate in their consumption, cultural norms may be altered. Simultaneously, however, hegemonic norms may also be maintained.

Judith Butler (1998, 2004), a feminist philosopher, has argued that lesbians and gays are rigorously excluded from state-sanctioned notions of the family. While she does not argue for their inclusion, she both provides evidence of this exclusion and raises several questions. Her evidence includes the ways lesbians and gays are denied visitation rights, executorial rights, and inheritance rights; selectively denied the status of citizenship; and denied the questionable benefit of being a member of the military who might speak his or her desire (Butler 2004). This provokes several questions: Are these exclusions not the effects of maintaining the traditional family? Are they not another variant of heteronormativity? And, finally, are these exclusions part of the state's distribution of recognition through legal and economic entitlements? (ibid.) In the next and final chapter of this book I apply these questions to the practices of and discourses about assisted reproduction.[12]

Lesbians are not the scripted or imagined "users" of sperm banks, nor are they granted kinship privileges. Nonetheless, through their consumer-driven interactions with sperm banks, lesbians challenge heteronormativity, demanding access and making choices that maximize their recognition as families and, therefore, their cultural legitimacy. However, lesbian sperm-donor selections also recreate geneticization narratives of U.S. culture. They rely on essentialist, biological notions of human characteristics, and they often reify these in ways that mirror U.S. hierarchical classifications of attributes such as race, ethnicity, and physical and social qualities. That is, in their reproductive practices lesbians maintain race, gender, cultural, and health hierarchies.

Yet, this research has revealed that kinship itself is a kind of doing, an assemblage of meanings and practices that are interlinked with other cultural, social, political, and economic phenomena. Boundaries between kinship and community, between the biological and the social, are rendered porous, decentering traditional notions of family, kin, and belonging.

Seven

Imagining Futures of Belonging

WHEN SHOULD A RESEARCHER STOP trying to capture unfolding events that take place as she analyzes and writes her findings? Certainly, much has ensued since I began the research for this book in 1998. It would have been difficult to imagine fully the conservative wave that followed the 2001 attacks on the United States. Heightened attention to security has been accompanied by a new emphasis on protecting the status quo. Political and military efforts to spread democratic principles around the globe have intensified efforts to protect so-called family values at home. Questions remain: what will this new century bring? What forms of critical imagination will shed light on the complexities that constitute social life? Like previous generations, one asks in what ways life might be better, more just, more inclusive, and one fears the new (and old) stratifications that always come with "progressive" change.

A moving target is not easily captured. As Avery Gordon (1997) says, "Life is complicated" (3), and the methods that have been devised to capture complex subjectivities, power relations, and dynamics of social change are not precise enough to do so. The categories and concepts established so far are inadequate to capture the density such terms comprise. There are no universal, definitive realities, only "partial truths" and "situated knowledges" (Haraway 1988). To understand them, one must be willing to confront the ghosts: the realities and concepts that are not there; the things that are implicated, behind or beyond the scenes, out of sight. One must be willing to see the real in fiction and the fiction in the real.

Beginning Questions

I began my research with a set of rather simple questions: in what ways can I understand and give meaning to my childhood as the daughter of a "lesbian mother" as at once part of a normative heterosexual family and participant in many queer family forms? As an observer and participant in lesbian cultures throughout the 1970s, 1980s, and 1990s, I often wondered: is lesbians having children a transgressive act, or does it represent a variant of the enduring social norms of gender and its concomitant social form — heterosexual reproduction? It seemed to me that lesbians having children reaffirmed the sociocultural expectation that women will reproduce, thereby naturalizing women's bodies as reproductive. My "experience" (always already interpretable) also confirmed that the idealized kinship structure of the nuclear family (with two parents of the opposite sex) was no longer salient in social practices, at least in my own life. Yet its dominance remained ideologically and politically hegemonic.

Of course, no childhood takes place entirely outside of heterosexuality; childhood is given meaning and produced through it. In what ways do lesbian reproductive practices challenge and destabilize this long-standing ideological structure? And in what ways do lesbians participate in its very reinforcement by providing the deviant "other" on which its meaning is formed?

In examining these questions, I began with the sociocultural histories of medical reproductive technologies and the medicalization and demedicalization of (homo)sexualities, complex interactions that reflected the unintended meeting of sex without reproduction and reproduction without sex. I attempted to partially engage with the presence of those subjected to forced institutionalization, sterilization, and other assaults on sexual and reproductive liberties, as well as those who navigated these landmines by passing, conforming, or finding communities to call home. These phantoms, from mannish women to those expressing perverse desires, were discursively produced along with women and men who fit rigid matrices of sex, gender, race, and sexuality. It is this latter group who were not only given support to reproduce but encouraged and "assisted" in doing so. These co-constitutive social practices partially produced and continue to give meaning to Fertility Inc. and to various queer social movements that formed during the past thirty years. I, and the thirty-six women interviewed, have told of the effects of power relations. I have attended to such power relations by looking in the shadows of the past and acknowledging their presence in the cultural landscape. Together, these power relations shape lesbian lives and their (new) social forms and (new) subjectivities. They both shape emergent possibilities and cultural backlashes to those possibilities.

A confluence of women's and lesbian health movements variously espoused slogans of women's empowerment and reproductive rights. Throughout the twentieth century feminists set out to ensure that sexual freedom and control over one's reproduction were not only protected but maximized. The two were understood as deeply connected and in need of both legal protection and cultural and political recognition. Lesbian feminist movements in the 1960s and 1970s continued to insist on these demands. By the mid-1980s, the meeting of sex without reproduction and reproduction without sex consolidated into a lesbian paradigm reflecting a shift for some from "playing softball in the park to pushing strollers down the avenue" (Jetter 1996). Furthermore, the self-empowerment slogans from women's health movements are expressions of what Ulrich Beck (1992) calls "a social surge of individualization" (87) that require constant self-monitoring so that "we are, not what we are, but what we make of ourselves" (Giddens 1991, 75). Self-empowerment has become a concept integral to Fertility Inc. and contemporary lesbian reproduction.

Summing It Up

At the heart of this book are my interviews with lesbians, who describe their experiences with reproductive technologies and services. In arguing that the present is productive of new reproductive subjectivities and material practices, I make six key assertions.

First, increasingly complex processes of biomedicalization have transformed lesbian insemination from a lay social movement exemplified by a low-tech, do-it-yourself approach into an elaborate event requiring the assistance of multiple actors and technologies, new information sources, and new forms of social relations. Assisted reproduction for lesbians has traveled far from the turkey-baster technology of the 1970s and now tends to be a highly biomedicalized process.

The shape of the shift toward biomedicalized reproduction is varied, but its defining characteristics include a supplanting of low-tech procedures with high-tech ones (ovulation detection; the use of frozen, washed semen from commercial sperm banks; nitroglycerin tanks; and needleless syringes); an increased reliance on sperm banks as key providers of technosperm, information, and training; and the use of intrauterine and more advanced technological procedures, often as first-line interventions.

When low-tech options are displaced, the stakes are high. Feminist health ideals may be undermined as "control" shifts from users to practitioners; access is compromised as more expensive technologies and services, often coupled with the ideology of infertility medicine, become the most widely available; and technology comes to shape both real and imagined possibilities.[1] Overall, as using advanced options becomes a routine and standard practice, those options are constructed as not only the "best" but as the *only* valid approach (Becker 2000a); other options are no longer envisioned or available. In addition, the practices of precise diagnosis and conservative treatment (of moving up a "ladder of care" rung by appropriate rung) are being rapidly displaced by protocols that advocate immediate use of hormone therapy and/or IVF. This move is apparent in the advertising and practices of many IVF clinics that guarantee "pregnancy or your money back."[2] This guarantee is achieved by amping up interventions as the first line of treatment. Thus, the new options concretely structure available choices. These so-called choices are further enforced through laws and regulations that, while not necessarily enforced, continue to govern and stratify conception trajectories and parenthood itself.

Each of these shifts represents a moment for potential discrimination — embedded and overt — as well as a potential avenue for challenging and subverting constraints or queering the terms of the landscape. While the overall shift has been toward increased technoscientific knowledges and applications, lesbians have actively brought forward a variety of ideals such as their subjectivity; a reliance or trust in embodied, subjective knowledge; and an enterprising, do-it-yourself control over settings, meanings, and practices. These are complex negotiations that rework the stability of the meanings and practices of reproduction itself.

Second, constitutive of the shift from do-it-yourself to biomedicalized reproduction are normalization processes embedded within fertility and infertility medicine. These reflect instances of embedded discrimination by defining and classifying a normative (i.e., heterosexual) infertility user, constructing "normal" treatment options (those targeting biophysiological infertility), and applying standard protocols of care. Throughout the latter half of the twentieth century, assisted-reproduction technologies reinforced childrearing as the proper activity of the heterosexual couple. The affirmation of heterosexual sex as the only appropriate route to making a baby took place even as conception was being rerouted through the biomedical clinic and despite the medicalization of the woman and/or couple as infertile. That is, a narrow view of sexuality as heterosexual and reproductive was sustained even in the absence of some biogenetic inputs and requisite sex acts. Yet today the ambiguous biomedical terms *fertility* and *infertility* serve multiple purposes and connote a variety of meanings. A discursive shift has taken place from infertility to fertility difficulties to fertility as part of every woman's (and man's) wellness. This shift has partially driven a wider market (and acceptance) of fertility users, yet insurance classification guidelines and coverage have not followed.[3]

In my interpretation, the assumption of Fertility, Inc. is that heterosexual sex (thus heterosexuality itself) is ubiquitous and that its outcome is what needs to be controlled and/or assisted. This assumption reinforces the hegemony of heterosexuality itself. The result is the construction of legitimate and illegitimate forms of sex, gender, and sexuality and the reinforcement of a cultural ideal of "compulsory heterosexuality" (Rich 1980). Moreover, infertility medicine appropriates compulsory heterosexuality and transforms it into "compulsory reproduction." The new grounding assumption becomes "If you *can* achieve pregnancy, you *must* procreate."

Being a lesbian generally means preferring the company of and intimacy with a female partner. It is a social category. At times, biomedical services and providers translate the social status of being a lesbian into a medical diagnosis of infertility. This can be read as a strategic lessening of barriers to reproduction for lesbians, but it also continues their historical medicalization by bringing them into the sphere of biomedicine as patients seeking solutions to social problems—in this case, the absence of sperm. Once a lesbian enters infertility medicine, all kinds of discursive constructions evolve to address the "newcomer."

Having once been seemingly invisible social actors in infertility services, lesbians continue to be implicated actors, this time as the subject of biomedical normalization processes. New forms of stratification are enacted—maneuvers that are historically contiguous with previous understandings of lesbians as nonprocreative deviants. Today, selectively taking on an infertility diagnosis—once relegated to heterosexual women—has become "routine" and childlessness has come to mean "not yet pregnant." This trend continues to consolidate, making fertility services part of everyday wellness for lesbians who desire pregnancy, whether or not an infertility diagnosis is made.

In short, being a lesbian, once a social designation, has been transformed into a fertility "risk" factor, giving every lesbian a biomedical classification that makes her an appropriate candidate for treatment and directs her into biomedical services. The social category has become conflated with a fertility status. The language shift from "infertility" to "fertility" services was taking place as I conducted this research. When I began in the mid-1990s, the concept of infertility was largely used and mobilized inside and beyond medical services. When I completed the research, the medical community largely referred to fertility services, which indicate a reframing of such services from treating pathology to offering wellness: a diagnosis is no longer necessary, and all women can access treatments for a fee.

Third, lesbian reproductive practices today occur in the context of the postmodern era, in which the creation of flexible consumer-citizens is the goal of the corporate, global economy. In this setting, the consumer must choose from a preset selection of menu items as a means to fulfill their goals, desires, and identities. Infertility medicine offers a range of sperm, egg, and conception options, and one's reproductive choices are structured and conditioned by the physical and social characteristics represented in this menu. Fertility services and sperm banks thus constitute new subjectivities: lesbian mothers, gay fathers, and new family arrangements brought into being through consumption. Reproduction is yet another do-it-yourself project —a way to transform oneself and one's identity: "We are, not what we are, but what we make of ourselves" (Giddens 1991, 75). This do-it-yourself project is brought to you by pharmaceutical products, specialist services, and other medical technologies that promise happiness from the inside out. Self-empowerment, direct from women's movements, has been co-opted as a marketing slogan looking to attract the lucrative market of in/fertility users.[4] This slogan appeals to women in their forties who came of age with various social movements of the 1970s, but more important, it appeals to women who grew up taking for granted many of the social changes that had occurred with women's, gay and lesbian, and civil-rights movements and the identity politics that followed. Self-empowerment offers an image of womanhood that is about possibility, limitless potential, and the promise of control over the future. Embedded in the concept of self-empowerment is the sense that a life of motherhood (and careerism) is within reach of women who learn the skills, navigate the system, and/or have the characteristics necessary for continual self-invention.

Of course, stratifications shape options, and the most significant constraint is economic resources. In a fee-for-service healthcare system like that in the United States, it is those who can pay who can also most easily transform themselves. As a result, uneven biomedicalization is a characteristic of assisted-reproduction technologies. Reproductive healthcare specialists and insurance guidelines do not provide or allow for services to be equally available and utilized across all persons or groups. Medical technologies are generally expensive, and access to such treatments is often limited to those who can pay or who are well-insured. As such, the use of reproductive technologies is a sexuality-based and class-based phenomenon. Thus, the biomedicalization of fertility is stratified: it reproduces U.S. class-, race-, and sexuality-based hierarchies by continuing to ensure the reproduction of middle-class (usually white) heterosexual families. Practices of classifying and categorizing health and illness constitute uneven biomedicalization by valorizing some points of view and silencing others (Bowker and Star 1999).

Constraints of age, physiology, economic resources, and/or sexual desire limit this bright future, but they do so in covert as well as overt ways. Society's message is that individuals with agency can overcome constraints with the right attitude, knowledge, drive, and choices. Many embrace this mandate, while others find its promise out of reach. The concept of choice is central to the problematic of empowerment versus constraint: choice is highly bound both by one's embodied, economic, and cultural resources as well as by what is being offered. As a result, Fertility Inc. and its entrepreneurial messages of empowerment and choice raise questions concerning the nature of identity and social relationships in an increasingly commodified world and participate in shaping new queer citizens ready and willing to participate in consumer culture (see Davis-Floyd 1992; Strathern 1992; Edwards et al. 1999).

Fourth, kinship is extended in several ways. While biosocial kinship has largely been constructed as fixed and, therefore, as something beyond one's control, the choices enabled by assisted-reproduction technologies turn this construction on its head and offer possibilities for selecting one's family members and their characteristics. Today, the biomedical shaping of human

relatedness is elaborated through technoscientific innovations and is produced through negotiations with legal policies, cultural norms, and purchasing power. One example produced at this site of analysis is the ways
lesbians construct affinity ties and thus relatedness—a specific instance of
queering reproduction, yet a complicated one. As the very meanings of
social and biological ties are negotiated, family and extended kinship remain
durable as organizing principles in social life. One may be better served by
removing these altogether. Taking the lead from my respondents, who always and consistently referred to family, I used the term *affinity ties* to signal
the deliberate construction of relatedness enabled through assemblages of
meanings of blood, genes, and social and cultural connection. As my respondents indicated, these forms of sociality lie within and between the
family one chooses and the family one is given in "nature." Lesbians mobilize affinity ties to negotiate legal and ideological norms and in doing so
offer constructions of family based on shared cultural and social characteristics as well as on biology. These constructions amount to a form of neo-
Lamarckism in which "natureculture" is once again combined and acquired
characteristics are mobilized in the genetic imaginary.

Fifth, uses of assisted-reproduction knowledges, services, and technologies are choreographies that reveal the complexity of what sociologists call
the agency-structure dilemma. Navigating pathways to conception includes
free will and structural constraint, but, more important, it includes "embodied subjectivity" and what science studies scholars call "scripted technologies." Users and their embodied subjectivities matter, as do the ways these
interact with material things. In examining material practices of achieving
pregnancy, I intended to work within the ontological privileging of science
and technology studies that highlight the importance of material things
(i.e., nonhuman objects such as the needleless syringe), yet to simultaneously focus on the social and the embodied. Doing so brought me to
conclude that achieving pregnancy for lesbians involves practices that people, their bodies, artifacts, and ideas do together.[5]

Lesbian users of reproductive technologies interpret and "make sense" of
these technologies in a variety of ways. Thus, while assisted-reproduction
technologies are developed and marketed with particular users and actions
in mind (Akrich 1995), in the hands of users these can be reinterpreted and
negotiated (Cowan 1987; Bijker, Hughes, and Pinch 1987). Regulatory
ideals can thus be disrupted. Sexuality and gendered norms and assump-

tions may be read as both "inputs" and "outputs" of the social and cultural construction of assisted reproduction. One's always *already* inscribed attitudes and understandings of sex, gender, and sexuality influence the manufacture and diffusion of these technologies and vice versa. Users can and do modify and/or subvert a technology's intended meaning or ideal use (Moore 1997).[6]

As the particular choreographies discussed herein reveal, some women follow given technological scripts while others create their own interpretations and meanings for the technologies and associated practices, thus subverting the expectations and scripts of the developers, marketers, and services organized around the technologies. Analyzing their negotiations allows one to see how lesbians navigate shifting control loci by variously resisting, accommodating, ignoring, and otherwise transforming the normative ideals of reproduction, pregnancy, and social relations. One must be cautious not to reproduce a colonial interpretation that characterizes the world as two-dimensional: control versus resistance, oppositional consciousness versus hegemonic structure, agentic actors versus those constrained by social forces. Instead, one must see that all new freedoms bring new controls, that all expansions come with accommodation and incorporation, and that the imagined and the actual, the material and the semiotic coexist.[7]

A paradox exists here: while the transformation of heteronormativity is possible, so, too, is its enforcement. Users' actions can be read as their means of inflecting dominant codes for their own purposes, of undermining truth claims regarding desire, and of making new social formations. The lesbian body is transformed: no longer "not a woman," instead a woman with agency — ready, willing, and able to use cultural constructions of womanhood for her own purposes. Further, hybrid-technology practices reveal transformative possibilities in the meanings applied to technologies themselves. Practices that involve cobbling together various types of technologies and technoscientific procedures as well as many forms of expertise, then putting them to use in a diversity of settings and with multiple social actors, reveal that "standards" are not required and certainly not enforced.

Sixth, lesbians' use of these technologies functions culturally as a stage for the enactment of the heterosexual matrix — a system of sex/gender/sexuality. If these markers are removed from their natural assumptions and understood for their categorical labeling, which serves the political purposes of

reproductive heterosexuality, then, as Monique Wittig (1981) argued, lesbians are not women. These actors are figures variously produced in time and
place. Yet, as my research has demonstrated, certain material-discursive
places make them into women. Fertility Inc. is one such space. What happens
to their lesbianism, their actual sexuality, and thus their subversion? Is it still
the lesbian — unsexed, unwoman — who refuses the heterosexual matrix of
epistemological domination, who can subvert the hierarchy of knowledge
and subjectivity? Or will lesbians be redefined once again to exclude them
from the category *woman*? Perhaps some lesbians will refuse inclusion and
intelligibility in favor of dodging gender norms altogether.

It may be that the actions of lesbians achieving pregnancy no longer
completely erase the "sexed" hierarchy of knowledge and subjectivity, as
these women become mothers despite their refusal of heterosexuality.
However, their actions may at once be complicit with hierarchical organizations based on sex, gender, and sexuality. However, what also emerges is
that queer uses of technoscientific practices are able to rock the heteronormative boat of reproduction, with its "appropriate" reproducers and "real"
parents. In this way, queer reproduction destabilizes the cultural site of
assisted reproduction, a site previously reserved for heterosexual, infertile,
married couples.

While the heterosexual paradigm remains strong in all areas of public
life — including biomedical life, its enforcement is porous and depends on
the "right" doctor, diagnosis, and economic and cultural capital to maintain
its hold. Yet compulsory heterosexuality continues to maintain and, at
times, create certain forms of biomedical protocols, technologies, and practices of assisting reproduction. Lesbians, as part of public and biomedical
life-worlds, have entered biomedicine and taken on and negotiated its classification systems, forms of technologies, and embedded assumptions. The
results are not monolithic. At times heterosexuality is reiterated and reinforced; at other times it is resisted, parodied, and even changed. The differences can be found in individual women's pragmatic negotiations, which
are always formed with the goal of pregnancy in mind.

As a result, while heterosexuality and the biological family are cultural
constructions, they remain very powerful ideas that do not evaporate or
cease to hold sway over social interactions. Compulsory heterosexuality and
reproduction have given rise to the biomedical social form of Fertility, Inc.
While current practices of achieving pregnancy are no longer confined to a

binary matrix (legitimate versus illegitimate uses, users, and settings), the regulatory ideals of heterosexuality remain powerful, if far less stable.[8] I therefore conclude with a return to the concept of queer formation — an array of sociohistorical processes whereby categories and meanings distinguishing types of sexual behaviors, beings, forms of kinship, and social relationships are created, transformed, and destroyed (Omi and Winant 1994, 55). I argue that the institutional, sociocultural, political, and discursive practices that organize local cultures of getting pregnant among lesbians in the San Francisco Bay Area are queer formations. Yet these formations are not absolute in the extent to which they queer social life itself. As chapter 2 demonstrated, a logic of normative time organizes lesbians' "getting ready" practices, biological clocks, and lifecourse stages. If dominant modes of organizing space-time must be altered in order for queering to occur, then no queering exists here. However, if we instead view the benchmark as producing new identifications, social connections, and ways of living together, then much is queered here. Questions remain: Are these practices part of a larger move to sexualize — homosexualize or heterosexualize — bodies, acts, desires, subjectivities, social relationships, and knowledges? Does lesbian assisted reproduction displace other modes of reproduction and parenting such as adoption, foster-parenting, and those more informal arrangements once touted as important to both help world-population growth and transform the hegemony of the nuclear family? Is sexuality in general, and lesbianism in particular, a distinctive feature of these practices? If so, does this feature challenge the institutions of reproduction and family?[9]

Past-Present-Future Assemblages

The future encompasses past-present-futures assembled anew in a variety of configurations, each embodying many complexities. Situated in postmodernity, the future is conceptualized as a set of "machinic assemblages" (Deleuze and Guattari 1977, 1987), that is, a state of becoming, an unfolding or process of interconnectedness of concepts that coparticipate in thought or meaning. Lesbian reproduction represents one such assemblage, produced and given meaning through a complex array of social forces, institutional structures, discursive fields, and material practices. Imagining the future of lesbian reproduction requires, first, a glance back to the past and to the early chapters of this book.

New dads Michael Thorne-Begland (left) and Tracy Thorne-Begland and hold their 4-month-old twins—daughter Logan (left) and son Chance. The twins were carried to term by a surrogate in a pregnancy that was the product of sperm from one of the partners and eggs donated by the sister of the other.

Fatherhood by a New Formula

Using an Egg Donor
And a Gestational
Surrogate, Some Gay
Men Are Becoming
Dads—and Charting
New Legal and
Ethical Territory

By SANDRA G. BOODMAN
Washington Post Staff Writer

It's a feeling the wealthy Washington entrepreneur likens to "stepping off into thin air," a gut-churning, middle-of-the-night realization that his life-changing choice is based on "some really big leaps of faith."

But most of the time, the single gay executive said, becoming a father using his sperm and eggs donated by a 24-year-old woman he met once in a downtown Starbucks to create embryos that were implanted in the uterus of a 22-year-old surrogate mother he barely knows, absolutely seems like the right thing to do.

It was, he said, the culmination of increasingly urgent soul-searching that accelerated as he hurtled toward 50.

"I've always loved children and I thought, 'What am I waiting for?' I want somebody to love me and I want somebody to love," said

Scott decided that he had the means and the motivation to become a single father. He rejected adoption because he wanted his own biological child. Instead Scott embarked on a two-year process, fraught with uncertainty, that will cost him $100,000 by the time he takes the baby, due in late June, home from the hospital.

Scott found his donor and surrogate through Creative Family Connections, a three-person law firm with offices in Tysons Corner and Bethesda. The firm often serves as a broker for would-be parents, finding both egg donors and surrogates and handling the associated legal work.

"We believe that everyone can build a family, and that's what we try to help people do," said the firm's founder, Diane S. Hinson. A Harvard Law School graduate, Hinson stopped practicing communications law to start the firm, a move she said was prompted by personal experience. Several years ago when she was single,

6   Sandra Boodman, *Washington Post*, 18 January 2005, F1. © 2005 by *The Washington Post*. Reprinted with permission.

As reported by the *Washington Post* article "Fatherhood by a New Formula" (Boodman 2005), one of the most visible new social forms in this first decade of the twenty-first century is the two-father family, produced through egg donation, surrogacy, and adoption (see fig. 6). The past is important in this development: the two-father family form shares ideological space with what is now the more domesticated lesbian mother. The practices, ideological continuities, stratifications, controversies, and possibilities offered by two-father and two-mother family forms overlap and hold their own distinctiveness, yet they require the same attention and analysis I have paid to lesbian reproduction herein.

This rise of two-father family forms must similarly be read as a gendered, raced, and classed social phenomenon "performing" complicated work in the popular imagination. Lesbian mothers have occupied this space for more than three decades. Of course, like lesbian mothers, gay fathers have always been part of the social fabric; their histories are also complicated, diverse, and used politically and socially for a variety of purposes. That is, while gay fatherhood may challenge and subvert the social order, it may also simultaneously reinforce the social order through its very marking as an other against which the natural stands strong. Further, two-father family forms will, and currently are, used for political maneuvering by many, whether they be neoconservative or progressive or something in between.

Although same-sex-father families and other queer family forms (e.g., transgender-parent families) are likewise constituted through the meeting of sex without reproduction and reproduction without sex, their distinctiveness requires research and theorization. The emergence of lesbian reproduction was enabled through the convergence of assisted-reproduction technologies with vibrant women's and lesbian health movements organized around issues of reproductive rights. Similarly the emergence of gay fatherhood is produced through more recent social movements around queer rights (including AIDS activism) and gay and lesbian inclusions in social entitlements (e.g., marriage, surrogacy, and adoption rights).

Today's emergent gay families are, in these ways, part of a thirty-year trend. They reflect a queer formation, and yet they are assemblages of their own. They are produced through the next wave of the two social forces shaping lesbian reproduction: gay and lesbian movements for equal rights and increased regenerative possibilities produced through "advances" in biomedical science (e.g., surrogacy). However, these are assembled through the technoscientific practices and political-economic trends of global capitalism that have formed since the mid-1980s. Gender, class, and race stratifications will shape two-dad, two-mom, and other parenting arrangements configured outside these dyads and outside these gender norms. In other words, both shared and divergent processes exist, raising new questions albeit with similar issues: who will provide the eggs and the wombs necessary to enable these family forms? From what towns, communities, and countries will the biomaterials be drawn? From whose gendered, raced, and classed bodies will they be drawn? Will reproductive services follow capitalism from the west to the rest to secure the bodies and labor necessary to fulfill American Dreams? Whatever forms future families take, and whatever means are used to produce them, transformative potentials as well as new controls will exist.

As biomedical innovations promising cure, treatment, risk reduction, or enhancement continue to flood the marketplace, questions must be asked about the controls and transformations they simultaneously allow, about the stratifications they produce, about the controversies they ignite, and about their intended and unintended affects on social life. That is, scientific innovations must be read as part of broader sociohistorical processes concerning the very fabric and meaning of life itself, of when and under what conditions life begins and ends, and what the contours of that life shall bring.

Further, when new sexual controversies and debates proliferate, they must be read as challenging particular forms of desire and social connection which transgress and/or stabilize heteronormativity, as constituting and deferring dominant knowledge, and as allowing new and old practices both within and beyond the confines of sexual acts, identities, and behaviors.[10]

Past-present-futures are often most salient in controversies. If one looks back to the beginning of the twentieth century, one sees that many controversies over reproduction and assisted reproduction have taken place since then. The issue of "artificial impregnation," for example, was heavily critiqued for its assumed altering of the so-called natural order. Guiding sperm was viewed as akin to adultery because it intervened, and thus interfered, in the relations between a husband and wife (Finegold 1976). Throughout the twentieth century, a Pandora's box of technical disruptions to the hegemonic sex act was unleashed.[11]

By the 1970s and 1980s controversies emerged as a large-scale infertility industry consolidated. Opposition came primarily from theologians, reproductive scientists, and a segment of feminists and women concerned with what they perceived as a decrease in opportunities to self-control reproductive processes. These groups shared a concern with assisted reproduction's perceived disruption to the meaning of marriage and parenthood: "Fertilization without sexual intercourse permits a separation of genetic from social fatherhood, a separation of a child's genetic and social identities, a separation of genetic communication which are integral components of human sexual intercourse. These separations effect the biological and social origins of personhood, parenthood, marriage, and the family" (anonymous, quoted in Blank 1984, 39). Others opposed assisted-reproduction technologies for what they perceived as a "dehumanizing of parenthood through its move of conception from the bedroom to the laboratory. Nonetheless, what became infertility medicine garnered support and today is a large-scale, lucrative, and mostly accepted medical practice. Benefits were seen to outweigh risks as the despair of innocent couples unable to naturally produce was overcome" (Finegold 1976).

When the physicians Robert Edwards and Patrick Steptoe announced the birth of a child conceived through IVF in 1978, the controversy over assisted reproduction heated up. Initially, IVF was attacked for its presumed nontherapeutic nature (i.e., it diverted money from more life-saving procedures) and its perceived unnaturalness (i.e., it separated the "physical" dimensions of reproduction — intercourse — from emotional ones). The primary concern was that procreation was transformed from being the intimate act of a heterosexual couple into a technical act, with the associated opportunity for people to apply technologies for their own purposes. The rhetoric of these arguments is quite similar to much of the language used in today's controversy over the use of cloning technologies. Do they challenge nature in ways that have not previously been done? In the 1980s surrogacy (and particularly the practice of paying egg donors) was another site of reproductive controversy. While sperm donors have been paid for decades for their "altruistic" donations, compensating women for their "gifts" of surrogacy has met with much, and a variety of, disapproval. More recently, IVF is at the center of various controversies, including those that revolve around the blastocytes that are not used and around the use of IVF in surrogacy, including cases in which gay fatherhood and lesbian motherhood is achieved through surrogacy and/or egg donation.

New technologies allow for the increased integration of biological and information science, further blurring the bounds between health and illness, animal and machine, human and nonhuman. In the case of the reproductive and regenerative technologies offered, the controversies that emerge are likely to concern the boundaries of human sexuality, reproduction, and kinship; the parameters of legitimate and illegitimate sexual expressions; and the lines between sanctioned and unsanctioned linkages among sexuality, marriage, procreation, and family (Franklin 1993, 1995; Haraway 1995; Strathern 1995). Cultural changes in reproductive science and practice are often most visible by the controversies they provoke. Yet overt discrimination has rarely been a part of the lesbian reproductive practices, as I herein document. The location of San Francisco, California, has a lot to do with this finding. But despite location, ideological continuities exist that continue to shape the meanings and practices of lesbian reproduction even in those places where being a lesbian parent-to-be is widely accepted.

In the case of lesbian procreative practices in the 1970s and 1980s, the partial cultural shift from lesbians as nonprocreative to a "lesbian baby boom" was not without controversy. Similar to other reproductive controversies, it raised eugenic questions regarding who should and should not reproduce, under what circumstances, and by what means. Past controversies erupted over the appropriate recipient of donated sperm as well as the appropriate donor. The existence of controversies about reproductive technologies illustrate that "not only are individuals being reproduced, but so too are the social relations that organize them and render them recognizable as such" (Hartouni 1997, 119).

Today's controversies appear to be most pronounced in the areas of reproductive and therapeutic cloning, stem-cell research, and genetic modification. However, they continue to reappear in the more mundane practices of lesbian insemination. In a recent case in San Diego, California, Guadalupe Benitez was refused services from her medical group because of the "personal religious beliefs about gay people held by numerous members of the clinic's staff" (Lambda Legal 2006, paragraph 4). Benitez was told to go elsewhere for the procedure. The case provoked much controversy as groups such as the California Medical Association and the Christian Medical and Dental Associations filed friend-of-the-court briefs in support of the doctors.[12] Fifteen civil-rights, medical and community-health organizations joined together in a friend-of-the-court brief supporting Benitez and opposing religiously motivated discrimination in healthcare (ibid.). Benitez won the case; the clinic, however, is currently appealing the ruling.

Such cases are controversial because of their very imbrications with queer reproduction — that is, their potential for creating one-parent and same-sex-parent families and for allowing the selection of family characteristics (including the gay gene). Technoscientific advances, such as the cloning techniques pioneered on Dolly, the first cloned sheep, may soon permit same-sex biological parents. Scenarios include those in which both members of a gay male couple procreate using their DNA and a woman surrogate, and in which both members of a lesbian couple procreate using one partner as the birth mom and the other as the DNA donor.[13] Such possibilities have already been announced. Several newspapers announced the possibility of "two biological dads" (Kelly 2001) and "babies without fathers" (Zonneveldt 2001). Orly Lacham-Kaplan, an Australian embryologist at the Monash IVF centre in Melbourne, Australia, stated that it was theoretically possible to use a human cell to fertilize a woman's eggs (Nationwide News Party Limited 2001).

As early as 1997, Lee Silver (1997), a molecular biologist at Princeton University, presented a futuristic (circa 2009 and beyond) account of a world divided into two social classes, the GenRich (genetically enhanced, gene-enriched) and the Naturals, who are unable to financially afford genetic enhancement. His account not only assumes that all who can will utilize genetic technologies, but he overtly argues that many lesbians will come to occupy a subset of the GenRich class. These possibilities might seem to be the realm of science fiction, but the knowledge needed to realize them is already in development. And they reflect a long-standing cultural imagination. That is, one can see ideological continuities in shifts from eugenics to genetic medicine, from infertility to fertility problems, and from nonprocreation as a product of unnatural gender to procreation for every woman and man.

Several artists and science-fiction writers play on the blurred boundaries between pasts, presents, and futures, science and fiction, real and imagined, and other borders previously thought secure. As Lori Andrews (2003) described in *Living with the Genie,* artists are already offering boutique medicines, selling genetic traits by appealing to individuals' desires to modify their personalities and other characteristics. In 1998 Tran T. Kim-Trang and Karl Mihail created a public-art installation, Gene Genies Worldwide, a retail space for a fictitious company offering to custom design clients' genetic codes. The Gene Genies Web site (www.genegenies.com) holds the phrase "human to human genetic traits" on the screen, as words such as "bargaining," "creativity," "novelty," "sinning," "difficulty following instructions," and others intermittently flash across the screen. These are visually brought together to demonstrate the shift from humanness to human genetic traits able to be reduced and/or enhanced at will. Part of the project's fiction is the "Gene Harvest Archive," with its "intent to harvest, store, and utilize the genetic codes for creativity collected from society's most exemplary and recognized creative individuals." Of course, these technologies are not yet available. Or are they? Certainly, "we all" are asked to imagine our selves anew through the consumption of products that promise self-transformation.

How different is this from the goal of the Repository for Germinal Choice, a sperm bank that opened in Escondido, California, in the early 1980s?[14] The intent was to offer sperm donors according to IQ, level of education, and professional attainment, and the operators prided themselves on offering sperm from several Nobel Prize winners. The repository was supposed to help reverse the genetic decay (i.e., degeneration, reverse evolution) that the director, Robert Graham, saw around him. The response was to preserve and multiply the best genes of his generation. By the time Graham's repository closed in 1999, it was said that his genius sperm had been responsible for the birth of more than 200 children (Plotz 2005). The intent was clear: to enhance the future, make "better babies," and allow potential parents to imagine their futures anew.

Imagining future possibilities through reproductive technologies and/or human genetics is not just an artistic venture. It is now not only a possibility but a reality that abortions are taking place after prenatal gender determination, albeit through a more routine sonogram. Genetic testing for disabilities and even carriers of disability traits are provoking similar moves. But where, one might ask, is the line from Tay-Sachs to Attention Deficit Hyperactivity Disorder? Who will decide?

What "we" will do with these possibilities is yet to be answered. What is emerging, however, are strange bedfellows created as pro-life groups join feminist activists to ban cloning, disability movements join the religious right, some queer movements join others willing to push the bounds of reproductive cloning, and so on. An opportunity to change the path arises with controversy as "black boxes" (Latour and Woolgar 1979) are opened to reveal the inputs and outputs that were previously obfuscated. That is, the presence of controversy is productive of an opportunity to create social change and to queer dominant assumptions and institutions.

There are many ways to imagine and read the present-futures of human reproduction. First, they enterprise-up "normality" and enforce stratifications. Marketing choices for the future is already underway as sperm banks advertise for educated, athletic, creative donors, and as egg-donation services seek young, smart, and beautiful donors (sending clear gendered, raced, and classed messages). Choice is not only enterprised-up but also globalized as potential parents scour the world for the eggs, sperm, and technologies necessary to fulfill their "hopes and dreams." Today, IVF clinics exist in more than thirty-eight countries, including Egypt, Malaysia, and Israel (see especially Kahn 2000 and Inhorn 1996).

A seemingly unrestrained profit motive fuels biomedical innovations and healthcare services. The future is here and it is profitable (for some). But, of course, the risks are high, the field is stratified, and, for the most part, it is an unregulated terrain. Insurance companies rarely pay for reproductive technologies, and this drives providers to compete for wealthy patients. Imagining somewhat desperate and usually very determined heterosexuals, biomedical providers push the bounds of what they sell; Gay Becker (2000b) has called this the selling of hope. Start-up companies entering the marketplace do the same as they seek venture capital to launch their services. And the patenting of genes is encouraging more and more companies to get into the business of gene testing and engineering.

This is not lost on cultural theorist Donna Haraway (1997), who uses the term "Genes-R-Us" to refer to the commodification of all things biological. Lori Andrews (2003) warns that the future will yield the patenting not only of human genes but also of human embryos, putting a price on human beings (again). While this may be old wine packaged in new bottles, these new commercial ventures are enabled by technoscience. The social controls of medicalization continue, yet they are enacted through the latest techno-scientific means within the context of a highly commercialized biomedical arena and discourses of biomedicine that travel widely. Such predictions of a highly technologized, "first" world populated by white, tall, rich people who enhance their progeny must be read against what we "know" about the demography of same-sex, co-habitating couples and their children. The 2000 U.S. Census, for example, found that the children being raised by same-sex couples in the United States reflect a greater racial and ethnic diversity than the population as a whole.[15] Compared to different-sex couples with children, same-sex couples with children have fewer economic resources to care for their children; they have lower household incomes ($12,000 lower per year), a 15 percent lower home ownership rate, and lower levels of education than different-sex parents, suggesting that the economic benefits provided by legal marriage would be helpful to these families. Finally, lesbian and gay parents are raising a higher percentage of adopted children than same-sex couples (Sears, Gates and Rubenstein 2005). This picture is far from the popular misconception that gay people are predominantly male, affluent, urban, white and childless. It also belies the assumption among some queer communities that gay and lesbian families are mere replications of heteronormativity.

As a result, a second way to imagine and read these present-futures is as a queering of family demography. Whether or not reproductive technologies and practices in general represent a queering is driven by one's definition of queering itself. If the benchmark is contesting dominant heteronormative assumptions and institutions, then lesbian and gay parent families may adhere to Lisa Duggan's (2003) analysis that these family forms are creating a "homonormativity." If queering is defined as subverting a norm, as I think it is, then these families can be read as productive of social change.

What was once a simultaneous medicalization of assisted reproduction as a legitimate means toward procreation for heterosexual couples and a medicalization of lesbian bodies as nonprocreative has today yielded a confluence of queer and regenerative possibilities, with each subverting and producing different degrees of normativity.

Questions remain. Who will be deemed legitimate users of these technologies? Will these users continue, transform, or reduce current forms of stratified reproduction? Will old variants of social control persist? Through what means will new variants of social control emerge and in what places? Similarly, the question is not *whether* possibilities will emerge for social transformations, but *for whom*. Gaining an "accurate" version of social realities requires interrogations of material cultures in practice. Such interrogations must explore the forms of particular forms of negotiations and trajectories employed to achieve pregnancy; the ways that kinship is enforced and altered symbolically and materially; the ways that sex, gender, and sexuality are reworked or maintained; and the ways that reproduction is raced, classed, and gendered. With cloning technologies and embryo-fusion techniques, will same-sex couples find ways to share biological parenthood? And will this be consequential for the shape and meaning of (hetero)normativity — the equation of humanity with heterosexuality (Warner 1993) — and of human reproduction itself?

Futures of Belonging and Recognition

The last thirty years of the twentieth century witnessed struggles for the expansion of citizenship rights under the names of immigration rights, civil rights, women's rights, and gay and lesbian rights. These identity-based movements are also movements for recognition and belonging. My research provokes questions about how to understand and think about the social changes underway in the intimate spheres of social life, that is, who one lives with, how one raises children, how one organizes and handles one's body, how one relates as a gendered being, how one lives as an erotic person, and so on (Plummer 1995). These questions arise within "arenas of intimacy" (Plummer 2001; Giddens 1991, 1992) that trouble contemporary constructions of citizenship and challenge cultural meanings of belonging and recognition.

Kinship has long stood as a hegemonic system of belonging — not only to a nuclear family but also to extended and ancestral kin. Kinship is fragile in contemporary America. Now is a time when, some people believe (and use their political and religious power to assert), the family must be reincorporated into its idealized form; these people view homosexuality as an assault on the very foundation of the family and on the very notion of the human. Yet now is also a time of sustained high rates of heterosexual divorce and remarriage, exile and migration. Ideas about a return to the heteronormative family emphasize the ways children move from having a family to having no family and from having no family to being with family, rather than emphasize moves from one family form to another. Today's children are likely to live in various family forms with multiple parents, aunts, uncles, and grandparents. A recent *New York Times* article, for example, featured the now common "experience" of having eight grandparents (Harmon 2005). In addition to eight grandparents, children may live in situations wherein more than one woman operates as mother and/or more than one man operates as father and/or there is no mother or father. Straight and gay families are often blended, and queer families emerge in nuclear and non-nuclear forms with longer and shorter durations. Dreams of a world populated by married, heterosexual, monogamous adults do not address the multiple family forms thriving today, and they certainly do not address the potential possibilities for living an emotionally engaged social life. What will the legacy of kinship be for queer families? What new schemes of intelligibility will make their lives legitimate?

State policies enable normative or idealized kinship forms — a basis of social order — to continue with their ability, both symbolic and material, to structure social rules that make culture possible and intelligible. However, by definition, idealized kinship forms cannot operate without producing and maintaining the specter of their transgression. State policies and other hegemonic ideals provide incentives for conformity, but in doing so they also produce a set of social configurations that exceed and defy the rules by which they are occasioned. Alterations in kinship demand a rearticulation of contemporary gender and sexual theory. Although nothing within biology demands the cultural nuclear family form, in the United States today it is this family that represents social order, idealized kinship, and legitimate citizenship. But cultural rules are open to negotiation and change; idealized norms are contingent and productive of agencies. In refusing to honor normative kinship arrangements, not only do queer reproducers defy cultural ideals, but they can also be read as holding possibilities for the defiance of the social order and the state. Yet, in many ways, dynamics of what counts as valuable knowledge in U.S. society continues to mirror society's predominant configurations of sex, gender, and sexuality. Despite the decoupling of procreation from sexual intercourse through contraceptive technologies, questions remain as to whether these technologies create new cultural enactments of sex, gender, sexuality, and kinship forms, or reinforce old ones.

Legitimate citizens cannot exist without illegitimate ones in the same way that "configured" users of assisted-reproduction technologies cannot exist without implicated ones and that normative heterosexuality cannot exist without queer desire. Biological reproduction is the taken-for-granted kinship signifier in Western culture, and assisted-reproduction technologies intervene in this biological foundation. Persons recognized as kin primarily divide into those related by blood and those related by marriage. Procreation connects the two. Strathern (1995) also argued that reproductive technologies afford new ways of knowing about kinship, which she termed *dispersed kinship* to signal the multiplicity of procreators who are defined by their participation in the acts of conception.

Discussions of gay and lesbian kinship take place through two dominant cultural narratives: one reaffirms American kinship based on biogenetic and legal (marital) ties (Hayden 1995); the other denies the naturalness of lesbian and gay sexuality based on its assumed nonprocreative possibilities. Lesbians who conceive with assisted-reproduction technologies simultaneously affirm the importance of biogenetic ties as a symbol in American kinship and challenge the idea that "biology is a self-evident, singular fact and *the* natural baseline on which kinship is built" (Hayden 1995, 56). Instead of being a prerequisite for relatedness, biology is transformed into a mere signpost of parenthood.

The Politics of Recognition and Belonging:
Ending Questions

As part of my meditation on possible futures, I conclude by asking questions about a just society and the politics of recognition and belonging in such a world. In many ways the shifts in queer intimacies consolidated around regenerative possibilities offered through technoscience are part of LGBTQI challenges to and claims to the entitlements and benefits of state-sanctioned marriage, adoption, and reproductive rights. While these shifts provoke a rethinking of kinship markers, they also raise questions about belonging and recognition. How does one "know" and "recognize" to whom one belongs and who belongs with one?

Assisted reproduction is a medical practice shaped within a context of a corporate, mostly for-profit, healthcare system promoting individual choice (Clarke et al. 2003). Lesbian reproductive practices thus demonstrate the production of subjectivities, in particular consumer subjectivities. In some ways lesbian and gay reproduction are both part of the construction of the queer consumer-citizen who has emerged over the past three decades. This flexible citizen has been created within and through the shift from lesbian, gay, queer struggles for sexual liberation to LGBTQI battles for the right to marry, parent, and form relations in the same ways as heterosexuals do (Dominus 2004).

The flexible citizen has also been produced with and through the global economy. In global capitalism the imperative is to constantly expand one's market and diversify one's services. This mandate presents itself in U.S. assisted reproduction. Furthermore, border crossing is alive and well as lesbians and single women from "over there" buy sperm online to be sent through the mail. Stratifications are evident in such practices and shape who can and cannot become a consumer of Western biosperm.

In many ways the nonnormative, queer user of assisted-reproduction technologies challenges, through the kinship device of affinity ties, the very meaning of who and what makes a family. Yet, in other ways, these reproductive practices reveal a flexible citizen able to respond to the demands of consumer capitalism. Participation in normativity includes participation in the global trafficking in human sperm, eggs, and wombs.

Lesbian practices of reproduction have thus revealed fundamental questions regarding intimacy and belonging. What constitutes a family? What and who is a mother, a father, a parent? In what ways are the boundaries between heterosexual parenthood and queer parenthood regulated? Who is recognizable as a member of a family or group? How is relatedness formed and given meaning? In what ways do blood and genes signal relatedness? In what ways are intimacies through choice and affilial connection maintained or repositioned? In what ways, if any, are these questions shaped by and through the use of consumer-based medical reproductive technologies? And, finally, in what ways are these expressions of who one is as an individual and as a family member bound up with the public recognitions through which one defines oneself and through which one is defined through state, medical, and legal discourses? In all, these are questions of group-based treatment and identity formation in the context of social belonging.

Much of lesbian, gay, bisexual, transgender, queer, and intersex politics are concerned with expanding access to citizenship rights such as the rights to be married, to divorce, to pass benefits to one's partner at one's death, to adopt children, to visit one's partner in a hospital, and so on. Yet these struggles are also more generally about belonging and recognition. Who will one recognize as legitimate members of societies? How will one know who to let in and who to keep out? Struggles to expand citizenship rights do not come without a price tag, and these questions suggest some of the associated costs. Seeking belonging and recognition drives new complexities and troubles the "normal" in new ways (Warner 1999). That is, challenges destabilize traditional relationships between (hetero)sexuality and membership within the polity. Plummer (2000) argues that these changes are driven and shaped by a growing culture of individualization with its associated ideology of choice and self-reflexivity. Coupled with an emphasis on individual choice in Western societies is a broader range of "choices" concerning who one marries; with whom one cohabitates; if, when, and under what conditions one procreates; and with whom one has sex and in what form. A culture of consumption drives change, is deeply reflective of an ideology of individual choice, and offers an avenue through which access to citizenship, at least conceptually, can be secured. The struggles for inclusion and belonging, as well as the concomitant attacks on the rights and benefits afforded to gay men and lesbians, arise at the intersection of an ideology of individual choice, a culture of consumption, and a broad regime of normalization (Foucault 1979, 1980a).

Many of the recent shifts in sexual intimacies are driven by challenges to institutions of the law and consumer medicine. Challenges are taking place at the level of inclusion as reproductive (and consumer) citizens and are seen as a means through which to gain social legitimacy. As lesbians and gay men are slowly accepted into mainstream life through institutions of medicine and the law, as we experience increased tolerance, questions emerge. Through what means and at what cost are acceptance, tolerance, and expanded citizenship won? And what kinds of legal and political backlash will they bring? What new obstacles, at the state and federal levels of U.S. society, will result from reactions against the expansion of rights for gays and lesbians?

Political struggles for gay and lesbian citizenship rights in areas of intimacy are driven, at least in part, by acceptance of a new ideology and mandate: that gays and lesbians reproduce in the same way as heterosexual couples. Queer struggles for inclusion rights in the areas of marriage and reproduction take place within a context of biomedicalization in which medicine, the state, and a culture of consumption intertwine to produce normative juridical subjects, including the new citizen queer consumer. The concrete practices of achieving pregnancy among lesbians reveal that what was once an alternative practice driven by the ideology of a do-it-yourself women's health movement has today (mostly) become a consumer-based, highly biomedicalized process. The biomedicalization of *all* women's fertility and infertility accomplishes both the standardization of practice and the configuring of "normative" consumers-users-citizens be they gay, lesbian, heterosexual, or something else. What has been accomplished most of all is the production of subjectivities within the new economy of global capitalism.

In the context of recent geopolitical changes, several questions arise. How does one frame belonging? What are the parameters for inclusions and exclusions? How will determinations be made regarding who is and who is not entitled to inclusions and rights. In what ways will social belonging be sought and secured? Kinship is no longer regarded as "culture" itself (as anthropologists such as Claude Lévi-Strauss theorized), but is one cultural practice linked to material practices, political formations, and epistemologies of science, medicine and technologies. The study of kinship must be, and is already, expanded to include global-economic-political changes (see especially Franklin and McKinnon 2001; Butler 1998, 2004).

The above issues, of course, go beyond questions of the formation of families, to include the social and cultural assemblage of belonging, legitimacy, and recognition in general. Nonetheless, the material practices of creating family and securing legitimacy in the face of exclusion goes to the heart of creating a just sociality. That belonging is enabled through the co-construction of technoscience and kinship does not minimize the important question of the ways social pressures of hegemony encourage and constrain social formations and policies and politics of inclusion. In the context of recent geopolitical changes, what new pressures and constraints will be placed on the formation of families and the construction of affinity ties? The geopolitical assemblages of the time may be most responsible, through their strategies of normalization and governmentality, for the production of new citizen queer subjectivities. They may also provoke strategies by which other queer subjectivities prefer, or are forced, to remain illegitimate.

Notes

Introduction

1 I use the term *discourse*, following Foucault's notion of discursive apparatuses and technologies to refuse the distinction between ideas and practices or texts and lived experience; I instead approach them as co-productive (see Foucault 1979, 1980a).

2 The phrase "achieving parenthood" is borrowed from Ellen Lewin's (1993) and Faye Ginsburg's (1989) accounts of motherhood as an achievement. I use it here to signal the active and intentional aspects of getting to pregnant, that segment of the reproductive trajectory most distinctive for lesbians.

3 The mutual constitutiveness of sciences and sex-genders-sexualities is a key feminist concern (e.g., Haraway 1997) as these categories are shown to be overlapping (see, for example, Fishman, Wick, and Koenig 1999; Grosz 1994; Moore and Clarke 1995).

4 The sociology of knowledge is important throughout this book. I use the term *knowledge* in its plural to argue that many different knowledges exist and that they are produced by all kinds of people, under heterogeneous circumstances, and in a stunningly wide variety of situations (e.g., Mannheim 1946; Wright and Treacher 1982). Certain knowledges and their advocates have considerably more cultural and social power than others, and this varies across time and location, making the temporal and spatial distributions of knowledges two fundamental concerns in analyzing their stratification (Haraway 1991).

5 For recent elaborations of biopower, see especially Rose and Novas 2003 and Petryna 2002; on "psycho-power," see Orr 2006.

6 I engage here with a complicated and ongoing debate regarding the agency-structure dilemma: the degree to which gender (and gender inequality) is fixed within the body, culture, and society versus the degree to which such relations can be subverted through intentionality or free will. For an analysis of this tension, see Pitts 2005, which argues for a feminist perspective that shifts the focus from intentionality to technology.

7 The concept of co-constitutiveness is widely used in the field of science and technology studies to illustrate the ways scientific knowledge and culture, or social life, are produced simultaneously (see Shapin and Schaffer 1986). One doesn't exist without the other, and they in fact rely on each other for meaning (see Haraway 1985).

8 I borrow the term "stratified reproduction"—coined by Shellee Colen (1989) and later used in Faye Ginsburg's and Rayna Rapp's edited volume of feminist studies of reproduction (1995)—to denote the unequal distribution of reproductive controls and assistance.

9 The concept of hegemony is from Gramsci (1992), an Italian Marxist of the 1920s, who uses the term to describe relations of domination which are not inherently visible because they involve consent (not coercion) on the part of the dominated (or subaltern, as he puts it). Foucault's (1979) term, *governmentality,* is used in much the same way to refer to the cultural means used to produce conforming or "docile" bodies.

10 Theory and methods are deeply connected throughout this book. I take the social positions and perspectives of users' seriously as the "object" of focus. I begin with what people do and say they do in interactions with technologies and institutional practices. Users here are both agentic—able to modify or subvert a technology's intended meaning and/or ideal use (e.g., Moore 1997; Akrich 1995; Clarke and Fujimura 1992; Clarke and Montini 1993; Clarke and Olesen 1999; Cockburn and Furst-Dilic 1994; Garrety 1997; Shim 2000, 2006; Star 1995; Fosket 2000; Fishman and Mamo 2002; Mamo and Fishman 2001)—and constrained by economic, biological and other social positions. The consumption junction (Cowan 1987), where users may either follow given technological scripts or create their own interpretations and meanings for the technology, is thus brought forward (Cockburn and Furst-Dilic 1994) to reveal the ways heterogeneously situated users come together in particular ways.

11 Donna Haraway's (1997) and Bruno Latour's (1987) concept of technoscience signals their argument that sciences and technologies are co-constituted. Integral is an emphasis on "praxis," a concept borrowed from Marx to refer to human activity as the source of social and historical change. In the 1970s several theorists emphasized practice as a mediating factor between structure and agency (see Bourdieu 1984; Giddens 1979), and several material feminist scholars emphasized the ways knowledges and meanings are embedded in differing visions and social relations (see especially Haraway 1988).

12 Feminism and science studies share an attention to users' perspectives. While scholars of science and technology studies traditionally "study up" to understand the ways scientists and other experts create knowledge, feminism turns the focus around to study the ways people make sense of and interact with the social world. Theoretically, from the perspective of science and technology studies, meaning arises through interactions among users and technologies. Technologies are brought forward for the social and cultural work they accomplish as much as for their particular—intended—purpose. Technologies do not always work as they are idealized (see Timmermans 1999 for an example in the case of CPR). Different actors interact with technologies in various ways, transforming them into the "right tools for the job" (Clarke and Fujimura 1992). Users' identities, in particular gendered identities, are constructed by technologies and can be transformed in use (see especially Oudshoorn 2003).

13　Throughout this book I use the term *alternative insemination* specifically when discussing reproductive practices shaped by feminist health movements.

14　Lesbian reproduction is a set of material practices shaped by and able to modify cultural scripts (assumptions) embedded in institutions, technologies, and knowledges. The concept of a sexual script illustrates the complex ways "labels" (not nature) assign meaning (see Gagnon and Simon 1967; see also Gagnon and Simon 1973 on sexuality and the ways it is open to a wide range of sociocultural variations and is a symbolically and socially scripted phenomenon). Technology studies uses the concept of "script" similarly to argue that assumptions (and politics) are built in to technologies at the design stage, when users are imaged. In the hands of users, however, scripts can be described (Akrich 1995) and reinterpreted and negotiated (Cowan 1987; Bijker, Hughes, and Pinch 1987). Furthermore, users can and do modify and/or subvert a technology's intended meaning or ideal use (Moore 1997), but they also may reinforce these meanings.

15　Following technoscience, I take nonhuman actants (that is, technologies themselves) seriously as agentic in daily life (Callon 1985; Latour 1987), and I conjointly study meanings and materialities—including corporealities—as hybrid or cyborg (Casper and Koenig 1996; Gray, Figueroa-Sarriera, and Mentor 1995; Hayles 1999).

One　From Whence We Came

1　All names and identifying characters have been changed to ensure anonymity.

2　See Pfeffer 1993, 32. This definition can be found in writings by J. Matthews Duncan (1826–1890), an eminent Scottish physician specializing in obstetrics. Duncan outlined the leading medical theories of sterility and fertility during the 1800s in a book titled, *Fecundity, Fertility, Sterility and Allied Topics* (1871). His ideas were considered valid for almost fifty years.

3　For a cultural analysis of infertility from colonial era to the late 1990s, see Marsh and Wonner 1996.

4　Similar signs of "abnormal" genitalia were also interpreted by sexologists as possible indicators of homosexuality in women (Terry 1999, 205), which indicated a construction of lesbian bodies as nonprocreative.

5　There is a link between assisted reproduction and theories of degeneracy. Theories of degeneracy shaped eugenics policies, which interpreted social and biological "progress" in racial and socioeconomic terms and placed white, land-owning men at the top of the hierarchy. Degeneracy, and those deemed degenerate, were assumed to threaten the social order (on eugenics policies, see Larson 1995; Kevles 1985). The logic of degeneracy was part of the science of eugenics and of early-twentieth-century public policies and rhetoric, including "planned parenthood" and its equation of planned children with healthy children; public-health programs concerned with the "health" of populations (code for "good stock"); and the interests of scientific sex reformers, which were allied with the health and well-being of the modern, heterosexual, procreative family (Clarke 1998).

6 The history of the reproductive sciences has been well documented by Adele E. Clarke in her 1998 book, *Disciplining Reproduction*.

7 During his exam of the woman, Pancoast found what he called "the suction function of the uterus, which takes place during orgasm" (Hard 1909, 163). How he discovered this function is unknown.

8 Pancoast attributed this pathology to an earlier bout of gonorrhea and suspected that the lack of sperm was the cause of the couple's sterility.

9 Medical students were among the first to donate sperm and to take on the label of "sperm donors." This practice continued through the 1970s and 1980s, with many small cryobanks housed in physicians' offices.

10 Hard and others advocated artificial impregnation as a tool for eugenic reproduction and as a cure for what was then termed "race suicide." The threat of race suicide — read white-race suicide — gained cultural prominence in the early twentieth century, creating social alarm among whites about their declining reproduction (see Beisel 1997).

11 Knowledge that a combination of male sperm and a female egg is necessary to produce an offspring emerged in the early years of the twentieth century (see Finegold 1976). Clarke 1998 documents the large-scale transformation of American farming from a subsistence, cottage industry to a commercial enterprise that helped launch Fertility Inc.

12 In the nineteenth century little was accurately understood about the female cycle or the role of the ovaries in reproduction (see Laqueur 1990, 187). The first scientific article on the fertility cycle and menstrual charting was published in 1933 in *Birth Control Review* (Hartman 1933). On the ovarian cycle, see Garrison 1929; Gruhn and Kazer 1989; May 1995. Advances in understanding led to the rise of reproductive endocrinology from 1925 to 1940 (Parkes 1985) in three professional worlds: biology, medicine, and agriculture (Clarke 1998, 2000). For extensive histories of the development and use of artificial insemination in agriculture in the United States, see Perry et al. 1945; for the same in Britain, see Herman 1981.

   Until the discovery of hormones and their function in reproduction, doctors routinely advised women that their most fertile time was right after or during their periods (Parkes 1985). *Marshall's Physiology of Reproduction,* a landmark publication on reproductive biology, was published in 1910 (see Parkes 1952). It launched a new line of study: the reproductive sciences, including reproductive endocrinology (Clarke 1998).

13 The scientific knowledge of ovulation was part of work in reproductive endocrinology. By 1915, American embryologists believed hormones defined the man or the woman (Fausto-Sterling 2000; Oudshoorn 1994). In the 1920s and 1930s reproductive endocrinology was significant for both fertility and infertility and understandings of homosexuality. The American embryologist Frank

Rattray Lillie (1870–1947) concluded that "genes started the sex determination ball rolling, but hormones did the follow-through work" (Fausto-Sterling 2000, 163).

14 See Emily Martin (1991) on metaphors of menstruation and Thomas Laqueur (1990) on early understandings of male and female bodies.

15 See Michelle Murphy's (1999) discussion of the vaginal examination chart as a self-examination technology. Basal-body-temperature monitoring became significant for its long-standing support by Catholic birth-control movements that advocated child spacing and natural, not artificial (i.e., technical), means of contraception through the timing of pregnancies. The naturalness was constructed as achieved through periods of abstinence and timing of intercourse based on ovulation prediction.

16 Diagnosing and treating anovulation problems developed along two lines: clomiphene citrate and human menopausal gonadotrophins. Biochemical understandings of these substances produced medical treatments. Compounds for inducing ovulation provided "proof" that investment in the developments of pharmaceutical therapies could pay off in the long run. Although research using gonadotrophins for the induction of ovulation, which continued throughout the 1960s, resulted in the discovery of multiple problems with these substances (e.g., instability, difficult measurement, allergic reactions), Merrell Corporation's release of clomiphene citrate, an orally active, synthetic, nonsteroidal agent, under the brand name Clomid indicated the potential of drugs in infertility services (Gruhn and Kazer 1989). For histories of development of fertility treatments, see Taymor 1959, Pfeffer 1993, Clarke 2000.

17 In 1949 Piero Donini, an Italian chemist, successfully extracted and purified the first gonadotropin from postmenopausal urine, branded Pergonal. Throughout the early 1960s, clinical trials were conducted using varying doses of clomiphene citrate (see, for example, Greenblatt 1961; Whitelaw 1963; Roy et al. 1963). Although researchers did not (and still do not) fully understand how clomiphene citrate worked, they suspected that its antiestrogenic effects caused release of pituitary gonadotrophins (Chen and Wallach 1994). Specifically, Clomid is thought to successfully "block" the effects of estrogen throughout the body, causing the pituitary gland to detect low levels of estrogen in the bloodstream and to respond by increasing the output of follicle-stimulating hormone, thereby producing more estrogen, which is needed for ovulation.

18 Spermatozoa, unknown until described by Leeuwenhoek in 1674 (Gruhn and Kazer 1989), is a component found in semen, a mixture of prostaglandin, fructose, fatty acids and about 10 percent spermatozoa cells. While important aspects of sperm's function and origins were identified in the 1820s (Zorgniotti 1975; Finegold 1976), the exact relationship of sperm motility to human fertility was not known until the late 1860s (McGregor 1989; Finegold 1976). In 1929 Donald Macomber and M. B. Sanders published "Spermatozoa Count" wherein they described a sampling technique that closely resembles measurement

methods still in use and established early standards of both a "viable" minimum sperm count for achieving pregnancy and "effective" techniques for artificial conception (Zorgniotti 1975).

In the 1930s Arthur Walton of Cambridge, England, pioneered studies on the properties, storage, and handling of semen (Herman 1981, 3–4). In the late 1930s United States many agricultural colleges in the Midwest began using the practice of artificial insemination for their dairy herds, which led to the initiation and funding of research on spermatozoa, semen dilution, storage, shipping, and insemination techniques (ibid., 6).

In the 1950s, in both England and the United States, the technologies used to produce frozen semen originated in artificial insemination for livestock (Herman 1981; Parkes 1952, 1985). This agricultural work provided "evidence" that among the millions of calves produced from frozen sperm, no pattern of abnormalities occurred. Thus, when human sperm banks emerged, the evidence based on livestock insemination was extended to the human case to argue that insemination procedures would not cause birth defects.

19 By 1954, Bunge, W. C. Keettel, and Sherman (1954) reported four successful pregnancies from artificial insemination with frozen semen (taken from the women's husbands). While the basic science of freezing semen had been developing for decades (see Herman 1981), frozen semen did not yield successful conception until after World War II (Parkes 1985). Once freezing was accomplished, the next frontier was long-term storage. In 1949, work with red blood cells revealed that glycerol had to be removed slowly before cells could be inseminated or transfused (Polge, Smith, and Parkes 1949; Parkes 1985). The resulting slow-cooling technique proved successful, permitting the motility necessary for successful conception. In late 1950 the first successful conception using donor semen in cows was recorded (Parkes 1985). This knowledge was significant for assisting human reproduction as well as blood transfusions and tissue grafting.

20 Today, cryopreservation is also used for men who anticipate a course of chemotherapy and want to store their semen for future reproduction.

21 Once cryobanking was achieved, the development of criteria for selecting "appropriate" semen for artificial insemination became necessary. In the 1960s the physician Frances Shields established these criteria: a donor had to be free of syphilis, free from disease, and of unquestioned mental health (Chen and Wallach 1994).

22 Resistance to medical classifications and their controversial implications has been examined with regard to the American Psychiatric Association's Diagnostic and Statistical Manual's inclusion of premenstrual syndrome (Figert 1996), homosexuality (Kirk and Kutchins 1992), and, more recently, sexual dysfunction (Working Group 2000) and gender-identity disorder.

23 Gay Becker and Robert Nachtigall (1992) explore the medicalization of infertility and argue that placing problems within a medical framework does not

provide a solution to conditions that deviate from cultural norms: cultural norms are replicated in medical ideologies. Childlessness remains deviant within medicine, and childless heterosexuals are not spared their feelings of abnormality when medical legitimacy is applied. Medicalization thus undermines its own intent. Becker (2000a) also argues that for all women, being infertile presumes the desire for children rather than stemming directly from an inability to have them. Heterosexual infertility involves both a desire to have children and a physical inability to conceive. Most lesbians, by contrast, enter infertility services with only the desire to have children.

24 The definition of infertility as a disease was approved by the practice committee of the American Society for Reproductive Medicine (formerly the American Fertility Society) on 27 March 1993 and by the board of directors on 17 July 1993. The guidelines state, "The duration of the failure to conceive should be twelve or more months before an investigation is undertaken unless medical history and physical findings dictate earlier evaluation and treatment." Citing the 1988 edition of *Dorland's Medical Dictionary,* the guidelines add that infertility is "any deviation from or interruption of the normal structure or function of any part, organ, or system, or combination thereof, of the body that is manifested by a characteristic set of symptoms or signs, and whose etiology, pathology, and prognosis may be known or unknown" (see American Society for Reproductive Medicine, "Definition of 'Infertility,'" http://www.asrm.org).

25 In 1971 promising clinical trials of tamoxifen as a treatment for anovulatory disorders were announced; tamoxifen is a close relative of both clomiphene and diethylstilbestrol (DES), a synthetic estrogen originally used to prevent miscarriage but later linked to a rare vaginal cancer in offspring and confirmed as a teratogen, an agent that can cause malformation in an embryo or fetus.

26 When the patent for Clomid expired, a second drug, serophene, was released by the pharmaceutical company Serono. Together, these two drugs created a pharmaceutically driven market for infertility treatment.

27 In light of these risks and the DES crisis, many physicians were unwilling to prescribe these drugs, and potential patients were unwilling to take them. Nonetheless, throughout the 1960s and 1970s, few regulations governed the conduct of human research; as a result, women (mostly from Puerto Rico) were employed as research subjects in the area of reproductive medicine and were given DES and human-gonadotrophin stimulants (see Oudshoorn 1994). Robert Edwards and Patrick Steptoe used human-gonadotrophin stimulants in their research on in-vitro fertilization (Pfeffer 1993), research that later led to the birth of the first "test-tube" baby.

28 The population of infertile patients seeking the services of the new subspecialty included a large proportion of high-income patients, which enabled healthcare professionals to charge high fees to pay for their scientific research (Aral and Cates 1983).

29 Why the rates of infertility were higher among African American women is not known due to the ambiguity in the known causes of infertility. It is speculated that infertility is caused by such factors as delayed childbearing, exposure to toxins in both the workplace and the home, and sexually transmitted diseases.

30 Endocrinology-infertility was recognized as a subspecialty subject to board certification in 1974 and has expanded significantly ever since (see Aral and Cates 1983, 2330). Professionalization increased the jurisdiction of specialists over the parameters and treatments of fertility and infertility.

31 See Ehrenreich and Ehrenreich 1971 and Relman 1980 on the "medical-industrial complex"; see also an elaboration of the subject in Clarke et al. 2003.

32 Increased investor ownership is referred to as "corporatization" in McKinlay and Stoeckle 1988.

33 Pronatalist ideology embodies the belief that a person's social value is linked to procreation (Ulrich and Weatherall 2000). Berenice Fisher (1992) explains that most women face significant pressure to conceive and/or raise children. Thus, despite how the roles available to women in North America have expanded over the past three decades, motherhood is still emphasized as women's primary social role (Jordan and Revenson 1999). Pronatalist ideology perpetuates the belief that biological motherhood is the most valued path toward parenthood for women and that, therefore, a woman's social worth is inextricably linked to her ability to achieve biological motherhood.

34 In the early part of the twentieth century, sex reformers and sexologists expanded from the study of deviant or abnormal sexual behaviors to include research to construct the "normal": white, heterosexual, healthy individuals. The rhetoric of health replaced the eugenic ideology of "good stock" and became a primary objective of the Planned Parenthood Federation of America (Linda Gordon 1990). The shift in focus toward "health" is significant to contemporary practices of assisted reproduction.

35 As Siobhan Somerville (2000) documents so well, the classification of sex and race are intertwined. The classification of people's sexuality into two distinct categories took root in the late 1800s, largely due to the then recent definition of the color line. Just as with racial categories, bodies were labeled as either-or. As a result, society and its institutions were able to control and own sexual identity as though it were property (see also Ordover 2003).

36 Sexual pleasure was considered legitimate as long as it was a means to procreation (D'Emilio and Freedman 1988). In the nineteenth century, practices considered sinful deviations from procreation included sodomy, masturbation, and controlled fertility, which was espoused by women's movements. In various ways such practices were attacked for turning away from the "laws of nature" expressed in heterosexuality, marriage, and motherhood (Jackson 1994, 121). These ideas were perpetuated in early-twentieth-century U.S. medical and scientific commentary on homosexuality, which served as a vehicle for expressing conservative anxieties about gender and sexuality and for managing the diverse populations that were congregating in cities as a result of urbanization.

37 For an extensive history of biomedical constructions of homosexuality in America, see Terry 1999.

38 Recently, a wider range of sexual problems, including sexual dysfunction, have been placed under medical jurisdiction (see, e.g., Tiefer 1994; Laumann, Paik, and Rosen 1999; Mamo and Fishman 2001; Fishman 2004).

39 The science of sexology displaced the view of sexual perversions as morally sinful and under the control of the church. Instead, these perverse sexual behaviors were defined as medical deviations from normal sexuality and placed under the jurisdiction of medicine. It was within the context of medicine that what and whom one today refers to as lesbians were first socially defined. Part of the medicalization of lesbians included the construction of lesbian bodies as nonprocreative based on their presumed biophysiological abnormalities and social deviations relative to normal, procreative women.

40 The construction of lesbians as hormonally deviant is also consequential in light of ongoing research into sex hormones and their role in human reproduction (see Terry 1999).

41 Radclyffe Hall's book *The Well of Loneliness* (1928) described Stephen, the main character, as "naturally" masculine and therefore deserving of social acceptance (Bland and Doan 1998, 3).

42 Dickinson also studied heterosexuals. As Lisa Moore and Adele Clarke (1995) argued, while Dickinson's research took women's sexuality seriously, he constructed heterosexualizing consequence. For example, in his research for *Atlas of Human Sex Anatomy* (1933) he created "Norma" and "Norman" as female and male embodiments of "perfect measurements," thereby constructing normalcy in relation to deviant anatomy.

43 See also discussions of Saartje Bartmann by Anne Fausto-Sterling (1995).

44 In the late 1800s Richard Freiherr von Kraft-Ebbing categorized lesbians into four increasingly deviant and masculine types that ranged from those who did not betray their femininity yet were responsive to the approaches of "masculine" women to "the extreme grade of degenerative homosexuality . . . [whose] sentiment, action, even external appearance are those of the man" (quoted in Newton 1984, 287). Using the historical example of the all-girls boarding school, Somerville (2000) described how the color line of black-white could turn into butch-femme. Although in a somewhat modified manner, Havelock Ellis maintained this typology; when speaking of the "extreme" invert, he stated that the sexually inverted woman "ought to have been a man" (quoted in Newton 1984, 288). Thus, these women were a "third sex," neither man nor woman, and one can assume that they were regarded as having little or none of the natural proclivity toward motherhood and nurturance found in normal women. The female invert was associated with feminist transgressions of traditional gender roles (embodied by the "New Woman," as described in Newton 1984) such as motherhood, passivity, and subordination (see, for example, Newton 1984; Katz 1976; Weeks 1977; Vicinus 1989; Faderman 1991).

45 Scientific ideas and cultural norms are co-produced. The history of reproductive

medicine emerged alongside and shaped the social construction of both an idealized modern reproductive family and of groups viewed as deviating from this norm.

46 See, for example, Schwartz 1998; D'Ercole 1996; Magee and Miller 1997; Domenici and Lesser 1995; Lesser and Schoenberg 1999.

47 The lesbian sex wars exemplified this division well. For an excellent discussion of these struggles, see Duggan and Hunter 1995.

48 Lesbian and gay studies, a critical project that emphasizes the need to raise the standpoint of sexuality to a central position in academic and mainstream discourse, has contributed substantially to the formation of queer theories (see Parker and Gagnon 1995).

49 While the dominant medical and cultural narratives of lesbians as nonprocreative and psychosexually deviant circulated throughout the 1920s and into the 1960s, the lived experience of lesbians varied. Lesbians have, of course, always been mothers, but demographic research has not been adequately collected on this population group and their life trajectories. While there exists no comprehensive historical review of same-sex parenting in the pre-Stonewall era, one can assume that lesbians were not in any significant way participants in the infertility-medicine complex prior to the mid-1980s.

50 From the 1930s to the 1950s, working-class lesbians were able to give public expression to women's autonomy and sexual desire for other women by manipulating the hierarchical distinctions between male and female (Kennedy and Davis 1993; Nestle 1987). "Butch-femme" indicated sexual preference and sexual desire in a world that regularly sought to control and uproot same-sex desires, and it created the foundations on which some lesbian identities now stand.

51 *Boots of Leather and Slippers of Gold* demonstrates that during the late 1950s and early 1960s, regardless of gender identification, sleeping with men, either for pleasure, in marriage, or as sex-work often led to pregnancy and motherhood (Kennedy and Davis 1993).

52 A key aspect of some women's health movements was the organization of consciousness-raising groups. These were informal support, information, and, at times, political-theorizing groups that often took place at women's homes.

53 Margaret Sanger asserted this right in the early part of the twentieth century (Clarke 1998).

54 This question follows Foucault's (1979, 1980b) understanding of power as diffuse and often exerted locally and routinized in body practices, families, communities, and institutions.

55 Reproductive technologies are consumer goods, and any examination of them must go beyond individual choices and desires to include the social conditions and institutional resources under which personal actions are negotiated (Lury 1996; Slater 1997). Consumer goods are not neutral artifacts; they are social, economic, and institutional forces (Balsamo 1996, 159) that both influence and

reflect the organization of social positions (such as class, race, gender, and sexuality). Users of goods are consumers embedded in a network of social relations that limits, controls, and expands the "choice" they are capable of making (Cowan 1987). Thus, consumption is a social practice replete with cultural significance and meaning.

56 Biomedical cooptation also appears in AIDS activism (Epstein 1996).

57 This case resulted in a landmark legal decision in which a judge ruled that the lesbian couple could place both of their names on the birth certificate under the category of "mother" (Crummy 2000).

Two   "Real Lesbians Don't Have Kids"

1 In sociologist Arlene Stein's book *Sex and Sensibility* (1997), she analyzes shifts in lesbian identity and culture from the heyday of the "second" wave women's movement through the 1990s growth of alternative families. Part of her analysis includes a comparison of identity formation among two lesbian generations: one born between 1945 and 1961 (the baby boom generation) and coming of age in the early 1970s and the other born between 1961 and 1971 and coming of age a decade later in the 1980s and early 1990s. She argues that the first generation, highly influenced by lesbian feminism and the women's movement, engaged in complex struggles over the very meaning of identity, first centering lesbian identity as focal to their lives and communities and then integrating this identity into "lifestyle" issues of family, work, and well-being. This generation — often revolutionary in their resistance to dominant gender and sexual norms — shaped the contours of identity politics and constructed their personal lives in political terms. This baby boom generation contrasts with a younger generation born in the late 1960s and 1970s. This generation, in contrast, was less concerned with stabilizing their identity, and more concerned with recognizing the very instability of identity categories in general. While the salience of their lesbian identity did not differ significantly, the meanings of their identification did. Younger lesbians, Stein argued, were more apt to de-center lesbian identity, culture, and communities and allow for heterogeneity of desires and lives that were less confining and more accepting of a variety of choices and ways of living. In Stein's own construction, it would be too simple to interpret the de-centering of lesbian identity as a failure of lesbian politics. Instead, this may be an opening up of possibilities for the ways to live a queer life. The legacy of lesbian feminism and the controversies within both feminist and queer theories and politics were central for the women I interviewed as well.

2 Of course, my research is based on women who were trying to get pregnant and thus describes only those for whom a decision to pursue parenthood resulted.

3 I use the acronym LGBTQI throughout this book to reference lesbian, gay, bisexual, transgender, queer, and intersex identifications, practices, and communities.

4 There has been a long-standing pattern of both ignoring the high rates of African American infertility and/or attributing these high rates to sexual promiscuity (Collins 1999; Roberts 1997).

5 For a thorough review of access to insemination services globally, see Minot 2000.

6 See Lareau 2003 for the ways class shapes negotiation tactics.

7 See also Fosket 2000 for an analysis of the multiple knowledges women acquire in the context of breast cancer.

8 These are Pacific Reproductive Services (www.hellobaby.com), the Sperm Bank of California (www.thespermbankofca.org), and Rainbow Flag Health Services (www.gayspermbank.com).

9 There are five processes through which biomedicalization occurs: (1) through the political-economic constitution of the Biomedical TechnoService Complex; (2) through the elaboration of risk and surveillance biomedicine; (3) through the technoscientization of biomedicine; (4) through transformations of biomedical knowledge production, information management, and distribution; and (5) through transformations of bodies and the production of new individual and collective technoscientific identities (Clarke et al. 2003).

Three   Choosing a Donor

1 Heteronormative gender assumptions underpin this hegemonic view of the nuclear family. It has been argued that lesbian co-mothers manage their self-representation of family so as to minimize threats to familial legitimacy (see especially Reimann 2001; Sullivan 2001).

2 David Schneider (1968, 1964) argued that social ties can be found in culture (e.g., in marriage arrangements), not nature.

3 See especially Collier and Yanagisako 1989; Edwards et al. 1999; Franklin 1995; Modell 1994; Ragoné and Twine 2000; Strathern 1992, 1995; Weston 1991; Yanagisako and Delaney 1995). A central cultural foundation was a "folk model" of heterosexual reproduction hidden behind assumptions of the kinship (genealogical) model (Schneider 1968; Yanagisako and Delaney 1995).

4 Susan Kahn (2000), in her cultural account of assisted conception in Israel, partially disagrees with Strathern, arguing instead that in turning our gaze to kinship and reproduction, assisted reproductive technologies "reinforce and entrench" foundational cultural assumptions (159). In Kahn's research, she found that Israeli women maintain and reinforce the cultural imperative to reproduce.

5 It has been found that heterosexual couples have tended to select sperm in ways that maximize fatherhood. That is, they have chosen donors whose genetic characteristics most closely resemble the social father so that secrecy can be maintained. This tendency is changing as the culture shifts toward emphasizing the importance of "truth" and "knowing" on development (Becker 2000b; see also Agigian 2004).

6 The first children's book published on the topic of lesbian co-parenting, *Heather Has Two Mommies* gained notoriety in the late 1980s in New York, when the Brooklyn school district proposed its inclusion in their Rainbow Education Curriculum. Both the book's inclusion and the entire Rainbow curriculum were opposed by the school board.

7 It has been suggested that because HIV is understood as preventable and no longer thought of as a gay illness, community-based practices of donor insemination have re-emerged, with lesbians often choosing to know the donor's identity (Saffron 1994, 9).

8 I have been unable to locate an exact citation for this legal case. Thus, while it was frequently cited by respondents in this research, it may be folklore, not legal evidence.

9 The folklore of lesbian parental vulnerability is based on historical precedent. In her landmark analysis of family law, *Mothers on Trial: The Battle for Children and Custody* (1986), feminist psychologist Phyllis Chesler reported that lesbian mothers lost judicial custody of their children in 88 percent of custody cases and lost private custody in 83 percent of cases. Most importantly, she observed that lesbian mothers were very aware of their custodial vulnerability. A decade later, Mary Ann Mason (1999) found that informal sperm donors (i.e., directed and known donors) regularly had won paternity rights and in some cases a donor had won custodial rights. On a more positive note, however, in 2005, the California Supreme Court made several decisions to protect custody rights of lesbian mothers. In three cases, *Elisa B. v. Superior Court*, *K.M. v. E.G.*, and *Kristine H. v. Lisa R*, the court ruled that when a couple deliberately brings a child into the world through the use of assisted reproduction, both partners are legal parents, regardless of their gender or marital status. The California Supreme Court is the first state supreme court to reach this issue, and its holding in these three cases inevitably will influence courts in other states (National Center for Lesbian Rights 2005).

10 The National Center for Lesbian Rights was formerly the Lesbian Rights Project.

11 In the absence of a legally protected parental relationship, a child cannot claim financial support or inheritance rights from the second parent; is not entitled to Social Security benefits, retirement benefits, or state worker's compensation benefits if the second parent dies or becomes incapacitated; and is ineligible for health-insurance or other insurance benefits from the second parent's employer. Moreover, a seriously ill child may be denied essential care if the second parent is ineligible for parental leave under the Family and Medical Leave Act or, in the event of an emergency in which the legal parent is unavailable, is unable to consent to medical treatment for the child or even to visit him or her in a hospital emergency room. Second-parent or joint adoption is also critical to protect the child's right to financial support and to a continuing relationship with the second parent if the parents separate (National Center for Lesbian Rights 2004).

12 The "culture wars" over marriage and same-sex parenting are currently under
    way. Those in favor have employed large-scale social-science research on the
    children of same-sex parents to assure that these children "function" in the same
    way as children of heterosexual parents as measured by the Child Behavior
    Checklist (see Patterson, Hurt, and Mason 1998; Patterson 1994). Others argue
    that there are differences, but that these are positive signs of uniqueness and
    tolerance in the children raised in a same-sex household (Stacey and Biblarz
    2001). Judith Stacey has no quarrel with research suggesting that children of gay
    parents are as well-adjusted as their peers, but she does contest the idea that
    there is no difference when it comes to sexuality. Stacey and her coauthor,
    Timothy Biblarz, conclude that the evidence, "while scant and underanalyzed,"
    seems to suggest the possibility that children of gay parents "will be more likely
    to attain a similar orientation — and theory and common sense support such a
    view" (ibid., 177–78). They urge sociologists to examine the "contextual ef-
    fects" of differences such as being raised in urban and often progressive areas.
13 While some argue that a father is necessary for the well-being of children,
    sociological and psychological research has demonstrated this to be largely un-
    true (Stacey and Biblarz 2001).
14 See Rubin 1975 and Schwartz 1998 for thorough analyses of the potential dis-
    ruption to dominant theories of gender acquisition.
15 I borrow the term "postmodern family form" from Judith Stacey (1996). See
    also Amy Agigian's (2004) excellent analysis of lesbian alternative insemination
    as a theory of postmodern families.

Four   Negotiating Conception

1   In the arena of reproduction, a fundamental cultural assumption is that it is
    "natural" for "normal" couples to reproduce (or at least hold the potential to do
    so). In doing so, dominant ideals of sex, gender, and sexuality are upheld
    through the reinforcement of appropriate gender norms, heterosexual sex, and
    heterosexuality. Reproduction becomes the natural outcome when all three
    positions are firmly in line.
2   Biomedical normalization can also be found in the emergence and expansion of
    Resolve, a national consumer organization for infertility founded in 1973. Eliz-
    abeth Britt (1998) conducted an ethnography of Resolve and found that the
    organization deemphasized infertility as a health issue and used profamily rhet-
    oric to make medical treatment a "natural and necessary" response to infertility.
    Resolve's message, she argued, assumed parenthood as a natural feature of
    heterosexual union and motherhood as a basic female role. Technological inter-
    ventions into procreation were assimilated into the framework of "natural." By
    extension, Resolve helped to normalize technoscientific interventions into con-
    ception for heterosexual couples and not for others.
3   This in many ways mirrors Gayatri Chakravorty Spivak's (1988) concept of

strategic essentialism, which is used to legitimate the use of essentialist or realist epistemological assertions when they are more effective politically than the use of assertions of multiplicity and/or diversity.

4 The major conceptualization to date addressing technoscientific identities is Paul Rabinow's (1992, 241–42) notion of biosocial identities and biosocialities. Rabinow refers to the process of transforming cultural phenomena by naturalizing them as "biosociality." He anticipates that "nature will be known and remade through technique and will finally become artificial, just as culture becomes natural" (Rabinow 1996, 99). Several feminists have explored the processes by which technology is naturalized (see Clarke 1998; Yanagisako and Delaney 1995; Franklin 1997; Haraway 1997).

5 It is consistent with contemporary biomedicalization tendencies to bring aspects of health into the medical fold (Clarke et al. 2003).

6 For an extensive history of biomedical constructions of homosexuality in America, see Terry 1999.

7 Lesbians remain "implicated actors" (Clarke and Montini 1993; Clarke 2005) in infertility medicine as downstream users and consumers of the technologies. That is, they are not and have not been included at design stages of technological development. Although lesbians are no longer as invisible as they once were, having become physically present actors in reproductive medicine and services, they are generally silenced, ignored, or made invisible by those in power in those social worlds or arenas (Clarke 2005).

8 While the biomedical trajectories reported by participants are complex and nonlinear, those trajectories are crudely mapped in chapter 5, table 5.

9 Ovulation prediction became a technology with the appearance of the rhythm method (also termed natural fertility control) and the availability of the low-tech basal-body-temperature thermometer (for an analysis of natural fertility and medicalized technologies of ovulation, see DeNora 1996). Today, this technology is also involved with ongoing, highly competitive attempts to develop ovulation prediction as a marketable and profitable contraceptive method, "a jet-age" rhythm method (DeNora 1996).

10 Recent pharmaceutical developments include the use of "smarty pants," ovulation-detection pads, worn like panty-liners, that change color to "warn" women they are about to ovulate. They can also indicate whether a woman has an infection—or even when her period will start. Healthcare companies are scrambling to patent these new approaches.

11 OvuQuick joins the recent history of self-care diagnostic test kits. The first such kits were diabetic urine tests, followed in 1977 by the launching of the e.p.t. home pregnancy test. Despite controversy, the home pregnancy test became a big-selling item in pharmacies across America. Home pregnancy tests were the beginning of a new market for a variety of home diagnostic kits. Products designed to help women conceive followed soon thereafter.

12 Located in San Diego, California, Quidel is a medical-supply company that

develops, manufactures, and markets rapid diagnostics for detection of human medical conditions and illnesses, with a focus on women's and family health. The current incarnation of Quidel Corporation was formed by a 1991 merger between Monoclonal Antibodies, founded in 1979 in the Bay Area, and the original Quidel, founded in San Diego in 1981. The initial charter of both companies involved the commercial development of monoclonal antibodies into rapid diagnostic test kits for the detection of important medical conditions such as infertility, pregnancy, allergy, and infectious diseases. OvuQuick was part of the original Quidel's first product line, which was launched in 1986 and marketed to Johnson and Johnson and Becton Dickinson on an original-equipment-manufacturer basis.

13 Studies have found that IUI is more effective if the ovaries are first stimulated with oral (Clomiphene) or injectable (hMG) medications. As a result, it is often recommended that women include these pharmaceutical therapies when utilizing IUI methods.

14 When untreated semen or unwashed sperm are introduced into the vagina, the cervix separates prostaglandin from sperm.

15 IUI is often recommended twice per cycle at twelve-hour intervals. Associated costs can thus exceed $1,000 per month.

Five   Going High-Tech

1 In *The History of Sexuality* Foucault argued that in modernity the deployment of sexuality emerged as a powerful system of regulation. In late modernity a huge network of expert knowledges has developed, a network that has been accompanied by apparatuses and institutions, and built around the construction, reproduction, dissemination, and practice of such expert knowledges (Foucault 1980a). Furthermore, modern systems of liberal government have emphasized rule and the maintenance of order through voluntary self-discipline and normalization. A particular form of power, biopower, has come to work internally through the enforcement of regulatory ideals composed of definitions of normative social actions and sanctions for violating them.

2 These ideas are expanded in Thompson 2005.

3 In asking these questions I follow Cussins 1996.

4 See Fosket 2004 for an analysis of a similar move in breast-cancer risk assessment.

5 See, for example, Cole 1996 on AIDS discourses.

6 Age-related diagnostic categories include ovarian reserve counts and their associated use of antral follicle counts and test for levels of follicle stimulating hormone (FSH).

7 By chemicals, Sara meant synthetic hormones such as clomiphene, marketed as Clomid, and gonadotropin-releasing hormone, marketed as Lupron and Synarel.

8 Until now, the confluence of emotions, bodies, and technologies has not been

adequately theorized. Previously, however, technoscience studies theorized technologies and bodies (Gray, Figueroa-Sarriera, and Mentor 1995; Casper and Koenig 1996; Haraway 1991; Hayles 1999). Interfaces between bodies and technologies has led to what many are calling the emergence of "techno-bodies" (Balsamo 1996), "plastic bodies" (Bordo 1993), "posthuman bodies" (Halberstam and Livingston 1995), "cyborgs" (Haraway 1991; Hayles 1999), and even "monsters" (Lykke and Braidotti 1996). Queer theories also often emphasize corporeality and materiality (Butler 1993), although the overlaps are not usually theorized. In this book I bring theories of the body, embodiment, and emotions together with theories of technoscience. Of course, the sociology of health and illness has theorized bodies and emotions (Hochschild 1979, 1983, 1998; James and Gabe 1996; Mamo 1999; Olesen 2000; Olesen et al. 1990; Montini 1996; Williams and Bendelow 1998). I understand ways of being in the body as produced through culture and shaped by human and on-human artifacts alike (e.g., technologies, emotions, other people, ideas, etc.). That is, technological and ideological practices produce specific cultural effects on bodies and construct certain "truth effects" about users, including positional markers of gender and sexuality. Technologies themselves have the power to create and transform subjectivities (De Lauretis 1987; Balsamo 1996, 4). In other words, the ways in which emotions, being in the body, and engaging in technological experiences are mutually constituted remains undertheorized. By bringing materiality together with discourse, I argue the necessity of exploring the more inchoate social processes found at the level of the unconscious, the phenomenological, and the emotional.

9   I have used the term *switching* as a metaphor to apply to other aspects of achieving pregnancy as well. While many trajectory components (plans, technologies, donors) change, the language of the switch is used here to specifically indicate the act of moving from one partner as the receptacle or container for pregnancy to another.

10 See Lewin 1998b for a further complication of resistance and accommodation in lesbian reproduction.

Six   Affinity Ties as Kinship Device

1   Lamarck's (1809) conclusions were later discarded by most scientists as invalid.

2   The history of frozen semen dates back to the eighteenth century, when it was found that freezing stallion semen did not destroy motility (Herman 1981). This knowledge led to artificial insemination first for livestock (Herman 1981; Parkes 1952), then for humans (Bunge, Keettel, and Sherman 1954; Sherman 1954).

3   Intracytoplasmic sperm injection (ICSI) involves injecting a single sperm into an egg in the IVF lab. It is used when the man has weak sperm or a very low sperm count. If the ICSI procedure is successful, the fertilized egg is transferred to the woman's uterus using normal IVF procedures. Recent statistics show that

ICSI is used in about 47 percent of IVF procedures in the United States (Centers for Disease Control 2000).

4 I was unable to secure copyright permission to reproduce this image.

5 California Family Code 7613a reads: "If, under the supervision of a licensed physician and surgeon and with the consent of her husband, a wife is inseminated artificially with semen donated by a man not her husband, the husband is treated in law as if he were the natural father of a child thereby conceived. The husband's consent must be in writing and signed by him and his wife. The physician and surgeon shall certify their signatures and the date of the insemination, and retain the husband's consent as part of the medical record, where it shall be kept confidential and in a sealed file. However, the physician and surgeon's failure to do so does not affect the father and child relationship. All papers and records pertaining to the insemination, whether part of the permanent record of a court or of a file held by the supervising physician and surgeon or elsewhere, are subject to inspection only upon an order of the court for good cause shown" (*California Family Code* 2001).

6 Little has been known about how recipients actually select sperm donors for reproduction (exceptions include Hanson 2001; Jacob, Klock, and Maier 1999; Scheib, Riordan, and Shaver 2000). A significant content analysis of sperm-bank catalogs, however, was conducted by Matt Schmidt and Lisa Moore in 1998. Schmidt and Moore (1998) argue that donor catalogs are "discourse templates" that mirror personal ads and encourage clients to think of sperm purchasing as akin to a dating game. By listing *differences* (e.g., height and weight) among and within individual sperm donors, sperm banks encourage recipients to both "pick a winner" and rematerialize donor sperm as donors with full personalities and imagined social (and genetic) connections.

7 This is similar to the ways in which Charis Cussins Thompson (Cussins 1996, 1998; Thompson 2001, 2005) describes heterosexual recipients of egg donation as mapping genetics back onto cultural (and socioeconomic) factors in their emphasis on "genetic similarity" and shared cultural heritage as significant signposts for relationships.

8 During the period from 1920 to the end of World War II, eugenics thrived as both a "science" and a social movement. Attempts at eugenic hygiene included identifying "genetic defectives" and controlling their procreation or assimilation into society through marriage, immigration, sterilization, and imprisonment policies. Prior to World War II, hereditary theories of various diseases, conditions, and behaviors were rampant. The demise of the eugenics movement, at least under that name, came as social scientists began to criticize its assumptions and as the eugenics-based atrocities of Nazi Germany were uncovered in the 1930s and 1940s. By the 1950s eugenics per se had fallen into disrepute and was considered bad science. Troy Duster (1990) called the ways in which eugenic ideas and perspectives have survived and been reincarnated through other means "eugenics through the backdoor." Diane Paul (1998) doc-

uments how such ideas were incorporated into the emerging discipline of medical genetics.

9 The "new genetics" was launched in 1953 by James Watson and Francis Crick who discovered the double-helix structure of DNA. This led to the field of molecular biology, the development of research on genetic structure, and, by the 1980s, the cutting-edge field of genetic research (Conrad 1997).

10 American examples of reproductive stratification including regulations of black women's reproduction and childrearing in the name of science (Collins 1990, 1999; Davis 1983; Roberts 1997); forced sterilization of the so-called feeble-minded (Reilly 1991) and of members of groups deemed undesirable by state-sanctioned policies and eugenics programs, including Native Americans (Briggs 1998, 2002); the suppression of vice under the Comstock Act (Beisel 1997); subtle forms of sterilization such as lack of reproductive options, unnecessary hysterectomy, and economic and informational restraints on reproductive choices and access; and ideologies regarding appropriate family size and structure (Clarke 1984). Intersecting with the development of scientific knowledge aimed at identifying and developing racial differences was a science focused on sex and sexuality. Early sexologists developed criteria used to classify homosexuals as a distinct human type. These classification systems and cultural discourses provided an important framework for structuring subsequent debates and understandings of scientific, medical, and cultural understandings of homosexuality (Terry 1999; Somerville 2000).

11 For a history of twentieth-century research on genes, see Keller 2000.

12 Judith Stacey (Stacey 1990, 1996, 2003; Stacey and Biblarz 2001) attempted to empirically test these ideas as they relate to alternative family forms.

Seven Imagining Futures of Belonging

1 Discourses of women's health movements continue to shape lesbian trajectories. Ideologies of women-controlled and women-centered information are present in many accounts of achieving pregnancy. Some women described medical procedures as inherently characteristic of "loss of control" over their reproductive bodies, a language frequently used in 1970s women's health discourses, which demonstrated that women's-health-movement discourse was alive and well. Yet many principles of women's health movements have also been co-opted by biomedical entities. Many for-profit sperm banks, for example, market services with slogans that tout "freedom," and some "traditional" women's health resources and service providers have altered women's health principles to compete in the current biomedical climate — for example, the feminist health center that was transformed into a lesbian-owned, -run, and -identified sperm bank. While this organization maintains many feminist principles, they also sell products and information previously not commodified. This shift of control has also occurred in the historical development of contraceptives (Clarke 2000).

2   Shady Grove in the Washington, D.C., area offers a "money back guarantee."
3   My own healthcare coverage in the State of Maryland, for example, clearly states that "Member must be married" to receive coverage (see www.dbm.maryland .gov for more details).
4   Following Lisa C. Ikemoto (1996), I intend the slash in the term *in/fertility* to signal that the dominant understandings of infertility and the infertile are shaped with respect to cultural understandings of fertility and the fertile. In Ikemoto's analysis cultural understandings include the construction of fertile women (normative, middle-class, usually white women), too-fertile women (poor and working-class, usually brown and black women), and what she calls dysfertile women (lesbians and single women). Her powerful argument asserts that in/fertility is raced, classed, and inscribed with normative heterosexuality.
5   Important here is the involvement of bodily and technological processes, themselves simultaneously and inextricably emotional, embodied, and technical. The naturalistic framing of reproductive technologies shapes the cognitive and emotional experience of their use and vice versa (in multiple directions). The sociocultural meanings of hybrid-technology practices, for example, are themselves being transformed through who uses them and how they feel about them. Queer use of assisted reproduction and feelings of empowerment and pleasure at being able to create desired new social formations — new queer families — give those technoscientific innovations even more potency. It is my hope that this work will inform theories regarding the complex ways people variously construct meanings of technoscientific innovations and negotiate institutions in an effort to meet their personal needs.
6   My goal has been to move from the ontological to the interactional in an effort to allow a refiguring of the human body. The female body, consistently coded as the cultural sign of "the natural" and the "reproductive" and equated with the maternal body, can be reconfigured. While these codes serve as regulatory ideals and are embedded in the organization of reproductive technologies through the circulation of the "heterosexual matrix" (Butler 1990) as an organizational framework, analyzing the material practices of users embedded in these discursive worlds allows one to deprivilege such ideals. Material bodies, subjective "experience," and various knowledges interact with this organizational framework in a variety of ways that provoke a queering of such dominant codes.
7   In the case of LGBTQI rights more generally, examples include the recent "backlash" of the 2004 presidential election, in which eleven states voted to pass initiatives to amend their relevant state constitutions to limit marriage and marriage-related benefits to different-sex couples and recognize marriage as exclusively between a man and a woman at the state level. In a September 2004 ruling the 11th U.S. Circuit Court of Appeals allowed Florida to remain the only state with a complete ban on gay adoption (the law was passed in 1977 at the height of Anita Bryant's antihomosexual campaign). The events are part of the current trend to legislate against same-sex marriage and legitimize and

strengthen heterosexuality through its very opposition to an unnatural other. Queer politics and theories must take note and, instead of operating within these discursive, oppositional systems, begin to privilege differential consciousness that allows multiplicities and varieties, thereby destabilizing the heteronormative system without reproducing an either-or framework.

8   Foucault's (1988a; 1988b) analysis of technologies of the self and resistance to biopower offered entrance into exploring domination and agency as co-constitutive entities. Not only are agency and domination co-constitutive, but so, too, are sexualities and reproductive practices.

9   As E. V. Haimes and K. Weiner (2000) argue, one effect of drawing lesbians into the clinical framework of assisted reproduction is the containment of the challenges that alternative self-insemination poses to the family, the legal system, and the institution of medicine. They argue that in terms of medicine, self-insemination is analogous to self-help groups in that it is a radical nonmedicalized, nonprofessionalized social practice that emphasizes lay knowledges and user concerns.

10   The 2005 controversy over the life of Terri Schiavo is an example. As conservatives politicize her life in their enforcement of a "pro-life" agenda, they simultaneously contradict their position on the dominance of marriage. That is, in supporting Terri's parent's decisions, they are discounting not only her husband's decision but also the knowledge gained in the intimacies produced through their marriage.

11   In efforts to minimize controversy, during the early decades of artificial insemination by donor, doctors would mix the husband's sperm with the donor's in an effort to both mask "true" fatherhood and protect the naturalness of the heterosexual family. During the 1950s and early 1960s, Catholic anti-reproductive-intervention activists attempted to criminalize the use of artificial insemination and to subject all participants — the physician, the donor, and the couple — to fines and imprisonment (Andrews and Elster 2000). While no prohibitory laws were passed, laws had to be passed to protect the use of artificial insemination; at least thirty-five states adopted laws that facilitate artificial insemination by donor (in contrast to artificial insemination by husband) by declaring the consenting husband of the sperm recipient to be the legal father (ibid.).

12   The California Medical Association later withdrew its brief in support of the doctors.

13   Today, scientists work to make egg cells not only from female cells but also from male cells, indicating that even males have the biological capacity to make eggs. If the science holds true in humans as in mice — and several scientists suspect it will (Weiss 2003) — then a gay-male couple might before long be able to produce children through sexual reproduction, with one man contributing sperm and the other fresh eggs bearing his own genes. That scenario raises difficult questions, including whether the second man would be recognized as the child's biological mother (Weiss 2003).

14 For an excellent historical analysis of this sperm bank and the children born from its sperm, see Plotz 2005.

15 The Census data shed no light on how many single gay men and lesbians are raising children, as the Census does not ask directly about the sexual orientation and sexual behaviors of respondents. Furthermore, the Census most likely underestimates the number of same-sex couples, given either the unwillingness of gays and lesbians to "disclose" their sexuality or a motivated decision not to declare until the "marriage" box is allowed by law.

Works Cited

Agigian, Amy. 1998. Contradictory Conceptions: Lesbian Alternative Insemination. Ph.D. dissertation, Department of Sociology, Brandeis University, Waltham, Mass.

———. 2004. *Baby Steps: How Lesbian Alternative Insemination is Changing the World*. Middletown, Conn.: Wesleyan University Press.

Akrich, Madeleine. 1992. The De-Scription of Technical Objects. In *Shaping Technology/Building Society: Studies in Sociotechnical Change*, edited by Wiebe E. Bijker and John Law, 205–24. Cambridge, Mass.: MIT Press.

———. 1995. User Representations: Practices, Methods and Sociology. In *Managing Technology in Society: The Approach of Constructive Technology Assessment*, edited by Arie Rip, Thomas J. Misa and Johan Schot, 167–84. New York: Pinter, St. Martin's.

Allen, K. R., and D. H. Demo. 1995. The Families of Lesbians and Gay Men: A New Frontier in Family Research. *Marriage and the Family* 57: 111–27.

Alpert, Harriet. 1988. *We Are Everywhere: Writings by and about Lesbian Parents*. Freedon, Calif.: Crossing.

American Society of Reproductive Medicine. 1997. *Guidelines for Gamete and Embryo Donation: A Practice Committee Report, Guidelines and Minimum Standards*. Birmingham, Ala.: American Society of Reproductive Medicine.

Andrews, Lori B. 2003. Changing Conceptions. In *Living with the Genie: Essays on Technology and the Quest for Human Mastery*, edited by Alan Lightman, Daniel Sarewitz, and Christina Desser, 105–28. Washington, D.C.: Island.

Andrews, Lori B., and Nanette Elster. 2000. Regulating Reproductive Technologies. *Legal Medicine* 21, no. 1: 31–65.

Anspach, Renee R. 1993. *Deciding Who Lives: Fateful Choices in the Intensive-Care Nursery*. Berkeley: University of California Press.

Anzaldúa, Gloria. 1987. *Borderlands/La Frontera: The New Mestiza*. San Francisco: Aunt Lute.

Aral, Sevgi O., and Willard Cates. 1983. The Increasing Concern with Infertility: Why Now? *Journal of the American Medical Association* 250, no. 17: 2327–31.

Arnup, Katherine, ed. 1995. *Lesbian Parenting: Living with Pride and Prejudice*. Charlottetown, Prince Edward Island: Gynergy.

Aronson, D. E. 2000. Defining Infertility. *Public Health Reports* 115:6.

Balsamo, Anne. 1996. *Technologies of the Gendered Body*. Durham, N.C.: Duke University Press.

Bateman-Novaes, Simone. 1998. The Medical Management of Donor Insemina-
   tion. In *Donor Insemination: International Social Science Perspectives*, edited by Ken
   Daniels and Erica Haimes, 105–30. New York: Cambridge University Press.
Beck, Ulrich. 1992. *Risk Society: Towards a New Modernity*. Thousand Oaks, Calif.:
   Sage.
Becker, Gay. 1990. *Healing the Infertile Family: Strengthening Your Relationship in the
   Search for Parenthood*. New York: Bantam.
———. 2000a. *The Elusive Embryo: How Men and Women Approach New Reproductive
   Technologies*. Berkeley: University of California Press.
———. 2000b. Selling Hope: Marketing and Consuming the New Reproductive
   Technologies in the United States. *Sciences Sociales et Sante* 18, no. 4: 105–26.
Becker, Gay, and Robert D. Nachtigall. 1992. Eager for Medicalization: The Social
   Production of Infertility as a Disease. *Sociology of Health and Illness* 14, no. 4: 456–
   71.
Beisel, Nicola. 1997. *Imperiled Innocents: Anthony Comstock and Family Reproduction
   in Victorian America*. Princeton: Princeton University Press.
Belkin, Lisa. 1996. Charity Begins at . . . the Marketing Meeting, the Gala Event, the
   Product Tie-In. *New York Times Magazine* (22 December): 40–58.
Benkov, Laura. 1994. *Reinventing the Family*. New York: Crown Trade.
Bennett, Lisa. 1998. High-Tech Pregnancies: Lesbian Couples Are Increasingly
   Turning to Science for Help in Their Quest to Have Children. *Advocate* (22
   December): 47–50.
Bernstein, Mary, and Renate Reimann, eds. 2001. *Queer Families, Queer Politics:
   Challenging Culture and the State*. New York: Columbia University Press.
Berube, Allen, and Jeffrey Escoffier. 1991. Queer Nation. *Out/Look* 11:14–16.
Bijker, Wiebe E. 1987. The Social Construction of Fluorescent Lighting, or How an
   Artifact Was Invented in Its Diffusion Stage. In *The Social Construction of Tech-
   nological Systems: New Directions in the Sociology and History of Technology*, edited by
   Wiebe E. Bijker, Thomas P. Hughes, and Trevor J. Pinch, 75–102. Cambridge,
   Mass.: MIT Press.
Bijker, Wiebe E, Thomas P. Hughes, and Trevor J Pinch, eds. 1987. *The Social
   Construction of Technological Systems: New Directions in the Sociology and History of
   Technologies*. Cambridge, Mass.: MIT Press.
Birtha, Becky. 1991. "The Childless Women Poems." In *The Forbidden Poems*, by
   Becky Birtha, 20–23. Seattle: Seal.
Bland, Lucy, and Laura Doan, eds. 1998. *Sexology Uncensored: The Documents of
   Sexual Science*. Chicago: University of Chicago Press.
Blank, Robert H. 1984. *Redefining Human Life: Reproductive Technologies and Social
   Policy*. Boulder, Colo.: Westview.
Blumer, Herbert. 1958. Race Prejudice as a Sense of Group Position. *Pacific Sociologi-
   cal Review* 1:3–7.
Boodman, Sandra G. 2005. Fatherhood by a New Formula. *Washington Post*, 18
   January, p. F1.

Bordo, Susan. 1993. *Unbearable Weight: Feminism, Western Culture and the Body*. Berkeley: University of California Press.

Boston Women's Health Book Collective. 1971. *Our Bodies, Ourselves*. Boston: South End.

———. 1976. *Our Bodies, Ourselves: A Book by and for Women*. 2d ed. New York: Simon and Schuster.

———. 1984. *The New Our Bodies, Ourselves*. New York: Simon and Schuster.

Bourdieu, Pierre. 1984. *Distinction: A Social Critique of the Judgment of Taste*. Translated by Richard Nice. Reprint edition (September 1, 1987). Cambridge. Mass: Harvard University Press.

Bowker, Geoffrey C., and Susan Leigh Star. 1999. *Sorting Things Out: Classification and Its Consequences*. Cambridge, Mass.: MIT Press.

Briggs, Laura. 1998. Discourses of "Forced Sterilization" in Puerto Rico: The Problem of Speaking the Subaltern. *Differences* 10, no. 2: 30–66.

———. 2002. *Reproducing Empire: Race, Sex, Science, and U.S. Imperialism in Puerto Rico*. Berkeley: University of California Press.

Britt, Elizabeth C. 1998. Infertility as a Medical Problem: Recasting Feminist Accounts of Nature, Science, and the Law. *Science as Culture* 7, no. 2: 265–80.

Bunge, R. G., W. C. Keettel, and J. K. Sherman. 1954. Clinical Use of Frozen Semen: Report of Four Cases. *Fertility and Sterility* 5:520–29.

Bunge, R. G., and J. K. Sherman. 1954. Frozen Human Semen. *Fertility and Sterility* 5:193–94.

Butler, Judith. 1990. *Gender Trouble: Feminism and the Subversion of Identity*. New York: Routledge.

———. 1993. *Bodies that Matter: On the Discursive Limits of Sex*. New York: Routledge.

———. 1998. Merely Cultural (Non-material Leftist Movements). *New Left Review* 227, no. 33: 33–44.

———. 2000. *Antigone's Claim: Kinship between Life and Death*. New York: Columbia University Press.

———. 2004. *Undoing Gender*. New York: Routledge.

California Family Code. 2001. 7613a and b.

Callon, Michel. 1985. Some Elements of a Sociology of Translation: Domestication of the Scallops and the Fishermen of St. Brieuc Bay. In *Power, Action and Belief*, edited by John Law, 196–233. Boston: Routledge and Kegan Paul.

Carrington, Christopher. 1999. *No Place Like Home: Relationships and Family Life among Lesbians and Gay Men*. Chicago: University of Chicago Press.

Carsten, Janet. 2004. *After Kinship*. Cambridge: Cambridge University Press.

———, ed. 2000. *Cultures of Relatedness: New Approaches to the Study of Kinship*. Cambridge: Cambridge University Press.

Casper, Monica J. 1998. *The Making of the Unborn Patient: A Social Anatomy of Fetal Surgery*. New Brunswick, N.J.: Rutgers University Press.

Casper, Monica J., and Barbara Koenig. 1996. Reconfiguring Nature and Culture:

Intersections of Medical Anthropology and Technoscience Studies. *Medical Anthropology Quarterly* 10, no. 4: 523–36.

Centers for Disease Control. 2000. *Associated Reproductive Technology Success Rates.* Atlanta: Centers for Disease Control.

Chen, Serena H., and Edward E. Wallach. 1994. Five Decades of Progress in Management of the Infertile Couple. *Fertility and Sterility* 62, no. 4: 665–85.

Chesler, Phyllis. 1986. *Mothers on Trial: The Battle for Children and Custody.* New York: McGraw-Hill.

Clarke, Adele E. 1984. Subtle Sterilization Abuse: A Reproductive Rights Perspective. In *Test-Tube Women: What Future for Motherhood?* edited by Rita Arditti, Renate Duelli Klein, and Shelley Minden, 188–212. London: Pandora.

———. 1995. Modernity, Postmodernity and Reproductive Processes ca. 1890–1990, or "Mommy, Where Do Cyborgs Come from Anyway?" In *The Cyborg Handbook,* edited by Chris H. Gray, 139–56. New York: Routledge.

———. 1998. *Disciplining Reproduction: Modernity, American Life Sciences, and "The Problems of Sex."* Berkeley: University of California Press.

———. 2000. Maverick Reproductive Scientists and the Production of Contraceptives. In *Localizing and Globalizing Reproductive Technologies,* edited by Anne Saeton, Nelly Oudshoorn, and Marta Kirejczyk, 37–89. Columbus: Ohio State University Press.

———. 2005. *Situational Analysis: Grounded Theorizing after the Postmodern Turn.* Thousand Oaks, Calif.: Sage.

Clarke, Adele E., Jennifer R. Fishman, Jennifer R. Fosket, Laura Mamo, and Janet Shim. 2000. Technoscience and the New Biomedicalization: Western Roots, Global Rhizomes. *Sciences Sociales et Sante* 18, no. 2: 11–42.

Clarke, Adele E., and Joan H. Fujimura. 1992. *The Right Tools for the Job: At Work in Twentieth Century Life Sciences.* Princeton: Princeton University Press.

Clarke, Adele E., and Theresa Montini. 1993. The Many Faces of RU 486: Tales of Situated Knowledges and Technological Contestations. *Science, Technology and Human Values* 18, no. 1: 42–78.

Clarke, Adele E., and Virginia L. Olesen. 1999. Revising, Diffracting, Acting. In *Revisioning Women, Health, and Healing: Feminist, Cultural, and Technoscience Perspectives,* edited by Adele E. Clarke and Virginia L. Olesen, 3–48. New York: Routledge.

Clarke, Adele E., Janet Shim, Laura Mamo, Jennifer R. Fosket, and Jennifer R. Fishman. 2003. Biomedicalization: Theorizing Technoscientific Transformations of Health, Illness, and U.S. Biomedicine. *American Sociological Review* 68, no. 2: 161–94.

Clausen, Jan. 1980. *Mother, Sister, Daughter, Lover: Stories.* Trumansburg, N.Y.: Crossing.

———. 1982. *Sinking Stealing: A Novel.* Trumansburg, N.Y.: Crossing.

Cockburn, Cynthia, and Ruza Furst-Dilic. 1994. *Bringing Technology Home: Gender and Technology in a Changing Europe.* Philadelphia: Open University Press.

Cole, Cheryl L. 1996. Containing AIDS: Magic Johnson and Post[Reagan] America. In *Queer Theory/Sociology*, edited by Steven Seidman, 280–310. Cambridge, Mass.: Blackwell.

Colen, Shellee. 1989. "Just a Little Respect": West Indian Domestic Workers in New York City. In *Muchachas No More: Household Workers in Latin America and the Caribbean*, edited by Elsa M. Chaney and Mary Garcia Castro, 171–96. Philadelphia: Temple University Press.

Collier, Jane F., and Sylvia J. Yanagisako. 1989. Theory in Anthropology since Feminist Practice. *Critique of Anthropology* 9, no. 2: 27–37.

Collins, Patricia Hill. 1990. *Black Feminist Thought: Knowledge, Consciousness and the Politics of Empowerment*. New York: Routledge.

———. 1999. Will the "Real" Mother Please Stand Up? The Logics of Eugenics and American National Family Planning. In *Revisioning Women, Health and Healing: Feminist, Cultural, and Technoscience Perspectives*, edited by Adele E. Clarke and Virginia L. Olesen, 266–82. New York: Routledge.

Conrad, Peter. 1997. Public Eyes and Private Genes: Historical Frames, New Constructions and Social Problems. *Social Problems* 44, no. 2: 139–54.

Conrad, Peter, and Joseph W. Schneider. 1980. *Deviance and Medicalization*. St. Louis: C. V. Mosby.

Coontz, Stephanie. 1992. *The Way We Never Were: American Families and the Nostalgia Trap*. New York: Basic.

Corea, Gina. 1984. Egg Snatchers. In *Test-Tube Women: What Future for Motherhood?* edited by Rita Arditti, Renate Duelli Klein, and Shelley Minden, 37–51. London: Pandora.

———. 1985. *The Mother Machine: Reproductive Technologies from Artificial Insemination to Artificial Wombs*. New York: Harper and Row.

———. 1987. The Reproductive Brothel. In *Man-made Women: How New Reproductive Technologies Affect Women*, edited by Gina Corea, 38–51. Bloomington: Indiana University Press.

Cowan, Ruth Schwartz. 1987. The Consumption Junction: A Proposal for Research Strategies in the Sociology of Technology. In *The Social Construction of Technological Systems: New Directions in the Sociology of History and Technology*, edited by Wiebe E. Bijker, Thomas P. Hughes, and Trevor J. Pinch, 261–80. Cambridge, Mass.: MIT Press.

Crummy, Karen E. 2000. My Two Mommies: Court Backs Lesbian Couple. *Boston Globe*, July 24, p. 2.

Cussins, Charis. 1996. Ontological Choreography: Agency through Objectification in Infertility Clinics. *Social Studies of Science* 26, no. 3: 575–610.

———. 1998. "Quit Sniveling Cryo-Baby. We'll Work Out which One's Your Mama!" In *Cyborg Babies: From Techno-Sex to Techno-Tots*, edited by Robbie Davis-Floyd and Joseph Dumit, 40–66. New York: Routledge.

Dalton, Susan. 2000. Nonbiological Mothers and the Legal Boundaries of Motherhood: An Analysis of California Law. In *Ideologies and Technologies of Motherhood:*

Race, Class, Sexuality, Nationalism, edited by Helena Ragoné and France Winddance Twine, 201–20. New York: Routledge.

Daniels, Cynthia R. 2006. *Exposing Men: The Science and Politics of Male Reproduction*.
Oxford: Oxford University Press.

Davis, Angela Y. 1983. *Women, Race, and Class*. New York: Random House.

Davis-Floyd, Robbie. 1992. *Birth as an American Right of Passage*. Berkeley: University of California Press.

De Lauretis, Teresa. 1987. *Technologies of Gender: Essays on Theory, Film, and Fiction*.
Bloomington: Indiana University Press.

Deleuze, Gilles, and Felix Guattari. 1977. *Anti-Oedipus: Capitalism and Schizophrenia*. Translated by Robert Hurley, Mark Seem, and Helen R. Lane. New
York: Viking.

——. 1987. *A Thousand Plateaus: Capitalism and Schizophrenia*. Translated by B.
Massumi. Minneapolis: University of Minnesota Press.

D'Emilio, John, and Estelle B. Freedman. 1988. *Intimate Matters: A History of Sexuality in America*. New York: Harper and Row.

DeNora, Tia. 1996. From Physiology to Feminism: Reconfiguring Body, Gender
and Expertise in Natural Fertility Control. *International Sociology* 11, no. 3: 359–
83.

D'Ercole, Ann. 1996. Postmodern Ideas about Gender and Sexuality. *Psychoanalysis
and Psychotherapy* 13, no. 2: 142–52.

Dickinson, Robert L. 1933. *Human Sex Anatomy*. Baltimore: William Wood.

Domenici, Thomas, and Ronnie Lesser. 1995. *Disorienting Sexuality: Psychoanalytical
Reappraisals of Sexual Identities*. New York: Routledge.

Dominus, Susan. 2004. Growing Up with Mom and Mom. *New York Times Magazine* (24 October): 69–74.

Dornin, Rusty. 1998. Surfing for Sperm: Reproduction in Cyberspace. CNN.com,
http://www.cnn.com/HEALTH/9807/24/cyber.sperm (accessed February 16,
2007).

Duelli Klein, Renate. 1984. Doing It Ourselves: Self-insemination. In *Test-Tube
Women: What Future for Motherhood?* edited by Rita Arditti, Renate Duelli Klein,
and Shelley Minden, 382–90. London: Pandora.

Duggan, Lisa. 2002. The New Homonormativity: The Sexual Politics of Neoliberal-
ism. In *Materializing Democracy: Toward a Revitalized Cultural Politics,* edited by
Russ Castronovo and Dana D. Nelson, 173–94, Durham, N.C.: Duke University
Press.

Duggan, Lisa, and Nan Hunter, eds. 1995. *Sex Wars: Sexual Dissent and Political
Cultures*. New York: Routledge.

Duncan, Matthews J. 1871. *Fecundity, Fertility, Sterility and Allied Topics*. 2d ed.
Edinburgh: Adam and Charles Black.

Dunne, Gillian. 2000. Opting into Motherhood: Lesbians Blurring the Boundaries
and Transforming the Meanings of Parenthood and Kinship. *Gender and Society*
14, no. 1: 11–35.

Duster, Troy. 1990. *Backdoor to Eugenics*. New York: Routledge.

Edwards, Jeanette. 2000. *Born and Bred: Idioms of Kinship and New Reproductive Technologies in England*. Oxford: Oxford University Press.

Edwards, Jeanette, Sarah Franklin, Eric Hirsch, Frances Price, and Marilyn Strathern, eds. 1999. *Technologies of Procreation: Kinship in the Age of Assisted Conception*. 2d ed. London: Routledge.

Ehrenreich, John, ed. 1978. *The Cultural Crisis in Modern Medicine*. New York: Monthly Review.

Ehrenreich, Barbara, and John Ehrenreich. 1971. *The American Health Empire: Power, Profits, and Politics*. New York: Vintage.

Epstein, Steven. 1996. *Impure Science: AIDS, Activism, and the Politics of Knowledge*. Berkeley: University of California Press.

Estes, Carroll L., and Elizabeth A. Binney. 1989. The Biomedicalization of Aging: Dangers and Dilemmas. *Gerontologist* 29, no. 5: 587–96.

Faderman, Lillian. 1981. *Surpassing the Love of Men: Romantic Friendship and Love between Women from the Renaissance to the Present*. New York: Morrow.

———. 1991. *Odd Girls Out and Twilight Lovers: A History of Lesbian Life in Twentieth Century America*. New York: Columbia University Press.

Fausto-Sterling, Anne. 1995. Gender, Race, and Nation: The Comparative Anatomy of "Hottentot" Women in Europe, 1815–1817. In *Deviant Bodies: Critical Perspectives on Difference in Science and Popular Culture*, edited by Jennifer Terry and Jacqueline Urla, 19–48. Bloomington: Indiana University Press.

———. 2000. *Sexing the Body: Gender, Politics, and the Construction of Sexuality*. New York: Basic.

Figert, Anne E. 1996. *Women and the Ownership of PMS: The Structuring of a Psychiatric Disorder*. New York: Aldine de Gruyter.

Finegold, Wilfred J. 1976. *Artificial Insemination*. 2d ed. Springfield, Ill.: Thomas.

Finkler, Kaja. 2000. *Experiencing the New Genetics: Family and Kinship on the Medical Frontier*. Philadelphia: University of Pennsylvania Press.

Firestone, Shulamith. 1970. *The Dialectic of Sex*. New York: Morrow.

Fisher, Berenice. 1992. Against the Grain: Lives of Women Without Children. *IRIS* 2: 46–51.

Fishman, Jennifer. 2004. Manufacturing Desire: The Commodification of Female Sexual Dysfunction. *Social Studies of Science* 34, no. 2: 187–218.

Fishman, Jennifer, and Laura Mamo. 2002. What's in a Disorder? A Cultural Analysis of the Medical and Pharmaceutical Constructions of Male and Female Sexual Dysfunction. In *A New View of Women's Sexual Problems*, edited by Ellyn Kaschak and Leonore Tiefer, 179–94. Binghamton, N.Y.: Haworth.

Fishman, Jennifer R., Janice E. Wick, and Barbara A. Koenig. 1999. The Use of "Sex" and "Gender" to Define and Characterize Meaningful Differences between Men and Women. In *An Agenda for Research on Women's Health for the Twenty-first Century*, edited by Office of Research on Women's Health, 2–20. Washington, D.C.: National Institutes of Health.

Food and Drug Administration, United States Department of Health and Human
    Services. 2004. Eligibility Determination for Donors of Human Cells, Tissues,
    and Cellular and Tissue-Based Products. *Federal Register* 69, no. 101 (May 25):
    29785–834.

Fosket, Jennifer Ruth. 2000. Problematizing Biomedicine: Women's Constructions
    of Breast Cancer Knowledge. In *Ideologies of Breast Cancer: Feminist Perspectives*,
    edited by Laura K. Potts, 15–36. London: Macmillan.

———. 2004. Constructing "High Risk" Women: The Development and Standard-
    ization of a Breast Cancer Risk Assessment Tool. *Science, Technology, and Human
    Values* 29, no. 3: 291–313.

Foucault, Michel. 1972. *The Archaeology of Knowledge and the Discourse on Language*.
    Translated by Alan M. Sheridan Smith. New York: Pantheon.

———. 1979. *Discipline and Punish*. New York: Vintage.

———. 1980a. *The History of Sexuality: An Introduction*. Vol. 1 of *The History of
    Sexuality*. New York: Vintage.

———. 1980b. *Power/Knowledge: Selected Interviews and Other Writings, 1972–1977*.
    Edited by C. Gordon. New York: Pantheon.

———. 1988a. *The Care of the Self*. Vol. 3 of *The History of Sexuality*. New York:
    Vintage.

———. 1988b. Technologies of the Self: A Seminar with Michel Foucault. In *Tech-
    nologies of the Self: A Seminar with Michel Foucault*, edited by L. H. Martin, H.
    Gutman, and P. H. Hutton, 16–49. Amherst: University of Massachusetts Press.

———. 1991. Governmentality. In *The Foucault Effect: Studies in Governmentality*,
    edited by G. Burchel, C. Gordon, and P. Miller, 87–104. Chicago: University of
    Chicago Press.

Franklin, Sarah. 1990. Deconstructing "Desperateness": The Social Construction of
    Infertility in Popular Representations of New Reproductive Technologies. In *The
    New Reproductive Technologies*, edited by Maurren McNeil, Ian Varcoe, and Steven
    Yearley, 200–229. London: Macmillan.

———. 1993. Essentialism, Which Essentialism? Some Implications of Reproductive
    and Genetic Techno-Science. *Journal of Homosexuality* 24, nos. 3 and 4: 27–40.

———. 1995. Postmodern Procreation: A Cultural Account of Assisted Reproduc-
    tion. In *Conceiving the New World Order: The Global Politics of Reproduction*, edited
    by Faye D. Ginsburg and Rayna Rapp, 323–45. Berkeley: University of California
    Press.

———. 1997. *Embodied Progress: A Cultural Account of Assisted Reproduction*. London:
    Routledge.

———. 2000. Life Itself: Global Nature and the Genetic Imaginary. In *Global Nature,
    Global Culture*, edited by Sarah Franklin, Celia Lury, and Jackie Stacey, 188–27.
    London: Sage.

Franklin, Sarah, and Susan McKinnon, eds. 2001. *Relative Values: Reconfiguring
    Kinship Studies*. Durham, N.C.: Duke University Press.

Freedman, Estelle. 1996. The Prison Lesbian: Race, Class and the Construction of the Aggressive Female Homosexual, 1915–1965. *Feminist Studies* 22, no. 2: 397–423.

Freud, Sigmund. 1920. *Psychogenesis of a Case of Female Homosexuality.* Standard ed. Repr., London: Hogarth, 1955.

Gagnon, John H., and William Simon. 1967. Homosexuality: The Formulation of a Sociological Perspective. *Health and Social Behavior* 8: 177–85.

———. 1973. *Sexual Conduct: The Social Sources of Human Sexuality.* Chicago: Aldine de Gruyter.

Gamson, Joshua. 2000. Sexualities, Queer Theory, and Qualitative Research. In *Handbook of Qualitative Research*, edited by Norman K. Denzin and Yvonna S. Lincoln, 347–65. Thousand Oaks, Calif.: Sage.

Garrety, Karin. 1997. Social Worlds, Actor Networks and Controversy: The Case of Cholesterol, Dietary Fat and Heart Disease. *Social Studies of Science* 27, no. 5: 727–73.

Garrison, Fielding H. 1929. *An Introduction to the History of Medicine.* 4th ed. Philadelphia: W. B. Saunders.

Giddens, Anthony. 1979. *Central Problems in Social Theory.* Berkeley: University of California Press.

———. 1991. *Modernity and Self Identity.* Oxford: Polity.

———. 1992. *The Transformation of Intimacy.* Oxford: Polity.

Ginsburg, Faye D. 1989. *Contested Lives: The Abortion Debate in an American Community.* Berkeley: University of California Press.

Ginsburg, Faye D., and Rayna Rapp. 1995. *Conceiving the New World Order: The Global Politics of Reproduction.* Berkeley: University of California Press.

Glaser, Barney. 1978. *Theoretical Sensitivity: Advances in the Methodology of Grounded Theory.* Mill Valley, Calif.: Sociology Press.

Glaser, Barney, and Anselm Strauss. 1967. *The Discovery of Grounded Theory.* Chicago: Aldine.

Goffman, Erving. 1959. *The Presentation of Self in Everyday Life.* New York: Anchor.

Gordon, Avery F. 1997. *Ghostly Matters: Haunting and the Sociological Imagination.* Minneapolis: University of Minnesota Press.

Gordon, Linda. 1990. *Woman's Body, Woman's Right: A Social History of Birth Control in America.* 2d ed. New York: Viking.

Gramsci, Antonio. 1992. *Selections from the Prison Notebooks.* Translated by Quintin Hoare and Geoffrey Nowell Smith. New York: International.

Gray, Chris Hables, Heidi J. Figueroa-Sarriera, and Steven Mentor, eds. 1995. *The Cyborg Handbook.* New York: Routledge.

Greenblatt, R. B. 1961. Chemical Induction of Ovulation. *Fertility and Sterility* 12: 402–4.

Grosz, Elizabeth. 1993. Bodies and Knowledge: Feminism and the Crisis of Reason. In *Feminist Epistemologies*, edited by Linda Alcoff and Elizabeth Potter, 187–216. New York: Routledge.

———. 1994. *Volatile Bodies: Towards a Corporeal Feminism.* Bloomington: Indiana University Press.

Gruhn, John G., and Ralph R. Kazer. 1989. *Hormonal Regulation of the Menstrual Cycle: The Evolution of Concepts*. New York: Plenum Medical Book Company.

Guttmacher, Alan Frank. 1938. Practical Experience with Artificial Insemination. *Contraception* 3, no. 4: 76–77.

Haimes, E. V., and K. Weiner. 2000. "Everybody's Got a Dad": Issues for Lesbian Families. *Sociology of Health and Illness* 22, no. 4: 477–99.

Halberstam, Judith. 2005. *In a Queer Time and Place: Transgender Bodies, Subcultural Lives*. New York: New York University Press.

Halberstam, Judith, and Ira Livingston, eds. 1995. *Posthuman Bodies*. Bloomington: Indiana University Press.

Hall, Radclyffe. 1928. *The Well of Loneliness*. Repr., New York: Avon, 1981.

Hanson, F. A. 2001. Donor Insemination: Eugenic and Feminist Implications. *Medical Anthropology Quarterly* 15, no. 3: 287–311.

Haraway, Donna J. 1985. Manifesto for Cyborgs: Science, Technology, and Socialist Feminism in the 1980s. *Socialist Review* 80: 65–108.

———. 1988. Situated Knowledges: The Science Question in Feminism and the Privilege of the Partial Perspective. *Feminist Studies* 14, no. 3: 575–600.

———. 1991. *Simians, Cyborgs, and Women: The Reinvention of Nature*. New York: Routledge.

———. 1992. The Promises of Monsters: A Regenerative Politics for Inappropriate/d Others. In *Cultural Studies*, edited by Lawrence Grossberg, Cary Nelson, and Paula A. Treichler, 295–337. New York: Routledge.

———. 1995. Universal Donors in a Vampire Culture: It's All in the Family: Biological Kinship Categories in the Twentieth-Century United States. In *Uncommon Ground: Toward Reinventing Nature*, edited by William Cronon, 321–66. New York: W. W. Norton.

———. 1997. *Modest ＿ Witness@Second ＿Millennium.FemaleMan© ＿Meets ＿ Onco Mouse™: Feminism and Technoscience*. New York: Routledge.

Hard, Addison Davis. 1909. Artificial Impregnation. *Medical World* (April): 163–64.

Harmon, Amy. 2005. Ask Them (All 8 of Them) about Their Grandson. *New York Times*, 20 March, p. A1.

Hartman, Carl G. 1933. Catholic Advice on the Safe Period. *Birth Control Review* 17 (May): 117–19.

Hartouni, Valerie. 1997. *Cultural Conceptions: On Reproductive Technologies and the Remaking of Life*. Minneapolis: University of Minnesota Press.

———. 1999. A Study in Reproductive Technologies. In *Revisioning Women, Health, and Healing*, edited by Adele E. Clarke and Virginia L. Olesen, 254–65. New York: Routledge.

Hayden, Corinne P. 1995. Gender, Genetics, and Generation: Reformulating Biology in Lesbian Kinship. *Cultural Anthropology* 10, no. 1: 41–63.

Hayles, Katherine N. 1999. *How We Became Posthuman: Virtual Bodies in Cybernetics, Literature, and Informatics*. Chicago: University of Chicago Press.

Hellman, Lillian. 1934. *The Children's Hour*. New York: Knopf.

Hequembourg, A. L., and M. P. Farrell. 1999. Lesbian Motherhood: Negotiating Marginal-Mainstream identities. *Gender and Society* 13: 540–57.

Herman, Harry A. 1981. *Improving Cattle by the Millions: NAAB and the Development and Worldwide Application of Artificial Insemination*. Columbia: University of Missouri Press.

Hertz, Rosanna. 2002. The Father as an Idea: A Challenge to Kinship Boundaries by Single Mothers. *Symbolic Interaction* 25, no. 1: 1–31.

Hochschild, Arlie. 1979. Emotion Work, Feeling Rules, and Social Structure. *American Journal of Sociology* 85: 551–75.

———. 1983. *The Managed Heart: The Commercialization of Human Feelings*. Berkeley: University of California Press.

———. 1998. The Sociology of Emotions as a Way of Seeing. In *Emotions in Social Life: Critical Theories and Contemporary Issues*, edited by Gillian Bendelow and Simon J. Williams, 3–15. London: Routledge.

Hood, Jane C. 2002. The Power of Gametes Versus the Tyranny of Master Narratives: Commentary. *Symbolic Interaction* 25, no. 1: 33–39.

Hornstein, Francie. 1984. Children by Donor Insemination: A New Choice for Lesbians. In *Test-Tube Women: What Future for Motherhood?* edited by Rita Arditti, Renate Duelli Klein, and Shelley Minden, 373–81. London: Pandora.

Ikemoto, Lisa C. 1996. The In/fertile, the Too Fertile, and the Dysfertile. *Hastings Law Journal* 47, no. 4: 1007–56.

Inhorn, Marcia. 1996. *Infertility and Patriarchy: The Cultural Politics of Infertility and Family Life in Egypt*. Philadelphia: University of Pennsylvania Press.

Irvine, Janice M. 1995. Regulated Passions: The Invention of Inhibited Sexual Desire and Sexual Addiction. In *Deviant Bodies*, edited by Jennifer Terry and Jacqueline Urla, 314–37. Bloomington: Indiana University Press.

Jackson, Margaret. 1994. *The Real Facts of Life: Feminism and the Politics of Sexuality, c. 1850–1940*. London: Taylor and Francis.

Jacob, M. C., S. C. Klock, and D. Maier. 1999. Lesbian Couples as Therapeutic Donor Insemination Recipients: Do They Differ from Other Patients? *Psychosomatic Obstetrics and Gynaecology* 20, no. 4: 203–15.

James, Veronica, and Jonathan Gabe, eds. 1996. *Health and the Sociology of Emotions*. Sociology of Health and Illness, ed. J. Gabe. Oxford: Blackwell.

Jetter, Alexis. 1996. Lesbian Baby Boom. *Harper's Bazaar* (October): 66–70.

Jordan, Caren, and Tracey A. Revenson. 1999. Gender Differences in Coping with Infertility: A Meta-analysis. *Behavioral Medicine* 22: 341–58.

Joyce, Kelly, and Laura Mamo. 2006. "Graying the Cyborg: New Directions in Feminist Analyses of Aging, Science, and Technology." In *Age Matters*, edited by Toni Calasanti and Katherine Allen, 99–121. New York: Routledge.

Kahn, Susan Martha. 2000. *Reproducing Jews: A Cultural Account of Assisted Conception in Israel*. Durham, N.C.: Duke University Press.

Katz, Jonathan. 1976. *Gay American History*. New York: Crowell.

Keller, Evelyn Fox. 2000. *The Century of the Gene*. Cambridge, Mass.: Harvard University Press.

Kelly, Jen. 2001. Gay Men May Make Babies. *Herald Sun* (Melbourne), 4 January, News section, p. 15.

Kendell, Kate, ed. 1996. *Lesbians Choosing Motherhood: Legal Implications of Donor Insemination, Second Parent Adoption, Co-Parenting, Ovum Donation and Embryo Transfer*. 3d ed. San Francisco: National Center for Lesbian Rights.

Kennedy, Elizabeth Lapovsky, and Madeline D. Davis. 1993. *Boots of Leather, Slippers of Gold: The History of a Lesbian Community*. New York: Routledge.

Kevles, Daniel J. 1985. *In the Name of Eugenics: Genetics and the Uses of Human Heredity*. New York: Alfred A. Knopf.

Kirk, Stuart A., and Herb Kutchins, eds. 1992. *The Selling of the DSM: The Rhetoric of Science in Psychiatry*. New York: Aldine de Gruyter.

Klepfisz, Irena. 1977. "Women without Children, Women without Families, Women Alone." In *Dreams of an Insomniac: Jewish Feminist Essays, Speeches, Diatribes*, by Irena Klepfisz, 101–15. Repr., Boulder, Colo.: Eighth Mountain, 1990.

Kolata, Gina. 2002. Fertility Inc.: Clinics Race to Lure Clients. *New York Times*, 1 January, pp. D1, D7.

Krieger, Susan. 1983. *The Mirror Dance: Identity in a Women's Community*. Philadelphia: Temple University Press.

Lamarck, Jean-Baptiste. 1809. *Philosophie Zoologique*. Trans. by Hugh Elliot as *Zoological Philosophy: An Exposition with Regard to the Natural History of Animals* with introductory essays by David L. Hull and Richard W. Burkhardt Jr., Chicago: University of Chicago Press, 1984.

Lambda Legal Defense and Education Fund. 2006. Case: Benitez v. North Coast Women's Care Medical Group. http://www.lambdalegal.org/cgi-bin/iowa/cases/record?record=222 (accessed February 16, 2007).

Laqueur, Thomas W. 1990. *Making Sex: Body and Gender from the Greeks to Freud*. Cambridge, Mass.: Harvard University Press.

Lareau, Annette. 2003. *Unequal Childhoods: Class, Race and Family Life*. Berkeley: University of California Press.

Larkin, Joan. 1975. *Housework: Poems*. New York: Out and Out.

Larson, Edward J. 1995. *Sex, Race, and Science: Eugenics in the Deep South*. Baltimore: Johns Hopkins University Press.

Latour, Bruno. 1987. *Science in Action: How to Follow Scientists and Engineers through Society*. Cambridge, Mass.: Harvard University Press.

Latour, Bruno, and Steve Woolgar. 1979. *Laboratory Life: The Social Construction of Scientific Facts*. 2d ed. Princeton: Princeton University Press.

Laumann, Edward O., Anthony Paik, and Raymond C. Rosen. 1999. Sexual Dysfunction in the United States. *Journal of the American Medical Association* 281, no. 6: 537–44.

Law, John. 1987. Technology and Heterogeneous Engineering: The Case of Portuguese Expansion. In *The Social Construction of Technological Systems*, edited by

Wiebe E. Bijker, Thomas P. Hughes, and Trevor J. Pinch, 111–34. Cambridge, Mass.: MIT Press.

Leland, John. 2000. O.K., You're Gay. So? Where's My Grandchild? *New York Times*, 21 December, pp. B1, B14.

Lemert, Charles. 1993. *Social Theory: The Multicultural and Classic Readings*. Boulder, Colo.: Westview.

Lesser, Ronnie C., and Erica Schoenberg, eds. 1999. *That Obscure Subject of Desire: Freud's Female Homosexual Revisited*. New York: Routledge.

Lewin, Ellen. 1993. *Lesbian Mothers: Accounts of Gender in American Culture*. Ithaca, N.Y.: Cornell University Press.

———. 1998a. *Recognizing Ourselves*. New York: Columbia University Press.

———. 1998b. Wives, Mothers, and Lesbians: Rethinking Resistance in the U.S. In *Pragmatic Women and Body Politics*, edited by Margaret Lock and Patricia A. Kaufert, 164–77. New York: Cambridge University Press.

———, ed. 1996. *Inventing Lesbian Cultures in America*. Boston: Beacon.

Lippman, Abby. 1992. Led (Astray) by Genetic Maps: The Cartography of the Human Genome and Health Care. *Social Science and Medicine* 35, no. 12: 1469–76.

Lock, Margaret, and Deborah Gordon, eds. 1988. *Biomedicine Examined*. Dordrecht, Germany: Kluwer Academic.

Lock, Margaret, and Patricia A. Kaufert, eds. 1998. *Pragmatic Women and Body Politics*. New York: Cambridge University Press.

Lorber, Judith. 1989. Choice, Gift, or Patriarchal Bargain? Women's Consent to Invitro-Fertilization in Male Infertility. *Hypatia* 4: 23–36.

Lorde, Audre. 1978. *The Black Unicorn*. New York: Norton.

———. 1979. Man Child: A Black Lesbian Feminist Response. *Conditions* 4: 30–36.

Lupton, Deborah. 1997. Foucault and the Medicalization Critique. In *Foucault, Health, and Medicine*, edited by Alan Petersen and Robin Bunton, 94–112. New York: Routledge.

Lury, Celia. 1996. *Consumer Culture*. New Brunswick, N.J.: Rutgers University Press.

Lykke, Nina, and Rossi Braidotti. 1996. *Between Monsters, Goddesses, and Cyborgs*. London: Zed.

Lyon, Phyllis, and Del Martin. 1972. *Lesbian/Woman*. New York: Bantam.

Macomber, Donald and M. B. Sanders. 1929. Spermatozoa Count. *New England Journal of Medicine* 200: 981–82.

Magee, Maggie, and Diana Miller. 1997. *Lesbian Lives: Psychoanalytic Narratives Old and New*. Hillsdale, N.J.: Analytic.

Mamo, Laura. 1999. Death and Dying: Confluences of Emotion and Awareness. *Sociology of Health and Illness* 21, no. 1: 13–26.

Mamo, Laura, and Jennifer Fishman. 2001. Potency in All the Right Places: Viagra as a Technology of the Gendered Body. *Body and Society* 7, no. 4: 13–35.

Mannheim, Karl. 1946. *Ideology and Utopia: An Introduction to the Sociology of Knowledge*. Translated by Louis Wirth and Edward Shils. New York: Harcourt, Brace.

Marsh, Margaret, and Wanda Ronner. 1996. *The Empty Cradle: Infertility in America from Colonial Times to the Present*. Baltimore: Johns Hopkins University Press.

Martin, Emily. 1991. The Egg and the Sperm: How Science has Constructed a Romance Based on Stereotypical Male-Female Roles. *Signs* 16, no. 3: 485–501.

Mason, Mary Ann. 1999. *The Custody Wars: Why Children are Losing the Legal Battle, and What We Can Do About It*. New York: Basic Books.

May, Elaine Tyler. 1995. *Barren in the Promised Land: Childless Americans and the Pursuit of Happiness*. Cambridge, Mass.: Harvard University Press.

McGregor, Deborah Kuhn. 1989. *Sexual Surgery and the Origins of Gynecology: J. Marion Sims, His Hospital, and His Patients*. New York: Garland.

McKinlay, John B., and John D. Stoeckle. 1988. Corporatization and the Social Transformation of Doctoring. *International Journal of Health Services* 18, no. 2: 191–205.

McLaren, Angus. 1990. *A History of Contraception: From Antiquity to the Present Day*. Oxford: Blackwell.

McNair, Ruth, Deborah Dempsey, Sarah Wise, and Amaryll Perlesz. 2002. Family Matters. *Australian Institute of Family Studies* 63: 40–49.

Minot, Leslie Ann. 2000. *Conceiving Parenthood: Parenting and the Rights of Lesbian, Gay, Bisexual and Transgender People and Their Children*. San Francisco: International Lesbian and Gay Human Rights Commission.

Minow, Martha. 1998. Redefining Families: Who's In and Who's Out. In *Families in the U.S.: Kinship and Domestic Politics*, edited by Karen V. Hansen and Anita I. Garey, 7–19. Philadelphia: Temple University Press.

Modell, Judith S. 1994. *Kinship with Strangers: Adoption and Interpretations of Kinship in American Culture*. Berkeley: University of California Press.

Montini, Theresa. 1996. Gender and Emotion in the Advocacy of Breast Cancer Informed Consent Legislation. *Gender and Society* 10: 9–23.

Moore, Lisa J. 1997. "It's Like You Use Pots and Pans to Cook, It's the Tool": The Technologies of Safer Sex. *Science, Technology and Human Values* 22, no. 4: 343–471.

Moore, Lisa J., and Adele E. Clarke. 1995. Clitoral Conventions and Transgressions: Graphic Representations in Anatomy Texts, c. 1900–1991. *Feminist Studies* 21, no. 2: 255–302.

———. 2001. The Traffic in Cyberanatomies: Sex/Gender/Sexuality in Local and Global Formations. *Body and Society* 7, no. 1: 57–96.

Morgen, Sandra. 2002. *Into Our Own Hands: The Women's Health Movement in the United States, 1969–1990*. New Brunswick, N.J.: Rutgers University Press.

Murphy, Julien S. 2001. Should Lesbians Count as Infertile Couples? Antilesbian Discrimination in Assisted Reproduction. In *Queer Families, Queer Politics: Challenging Culture and the State*, edited by Mary Bernstein and Renate Reimann, 182–200. New York: Columbia University Press.

Murphy, Michelle. 1999. Self-Speculation and the Production of "Experience" as a Critique of Biomedicine. Paper read at Society for the Social Studies of Science conference, San Diego, Calif., October 28–31.

National Center for Lesbian Rights. 2004. Adoption by Lesbian, Gay and Bisexual Parents: An Overview of Current Law. National Center for Lesbian Rights. http://www.nclrights.org/publications/adptno204.htm (accessed February 16, 2007).

Nationwide News Party Limited. 2001. No-dad Babies Seen as Boon for Lesbians. *Mercury, Hobart*, 12 July.

Nestle, Joan. 1987. *A Restricted Country*. New York: Firebrand.

Newman, Leslea. 1989. *Heather Has Two Mommies*. Northhampton, Mass.: In Other Words.

Newton, Esther. 1984. The Mythic Mannish Lesbian: Radclyffe Hall and the New Woman. *Signs* 9: 557 75.

Noble, Elizabeth. 1988. *Having Your Baby by Donor Insemination: A Complete Resource Guide*. Boston: Houghton Mifflin.

O'Donnell, Mary, Val Leoffler, Kater Pollock, and Ziesel Saunders. 1979. *Lesbian Health Matters*. Santa Cruz, Calif.: Santa Cruz Women's Health Collective.

Olesen, Virginia. 2000. Emotions and Gender in U.S. Health Care Contexts: Implications for Stasis and Change in the Division of Labour. In *Health, Medicine, and Society: Key Theories, Future Agendas*, edited by S. J. William, J. Gabe, and M. Clanan, 315–32. London: Routledge.

Olesen, Virginia, Leonard Schatzman, N. Droes, D. Hatton, and Nan Chico. 1990. The Mundane Ailment and the Physical Self: Analysis of the Social Psychology of Health and Illness. *Social Science and Medicine* 30: 449–55.

Omi, Michael, and Howard Winant. 1994. *Racial Formation in the United States: From the 1960s to the 1990s*. New York: Routledge.

Orr, Jackie. 2006. *Panic Diaries: A Genealogy of Panic Disorder*. Durham, N.C.: Duke University Press.

Oudshoorn, Nelly. 1994. *Beyond the Natural Body: An Archeology of Sex Hormones*. New York: Routlege.

———. 1995. Female or Male: The Classification of Homosexuality and Gender. *Homosexuality* 28, nos. 1 and 2: 79–86.

———. 2003. *The Male Pill: A Biography of a Technology in the Making*. Durham, N.C.: Duke University Press.

Parker, Pat. 1985. *Jonestown and Other Madness: Poetry*. Ithaca, N.Y.: Firebrand.

Parker, Richard G., and John Gagnon, eds. 1995. *Conceiving Sexuality: Approaches to Sex Research in a Postmodern World*. New York: Routledge.

Parkes, Alan S. 1985. *Off-beat Biologist: The Autobiography of Alan S. Parkes*. Cambridge, U.K.: Galton Foundation.

———, ed. 1952. *Marshall's Physiology of Reproduction*. 3d ed. Vol. 2. London: Longmans, Green.

Patterson, Charlotte J. 1994. Lesbian and Gay Families. *Current Directions in Psychological Science* 3, no. 2: 62–64.

Patterson, Charlotte, Susan Hurt, and Chandra Mason. 1998. Families of the Lesbian Baby Boom: Children's Contact with Grandparents and Other Adults. *American Journal of Orthopsychiatry* 68, no. 3: 390–99.

Paul, Diane B. 1998. *The Politics of Heredity: Essays on Eugenics, Biomedicine, and the Nature-Nurture Debate*. Albany: State University of New York Press.

Pepper, Rachel. 1999. *The Ultimate Guide to Pregnancy for Lesbians: Tips and Techniques from Conception to Birth: How to Stay Sane and Care for Yourself*. San Francisco: Cleis.

Perry, Enos J., John W. Batlett, George E. Taylor, Joseph Edwards, Claire E. Terril, Victor Berlinger, and Fred P. Jeffrey, eds. 1945. *The Artificial Insemination of Farm Animals*. New Brunswick, N.J.: Rutgers University Press.

Petryna, Adriana. 2002. *Life Exposed: Biological Citizens after Chernobyl*. Princeton: Princeton University Press.

Pfeffer, Naomi. 1993. *The Stork and the Syringe: A Political History of Reproductive Medicine*. Cambridge, U.K.: Polity.

Pies, Cheri. 1988. *Considering Parenthood*. 2d ed. San Francisco: Spinster.

Pies, Cheri, and Francie Hornstein. 1988. Baby M and the Gay Family. *Out/Look* 1, no. 1: 78–85.

Pitts, Victoria. 2005. "Feminism, Technology and Body Projects," *Women's Studies* 34, nos. 3 and 4: 229–47.

Plotz, David. 2005. *The Genius Factory: The Curious History of the Nobel Prize Sperm Bank*. New York: Random House.

Plummer, Ken. 1995. *Telling Sexual Stories: Power, Change, and Social Worlds*. New York: Routledge.

———. 2000. Intimate Choices. In *Theory and Society: Understanding the Present*, edited by Gary Browning, Abigail Halcli, and F. Webster, 432–44. London: Sage.

———. 2001. The Square of Intimate Citizenship: Some Preliminary Proposals. *Citizenship Studies CISDFE* 5, no. 3: 237–53.

Polge, Chris, Audrey U. Smith, and Alan S. Parkes. 1949. Revival of Spermatozoa after Vitrification and Dehydration at Low Temperatures. *Nature* 164: 666.

Porter, Theodore M. 1995. *Trust in Numbers: The Pursuit of Objectivity in Science and Public Life*. Princeton: Princeton University Press.

Poynter, F. N. L. 1968. Hunter, Spallanzani, and the History of Artificial Insemination. In *Medicine, Science and Culture: Historical Essays in Honor of Owsei Temkin*, edited by Lloyd G. Stevenson and Robert P. Multhauf, 97–113. Baltimore: Johns Hopkins University Press.

Pratt, Minnie Bruce. 1989. *Crime against Nature*. Ithaca, N.Y.: Firebrand.

Putnam, Robert D. 2000. *Bowling Alone: The Collapse and Revival of American Community*. New York: Simon and Schuster.

R., Kate. 2000. The Crazy Mixed-Up World of Donor Insemination. *Volunteer Notes* (fall): 2–4.

Rabinow, Paul. 1992. Artificiality and Enlightenment: From Sociobiology to Biosociality. In *Incorporations*, edited by Jonathan Crary and Sanford Kwinter, 234–52. New York: Zone.

———. 1996. *Essays on the Anthropology of Reason*. Princeton: Princeton University Press.

Ragoné, Helena, and France Winddance Twine, eds. 2000. *Ideologies and Technologies of Motherhood: Race, Class, Sexuality, Nationalism*. New York: Routledge.

Rapp, Rayna. 1999. *Testing Women, Testing the Fetus: The Social Impact of Amniocentesis in America*. New York: Routledge.

Reilly, Philip R. 1991. *The Surgical Solution: A History of Involuntary Sterilization in the United States*. Baltimore: Johns Hopkins University Press.

Reimann, Renate. 2001. Lesbian Mothers at Work. In *Queer Families, Queer Politics: Challenging Culture and the State*, edited by Mary Bernstein and Renate Reimann, 254–71. New York: Columbia University Press.

Relman, Arnold S. 1980. The Medical-Industrial Complex. *New England Journal of Medicine* 303, no. 17: 963–70.

Resolve: The National Infertility Association. 2007. Advocacy: State Coverage Descriptions. http://www.resolve.org/site/PageServer?pagename=lrn_ic_coverage (accessed February 16, 2007).

Rich, Adrienne. 1976. *Of Woman Born: Motherhood as Experience and Institution*. New York: W. W. Norton.

———. 1980. Compulsory Heterosexuality and Lesbian Existence. *Signs* 5: 631–60.

Riessman, Catherine Kohler. 1983. Women and Medicalization: A New Perspective. *Social Policy* 14, no. 1: 3–18.

Roberts, Dorothy. 1997. *Killing the Black Body: Race, Reproduction, and the Meaning of Liberty*. 2d ed. New York: Vintage.

Rohleder, Hermann. 1934. *Test Tube Babies: A History of the Artificial Impregnation of Human Beings*. New York: Panurge.

Rose, Nikolas, and Carlos Novas. 2003. Biological Citizenship. In *Global Assemblages: Technology, Politics, and Ethics as Anthropological Problems*, edited by Aihwa Ong and Stephen J. Collier, 436–63. Malden, Mass.: Blackwell.

Rothman, Barabara Katz. 1986. *The Tentative Pregnancy: Prenatal Diagnosis and the Future of Motherhood*. New York: Viking.

Roy, S., R. B. Greenblatt, V. B. Mahesh, and E. C. Jungck. 1963. Clomiphene Citrate: Further Observations on Its Use in Induction of Ovulation in the Human and on Its Mode of Action. *Fertility and Sterility* 14: 575–95.

Rubin, Gayle. 1975. The Traffic in Women. In *Towards an Anthropology of Women*, edited by Rayna R. Reiter, 157–210. New York: Monthly Review.

Ruzek, Sheryl Burt. 1978. *The Women's Health Movement: Feminist Alternatives to Medical Control*. New York: Praeger.

Ruzek, Sheryl Burt, and J. Hill. 1986. Promoting Women's Health: Redefining the Knowledge Base and Strategies for Change. *Health Promotion* 1, no. 3: 301–9.

Saffron, Lisa. 1994. *Challenging Conceptions: Planning a Family by Self-Insemination*. London: Cassell.

Sawicki, Jana. 1991. *Disciplining Foucault: Feminism, Power, and the Body*. New York: Routledge.

Scheib, Joanna E., Maura Riordan, and Phillip R. Shaver. 2000. Choosing between Anonymous and Identity-release Sperm Donors: Recipient and Donor Characteristics. *Assisted Reproduction* 9, no. 5: 1–9.

Schiebinger, Londa. 1989. *The Mind Has No Sex? Women in the Origins of Modern Science*. Cambridge, Mass.: Harvard University Press.

———. 1993. *Nature's Body: Gender in the Making of Modern Science*. Boston: Beacon.

Schmidt, Matthew, and Lisa J. Moore. 1998. Constructing a "Good Catch," Picking a Winner: The Development of Technosemen and the Deconstruction of the Monolithic Male. In *Cyborg Babies: From Techno-Sex to Techno-Tots*, edited by Robbie Davis-Floyd and Joseph Dumit, 21–39. New York: Routledge.

Schneider, David. 1964. The Nature of Kinship. *Man* 64: 180–81.

———. 1968. *American Kinship: A Cultural Account*. Englewood Cliffs, N.J.: Prentice Hall.

Schwartz, Adria E. 1998. *Sexual Subjects: Lesbians, Gender, and Psychoanalysis*. New York: Routledge.

Scott, Joan. 1992. Experience. In *Feminists Theorize the Political*, edited by Joan Scott and Judith Butler, 22–40. New York: Routledge.

Scritchfield, Shirley A. 1989. The Infertility Enterprise: IVF and the Technological Construction of Reproductive Impairments. In *Research in the Sociology of Health Care: A Research Annual*, edited by Dorothy C. Wertz, 61–97. Greenwich, Conn.: JAI.

Sears, R. Bradley, Gary J. Gates, and William B. Rubenstein. 2005. *Same-Sex Couples and Same-Sex Couples Raising Children in The United States: Data from Census 2000*. Los Angeles: Williams Project on Sexual Orientation Law and Public Policy, UCLA School of Law.

Seidman, Steven. 1997. *Difference Troubles: Queering Social Theory and Sexual Politics*. Cambridge: Cambridge University Press.

Shapin, Steven, and Simon Schaffer. 1986. *Leviathan and the Air Pump: Hobbes, Boyle, and the Experimental Life*. Princeton: Princeton University Press.

Sherman, Jerome K. 1954. Freezing and Freeze-drying of Human Spermatozoa. *Fertility and Sterility* 5: 357–71.

———. 1979. Historical Synopsis of Human Semen Preservation. In *Human Artificial Insemination and Semen Preservation*, edited by Georges David and Wendel S. Price, 95–105. Paris: International Symposium on Artificial Insemination and Semen Preservation.

Shim, Janet K. 2000. Bio-Power and Racial, Class, and Gender Formation in Biomedical Knowledge Production. In *Research in the Sociology of Health Care*, edited by Jennie Jacobs Kronenfeld, 173–95. Stamford, Conn.: JAI.

———. 2006. Cultural Health Capital: A Theoretical Approach to Understanding Health Care Interactions and the Dynamics of Unequal Treatment. Unpublished manuscript.

Shreve, Jenn. 2004. The Gay-by Boom: Gay Couples No Longer Immune from Feeling the Pressure to Procreate. *SFGate.com*, 28 September. http://www.sfgate.com/cgi-bin/article.cgi?f=/g/archive/2004/09/28/gaybyboom.DTL# (accessed February 16, 2007).

Silver, Lee M. 1997. *Remaking Eden: How Genetic Engineering and Cloning Will Transform the American Family*. 2d ed. New York: Avon.

Slater, Don. 1997. *Consumer Culture and Modernity*. Malden, Mass.: Polity.

Snitow, Ann, ed. 1980. *Powers of Desire*. New York: Monthly Review.

Somerville, Siobhan B. 2000. *Queering the Color Line: Race and the Invention of Homosexuality in American Culture*. Durham, N.C.: Duke University Press.

Spivak, Gayatri Chakravorty. 1988. *In Other Worlds: Essays in Cultural Politics*. New York: Routledge.

Stacey, Judith. 1990. *Brave New Families: Stories of Domestic Upheaval in Late Twentieth Century America*. New York: Basic.

——. 1996. *In The Name of the Family: Rethinking Family Values in the Postmodern Age*. Boston: Beacon.

——. 2003. Cruising to Familyland: Gay Hypergamy and Rainbow Kinship. Paper read at New Sex: Changing Conditions of Gender, Sexuality, and Intimacy conference, George Mason University, spring.

Stacey, Judith, and Timothy J. Biblarz. 2001. (How) Does the Sexual Orientation of Parents Matter? *American Sociological Review* 66 (April): 159–83.

Stack, Carol. 1974. *All Our Kin: Strategies for Survival in a Black Community*. New York: Harper and Row.

Star, Susan Leigh, ed. 1995. *The Cultures of Computing*. Oxford: Basil Blackwell.

Starr, Paul. 1982. *The Social Transformation of American Medicine*. New York: Basic.

Stein, Arlene. 1997. *Sex and Sensibility: Stories of a Lesbian Generation*. Berkeley: University of California Press.

Strathern, Marilyn. 1992. *Reproducing the Future: Essays on Anthropology, Kinship, and the New Reproductive Technologies*. New York: Routledge.

——. 1995. Displacing Knowledge: Technology and the Consequences for Kinship. In *Conceiving the New World Order: The Global Politics of Reproduction*, edited by Faye D. Ginsburg and Rayna Rapp, 346–64. Berkeley: University of California Press.

Strauss, Anselm. 1987. *Qualitative Analysis for Social Scientists*. Cambridge: Cambridge University Press.

——. 1993. *Continual Permutations of Action*. New York: Aldine de Gruyter.

Strauss, Anselm, and Julie Corbin. 1990. *Basics of Qualitative Research*. Newbury Park, Calif.: Sage.

Sullivan, Maureen. 1996. Rozzie and Harriet? Gender and Family Patterns of Lesbian Coparents. *Gender and Society* 10, no. 6: 747–67.

——. 1998. Alma Mater: Family "Outings" and the Making of the Modern Other Mother. Paper read at the Pacific Sociological Association conference, San Francisco.

——. 2001. Alma Mater: Family "Outings" and the Making of the Modern Other Mother (MOM). In *Queer Families, Queer Politics: Challenging Culture and the State*, edited by Mary Bernstein and Renate Reimann, 231–53. New York: Columbia University Press.

——. 2004. *The Family of Woman: Lesbian Mothers, Their Children, and the Undoing of Gender*. Berkeley: University of California Press.

Taymor, M. L. 1959. Timing of Ovulation by LH Assay. *Fertility and Sterility* 10: 212–26.

Terry, Jennifer. 1991. Theorizing Deviant Historiography. *Differences* 3, no. 2: 55–74.

———. 1999. *An American Obsession: Science, Medicine, and Homosexuality in Modern Society*. Chicago: University of Chicago Press.

Thompson, Charis. 2001. Strategic Naturalization: Kinship in an Infertility Clinic. In *Relative Values: Reconfiguring Kinship Studies*, edited by Sarah Franklin and Susan McKinnon, 175–99. Durham, N.C.: Duke University Press.

———. 2005. *Making Parents: The Ontological Choreography of Reproductive Technologies*. Cambridge, Mass.: MIT Press.

Tiefer, Lenore. 1994. The Medicalization of Impotence: Normalizing Phallocentrism. *Gender and Society* 8, no. 3: 363–77.

Timmermans, Stefan. 1999. *Sudden Death and the Myth of CPR*. Philadelphia: Temple University Press.

Tober, Diane M. 2001. Semen as Gift, Semen as Goods: Reproductive Workers and the Market in Altruism. *Body and Society* 7: 137–60.

Ulrich, M., and A. Weatherall. 2000. Motherhood and Infertility: Viewing Motherhood through the Lens of Infertility. *Feminism and Psychology* 10: 323–36.

Vance, Carol, ed. 1982. *Pleasure and Danger*. New York: Routledge.

Vicinus, Martha. 1989. They Wonder to Which Sex I Belong: The Historical Roots of the Modern Lesbian Identity. In *The Lesbian and Gay Studies Reader*, edited by Henry Abelove, Michele Aina Barale, and David M. Halperin, 432–52. New York: Routledge.

Warner, Michael. 1999. *The Trouble with Normal*. New York: Free Press.

———, ed. 1993. *Fear of a Queer Planet: Queer Politics and Social Theory*. Minneapolis: University of Minnesota Press.

Weeks, Jeffrey. 1977. *Coming Out: Homosexual Politics in Britain from the Nineteenth Century to the Present*. London: Quartet.

Weiss, Rick. 2003. In Laboratory, Ordinary Cells Are Turned into Eggs. *Washington Post*, 2 May, p. A1.

West, Candace, and Sarah Fenstermaker. 1995. Doing Difference. *Gender and Society* 9, no. 1: 8–37.

West, Candace, and Don H. Zimmerman. 1987. Doing Gender. *Gender and Society* 1, no. 2: 125–51.

Weston, Kath. 1991. *Families We Choose: Lesbians, Gays, Kinship*. New York: Columbia University Press.

Whitelaw, M. J. 1963. Clomiphene Citrate: Newer Aspects of Its Use in Prevention and Treatment of Infertility. *Fertility and Sterility* 14: 540–46.

Wikler, Daniel, and Norma Wikler. 1991. Turkey-Baster Babies: The Demedicalization of Artificial Insemination. *Milbank Quarterly* 69, no. 1: 5–39.

Williams, Simon, and Gillian Bendelow, eds. 1998. *The Lived Body: Sociological Themes, Embodied Issues*. London: Routledge.

Wittig, Monique. 1981. One Is Not Born a Woman. *Feminist Issues* 1, no. 3: 47–54.
———. 1982. The Category of Sex. *Feminist Issues* 2, no. 2: 63–68.
Woolgar, Steve. 1991. Configuring the User: The Case of Usability Trials. In *A Sociology of Monsters: Essays on Power, Technology and Domination*, edited by John Law, 57–99. New York: Routledge.
Worcester, Nancy, and Marianne Whatley. 1988. The Response of the Health Care System to the Women's Health Movement: The Selling of Women's Health Centers. In *Feminism within the Science and Health Care Professions: Overcoming Resistance*, edited by Sue V. Rosser, 117–51. New York: Pergamon.
Working Group on a New View of Women's Sexual Problems. 2000. A New View of Women's Sexual Problems. *Electronic Journal of Human Sexuality* 3. http://www.ejhs.org/volume3/newview.htm (accessed February 16, 2007).
Wright, Peter, and Andrew Treacher, eds. 1982. *The Problem of Medical Knowledge: Examining the Social Construction of Medicine*. Edinburgh: Edinburgh University Press.
Yanagisako, Sylvia J., and Carol Delaney, eds. 1995. *Naturalizing Power: Essays in Feminist Cultural Analysis*. New York: Routledge.
Zola, Irving Kenneth. 1972. Medicine as an Institution of Social Control. *Sociological Review* 20: 487–504.
Zonneveldt, Mandi. 2001. No-dad Babies Uproar. *Herald Sun* (Melbourne), 11 July, News section, p. 2.
Zorgniotti, Adrian W. 1975. The Spermatozoa Count: A Short History. *Urology* 5, no. 5: 672–73.

Index

LAURA MAMO is an assistant professor of sociology and an affiliate assistant professor of women's studies and lesbian and gay studies at the University of Maryland.

443948

Library of Congress Cataloging-in-Publication Data

Mamo, Laura, 1969–
Queering reproduction: achieving pregnancy in the age of technoscience /
Laura Mamo.
p. cm.
Includes bibliographical references and index.
ISBN-13: 978-0-8223-4057-7 (cloth: alk. paper)
ISBN-13: 978-0-8223-4078-2 (pbk.: alk. paper)
1. Lesbian mothers — United States. 2. Self-insemination — United States. I. Title.
HQ75.53.M36 2007
306.874'30866430973 — dc22
2007010610